Y0-BRV-331

STUDIES IN
MEDIEVAL AND RENAISSANCE HISTORY

Volume IV

ADVISORY EDITORS

STUDIES IN Medieval and Renaissance History

Volume IV

Edited by
WILLIAM M. BOWSKY
University of California, Davis

UNIVERSITY OF NEBRASKA PRESS · LINCOLN
1967

Library of Congress Catalog Card Number: 63-22098

MANUFACTURED IN THE UNITED STATES OF AMERICA

CONTENTS

INTRODUCTION

Studies in Medieval and Renaissance History is a series of annual volumes designed for original major articles and short monographs in all fields of medieval and renaissance history.

The first impetus for the creation of this series came from a belief that there is a need for a scholarly publication to accommodate the longer study whose compass is too large for it to be included regularly in existing media but too small for it to appear in book form. The editors will consider articles in all areas of history from approximately the fourth through the sixteenth centuries—economic, social and demographic, political, intellectual and cultural, and studies that do not fit neatly into a single traditional category of historical investigation.

The editorial board hopes that the *Studies* will create another link between the work of medieval and renaissance scholarship; for many articles pertinent to both disciplines appear in publications consulted almost exclusively by either medieval or renaissance scholars.

Although this series is devoted primarily to the publication of major studies, it will contain occasional bibliographic essays and briefer articles dealing with unpublished archival or manuscript resources. The *Studies* will also make available in translation original articles by scholars who do not write in English.

Studies in Medieval and Renaissance History is not the official organ of any association or institution. Publication in the series is open to all historians whose research falls within its scope and fields of interest.

THE ORGANIZATION OF THE ENGLISH EPISCOPATE UNDER HENRY I

Everett U. Crosby

University of Virginia

ABBREVIATIONS

CHJ	*Cambridge Historical Journal* (after 1957 *The Historical Journal*)
Dugdale	*Monasticon Anglicanum*, ed. W. Dugdale (London, 1817–30)
EETS	*Early English Text Society*
EHD	*English Historical Documents*, ed. D. Douglas (London, 1953, etc.); Vol. I ed. D. Whitelock; Vol. II eds. D. Douglas and G. W. Greenaway
EHR	*English Historical Review*
EHS	*English Historical Society*
Feine	Hans E. Feine, *Kirchliche Rechtsgeschichte* (Cologne, 1964)
Haddan and Stubbs	*Councils and Ecclesiastical Documents Relating to Great Britain and Ireland*, eds. A. W. Haddan and W. Stubbs (3 vols.; Oxford, 1869)
HMCR	*Historical Manuscripts Commission Reports*
Le Neve	John Le Neve, *Fasti Ecclesiae Anglicanae* (London, 1716 and 1854)
PL	*Patrologiae Latinae Cursus Completus*, ed. J. P. Migne
Regesta	*Regesta Regum Anglo-Normannorum*, eds. H. Davis, C. Johnson, H. Cronne (2 vols.; Oxford, 1913, 1956)
RS	Rolls Series
TRHS	*Transactions of the Royal Historical Society*

THE ORGANIZATION OF THE ENGLISH EPISCOPATE UNDER HENRY I

I. The King's Bishops

The English episcopate during the reign of King Henry I (1100–1135) was a heterogeneous group of men, drawn from posts in the royal household and administration as well as from the monastic orders and lesser ecclesiastical offices; most of the bishops were chosen by the king and all of them required his approval before they were installed in their sees. By the twelfth century the bishops had become tenants-in-chief and held large estates by feudal military service, and it is understandable that Henry wished to maintain firm control over episcopal appointments.[1] Bishoprics were often bestowed on individuals for services performed, a practice that combined the advantages of a patronage system with a method of personal supervision. It is this double role of the bishop, as church officer and royal vassal, that underlies much of the history of the Anglo-Norman episcopate, although the extent to which an individual served his lord rather than his flock depended in large measure on the character and inclinations of the man himself.

In his description of the English monarchy, Walter Map speaks of the young Henry as "anxiously using every effort to gain the throne for he had not one of the bishops to aid him in his attempt; first, because Robert, his elder brother, was fighting in Jerusalem and, second, because Anselm was at that time in exile and of him with good reason they were afraid."[2] Although it is an exaggeration to say that Henry had not a bishop to help him in August of 1100, it is true that he did not have strong episcopal support in his bid for the crown. As Map states, the archbishop of Canterbury was abroad and did not reach England until late September of that year.[3] Thomas of York seems not to have been present at the coronation.[4]

1. The bishop of Rochester was an exception since he held of the archbishop of Canterbury rather than of the king (see p. 16).

2. Walter Map, *De Nugis Curialium*, in *Anecdota Oxoniensia*, ed. M. R. James, 4th ser., Vol. XIV (Oxford, 1914) and *Master Walter Map's Book*, eds. F. Tupper and M. B. Ogle (London, 1924), pp. 293 ff.

3. Eadmer, *Historia Novorum*, RS 81, p. 118.

4. Hugh the Chantor, *History*, ed. C. Johnson (London, 1961), p. 10: "audito T[homas] archiepiscopus qui tunc erat in Ripun de morte regis, accelerans versus Lundoniam, obtunc audivit Henricum regem esse consecratum . . . ." Thomas first witnessed a royal charter September 14, 1100, at Westminster (*Regesta*, II, 492).

Ranulf Flambard, the controversial bishop of Durham, would soon be seized and imprisoned in the Tower, and therefore, as the public victim of Henry's program of reform, was not in a position to lend outright support.[5] And two important sees, Salisbury and Winchester, were vacant and had been in the hands of the king.[6] Thus at the time of the coronation the bishops who held office and were able to perform their ecclesiastical functions were John (Bath), Ralph (Chichester), Osbern (Exeter), Gerard (Hereford), Robert (Chester), Robert (Lincoln), Maurice (London), Herbert (Norwich), Gundulf (Rochester), Samson (Worcester), Thomas (York), and the three bishops of Wales, Hervey (Bangor), Herewald (Llandaff), and Wilfrid (St. David's). Of these fourteen individuals, only Maurice of London, Gerard of Hereford, and Gundulf of Rochester appeared with the lay magnates at Westminster in August.[7] By September 14, Thomas of York and Robert of Chester were at Westminster, and probably by late September Robert of Lincoln had joined the court.[8]

By way of comparison, Stephen, on his accession in 1135, was able to count far more heavily on support from the episcopal baronage. Of the twenty sees in existence, only Bath, London, and Llandaff were vacant, and by April of 1136, when the great court was held at Oxford, Robert had been consecrated bishop of Bath.[9] Moreover, among the witnesses to the Oxford charter were the chief prelates of the realm: William of Canterbury, Henry of Winchester (the king's younger brother), Roger of Salisbury and his nephews Alexander of Lincoln and Nigel of Ely, Everard of Norwich, Simon of Worcester, Robert of Hereford, John of

5. H. Craster, "A Contemporary Record of the Pontificate of Ranulf Flambard," *Archaeologia Aeliana*, 4th ser., Vol. VII (1930); R. W. Southern, "Ranulf Flambard and Early Anglo-Norman Administration," *TRHS*, 4th ser., Vol. XVI (1933). Flambard attested as bishop on September 3, 1101, at Windsor (*Regesta*, II, 544).

6. Roger and William Giffard were named to the sees of Salisbury and Winchester, respectively, soon after Henry's accession, but were not consecrated until 1107, at the settlement of the investiture conflict. William attested the letter of Henry I to Anselm in August, 1100, as bishop-elect (*Regesta*, II, 491) and a royal charter to St. Peter's, Bath, on September 14 as bishop (*ibid.*, 492). Roger attested as chancellor and as bishop in two charters, probably in 1102 (*ibid.*, 595, 596). In addition to Canterbury, Salisbury, and Winchester, eleven of the largest and wealthiest abbeys also were in the king's hand; see H. Böhmer, *Kirche und Staat in England und in der Normandie im XI und XII Jahrhundert* (Leipzig, 1899), p. 155.

7. *Regesta*, II, 488*a*, 488*c*.

8. *Ibid.*, 492, 493, 495, 498.

9. See F. M. Powicke and E. B. Fryde, *Handbook of British Chronology* (London, 1961), p. 205.

Rochester, Adelulf of Carlisle, and Bernard of St. David's. The terms of the coronation charter of Henry I in 1100 and of Stephen in 1136 cast additional light on the development in the importance of the Anglo-Norman episcopate; Henry's promises were calculated to be most acceptable to the lay baronage but Stephen's were a firm bid for ecclesiastical support.

Henry, for example, promised the freedom of the church, that he would neither sell nor put at farm anything belonging to it, nor enjoy the revenues during archiepiscopal, episcopal, or abbatial vacancies; but the rest of the document lists the *malas consuetudines* by which the realm was oppressed and for which Henry promised relief. His main objective seems to have been the establishment of a satisfactory relationship between himself and his tenants-in-chief through which he could feel assured of their loyalty.[10]

Stephen's charter reveals greater dependence on the ecclesiastical magnates; indeed, to the author of the *Gesta Stephani* it was upon the king's brother, the bishop of Winchester, that "the whole effort rested."[11] Henry, like Stephen, promised that vacant sees would not be taken by the king, as was normal procedure, but where Henry's charter to Worcester has "nor . . . will I take anything from the demesne of the church or from its vassals during the period of vacancy until a successor is installed (*donec successor in eam ingrediatur*)," Stephen's charter states more fully: "when sees are vacant . . . I will give them into the hand and care of clerks and good men of the church until a shepherd is canonically appointed (*donec pastor canonice substituatur*)."

Where Henry promised freedom for his barons to dispose of their property, or, if they died intestate, the same freedom to their widows, children or relatives, Stephen's corresponding clause in his charter was addressed to his bishops, abbots or other ecclesiastics, who could dispose of their property as they wished, or, if they died intestate, disposal would be made, in each case, by the church. Other clauses in Henry's charter were addressed specifically to his barons, but Stephen promised free tenure of all ecclesiastical possessions held from the year 1087, confirmed

10. See *Select Charters*, ed. W. Stubbs (Oxford, 1948), 9th edition, pp. 117 ff., 142 ff. Stubbs and J. H. Round have pointed out the important comparisons of the coronation charters, but mainly in connection with Stephen's claim to the throne (J. H. Round, *Geoffrey de Mandeville* [London, 1892], pp. 25 ff.). For a discussion of the problems of interpretation in regard to royal interference *sede vacante,* see M. Howell, *Regalian Right in Medieval England* (London, 1962), pp. 20 ff.

11. *Gesta Stephani,* ed. K. Potter (London, 1955), p. 5.

immunities by charter as well as ancient customs of the church, and gave the bishops authority over all ecclesiastics and disposal of church lands. Even if Stephen, like Henry, was better at making promises than keeping them, the former owed much to the church, particularly to the episcopal power and to the groups represented on one side by Henry of Winchester and on the other by Roger of Salisbury.

These differences would point to the fact that during the period 1100–1135 the strong basis for episcopal power that was created through Norman influence, particularly after the conquest (by transferring sees to urban centers and increasing the bishop's diocesan control, by incorporating the prelates into the feudal military structure, and by separating lay and ecclesiastical courts), was broadened considerably by Henry I who came to depend in important ways on the service and support of his bishops. This conscious effort on the part of the king to strengthen his hand can be seen, for instance, in the long series of grants and confirmations made to certain of his ecclesiastical barons. Not all of them, of course, achieved equally favored positions. Some are seen continually in attendance upon the king, while others hardly ever appear and, as will be shown in the following discussion, a correlation can be made between status and service on the basis of the difference between secular and monastic bishops, and between those individuals drawn from the royal household or from outside it.

With the information provided by William Farrer in his *Itinerary*,[12] and the charter evidence in the second volume of the *Regesta Regum Anglo-Normannorum* it is possible to compile a list of the bishops under Henry I in the order of frequency of appearances as witnesses to the granting of royal charters. Most of the bishops of course, held their sees for varying lengths of time, and to adjust this difference a factor has been obtained by dividing an individual's total appearances by the number of years he was in possession of his bishopric between 1100 and 1135.[13] Although there would be a variation in the order if more information were found for an individual's place in the *curia regis*, this compilation permits a statistical approximation of the political importance of Henry's bishops. Of forty-four bishops the fifteen who rank highest in our list are Roger of Salisbury, Robert of Lincoln, Henry of Winchester, Turstin of York, Nigel of Ely, Alexander of Lincoln, Ralph of Canterbury, William of Winchester,

12. W. Farrer, "An Outline Itinerary of King Henry I," *EHR*, XXXIV (1919), 303 ff., 505 ff.

13. Ralph of Rochester, Gerard of Hereford, and Hervey of Bangor each appear twice, as archbishops of Canterbury and York, and bishop of Ely, respectively.

Anselm of Canterbury, Bernard of St. David's, William of Canterbury, Geoffrey of Durham, Maurice of London, Robert of Hereford, and Ranulf of Durham. It will be seen from the following discussion that other evidence supports the conclusion that these men enjoyed a superior position in the political life of the realm.

STATISTICAL RANKING OF THE POLITICAL IMPORTANCE OF THE ENGLISH BISHOPS DURING THE REIGN OF HENRY I, BASED ON FREQUENCY OF APPEARANCES AS WITNESSES TO THE GRANTING OF ROYAL CHARTERS

Bishop	*Appear-ances*	*Years in See*	*Factor*	*Bishop*	*Appear-ances*	*Years in See*	*Factor*
1. Roger of Salisbury	143	29	4.93	25. Gilbert of London	7	8	0.87
2. Robert of Lincoln	110	24	4.58	26. Thomas of York	5	6	0.83
3. Henry of Winchester	20	7	2.85	27. John of Bath	18	23	0.78
4. Turstin of York	48	17	2.82	28. Osbern of Exeter	3	4	0.75
5. Nigel of Ely	8	3	2.66	29. Ralph of Chichester	17	24	0.70
6. Alexander of Lincoln	34	13	2.61	30. Robert Limesey of Chester	12	18	0.66
7. Ralph of Canterbury‡	20	9	2.22	31. Everard of Norwich	9	15	0.60
8. William of Winchester	49	23	2.13	32. Herbert of Norwich	11	20	0.55
9. Anselm of Canterbury	21	10	2.10	33. Theulf of Worcester	5	9	0.55
10. Bernard of St. David's	44	21	2.10	34. Simon of Worcester	6	11	0.54
11. William of Canterbury	22	13	1.69	35. Hervey of Bangor‡	5	10	0.50
12. Geoffrey of Durham	5	3	1.66	36. Gerard of Hereford‡	3	6	0.50
13. Maurice of London	13	8	1.62	37. Hervey of Ely‡	11	23	0.47
14. Robert of Hereford	7	5	1.40	38. Godfrey of Bath	6	13	0.46
15. Ranulf of Durham	35	29	1.20	39. John of Rochester	5	11	0.45
16. Robert Pecce of Coventry	8	7	1.14	40. Ralph of Rochester‡	2	7	0.28
17. Richard of Hereford	8	7	1.14	41. Regenhelm of Hereford	2	9	0.22
18. Richard of London	20	20	1.00	42. Ernulf of Rochester	2	10	0.20
19. Samson of Worcester	13	13	1.00	43. David of Bangor	3	16	0.18
20. Seefrid of Chichester	11	11	1.00	44. Roger of Coventry	1	7	0.14
21. Adelulf of Carlisle	3	3	1.00	45. Urban of Llandaff	3	27?	0.11
22. William of Exeter	27	29	0.93	46. Geoffrey of Hereford	0	6	0.00
23. Gundulf of Rochester	8	9	0.88	47. Wilfrid of St. David's	0	16	0.00
24. Gerard of York‡	7	8	0.87				

‡ V. p. 6, note 13.

In regard to ecclesiastical appointees, the king usually was free upon the death or removal of an individual bishop to suggest a candidate without fear that the *temporalia* would be claimed by an heir (there are several instances in which bishops of the period were able to provide for their offspring or close relatives but it is difficult to determine whether the wealth belonged to the see or to the bishop). Sometimes he would delay the appointment because the clergy could not be expected to contribute various feudal dues, as for marriage and wardship, and since these were lost to the lord, Henry doubtless attempted to make them up through revenue from vacant sees. A bishopric, however, that provided considerable income and conferred an assured status was eagerly sought by various men. During the period from the last years of William I to the death of Henry I, for instance, Herbert Losinga (whose simoniac character inspired a short poem) paid his way into the see of Norwich, at last repented, and sought forgiveness at Rome.[14] Robert Bloet, it is said, gave the king several thousand pounds for consideration for the see of Lincoln;[15] and Theulf, a royal chaplain, if we may believe William of Malmesbury, seems to have bought his office at Worcester.[16] The grant of a bishopric also was a means by which Henry could reward a competent and faithful servant for services rendered, such as Roger of Salisbury, who also became one of the chief advisors of the king in the decade of 1120. Or it could be a means by which a politically important figure was satisfied and made useful, as was Nigel of Ely (Bishop Roger's nephew), who also became a royal treasurer—or a means by which someone like Ranulf of Durham could be brought back into the royal service. Henry, continuing a practice of his father and brother, promoted men to important offices from groups well known to him, particularly from the royal household and, as one of the groups from which bishops were chosen, it has been established that more than half of the English and Welsh episcopate during Henry's reign came from this source.

The *Constitutio Domus Regis*, drawn up shortly after the death of Henry I, tells us the office of chancellor was of greatest importance, and it is of interest to note that the bishops who were appointed to the most important sees often had served in this capacity[17]: Gerard of York,[18] Geoffrey of Durham,[19] Maurice of London,[20] Roger of Salisbury,[21] William of Winchester,[22] and Robert of Lincoln.[23] Regenhelm and Bernard were chancellors of the queen before their elevation to the sees of Hereford and

14. A. L. Poole, *From Domesday Book to Magna Carta* (Oxford, 1951), p. 169.
15. Henry of Huntingdon set the figure at £5,000 (RS 74, p. 217).
16. William of Malmesbury, *Gesta Pontificum*, RS 52, p. 151.
17. *Red Book of the Exchequer*, RS 99, I, 808 ff. A full discussion is provided by G. H. White in "The Household of the Norman Kings," *TRHS*, 4th ser., Vol. XXX (1948); cf. J. H. Round, *The King's Serjeants and Officers of State* (London, 1911), 52 ff.
18. *Regesta*, II, ix.
19. Robert of Torigni, *Chronicon*, RS 82, *anno* 1133; cf. *Waverley Annals*, RS 36, Vol. II, *anno* 1133.
20. *Regesta*, I, 147, 285; see also William of Malmesbury, *GP*, RS 52, p. 145.
21. *Regesta*, II, 507, 521, 1211, 1488, 1514; see Symeon, *Historia*, RS 75, p. 184.
22. *Regesta*, I, 415, 427.
23. *Ibid.*, 315, 337.

St. David's,[24] and Godfrey of Bath also may have been a chancellor of the queen, for he is called *capellanus reginae* by Matthew Paris (but *cancellarius reginae* by Roger of Howden and simply *cancellarius* by Henry of Huntingdon).[25] Turstin and Thomas II of York, although from the royal household, are not mentioned as chancellors, nor the archbishops of Canterbury, but the correspondence shows that men who achieved suitable recognition to have become chancellor were later given bishoprics commensurate to their previous position. The only exception to this was Ranulf, a chancellor, who became lord of Berkhampstead, in Hertfordshire—the honour of William of Mortain, who rebelled against the king in 1106. Ranulf, who died in 1123, did not become a bishop.[26]

Other individuals were advanced to episcopal office from the royal chapel: Theulf to Worcester, Everard to Norwich, and Thomas and Turstin to York.[27] William Warelwast, who became bishop of Exeter in 1107, had served as a royal chaplain, as a judge in the *curia* of William II, and—during Henry's reign—was a favorite courtier and royal agent.[28] Samson, who was a chaplain, and Simon, who had been a chaplain to the queen, were appointed to the see of Worcester; Herbert Losinga acquired Norwich and John of Tours became bishop of Bath.[29] Robert de Limesey, bishop of Chester, who had been a chaplain at the time of his appointment in 1086, died in 1117 and was succeeded by Robert Pecce in 1121, after a four-year vacancy. The latter first attested charters as chaplain in 1101, and after twenty years of service was rewarded with a see.[30] Other members of the household who were elevated were Richard, *custos sigilli regis*, who became bishop of Hereford in 1119, and Roger, the royal larderer, who died before his consecration in the same see—and so perhaps added to the legend of the short-lived bishops of Hereford.[31] Osbern Fitz-Osbern, bishop of Exeter until 1103 and brother of William Fitz-Osbern, earl of Hereford, seems to have been a member of the royal household before the Conquest;[32] and Nigel of Ely served as a treasurer of

24. *Regesta*, II, 544, 624.

25. Matthew Paris, *Chronica majora*, RS 57, p. 150; Roger of Howden, *Chronica*, RS 51, *anno* 1120; Henry of Huntingdon, *Historia*, RS 74, p. 245.

26. *Regesta*, II, 810; see also I. J. Sanders, *English Baronies* (Oxford, 1960), p. 14.

27. Hugh the Chantor, *op. cit.*, pp. 15, 33.

28. *Regesta*, I, 423, and II, 544. For a description of William, see Eadmer, RS 81, p. 187.

29. *Regesta*, I, xx, 146*a*, 147, 158, 315; Ordericus Vitalis, *Historia Ecclesiastica*, ed. Le Prévost, 5 vols. (Paris, 1840), IV, 11–12.

30. *Regesta*, II, 544, 684, 800, 1015, 1183, 1204, 1226.

31. William of Malmesbury, *GP*, RS 52, pp. 303 ff.

32. *Ibid.*, p. 201; see also J. H. Round, *Feudal England* (London, 1895), p. 320.

Henry I.[33] Geoffrey of Hereford is listed as a royal chaplain in the Godwin catalogue of 1601.[34]

If the court supplied many important sees with competent men who, from the traditional view of the church were not always good bishops, many sees were filled from the ranks of the monastic orders.[35] It might be thought that the monastic bishops, on the average, were less influential in the royal administration than those drawn from the household, but the evidence does not support this conclusion, even though the monastics were outnumbered by the seculars by more than three to one (ten monastics and thirty-five seculars). The archbishops of Canterbury were often present in the *curia regis*, Henry of Winchester can hardly be thought of as a monastic recluse, and Seefrid of Chichester, who had been abbot of Glastonbury, appears fairly often, as does Robert de Betun of Hereford, formerly an Austin canon and prior at Llanthony. Adelulf of Carlisle, prior of St. Oswald, and another Austin canon, although in office only three years under Henry, was regularly present. Herbert of Norwich, formerly abbot of Ramsey and a royal chaplain, and Gundulf and Ernulf of Rochester appear less often, but the fact that at least the latter two considered themselves monks first and bishops second may have been decisive.

Other individuals cannot be identified with either the monastic or the secular group. Richard de Belmeis, who, although closely attached to the Montgomery-Belême family wisely chose to remain loyal to the king during the rebellion in 1102, was named sheriff of Shropshire that same year and received the see of London in 1108,[36] Gilbert of London was a royal minister abroad and noted for his learning.[37] Roger de Clinton of Chester-Coventry was a nephew of Henry's treasurer and chamberlain, Geoffrey de Clinton.[38] Ralph Luffa of Chichester was a justiciar in the time of William II.[39] Hervey the Breton was bishop of Bangor and Ely,[40]

33. *Dialogus de Scaccario*, ed. C. Johnson (London, 1950), p. 50. For a notice of Nigel as treasurer in Normandy, see *Regesta*, II, 1691.

34. Francis Godwin, *Catalogue of the Bishops of England since the first planting of Christian religion in this Island* . . . (London, 1601). Geoffrey's chaplaincy, however, is not confirmed by other sources.

35. D. Knowles, *The Monastic Order in England* (Cambridge, 1950), pp. 709 ff.

36. *Regesta*, II, 900, 1473; see also R. W. Eyton, *Antiquities of Shropshire* (London, 1854–60). For the possibility that he may also have been sheriff of Sussex at the same time, see *Regesta*, II, 614, 810.

37. Hugh the Chantor, *op. cit.*, p. 127.

38. William of Malmesbury, *GP*, RS 52, p. 311.

39. *Regesta*, I, xxviii, 424; see also M. E. C. Walcott, "Early Statutes of Chichester," *Archaeologia*, XLV (1877), 95.

40. E. Miller, *The Abbey and Bishopric of Ely* (Cambridge, 1951), pp. 3–4.

and Alexander of Lincoln was promoted to his see—as the chronicler has it—because "of Henry's great love for Bishop Roger."[41]

Of the Welsh bishops during this period, Bernard of St. David's—as has been mentioned, was in the curial group. Wilfrid, his predecessor, was also a Welshman, and probably was nominated in the tradition of the *clas*.[42] David of Bangor had served in the court of Henry V, son-in-law of the king, and later returned to Wales.[43] Herewald of Llandaff, elected by the "people of the diocese,"[44] was invested by William I and consecrated by Lanfranc. Urban, who became bishop of Llandaff after a vacancy of four years, is called a priest of Worcester.[45] It did not seem to matter whether a bishop in a Welsh see was a native or a Norman who had been appointed outside the *clas*; what was important was his loyalty to the king—or apart from loyalty, the need of the moment might dictate the choice of bishop. On the death of Wilfrid, for instance, it is reported that the local clergy elected Daniel ap Sulien but that Henry dismissed him "against the will of the Britons" and gave the see to the royal favorite, Bernard; but David Scotus of Bangor, who was "elected by the Welsh prince and the clergy and people of Wales," retained his see for nineteen years.[46]

Henry tried to keep a firm hand upon his episcopate, but there is at least one important instance in this period—in connection with the vacancy at Canterbury after 1109—in which the candidate recommended by the king did not become the bishop. Henry, soon after his coronation, granted the abbey of Abingdon to Faritius, formerly a monk at Malmesbury and a physician to King Henry. Faritius was known as a competent and intelligent abbot, and undoubtedly found his connections with the royal household an advantage (a monk of Malmesbury sang his praise in a rhymed panegyric of twenty-eight lines). After the death of Anselm the king desired that the abbot take the archbishopric, but the important

41. *Anglo-Saxon Chronicle*, RS 23 *anno* 1123. See Henry of Huntingdon, *De contemptu mundi*, RS 74.

42. J. Davies (ed.), *Episcopal Acts Relating to the Welsh Dioceses* (1946), I, 132. The *clas* was a semi-monastic group, in some cases under the direction of a bishop, and often composed of clergy and laymen, following a local custom rather than the discipline of a regular order. See page 32.

43. Ordericus Vitalis, *op. cit.*, IV, 77; see also K. Leyser, "England and the Empire in the Early Twelfth Century," *TRHS*, 5th ser., X (1960), 77.

44. *Episcopal Acts*. L.4. The phrase, of course, may be nothing more than a figure of speech.

45. *Cartae et alia munimenta quae ad dominum de Glamorgancia pertinent*, ed. G. T. Clark (Cardiff, 1910), I, charter 38.

46. Haddan and Stubbs, I, 308. *Brut y Tywysogion*, RS 17, p. 118. See Walter of Coventry, RS 58, *anno* 1120. Again, the phrase may not be literally true.

curial bishops of the realm, meeting in council at Windsor, opposed the choice. According to William of Malmesbury, they feared the domination of such a man in the primacy; also, being seculars, they preferred a secular archbishop. The prior and monks of Canterbury then proposed Ralph of Rochester and it was finally agreed to promote him. Although a monk, Bishop Ralph was an obvious choice for he had administered the archiepiscopal see during the vacancy, and, unlike Faritius, seemed to be of an accommodating spirit.[47] From the time of his installation as abbot, Faritius had been the beneficiary of at least nineteen grants or confirmations by the king, including (on some of his lands) an exemption from the aid of three shillings on the hide that Henry levied, with the consent of his barons, to reimburse himself for expenses incurred at the time of his marriage to Matilda, daughter of the Salian Henry V.[48] In the case of Faritius, whose position was comparable to that of other barons who enjoyed special favor and received a bishopric, the king failed to advance a member of his household and the abbot failed to gain the reward for his services. That Henry evidently was willing to reconsider in the face of opposition from the bishops (such men as Robert of Lincoln and Roger of Salisbury, *qui summi erant in regno*) suggests the importance of the leading episcopal barons.[49] In the Canterbury election of 1123, for example, when the monks wanted one of their own, the bishops, this time supported by the king, proposed a clerk and the choice finally fell on William of Corbeil, an Austin canon and prior of St. Osyth, which broke the long tradition that archbishops were drawn from the abbey of Bec.

The charter evidence in the *Regesta* and the accounts in the Pipe Roll for Henry's reign make it clear that some of the bishops enjoyed important grants of lands and churches, grants of fairs, markets and tolls, and exemptions from the *murdrum* and Danegeld assessments; and some of those most favored in this respect are the bishops who appear most often in the witness lists as members of the *curia*. A summary of some of the most significant grants will help illustrate the point and will indicate the diversity of benefits conferred. We will consider only grants that were made directly to a bishop; grants made to a bishop and chapter, or to a

47. *Chronicon Monasterii de Abingdon*, RS 2, II, pp. 45 ff.; William of Malmesbury, *GP*, RS 52, pp. 125 ff., 192; Eadmer, RS 81, p. 222; see also D. Knowles, *Monastic Order*, pp. 180 ff.

48. *Regesta*, II, 959; also K. Leyser, *op. cit.*, pp. 64–65. For the grants, see *Regesta*, II, 498, 520, 550, 565, 567, 613, 615–16, 676, 701–3, 728, 854, 858, 952, 972, 980, 982, 1037, 1089, 1092, 1110, 1128, 1132–33.

49. Henry of Huntingdon, RS 74, p. 2.

bishop and monks, or to the church are not cited, even though there were many of these and the favor an individual enjoyed might well have been the reason for the king's action.[50]

Robert, bishop of Lincoln, in a charter granted probably no later than 1106, was given the manor of Tixover (formerly part of the royal demesne) by Queen Matilda at the king's request; shortly thereafter Robert was given the churches of three manors, Coxwold, Kirkby Moorside, and Hovingham in Yorkshire, and was ordered reseised of the church of Hough-on-the-Hill by Geoffrey, the steward of Count Stephen.[51] Other gifts followed: the churches of Caistor and Kirton, and of Barkstone and Uffington in the honour of Belvoir, and the Domesday barony of Robert de Todeni in Leicestershire.[52] Further, the king ordered the boundaries reviewed between his manor of Torksey and the bishop's manor of Stow, according to the formula "that the king wishes the bishop to hold well and honorably that which his predecessors possessed."[53] In the Leicestershire Survey, in the latter part of Henry's reign, the only change noted in the episcopal holdings as compared with Domesday Book was a gain of one estate, although the archbishop of York lost several estates to the lay magnate, Henry de Port.[54] In a notification before 1115, Henry made it known he had given the bishop permission to make an opening in the wall of the king's castle at Lincoln for the convenience of the bishop's house.[55] Robert's successor, Alexander, also enjoyed a series of royal favors. Shortly before 1133 he was given permission to divert the king's road at Newark and to enlarge his fishpond. (It is quite possible, however, that this favor cost the bishop twenty marks silver and one mark gold—the amount Goislinus, the bishop's steward, accounted for in 1130 "for the causeway made in the king's road.")[56] Alexander also was allowed to

50. For instances, see *Regesta,* II, 558, 628, 947 for Winchester; 837, 839 for York; 918 for Durham; 1421, 1576, 1620 for Ely; 1265 for Hereford; 617 for Chichester; 573, 1762 for Bath; 548 for Norwich; 868 for Rochester.

51. *Regesta,* II, 743–44, 977, 1115. It may be that the churches referred to in the grant at Woodstock (No. 977) were in the hands of Nigel d'Albini, who was named in the address and who was the sole witness. See I. J. Sanders, *English Baronies,* p. 37, for *Cottingham.*

52. *Regesta,* II, 1117, 1152. For the earlier grants of "Kirkton" and "Caistor," see *Regesta,* I, 283, 407.

53. *Regesta,* II, 1116.

54. *The Leicestershire Survey,* ed. C. F. Slade (Leicester, 1956), p. 95.

55. *Regesta,* II, 1118.

56. *Ibid.,* 1660–61. By comparison, the penalty of *straetbreche* in Henry's time is reported as 100*s.* (D. M. Stenton, "Communications," in *Medieval England,* ed., A. L. Poole (Oxford, 1958), I, 198.)

exchange land with Richard de Vernon in order to enlarge his park at Thame; he was given the right to build over the Trent, at his castle at Newark, where he held a five-day fair; the east gate of Lincoln was granted to him as a lodging; he was allowed to assign a third part of the knight-service of his bishopric to Newark Castle; and he was given free warren in all his lands in Lincolnshire.[57]

Alexander's uncle, Roger of Salisbury, as one might expect, was a beneficiary on many occasions. Henry lavished estates, churches, prebends, and abbeys upon Roger, who also received the tithes of hunting in the New Forest (and elsewhere) and the customs of the fairs of St. Frideswide in Oxford. In 1106 the king granted Bishop Roger the marcher lordship of Kidwelly, in southern Wales, and between 1107 and 1115 Roger gave a carucate of land to the church of Sherborne. In the charter that pertains to this gift the bishop mentioned a new ditch, a new mill, and the castle at Kidwelly. Although it is not known how much of the castle defenses he was responsible for, he had evidently been increasing the value of his lordship, which later passed into the hands of the London family, the first lay lords of Kidwelly.[58]

Other bishops who figure prominently as royal grantees are Ranulf of Durham, who received extensive confirmations (after his restoration) of lands and goods—those that belonged to the bishopric as well as those he had earlier owned.[59] Hervey of Ely, among other privileges, was permitted to have his service of castle guard in the Isle of Ely rather than at Norwich castle, although he was amerced £1,000 (of which he had paid only £364 before his death).[60] In 1127, William of Canterbury (and his successors forever) was given the custody and constabulary of the king's castle at Rochester, with permission to fortify it as he chose and with lodgings in the bailey.[61]

These grants to the episcopal baronage compare favorably with grants King Henry made to the greater lay magnates: to William de Albini, *pincerna*, the butler of the king, whose successors were the earls of Arundel;[62]

57. *Regesta*, II, 1707, 1770–73, 1784, 1792, 1899. See F. M. Stenton, *The First Century of English Feudalism* (Oxford, 1950), p. 212.

58. *Regesta*, II, 1162–64, 1362, 1957; see also *Episcopal Acts*, I, D.27, and pp. 113–14; J. Lloyd, *History of Wales* (London, 1939), II, p. 429.

59. *Regesta*, II, 540, 546, 560, 562, 575, 589–90, 642, 925, 1181.

60. *Ibid.*, 1420, 1503, 1656. See F. M. Stenton, *loc. cit.*

61. *Ibid.*, 1475, 1606. Lincoln, Ely, and Canterbury may have been included in *castallariae* grouped around Newark, Norwich, and Rochester castles (see Stenton, *op. cit.*, pp. 193, 207).

62. *Regesta*, II, 848, 911.

to Walter de Beauchamp, a royal dispenser and sheriff of Worcestershire, who married the daughter of Urse d'Abitot and received lands in Worcestershire after the exile of Urse's son, Roger (about 1110);[63] to Eudo, *dapifer*; to Walter and Miles of Gloucester, royal constables; to William Maudit, chamberlain of the exchequer; to Aubrey de Vere, master chamberlain; to Robert and Henry of Beaumont, earls of Leicester and Warwick, respectively; and to the king's nephew, Stephen, count of Boulogne, the future king of England.[64]

Examination of the extant portion of the Pipe Roll for Henry's reign indicates that although the episcopal group was a source of income for the king, a few of its members also received great benefits. In rough figures for purposes of comparison, the bishop of Salisbury was granted £160 in exemptions from the Danegeld and £560 in other reductions, as the *murdrum* and sheriff's aid. The bishop of Lincoln's Danegeld was reduced £30, but he showed a debt of £120. The bishop of Winchester was pardoned £50 in Danegeld assessments and £25 in miscellaneous amercements, but he owed £112. Others who were favored in one way or another were the archbishops of Canterbury and York and the bishop of London.[65] Hervey of Ely, however, owed an enormous amount, more than £1,400; the bishop of Rochester owed £40 and the bishop of Exeter £25. The farms of the bishoprics of Durham and Hereford, then vacant, were accounted for like other revenues that came into the royal exchequer.[66] These various grants and releases seem to have been in the form of outright gifts, although Henry seldom allowed his practical sense to be clouded by favoritism, and, like his Norman predecessors, used every device that would maintain or increase his income.[67]

On the basis of their military power as well, in the eyes of the king and in the life of the realm, bishops often enjoyed prestige and power that was little different from that of the most important lay lords. Comparison of the episcopal returns in the *Cartae Baronum* of 1166 shows that eleven of the fifteen archbishops and bishops represented had enfeoffed knights

63. *Ibid.*, xvi, 1024–25, 1034–35, 1062, 1550, 1710; see also I. J. Sanders, *op. cit.*, p. 75, for *Salwarpe.*

64. *Regesta*, II, 519, 552, 661 for Eudo; 998, 1268, 1280, 1395, 1552, 1622, 1723 for Gloucester; 729, 1255, 1719, 1846–47 for Maudit; 849, 1777–78, 1876 for de Vere.

65. *Pipe Roll*, 31 Henry I, ed. J. Hunter (London, 1929), *passim.*

66. J. H. Ramsey, *Revenues of the Kings of England*, 2 vols. (Oxford, 1925), I, p. 56.

67. The barons of the exchequer were said to be quit of Danegeld and *murdrum* fines (*Dialogus de Scaccario*, p. 56), which would mean Roger of Salisbury and Robert of Lincoln, and probably Nigel of Ely. Roger and Robert appear as members of the *curia regis* that sat for judicial business in 1119 (*Regesta*, II, 1211).

in excess of their quotas prior to the death of Henry I.[68] Canterbury, York, Ely, Exeter, Lincoln, London, Salisbury, and Winchester are the most important in this group. Those who had granted less than their quota were Bath, Chester, Norwich, and Worcester, and if under-enfeoffment meant lack of adequate resources, the picture here, at least as far as the first three sees are concerned, is not surprising. It will be recalled that the bishop of Ely was willing to pay the sum of £240 to the king in 1127 to be relieved of paying £40 of scutage on his surplus knights;[69] and Henry was quite willing to privilege his higher barons—for a price. We do not have the accounts for Carlisle and Rochester because, in the former case, Augustinian houses held by free alms, and therefore Carlisle did not owe military service to the king; and the bishop of Rochester owed his service to the archbishop of Canterbury (just prior to 1100 he was responsible for sending ten knights to his metropolitan).[70]

In addition to the *servitia debita*, the records of the knights' fees support the contention that the leading bishops were as important as the greatest lay magnates on the basis of military power. Before 1135 the bishop of Lincoln had granted the large number of 100½ fees, the archbishop of Canterbury 84¾, and the bishop of Winchester 70⅓. The bishop of Durham had granted 62⅔ fees, the bishop of Worcester 57, the bishop of Ely 56¼, the archbishop of York slightly over 44, the bishop of Salisbury about 39, the bishop of Exeter 33½—down to the bishop of Chichester, who had granted 9⅔.[71]

Closely connected with the military aspect of their power (and already mentioned in passing) was the program of castle building entered upon with a great deal of energy by a number of bishops. Roger of Salisbury

68. H. Chew, *Ecclesiastical Tenants-in-Chief and Knight Service* (Oxford, 1932). The bishop of Worcester had enfeoffed fifty-seven knights' fees before 1135, and his quota was set at sixty; he later claimed, however, that he owed only fifty (*Pipe Roll*, 2 Henry II, p. 63). If this was true, the total should be twelve instead of eleven.

69. *Regesta*, II, 1499; *Pipe Roll*, 31 Henry I, p. 44. For the implications of this action in the history of English feudalism, see F. M. Stenton, *op. cit.*, pp. 179 ff., S. Painter, *Studies in the History of the English Feudal Baronage* (Baltimore, 1943), p. 34, and E. Miller, *op. cit.*, pp. 155–62.

70. In regard to Carlisle, I. J. Sanders suggests that the date the military service was fixed lay between 1109, when the see of Ely, which owed forty knights, was founded, and 1133, when Carlisle cathedral church was founded, *Feudal Military Service in England* (Oxford, 1956), pp. 16–17; but 1133 seems questionable as a terminal date because of the special tenure involved. For Rochester, see D. Douglas, *Domesday Monachorum of Christ Church* (London, 1944), p. 105.

71. *Red Book of the Exchequer*, RS 99, Vol. I. In the case of Canterbury it is uncertain how many of these fees were granted between 1135 and 1166, but probably only a few.

built at Sherborne and Devizes, and probably at Kidwelly (as noted); at Malmesbury, he began his castle in the churchyard, and he obtained the royal castle at Salisbury for his use.[72] Alexander of Lincoln had castles at Newark and Sleaford.[73] The bishops of London acquired Stortford.[74] Bishop Ranulf fortified Durham; indeed, he made the castle so strong that, in the words of the poet Laurence, "it was impenetrable, impregnable and impossible to take by siege."[75] Ranulf also built at Norham, on the Tweed, and the castle became an important fortress in the north.[76]

It was only natural that the bishops should have desired their own castles, and if Henry counted them loyal to him and stood to profit by their industry he allowed them this freedom.[77] After Henry's death a number of lay barons who were not in sympathy with what they termed "the bishops' rage for castle building" helped convince Stephen of the bishops' bad faith and particularly accused Roger of Salisbury (but not Henry of Winchester), which led to Roger's arrest in 1139.[78] The reasons for this move have not yet been satisfactorily explained, and the king may have acted with more sense than he has heretofore been credited;[79] at any rate, the incident illustrates the potential danger of the bishops as great barons. The bishop of Ely, who had escaped arrest, upon hearing of his uncle's death, "abandoned the weapons of the gospel" and hired a private guard to avenge the crimes of the king.[80] During the reign of Henry I, however, the bishops were building their power and the king was able to keep them under control.

Since a number of references have been made to bishops' relatives in the course of this discussion, it might rightly be asked to what extent there was an attempt to establish their power, military or otherwise, on the basis of family relationships. It seems clear that, although more than half of the bishops in office during Henry's reign advanced their relatives

72. William of Malmesbury, *Historia Novella*, ed. K. Potter (London, 1955), p. 25.

73. *Gesta Stephani*, ed. K. Potter (London, 1955), p. 49, n. 1.

74. *Early Charters of . . . St. Paul*, ed. M. Gibbs (London, 1939), p. 31; see also *Regesta*, I, 211.

75. *Dialogi Laurentii Dunelmensis monachi ac prioris*, ed. J. Raine (London, 1880), Vol. LXX.

76. *Symeon of Durham*, RS 75, Vol. II.

77. Episcopal support of the king during the rebellions of 1088 and 1102 has been described as decisive (A. L. Poole, *From Domesday Book to Magna Carta*, pp. 101, 116).

78. William of Malmesbury, *Historia Novella*, pp. 26 ff.

79. *Gesta Stephani*, p. 48.

80. William of Malmesbury, *op. cit.*, and *Gesta Stephani* (pp. 64–66). See A. L. Poole, *op. cit.*, p. 137.

to positions of wealth and authority, and although several bishops doubtless owed their promotion to their relations with important families, there was no successful movement by a family group to "pack" the episcopate. Perhaps six bishops of Henry's reign came from important baronial families but only four of them[81] can be traced with certainty, and in no case is there enough evidence to justify the conclusion that there was a plan for dynastic advancement beyond normal needs. The power to give away tenements and livings, of course, added considerably to a bishop's authority and prestige, and this was frequently done; he could also appoint members of his family to household positions, and usually could bestow archdeaconries as he chose. At no time, however, not even in the last years of the reign, when one encounters the power bloc represented by Roger of Salisbury and his nephews, did a single family dominate the episcopate.

It might be wondered whether the ecclesiastical promotions of bishops' relatives tended to decrease the authority and efficiency of the offices, but there is not enough information here for a definite answer. There is no way of knowing how well an individual carried out his duties, except in a few cases, and these concern bishops, not the lower orders—and there is the problem of standards for judgment: an ecclesiastic who was a good administrator (like John of Bath's son) might advance the power but not the "name" of the church. It seems safe to consider the episcopal relatives who became bishops as no worse than some of their predecessors. In any case, there are no indications of widespread incompetence; it is likely that John of Salisbury would have made the same harsh remarks about archdeacons even if family members had not been given the posts.[82]

Family connections are of interest insofar as they illustrate the relationships between the individuals who were most important in the ecclesiastical life of the realm and the fact that there was never a strict compliance with the rules on clerical celibacy and the buying of church promotions.[83] At Canterbury, the background of Anselm is obscure, but

81. The bishops are Henry of Blois, Everard of Montgomery, Roger de Clinton, Osbern Fitz-Osbern, William Giffard, and Robert de Limesey. Although the surnames of the last two can be connected with prominent baronial families, the individuals cannot. See below.

82. Johannis Sarisberiensis, *Opera*, ed. J. A. Giles (Oxford, 1848), I, 260.

83. The Council of London, under Anselm, laid the rules down—in 1102. There is doubt, however, that the rules were strictly enforced, as it was thought that absolute obedience was impossible and that the priests might be led into more monstrous practices (Henry of Huntingdon, RS 74, pp. 234 ff.). That the decrees were not obeyed is proved not only by the histories of several bishops but also by the fact that other councils at

it is known that his sister, Richesa, married a man named Burgundius, and their son, also named Anselm, was treated with favor and given protection by his uncle. He came to England, evidently held a legatine commission, and became abbot of Bury St. Edmunds—and possibly a candidate for an English bishopric.[84] Although the archbishop also speaks of his other relatives (*consanguinei*), and some of these are known by name, none of them seems to have held church office in England.[85] Anselm's successor at Canterbury, Ralph of Rochester, had a brother, Pelochin (also called Sigfrid), who was sent as royal representative to Rome (in March of 1123) with Anselm of Bury St. Edmunds and several bishops.[86] Pelochin became abbot of Glastonbury, and was later made bishop of Chichester.[87] A similar case is that of Ralph's nephew, John, to whom the archbishop gave an archdeaconry in Canterbury and who is mentioned as having made a journey to Rome for the *pallium* in the company of William Warelwast, bishop of Exeter, in 1114. A relation of the archbishop, a cathedral dignitary, and active on a mission to the pope with an important curial bishop, it is not surprising that John became bishop of Rochester (in 1125).

In the archbishopric of York, Gerard, who had been bishop of Hereford, was a nephew of Walkelin, the bishop of Winchester.[88] Gerard's successor, Thomas II, was the son of Samson, bishop of Worcester in 1096 and *de nobilissima Normannorum prosapia oriundus.*[89] Thomas II also was the nephew of Thomas I, Gerard's predecessor at York,[90] which would appear to make Samson the brother of Thomas I. Samson's other son was Richard, who became bishop of Bayeux (where Samson had been

---

London (in 1125, 1127, and 1129) again issued the same pronouncements. *Concilia Magnae Britanniae et Hiberniae*, ed. D. Wilkins (London, 1737), I, 410.

84. *Letters of Osbert of Clare*, ed. E. W. Williamson (Oxford, 1929), p. 193. There is a brief discussion of the problem in R. W. Southern, *St. Anselm and his Biographer* (Cambridge, 1963), pp. 10–11. *Nepos* here means "nephew," although at other times it may be a euphemism for an illegitimate son. As Coulton once remarked, quoting Giraldus Cambrensis: "When God deprived bishops of sons, the Devil gave them nephews," G. G. Coulton, *Medieval Panorama* (Cambridge, 1947), p. 129.

85. *Sancti Anselmi . . . Opera Omnia*, ed. F. S. Schmitt (5 vols.; Rome and Edinburgh, 1938–51), IV, 290.

86. Symeon, RS 75, II, 268–69; Hugh the Chantor, *op. cit.*, p. 111.

87. In 1125 by a royal charter in favor of "Seefrid Polek(in)" (in *Regesta*, II, 1424).

88. William of Malmesbury, *GP*, RS 52, p. 258. At the time Walkelin died, Gerard was at Hereford, although he remained there only six years.

89. *Ibid.*, p. 260; see also the York archiepiscopal chronicle (RS 71, II, 522).

90. Hugh the Chantor, *op. cit.*, p. 15.

Cathedral treasurer).[91] The possession of the three sees was a family affair, so that Hugh the Chantor speaks of a *jus hereditarium* at York with the succession of Thomas II.[92] Turstin, the last of the York archbishops in this period, was not part of the Samson family but was able to provide for his own. His father had been a canon at St. Paul's, London, and his brother was Audoen, bishop of Evreux, in whose favor he is reported to have wished to resign his see.[93] Turstin's nephew, Osbert, was given the archdeaconry of Richmond.[94]

The family of John of Tours did well in the see of Bath. The bishop's brother, Hildebert, was given the farm of the church lands at Wells at a rent of sixty shillings, and, upon Hildebert's death, John, the bishop's son, who had been promoted to archdeacon, seized the lands despite the efforts of Bishop Godfrey to restore them to the canons.[95] Bishop John's nephew, Reginald, presumably the son of Hildebert, achieved the post of precentor in the cathedral church.[96]

At Durham, Ranulf Flambard, who was closely associated with the *curia regis*, had a number of relatives and provided for many of them. In the opening years of the twelfth century he took over the see of Lisieux—in trust, as it were, for his son, Thomas, who was a minor.[97] An older brother, Fulcher, later held Lisieux for seven months, and upon his death young Thomas was given the see. Another brother, Godfrey, appears in the Pipe Roll (31 Henry I) for Gloucestershire with a daughter who paid ten pounds to a certain Elyas Giffard. As Ranulf died in September, 1128, and the see was vacant until 1133, the bishop's niece may well have been acting on her late uncle's behalf in respect to an outstanding debt.[98]

Ranulf had several children by his mistress, Alveva of Huntingdon, and a son named Elias appears in 1115 as a co-prebendary of Lincoln with his father, holding lands in King's Sutton (Northamptonshire) and

91. S. E. Gleason, *An Ecclesiastical Barony of the Middle Ages* (Cambridge, Mass., 1936), p. 23.

92. Hugh the Chantor, *loc. cit.* The sees of York and Worcester were united, at irregular intervals between 972 and 1062.

93. C. N. L. Brooke, "Gregorian Reform in Action," *CHJ*, XII (1956), 16.

94. *Ibid.*

95. C. M. Church, *Chapters in the Early History of the Church of Wells* (London, 1894), pp. 6 ff.; see also *Historiola de Primordiis Episcopatus Somersetensis*, ed. J. Hunter (London: Camden Society, 1840), VIII, 22.

96. *HMCR*, X, Appendix III (Wells MSS), p. 18.

97. Ordericus Vitalis, *op. cit.*, IV, 116–17; Ivo of Chartres, *Letters*, *PL*, 162, col. 162 ff.

98. *Pipe Roll*, 31 Henry I, p. 79. Giffard probably was Elias II in descent from Osbern Giffard of Domesday Book.

in Horley (Oxfordshire).[99] The bishop also granted lands from the bishopric of Durham, with royal permission, to William Fitz-Ranulf, who may have been another son.[100] Ranulf's brother, Ulricus, gave the manor of Blakeford to the monks of Glastonbury.[101] A nephew, Richard, was given lands in the bishopric, possibly in 1129, after the bishop's death; and another nephew, Osbert, possessed the manor of Middleham—and, it seems, the office of sheriff.[102] Of Ranulf's successor, Geoffrey Rufus, little is known, except that he was married and had a daughter and a nephew of unknown importance.[103]

The family group at Ely needs little comment. Hervey, it seems, had two nephews, Richard and William, and William was made archdeacon during the bishop's term in office.[104] Bishop Nigel, a nephew of Roger of Salisbury, had a son, Richard Fitz-Neal, who was a royal treasurer and the bishop of London during the reign of Richard I.[105] At Coventry, Robert Pecce made his son, Richard, archdeacon, and the son later became bishop (in 1161).[106] The Pecce (Peche) family was widely dispersed in the south and had important holdings in Suffolk and Cambridgeshire.[107]

Robert Bloet, bishop of Lincoln and a frequent attendant on the king,

99. Christina of Markyate, *Life*, ed. C. H. Talbot (Oxford, 1959), p. 41.

100. *Regesta*, II, 1564.

101. *Johannis Glastoniensis Chronica . . .*, ed. T. Hearne (Oxford, 1726), p. 164. See *Regesta*, I, 293, where Blakeford is mentioned in what may have been an early grant.

102. *Regesta*, II, 1603; R. Surtees, *History and Antiquities of the County Palatine of Durham* (Sunderland, 1908), p. 188, n. c; G. T. Lapsley, *The County Palatine of Durham* (New York, 1900), pp. 80–81. Surtees (*loc. cit.*) suggests, but without convincing proof, that *nepos*, as it is used, means a natural child and not a nephew.

103. Symeon, RS 75, II, 316; *Inventarium Prioratus Dunelmensis*, ed. W. Greenwell (London: Surtees Society, 1872), LVIII, 140.

104. *Pipe Roll*, 31 Henry I, pp. 44–45; *Regesta*, II, 1502.

105. *Regesta*, II, 1562; *Dialogus de Scaccario*, p. 50.

106. Ralph de Diceto, RS 68, I, 305; A. Saltman, *Theobald, Archbishop of Canterbury* (London, 1956), p. 129.

107. Sanders, *English Baronies*, p. 48, for *Great Bealings*. Hamo Peccatum appears in a confirmation of 1121 X 1148 (*Feudal Documents from . . . Bury St. Edmunds*, ed. D. C. Douglas [London, 1931], p. 179). William Peccatum and his wife, Elfeven, held land in Cambridgeshire, as did Ralph Peche (*Regesta*, II, 1629, 1776). Geoffrey Pecche is mentioned in connection with the royal household early in the reign (*ibid.*, 693, 699), and Galfridus Peccatum held a small estate from the bishop of Coventry after 1135, which might connect him with the episcopal family (*Red Book of Exchequer*, RS 99, I, 264). The same problem occurs with the Limesey family, which preceded the Pecces at Chester-Coventry; the place of Robert de Limesey, for instance, in relation to the families of Ralph I and Ralph II, lords of the Cavendish barony in Suffolk, has not been determined.

had a son, Symeon, when the bishop was chancellor to William II, who became dean of Lincoln.[108] Two *nepotes*, Ralph and William, were sons of the bishop's brother, and perhaps there was a third son, Robert, whom Henry of Huntingdon mentions as archdeacon of Northamptonshire. Although no date is given, Robert is said to have held office between the archdeaconries of Nigel and William; since Nigel died early in Henry's reign and William was archdeacon in the time of Alexander, Robert could have been alive in 1130, and may therefore be the *Robertus nepos episcopi* who is mentioned in the Northamptonshire returns of the Pipe Roll.[109] The bishop of Lincoln is also thought to have had a relative, Richard, who became abbot of St. Alban's.[110]

Alexander of Lincoln was well known as a member of the family to which Roger of Salisbury and Nigel of Ely belonged. Alexander's brother, David, was made archdeacon of Buckingham, and his nephew, William, archdeacon of Northampton.[111] An interesting document relating to Nottinghamshire showing possible descent of an ecclesiastical estate contains evidence of the grant of land by Alan, earl of Richmond, to Alexander for the service of one knight. It also devised that Robert de Alvers, the son of the bishop's niece, should be Alexander's heir unless the latter chose to give his property as an inheritance to another relative during his lifetime.[112]

The family group at London has been investigated by Stubbs and others but it may be helpful to review the situation and to add one or two items.[113] William, a nephew of Richard Belmeis I by the bishop's sister, Adeline, was dean of St. Paul's from 1111 to 1138;[114] and Walter, the bishop's brother, had two sons, Ralph of Langford and Richard Belmeis II. Ralph may be the Ranulfus de Belemeins who is known to have held a knight's fee before 1135 in the barony of Herbert de Castello in Shropshire, the family county.[115] The second Richard Belmeis was granted the lands

108. Henry of Huntingdon, *De Contemptu Mundi*, RS 74, p. 6.

109. *Regesta*, II, 1969; *Pipe Roll*, 31 Henry I, p. 82.

110. D. Knowles, *Monastic Order*, p. 187.

111. Henry of Huntingdon, *loc. cit.*

112. *Early Yorkshire Charters*, eds. Farrer and Clay (2 vols.; London, 1914, 1937), IV, i (No. 15).

113. Ralph de Diceto, *Opera*, RS 68, I, xx, 251ff.; R. W. Eyton, *Antiquities of Shropshire* (London, 1854–60), II; L. Loyd, *Origins of Some Anglo-Norman Families* (London: Harleian Society, 1951), CIII, 13.

114. Ralph de Diceto, *loc. cit.*

115. *Red Book of the Exchequer*, RS 99, I, 275. In the *Liber Niger* the surname is Belmeis; and Radulfus de Langeford appears in the witness list for a charter of the D and C of London, 1111 X 1138 (*Early Charters*, No. 218).

of his uncle in 1127 by Henry I, and in 1152 followed in his uncle's footsteps by becoming the bishop of London.[116] Bishop Richard I also had a son named Walter, who was a canon of Newington and appeared in the Pipe Roll for London as owing ten marks silver that he might have the right of justice in the church of Ealing.[117] William de Belmeis (*Bello Manso*), who is mentioned by John of Salisbury as an archdeacon of London in 1148, must have been a member of the same family.[118] This extensive distribution of tenancies among the bishop's relatives during the period is a striking illustration of the power of the episcopal office.

At Norwich, Bishop Herbert Losinga bought the abbacy of Winchester for his father, Robert.[119] Herbert's successor, Everard, a man of powerful connections, was of the house of Montgomery and the son of Roger, earl of Shrewsbury, one of the great barons of William I.[120] Arthur, a brother of Everard, became a member of the episcopal household and his three sons, Richard de Colekirk, William, and Richard, appear as witnesses to an episcopal charter.[121] Everard had several *nepotes episcopi*, for Reginald and Adam and Walter are found in other attestations—although their positions and power are not known.[122]

The celebrated Roger of Salisbury had a brother, Humphrey, who evidently did not fare as well as the bishop's nephews as nothing more is known of him;[123] but the bishop had a son by his mistress, Matilda of Ramsbury, who is said to have been a royal scribe (*antigraphus*) to King Stephen in 1139.[124] The son, if he carried his father's name, may have

116. *Regesta*, II, 1492.

117. *Early Charters*, No. 218; Ralph de Diceto, RS 68, I, 215; *Pipe Roll*, 31 Henry I, p. 146. Illing (Ealing) had long been a part of the London endowment.

118. John of Salisbury, *Historia Pontificalis*, ed. M. Chibnall (London, 1956), p. 46.

119. Ordericus Vitalis, *op. cit.*, IV, 11. Robert de Losinga (d. 1095) was bishop of Hereford.

120. Roger of Montgomery (d. 1094) had married Mabel of Belême and Adele, daughter of Everard de Puiset; thus Bishop Everard was closely related to the powerful du Puiset–Blois family, which was active in England in the decade of 1130 and afterward.

121. *Primum Registrum Norwicense*, ed. H. W. Saunders (Norfolk: Norfolk Record Society, 1939), XI, fol. 11.

122. *Ibid.*, fol. 10; *HMCR*, LXII, Marquess of Lothian (1905), p. 37. It may be that Walkelin, archdeacon of Suffolk, was another nephew (*Dictionary of National Biography*, XVI, "Everard").

123. *Regesta*, II, 1042.

124. *Gesta Stephani*, *op. cit.*, p. 52. The editor identifies him as "Roger le Poer, the king's chancellor," which seems to confuse the son with the father (see *Regesta*, II, ix–xi). John of Hexham, however, called the son a royal chancellor (Johannis Prioris Hagustaldensis, *Historia*, in *Scriptores Decem*, ed. R. Twysden [London, 1652], col. 266).

become a cathedral dignitary at Salisbury since Roger the archdeacon and Roger *capellanus episcopi* appear about 1122 in a notification by the bishop[125] (a Rogerus de Remesberie was a canon at Salisbury, as was his brother, Azo[126]). When King Stephen seized the family possessions (in 1139), the son was taken as a hostage and held in chains;[127] he may have improved his fortunes later, but according to one account he was banished from the realm.[128]

At Exeter, Bishop Osbern Fitz-Osbern was a brother of William Fitz-Osbern, the steward of William I and earl of Hereford.[129] William Warelwast, Bishop Osbern's successor, advanced his own nephew, Robert, to an archdeaconry in the diocese. Evidently a man of ambition, Robert became dean of Salisbury and finally bishop of Exeter.[130] Little is known of the Winchester episcopal family, despite the fact that it had two bishops of wide reputation, but it is likely that Bishop William Giffard was related to the Giffards of Buckinghamshire.[131] Henry of Blois, the brother of King Stephen, upon the death of Roger of Salisbury tried to have his nephew, Henry de Solley, elected to the vacant see which the former was administering but was opposed by Stephen, who wished to appoint his chancellor; the vacancy was not filled until 1142, when Jocelin, archdeacon of Winchester, became the bishop.[132] Although a bishop could appoint members of his family to positions in the diocese and the household, when a bishopric was in question it was no longer entirely up to him. William, another nephew of Henry of Blois (the son of his half-sister, Emma), became treasurer at York and later archbishop.[133]

The bishops of Wales, no less than their English contemporaries,

125. *Regesta*, II, 1324.

126. *Vetus Registrum Sarisberiense* . . . , RS 78, I, 349–51.

127. *Gesta Stephani*, *loc. cit.*

128. John of Hexham, *loc. cit.* In the returns to the Inquest of 1166 a Rogerus le Poher is listed as holding a knight's fee from the bishop of Hereford, but it is not certain that he was Salisbury's or that the enfeoffment was made after 1139 (*Red Book of the Exchequer*, I, 278).

129. William Fitz-Osbern and Osbern Fitz-Osbern were sons of Osbert and Emma; it is uncertain which of the Herefordshire estates (if any) were in possession of the bishop.

130. A. Saltman, *Theobald*, p. 127; *Crawford Collection of Early Charters and Documents* . . . , ed. A. S. Napier and W. H. Stevenson (*Anecdota Oxoniensia*, pt. VII, Oxford, 1895), XIII, 29.

131. A nephew, Nicholaus, appears in a privilege of Innocent II that is dated December 21, 1136 (*Papsturkunden in England*, ed. W. Holtzmann [Berlin and Göttingen, 1930, etc.], III, No. 30). A number of Giffards held of the bishop of Winchester in 1166 (*Red Book of The Exchequer*, RS 99, Vol. I).

132. A. Saltman, *op. cit.*, pp. 97–98.

133. R. L. Poole, "The Appointment and Deprivation of St. William, Archbishop of York," *EHR*, XLV (1930), 276.

exercised rights of patronage in their sees. The legitimate son of Herewald of Llandaff, Lifris, was made archdeacon of Glamorgan,[134] and a nephew, Bertutis, was a physician in the bishop's *familia*.[135] Herewald's successor, Urban, raised his brother, Ensi, to the deanship of the cathedral.[136] At St. David's, Daniel, the disappointed son of the pre-Conquest bishop, Sulien, became archdeacon of Powys.[137] Bernard, who was bishop in 1115, had a nephew to whom he gave a prebend because "he had no one of his own family," as Giraldus put it. The nephew may have been Herbert, who also was a member of the episcopal household.[138]

Besides appointing household officers to bishoprics whenever possible, Henry continued to make use of their services after they were in possession of their sees—a practice that had been employed by Henry's predecessor and that was to continue into the reigns of the Angevins, and beyond. One of the barons appointed to carry out the Winchester Survey (1103 X 1115) was the former chancellor, William, bishop of Winchester.[139] During Henry's dispute with Anselm, in 1102, the bishops Herbert of Norwich and Robert of Chester and Archbishop Gerard of York were sent as the king's envoys to try to obtain a settlement for the vexing problem of investitures. (Gerard took advantage of his stay to plead—unsuccessfully—for the *pallium* and Herbert for the repeal of various rights enjoyed by the wealthy abbey of Bury St. Edmunds in his diocese.[140]) William of Exeter, whom Anselm called *regis nostri legatus*, represented Henry at Rome in 1103, in the presence of the archbishop, and was abroad in 1120 on royal business, requesting legatine authority for Canterbury.[141] In 1121, Bernard of St. David's was sent by the king to meet the papal legate in Normandy before he reached England, and two years later Bernard was in Rome as the royal agent in the Canterbury–York dispute.[142]

It is, of course, the career of Roger of Salisbury—although far from free of enigmatic aspects—that illustrates the mutually dependent

134. *Episcopal Acts*, Vol. II, L.3, L.6.

135. *Ibid.*, L.2.

136. *Ibid.*, L.36.

137. *Brut y Tywysogion*, RS 17, p. 152.

138. Giraldus Cambrensis, *De jure*, RS 21, III, 153 f.; see also *Episcopal Acts*, Vol. I, D.148.

139. *Victoria County History, Hampshire*, I, 527 f.

140. William of Malmesbury, *GP*, RS 52, p. 107; Eadmer, *op. cit.*, RS 81, pp. 137 ff.

141. *Epistolae Anselmi*, *PL*, 159, col. 79; Eadmer, *op. cit.*, pp. 152 ff.

142. *Episcopal Acts*, I, D.48, D.53, D.56.

relationship between king and bishops.[143] Roger's activities on Henry's behalf were varied and often significant: acting on the king's writ to order the royal foresters of Yorkshire to allow Archbishop Turstin an easement in the woods of his archbishopric[144] confirming a grant by Henry to the abbot of St. Augustine (Canterbury).[145] In a charter the king sent from France to Roger, the justiciars and sheriffs in England, Normandy, and the sea ports, Henry instructed the bishop to implement a franchise of the monks of Montebourg in England;[146] on another occasion Roger was instructed to ensure the exemptions from all tolls and customs of French ships of St. Ouen that put into British ports.[147] Roger, also on the king's orders, granted a moneyer in London to the abbot and monks of Reading;[148] he was to see that the abbey of Bury St. Edmunds received the revenue due it,[149] and in 1125 (it is said) he sent warrants throughout England for the arrest of false moneyers and their punishment at Winchester.[150]

Most of these documents fall within the decade of 1120, when the king was abroad for long stretches of time. From 1120 until his death at Lyon-la-Forêt in 1135, Henry was out of England approximately seven years, in two periods of two and a half years each and two periods of one year each, and he needed an officer who was capable of managing the affairs that demanded attention in his absence—including direction or joint direction of the exchequer. There is no indication, however, that the bishop exercised powers that exceeded those of a temporary vice-regent, and Henry upon his return to England reassumed his administrative

143. For the latest treatment of Roger's career, see H. G. Richardson and G. O. Sayles, *The Governance of Medieval England* (Edinburgh, 1963), pp. 156 ff. Although the authors' interpretation of the evidence suggests that the office of the justiciar was unique and well defined during Henry's reign and that the justiciar assumed vice-regal powers in the absence of the king, the argument is not fully convincing. Such a development had certainly begun, but during Henry's reign the dignity existed only upon the appointment by the king of a suitable individual. The information presented by L. Boivin-Champeaux in *Notice sur Roger le Grand, éveque de Salisbury et premier ministre d'Angleterre au XIIe siècle* (Evreux, 1878) is of little value, although it is an early appreciation of the bishop's importance.

144. *Regesta*, II, 1989.

145. *Ibid.*, 1814.

146. *Ibid.*, 1682.

147. *Ibid.*, 1573.

148. *Ibid.*, 1472. See D. M. Stenton, *EHR*, XXXIX (1924).

149. *Feudal Documents from . . . Bury St. Edmunds*, ed. D. Douglas, No. 47.

150. *Anglo-Saxon Chronicle*, *anno* 1125.

duties.[151] Roger of Salisbury's good fortune, however, did not last after Henry's death; although William of Malmesbury reports Stephen as saying he would give the bishop half of England if he asked for it, Stephen soon had him arrested and he died shortly thereafter.[152] It is significant that after the reduction of the episcopal power by Stephen, in 1139, Aubrey de Vere, formerly the master chamberlain of Henry I, defended the barons' right to seize the bishop without submitting the case to an ecclesiastical court by insisting that Roger had been arrested not as a bishop but as a servant of the king.[153]

One may conclude, then, that King Henry followed no fixed policy in choosing men to serve as advisers and administrators. In regard to ecclesiastical appointments, however, there is always the subtle but insistent theme of compromise. It was important to the king who could not demand of his bishops that they conceive of their roles in purely secular terms, forgetting their position as consecrated clergy (although several of them seem to have had few scruples in this respect); and it was important to the bishops who, while they might consider their mission in the church their primary concern, could not pursue this end to the exclusion of the king's interests. Except for the troubled years of Anselm's archiepiscopate at the beginning of the reign (and even in this case a compromise was finally reached), the balance between commitments to the *regnum* and the *sacerdotium* on the part of king and bishops was never seriously disturbed before Henry's death in 1135. Each side realized the advantages to be had from the establishment of an acceptable *modus vivendi* in which the positive contributions that monarchy and episcopacy might make were emphasized. It was a relationship, however, that existed because it was not subjected to rigorous examination or definition by either side. When this occurred under Stephen in the case of Archbishop William of York and under Henry II with Thomas Becket it was a sign that changes were

151. W. Farrer, *An Outline Itinerary of King Henry I.* William of Malmesbury, however, makes the point that Henry entrusted the business of the kingdom to Roger even when he was in England (*Historia Novella*, p. 37).

152. William of Malmesbury, *Historia Novella*, p. 39.

153. *Ibid.*, p. 31. This argument should be compared with Lanfranc's comment about the bishop of Durham at Durham's trial in 1088, when a distinction was made between the bishop as ecclesiastic and as baron. He was summoned, Lanfranc declared, to be judged in respect to his fief, not his bishopric, and he could not, therefore, take refuge in the law of the church which would have placed his case under papal jurisdiction. Odo of Bayeux also was so distinguished as earl, not bishop (Symeon of Durham, RS 75, I, 170). For a discussion of the date of the account of the trial, see H. S. Offler, *EHR*, LVI (1951).

taking place which would affect the whole position of the church in England. In the early twelfth century, however, Henry I remained in firm control of the episcopal leadership. As tenants-in-chief the bishops had specific responsibilities to their lord and if Henry conducted a patronage market in regard to high church office, this was simply a part, an important part, of the personal government of the time. Henry seems to have chosen individuals who served him well; if they also served themselves they at least formed no party of opposition to the royal will. A description of the episcopate under Henry VIII also applies to the episcopate under Henry I: "The rulers of the English Church were the servants of the English king, and it was because they served the king that they were allowed to rule the church."[154]

II. THE BISHOP AS DIOCESAN

The locations of the English and Welsh episcopal seats at the beginning of the twelfth century often were the results of arrangements that had been made during the preceding hundred years;[1] for reasons of safety or prestige or for personal wishes, seats had been transferred from Chester-le-Street to Durham,[2] from Crediton to Exeter,[3] from Selsey to Chichester,[4] from Dorchester to Lincoln,[5] from Sherborne to Salisbury (to what is now Old Sarum),[6] and from Elmham to Norwich (by way of Thetford).[7]

The bishops of Lichfield moved their seat to Chester toward the end of the eleventh century, but Robert de Limesey, bishop in 1086, struck with the wealth of the abbey of Coventry, made the abbey his cathedral church and was said to have been buried there in a posthumous gesture of substantiating this irregular claim. Robert Pecce, his successor, although he carried on an extensive building program at Lichfield during his administration, also was buried at Coventry.[8] Thus three locations were favored from time to time, and this unusual arrangement was noted by contemporary

154. S. T. Bindoff, *Tudor England* (London, 1961), p. 81.

1. F. M. Stenton, *Anglo-Saxon England* (Oxford, 1943), pp. 658 ff.; see also Frank Barlow, *The English Church: 1000–1066* (Aberdeen, 1963), pp. 162 ff.

2. Stenton, *loc. cit.*

3. *Ibid.*, p. 461.

4. *Regesta*, I, 26, 64.

5. *Ibid.*, 283.

6. *Ibid.*, 64, 125.

7. *Ibid.*, 138, 385.

8. William of Malmesbury, *Gesta Pontificum*, RS 52, pp. 307–11.

writers: Thomas I of York calls Lichfield "Chester";[9] the author of the Chronicle speaks of the bishopric of Chester in 1123 and of the bishopric of Coventry in 1130, first under Robert Pecce (1121–1127) and then under Roger de Clinton (1129–1148);[10] and Robert de Monte, writing in 1133, "solves" the problem by saying that all three sites belong to the bishopric.[11]

At Wells, John of Tours, a highly considered member of the king's court, wished to move to Bath, where there was a market and a well-endowed monastery.[12] In 1088 he was granted the abbey of Bath, where he established his seat, and between 1089 and 1091 he was given the entire city, with its customs, tolls and a mint.[13] William of Malmesbury reports that John purchased the city from King Henry I for £500 but this, more than likely, refers not to the original purchase but to a payment for a royal confirmation of the privileges (in 1101).[14]

These eight newly established sees, together with Canterbury, Rochester, Winchester, London, York, Hereford, and Worcester, comprised the fifteen English sees that existed in 1100. (With the exception of the two later foundations, Ely and Carlisle, under Henry I, this diocesan pattern remained essentially unchanged for the next four hundred years.) At Nottingham, in the fall of 1109, in the council of his prelates and barons and with papal consent Henry I created the bishopric of Ely, and Hervey, formerly bishop of Bangor, attested the charter as the first incumbent of the new Cambridgeshire see,[15] whose jurisdictional area was taken from the diocese of Lincoln because, as William of Malmesbury put it, "Lincoln was too big."[16] To compensate the bishop of Lincoln for the consequent loss of income, he was given the manor of Spalding, which had belonged to Ely abbey.[17]

Hervey, having tried to force his program of reform upon the Welsh

9. *Ibid.*, p. 41.

10. Anglo-Saxon Chronicle, in *EHD*, II, 189, 196.

11. Robert of Torigni, *Chronicle*, RS 82, *anno* 1133. See also *Handbook of British Chronology*, eds. F. M. Powicke and E. B. Fryde (London, 1961), p. 232, n. 1.

12. *Historiola de Primordiis Episcopatus Somersetensis*, ed. J. Hunter (London: Camden Society, 1840), VIII, 22.

13. *Regesta*, I, 314, 326.

14. William of Malmesbury, *op. cit.*, p. 194; *Regesta*, II, 544.

15. *Regesta*, II, 919.

16. William of Malmesbury, *op. cit.*, p. 325. See also the letters from Pope Paschal (note 22 below).

17. Florence of Worcester, *Chronicle*, ed. B. Thorpe, in *EHS* (London, 1848–49), I, 278; Ralph de Diceto, *Opera*, ed. W. Stubbs, in RS 68, II, 302.

and meeting with serious opposition, may have written to Pope Paschal II as early as the fall of 1102 in the hope of being translated from Wales to another see, for on December 12, 1102, Paschal had written to Anselm to request that he dispose of the case of the "Welsh Bishop,"[18] which Anselm apparently was reluctant to do. From a letter Anselm sent Henry I before 1107, it appears that Hervey had appealed to the king and that Henry, through the bishop-elect of Winchester, had asked Anselm to transfer Hervey to the see of Lisieux, which was vacant at the time. Jealous of his metropolitan rights and sensitive over the issue of lay investiture, Anselm was unwilling to give his consent and he reminded the king that a bishop could not be translated without the counsel and consent of the archbishop and the bishops of the province in which he had been consecrated.[19] Hervey, however, still hopeful despite the attitude of his metropolitan, continued to make himself heard, and Paschal soon wrote to the king requesting Hervey's appointment to a vacant see in England.[20]

During this time the bishop had been in touch with the court, for he appears as witness to charters in February, 1105, and August, 1107.[21] Finally, in 1108, Anselm wrote to the pope for confirmation of the plan for the proposed episcopal foundation at Ely. The letter was carried by Hervey, who returned to England with four replies—two addressed to the king, one to Anselm, and one to Anselm and the bishops of his province (all dated late November, 1108)—in which Paschal consented to the new diocese and recommended Hervey as its bishop.[22] Anselm must have assumed that Hervey would make a case for himself in Rome, although it is possible that he did not approve of the negotiations. The royal charter warranting the establishment of Ely as a bishopric was not issued until after Anselm's death, in the spring of 1109.

The other diocese created during the reign of Henry I was that of Carlisle. As early as 1092, William II had fortified this town in the northwest corner of his kingdom, and about 1122 Henry I repaired its defenses and bestowed a series of grants on the priory of St. Mary's. Then, in 1133, he approved the creation of a bishopric, removing part of

18. Eadmer, *Historia Novorum*, in RS 81, p. 139.

19. *PL*, CLIX, col. 163; *Anselmi Opera Omnia*, ed. F. Schmitt (Edinburgh, 1938 *et seqq.*), No. 451; see also Feine, p. 365.

20. *PL*, CLXIII, col. 450.

21. *Regesta*, II, 683, 828.

22. J. Bentham, *History and Antiquities . . . of Ely* (Norwich, 1812), Appendix VI, i–v, where the texts of the different letters are printed.

the archdeaconry of Richmond from the jurisdiction of the archbishop of York and transferring it to Carlisle. St. Mary's became the cathedral church, with a chapter of Augustinian canons.[23]

In addition to the fifteen English sees, the three dioceses in Wales are important for this study because of their Norman incumbents and their relationships with some of the English dioceses, including the claim of Canterbury to be their metropolitan.[24] The plan by which episcopal *capita* were moved from villages to towns had never been applied to the Welsh foundations, and the cathedral churches at Bangor, Llandaff, and St. David's remained apart from the larger centers of settlement until the Norman advance. Henry of Huntingdon speaks of them as "bishoprics without episcopal cities," and in the letter of 1108 Paschal II writes, although perhaps in a figurative sense, of the Welsh "barbarians" who ejected the bishop of Bangor.[25] Nevertheless, with the gradual conquest of the country by the earls of Chester in the north and by the earls of Shrewsbury and the lords Fitz-Hamon, de Neufmarché, Braose, and Clare in the south, the Welsh bishoprics were caught up in the royal net; of the six bishops whose tenures fell within the reign of Henry I, only two—Herewald of Llandaff, who became bishop before 1066, and Wilfrid of St. David's, who was elected in 1085, before that part of Wales was subjected to the Norman advance—could be considered to have obtained their sees without the approval of the English king.[26]

To be sure, the successful introduction of Normans into the ecclesiastical life of Wales was affected by the political stability of the country. In the great rebellion of 1094, for example, Anglesey and part of Gwynedd were recovered, the cathedral church of Bangor was captured, and Bishop

23. *Regesta*, II, 1617; Symeon of Durham, RS 75, II, 267; see also D. Knowles, *Religious Houses of Medieval England* (London, 1940), p. 132.

24. Henry of Huntingdon, in a general and brief description of the Welsh dioceses, named three: "Sed in occidentali parte Brittanniae quae vocatur Wallia tres supersunt episcopatus. Unus apud Sanctam David, alius apud Bangor, tertius apud Clamorgan" (*Historia Anglorum*, RS 74, p. 10). Hugh the Chantor gives evidence for a fourth diocese: ". . . ut Cantuariensis archiepiscopus de provincia sua magna Eboracensi archiepiscopo tres episcopatus concederet, Cestrensem, Pangorensem, et tercium inter hos duos medium set pro vastitate et barbarie episcopo vacantem" (*History of the Church of York*, ed. C. Johnson (London, 1961), pp. 122–23). This "middle see" later was called St. Asaph, but it lay vacant until 1143. For a discussion of the problem, see J. Davies (ed.), *Episcopal Acts*, I, pp. 83 ff.

25. Henry of Huntingdon, *loc. cit.*; Eadmer, *Historia Novorum*, RS 81, p. 139. See *Magna Vita Sancti Hugonis*, eds. D. Douie and H. Farmer, I, p. 118.

26. *Episcopal Acts*, I, 129. Even David of Bangor, who was said to have been elected by the prince of Gwynedd and the local clergy, was no exception (*ibid.*, p. 100).

Hervey was forced out (it was not until the next reign, as we have seen, that he was able to effect his translation to the new see of Ely). The organization of the chapters in the Welsh cathedrals rested on the *clas*, the religious community with common property, family livings, and hereditary tenure. Thus the rules on celibacy had little effect, and it was only when Normans were appointed to Welsh sees that a diocesan organization was developed that was similar to that of England. Indefinite diocesan boundaries gave rise to the celebrated disputes between the bishops of Llandaff, and Robert, the earl of Gloucester, and the bishop of St. David's (in the decade of 1120); and only gradually did groups of secular canons become the normal composition of the cathedral chapters.[27]

With the shift of cathedral churches, the consolidation of episcopal jurisdictions, the creation of new dioceses, and the attempts by various bishops to form new territorial units the geographical arrangement of diocesan lands underwent important changes between the pre-Conquest period and the time of Henry I. Diocesan boundaries in the first half of the eleventh century have been described in terms of the provinces, but by the early twelfth century this had been modified in several ways.[28] Salisbury, with its episcopal seat at Old Sarum, comprised the counties of Wiltshire, Berkshire, and Dorset, which previously had been divided between Sherborne and Ramsbury. Exeter had taken Devon and Cornwall from Crediton and St. Germans. Bath, by 1101, was the first church in Somerset, a position it shared occasionally with Wells. The diocese of Lincoln, after the creation of Ely, contained Lincolnshire, Northamptonshire, Huntingdonshire, Bedfordshire, Buckinghamshire, Oxfordshire, and part of Hertfordshire—most of which had formerly belonged to Dorchester.[29] The counties of Norfolk and Suffolk in the East Anglian area of Elmham came under the jurisdiction of the see of Norwich, while Hereford, in the west midlands, was expanded to include Herefordshire, Shropshire, and part of Gloucestershire. Adjacent to Hereford lay

27. *Cartae . . . quae ad dominum de Glamorgancia pertinent*, ed. G. T. Clark (Cardiff, 1910), I, n. 50; A. H. Thompson, "Welsh Dioceses in the Middle Ages," *Journal of the Historical Society of the Church in Wales*, I (1947), 102; Giraldus Cambrensis, *De Jure*, in RS 21, III, 153 ff.

28. Frank Barlow, *The English Church*, pp. 162–63.

29. For these and other dioceses, see the Ordnance Survey *Map of Monastic Britain*, 1954–55 (two sections), which, although helpful, covers the period 1066–1540, and therefore is not always as precise on diocesan boundaries and peculiars for the time of Henry I as one would like. Further references on the geographical extent of these dioceses are to be found in William of Malmesbury, *GP*, RS 52, p. 175; Robert de Monte, RS 82, *anno* 1114; *Regesta*, II, 779; and A. Morey, *Bartholomew of Exeter* (Cambridge, 1937), p. 217.

Worcester, with Worcestershire, most of Gloucestershire, and part of Warwickshire.[30] To the north was the large diocese of Chester (Lichfield-Coventry-Chester), which included Cheshire, Derbyshire, Staffordshire, part of Lancashire (to the river Ribble), and parts of Shropshire and Warwickshire. (In the case of shared counties, as in Warwickshire, disputes over the boundaries were common—such as the argument between Worcester and Lichfield over the town and castle of Dudley, which lay on the line.[31]) In the far north, except for the see of Durham, the archbishop of York held the lands north of the Humber and the Chester boundary, and the northern portion of Lancashire and Nottinghamshire, all the way to the Scottish border.[32] Durham included the land of St. Cuthbert between Tyne and Tees, and Northumberland as far as the Tweed, and its boundary probably followed the line of the Cheviot Hills.[33] The other dioceses seem to have been changed very little in the course of the late eleventh century: Kent was shared by Canterbury and Rochester; London comprised Middlesex, Essex, and part of Hertfordshire; Winchester held Hampshire and Surrey; and Chichester lay with Sussex, in the south.[34]

As a result of the dispute on diocesan limits between the bishops of Llandaff and St. David's (in which the bishop of Hereford also had a part) a document was drawn up that defined not only the territory of the church of Llandaff but the exact extent of the bishopric, by naming its settlements, churches, and villages.[35] Bishop Urban of Llandaff had

30. W. Holtzmann, *Papsturkunden in England* (Berlin, 1932 et seqq.), II, 8; *Regesta,* II, 1243; *Cartularium Ecclesie Wigornensis Hemingi,* ed. T. Hearne (Oxford, 1723) II, 527.

31. William of Malmesbury, *Gesta Regum,* in RS 90, I, vi. In assigning part of Warwickshire to Hereford, which is doubtful from the point of view of the topography, Malmesbury may have had in mind some "peculiar" jurisdiction of Hereford. The Dudley dispute was settled early in the thirteenth century: "Ita quod tota villa de Duddeleia pertinebit ad episcopum Wigorn. situs vero castri ejusdem villae . . . pertinebit ad episcopum Coventrensem" (*Annales Prioratus de Wigornia,* in RS 36, IV, 429).

32. William of Malmesbury, *GP,* pp. 41 ff.

33. A confirmation by Archbishop Thomas I (prior to the twelfth century) described the bishopric as "tota terra quae est inter Tese et Tyne, Northum'land, Thevietdale, Tindale, Carledun Werdale" (*Historians of the Church of York,* RS 71, III, vi); but the charter is suspicious, and the author may have exaggerated the claims of St. Cuthbert's monks.

34. William of Malmesbury, *GP,* p. 175; Henry of Huntingdon, RS 74, p. 9; *Regesta,* II, 1060, 614, 810. See the interesting, if extravagant, description of the episcopal cities of England fifty years later by Richard of Devizes (*Chronicon Richardi Divisensis,* ed. J. T. Appleby [Edinburgh, 1963], pp. 66–68).

35. *Cartae . . . de Glamorgancia,* I, lxiv.

entered his first complaints at the papal *curia* about 1119, particularly in regard to five districts, four of which were claimed by the neighboring bishop of St. David's and one by the bishop of Hereford.[36] The controversy was not settled until 1134, after the deaths of Bishop Urban, the bishop of Hereford, and two popes, when the districts were awarded to Hereford and St. David's. (Ambitious bishops of Hereford, it is clear, would try to extend the jurisdiction of that frontier diocese into areas that had only recently been conquered.[37])

The fact that a catalogue of diocesan possessions could be compiled for Llandaff meant there was an accurate idea of the diocesan limits, and it would seem that the limits and properties of the other sees in England must have been equally well known. Henry's grant to the bishop and monks of Rochester of all tithes from whales taken in the waters of the bishopric presupposed knowledge of the diocesan boundaries,[38] as did Anselm's letter addressed to all who had lands in the bishopric of St. David's, and the mention of the bishop's land at Norwich and the *baneleuca*.[39] There is further evidence, as in the case of Llandaff, that uncertain boundaries were often "surveyed" to determine the possessors. About 1100 a detailed list of London properties belonging to Christ Church, Canterbury, was made, which consisted largely of churches and lands.[40] In a writ issued between 1100 and 1114, King Henry ordered the earl of Chester, the sheriff, and others "to go and view the boundary" between the royal manor of Torksey and the manor of Stow (which belonged to the bishop of Lincoln) and "to cause the boundary to be defined by good men of the country."[41] In a charter issued by Roger of Salisbury between 1107 and 1115, the bishop confirmed the gift of a carucate of land at Kidwelly that

36. *Ibid.*, xlvii. The district of Erging was disputed by the bishop of Hereford, and Ystrádyw, Gower, Kidwelly, and Cantref Bychan were disputed by the bishop of St. David's.

37. "Hereford in Wales," in fact, appears in several documents: (*a*) *Regesta*, II, 399*a*, 404; (*b*) the Hereford returns to the Inquest of 1166 are recorded "Hereford in Wallia" (*Red Book of the Exchequer*, RS 99, I, 278); and (*c*) a reference in the chronicle of Roger of Howden in the time of Richard I mentions "H. Cant. archiep . . . fuit in Gwallia apud Herefordense . . ." (RS 51, IV, 35).

38. *Regesta*, II, 516.

39. *PL*, CLIX, Ep. XXII; *Regesta*, II, 762.

40. B. W. Kissan, "An Early List of London Properties," *London and Middlesex Archaeological Society Transactions*, n.s., VIII.

41. *Registrum Antiquissimum*, ed. C. W. Foster (Lincoln: Lincoln Record Society, 1931), I, 28.

he had made to the church at Sherborne and specified the extent of the land as he himself had measured it.[42] Although there were many disputes between bishops over particular churches or villages, it seems only reasonable that most parish priests would have had no doubts about their ecclesiastical superior or the extent of the area in which they performed their duties. Moreover, the creation of archdeaconries in all the dioceses during this period would have further defined the limits of a bishop's authority.[43]

Rights of jurisdiction, inseparable from rights to hold pleas and collect the benefits of justice, extended throughout a diocese, and in many instances early-twelfth-century bishops enforced these prerogatives or granted concessions in respect to them; between 1070 and 1103, for example, "the bishop of Norwich made persistent efforts to deprive St. Edmund's abbey of its exemption from episcopal control."[44] This was the period of the most intensive campaign by the bishops to encroach upon the abbey's jurisdiction, and it was first placed under papal protection and committed to the care of Archbishop Lanfranc in 1081. Even as late as 1129 there were disputes between Norwich and St. Edmunds.[45] At Lincoln, Robert Bloet revived the claim of giving benediction to the abbots of Ely, but the abbot, Richard, refused to submit and the dispute died out.[46] Robert was more successful at St. Albans, where the abbot, another Richard, and a relative of the bishop, subjected the abbey to episcopal authority *ut sic monachos suos rigidius, ut dicitur, gubernaret.*[47]

A frequently used means of gaining control of a church within a diocese or of subjecting one that lay outside was for a bishop to assert authority during a vacancy over rights to revenues and appointments

42. Dugdale, IV, 64 ff.: ". . . et pro salute animae meae et parentum meorum et antecessorum meorum do sanctae Shyrbornensi ecclesiae . . . unam carucatam terrae apud Cadweli sicut perambulabi eam . . . ." The task of walking the bounds was made easier because the land was naturally defined by brooks and streams.

43. See the list of archdeacons, Appendix II.

44. V. Galbraith, "The East Anglian See and the Abbey of Bury St. Edmunds," *EHR*, XL (1925), 40. For a discussion of ecclesiastical immunities and monastic foundations, see D. Knowles, *Monastic Order in England* (Cambridge, 1950), pp. 600–6; M. D. Lobel, *Ecclesiastical Banleuca in England* (Oxford, 1934); and N. M. Trenholme, *The English Monastic Boroughs*, in *University of Missouri Studies*, II (1927), 3.

45. *Regesta*, II, 1443, 1605.

46. According to J. Bentham, *History and Antiquities of Ely*, p. 113, who does not elaborate.

47. Dugdale, II, 183.

that lay within his grasp. At Canterbury, the abbots of St. Augustine claimed *exemptio plena* from jurisdiction of the archbishop, but the archbishop (as well as the priors of Christ Church) demanded the submission of the monastery when the see was vacant. A series of law suits developed, and ended about 1151, when Abbot Sylvester professed obedience to Archbishop Theobald, following a precedent reported to have been set in 1099.[48] At Durham, in 1099, Ranulf Flambard apparently held several abbeys as *custos*, and just prior to his elevation is said to have had sixteen combined vacancies in hand.[49] Henry of Blois, when he came to Winchester in 1129, retained the wealthy abbey of Glastonbury and did not appoint a new abbot. It cannot be denied that he increased the abbey's value during his administration, and although as a pluralist he enjoyed an exceedingly high income for several years, one might say that he collected only the "dividends" on his investments.[50] Roger of Salisbury acquired the abbey of Malmesbury in 1117, evidently expelled the abbot, Edulf, and retained the abbey until his death, in 1139.[51] Roger was particularly active in Dorset, which also lay within his diocese. As custodian of the abbey at Abbotsbury he granted two hides of the land, despite the objections of the convent, to one Nicholas de Meriet for the marriage of Nicholas' nephew. At Middleton, during a vacancy of five years—and again against the wishes of the monks—he converted two tenements into knights' fees, which had been held *in feodo censuali*.[52] Upon the bishop's demise, Malmesbury and Abbotsbury, which had been made

48. *HMCR*, V (Canterbury D. and C.), p. 431.

49. *Annales Monasterii de Wintonia*, RS 36, *anno* 1097; see Margaret Howell, *Regalian Right in Medieval England* (London, 1962). Chap. I and its references.

50. For the amount of his income, see D. Knowles, *Monastic Order*, p. 282.

51. *Charters and Documents of Salisbury*, RS 97, VI. The charter appears in a manuscript of the fourteenth century, with the address: "Henricus dei gratia rex Anglorum et dux Normannorum archiepiscopis, episcopis, abbatibus . . . ." Although the formula *dei gratia* became the rule in royal charters after 1172 (A. L. Poole, *From Domesday Book to Magna Carta*, p. 3, and T. A. M. Bishop, *Scriptores Regis* (Oxford, 1961), pp. 11 ff., 18 f.), there are many charters in which Henry I is so styled, some as early as 1101 (*Regesta*, II, 533, 556, 579, 620, 752, 756, 827, 860, 877, 918, 989, 1061, 1127, 1225, 1246, 1314, 1346, 1347, 1348, 1368, 1403, 1646, 1649, 1715, 1717, 1718, 1802, 1803, 1896, 1922). The formula also was used in several charters in the period 1066–1100 (*Regesta*, I, 53, 163, 215, 240, 248, 396, 417, 487).

52. *Red Book of Exchequer*, RS 99, I, 210–11. As it was, Roger had a *servitium debitum* of thirty-two, but he had made enfeoffments in only slightly more than thirty-eight knights' fees before 1135; he died in 1139, and there was no spectacular increase before 1166 (*ibid.*, pp. 236 ff.).

his "handmaids," were taken into the king's hands and restored "to their former splendor."[53]

Very often, however, rather than peremptorily assert his authority, a bishop might agree to a settlement of disputed claims with a diocesan foundation. The result would be a private bargain, a *compositio amicalis*, and the conditions accepted in one case did not necessarily resemble the conditions agreed upon in another. The only recurrent aspect is that of exemptions from payment of chrism dues and from attendance at synods, exemptions that were especially prized.[54] York relinquished the privilege of collecting chrism dues in 1121; similarly, the bishop of Chichester, after a hearing before the cathedral chapter, agreed to give up all episcopal customs and penalty payments, as well as chrism dues, that he had exacted from the abbey of St. Mary *extra murorum*.[55] In a grant to Godstow abbey in Oxfordshire, probably late in the decade of 1130, Alexander of Lincoln conceded exemptions from archidiaconal jurisdiction (but with the approval of the influential Walter, archdeacon of Oxford), allowing the abbey freedom from providing hospitality on archidiaconal visitations and from synodal attendance and chrism payments.[56] In a confirmation by Theobald (1150 X 1161), the same privileges were granted by Robert, bishop of Chester, to Burton abbey in Staffordshire, as well as the right to a court to hear pleas.[57] At Winchester, in the time of William Giffard, in respect to the abbey church recently removed to Hyde, the same kind of settlement was reached, although of a more conservative nature, for there is no mention of a comprehensive exemption for the abbey.[58] In

53. *Gesta Stephani*, ed. K. R. Potter (Edinburgh, 1955), p. 65. See the note on the Malmesbury levies of Henry II in M. Howell, *Regalian Right*, p. 42, n. 7, and p. 43. Roger may also have profited from a portion of the revenues from the vacant abbey of Battle (c. 1125). The Chronicle asserts that while the king was abroad the news of the vacancy reached Roger, *qui tunc per Angliam regia jura administrabat*. He dispatched a deputy, John Belet, to have an inventory made, and Belet seems later to have assumed the custody of the church—with some advantage to himself and doubtless to the bishop as well (*Chronicon de Bello*, ed. J. S. Brewer [London, 1846], p. 60).

54. Payment for chrism implied a proprietary church, and was a custom that was slowly dying out. Exemption from synods often meant relief from the offerings that were made at such times to the mother church of the diocese. In regard to synods, see a later charter of Archbishop Theobald (1150 X 1161) regarding prompt payment of the synodal pennies (in A. Saltman, *Theobald, Archbishop of Canterbury* [London, 1956], no. 49).

55. *Chronicon de Bello*, p. 56. St. Mary's was a dependent parish church of Battle Abbey.

56. *Early Register of Godstow*, ed. A. Clark, *EETS*, o.s. (1911), pp. 644 ff.

57. A. Saltman, *Theobald*, n. 23; but only *quamdiu justicia non defuerit*.

58. *Regesta*, II, 1070.

Wales, Wilfrid of St. David's made peace with the abbot of St. Peter's, Gloucester, by granting lands and churches in the diocese to the monks but retaining the privilege of receiving the customary dues. He acknowledged the abbot's gift of a pastoral staff, for which he sent a letter of thanks that confirmed his promises to protect the rights of St. Peter's if the monks would respect his rights as bishop.[59]

At times the king or the pope might be asked to sanction a settlement or to bring pressure on one side or the other, as in the Evesham abbey settlement of April, 1100, which took place *coram rege* in favor of the abbot against claims advanced by Samson, bishop of Worcester. It was ordered that the church of Evesham was to hold its *honour* as well as it did T.R.E. and of the two Williams, as the abbot proved his right against the bishop in the king's court. Furthermore, if Samson made any claims beyond what had just been settled, the abbot was to answer him only in the royal court; and no bishop was permitted to hold ordinations or synods at Evesham unless invited to do so by the abbot.[60] This is a good illustration of the king's ability to enter into disputes between his tenants and to rule on diocesan rights; it also suggests the serious concern of many bishops over the extent of jurisdictional peculiars that encroached on their power and that often emphasized the growing consciousness of their diocesan rights.[61] As will be seen shortly, not only other prelates but numerous monastic foundations held "islands" in his see, into which a bishop could not go and over which he had little or no control.[62]

Episcopal jurisdiction was not confined within diocesan boundaries; the twelfth-century bishop functioned as a key church officer and *christianae plebis pastor*, as well as an important feudal lord who held lands *in capite* of the king, and in both capacities his power was felt within his

59. *Historia et Cartularium . . . St. Petri Gloucestriae*, RS 33, I, 206, 265–66.

60. *Regesta*, I, 429.

61. Similar cases are those of Eynsham abbey, a proprietary church of the bishop of Lincoln (see *Eynsham Cartulary*, ed. H. Salter [Oxford: Oxford Historical Society 1907] (XLIX), pt. I, 36); St. Alban's, where the monks claimed their canonical right to free election of the abbot, and gained the king's consent in 1119 (see *Gesta Abbatum Monasterii Sancti Albani*, RS 28, I, 73); the case of *Blyth Abbey* v. *Archbishop Thomas of York* (see *Regesta*, II, 1076); and a London dean's appeal to the king against the bishop concerning his pleas (see *Pipe Roll*, 31 Henry I, ed. Hunter, p. 148). For an example of papal interference, see the mandate of Innocent II to Reading abbey (1130 X 1135) for the admission of secular clerks, canons, archdeacons, et al., to the abbey without archiepiscopal or episcopal pressure (Hotzmann, *Papsturkunden*, III, 29). Reading may have been a special case, however, as Abbot Hugh was in the service of the papal *curia* (*ibid.*, pp. 15, 22).

62. See n. 44 in regard to ecclesiastical immunities.

diocese, and beyond it. In his bishopric, as spiritual lord, he was concerned with the care of the people, land, and buildings under his control;[63] it often happened, however, that he spent very little time in his church and that the routine ecclesiastical administration was left in the hands of his household, of the cathedral clergy, and of the diocesan officers. This was especially true if a bishop had secular interests and found the business of the *curia regis* more fascinating—not to say more profitable—than the work for which he had been constituted in the eyes of the church. Frequently, a bishop held lands outside his own diocese, in the diocese of another bishop, and although the difficulty of conflicting jurisdictions had been encountered long before the twelfth century,[64] the problem is illustrated by a letter of Lanfranc to the bishop of Chichester. The archbishop held various estates in the diocese of Chichester, in Sussex, and the Sussex clergy who were under the jurisdiction and care of Canterbury had evidently been amerced by the archdeacons of Chichester. Lanfranc scolded the bishop of Chichester for allowing his archdeacons such license, ordered that the clergy subject to the archbishopric were not to attend synods in Chichester, were subject only to himself, and that he would inquire into the state of their morals on his visitations. The only way in which the bishop of Chichester could claim jurisdiction over the Canterbury priests was by exercising his right to collect payments for the chrism they obtained at Chichester.[65]

Because almost all the bishops of the time held lands in other dioceses, it seems reasonable to assume that they retained control over their distant clergy and received income from these lands, although one cannot always be sure of the kind of control they enjoyed. An examination of the Domesday episcopal holdings shows how widespread were the "detached" properties throughout the counties of England, although the largest concentration of holdings in each case was in the home county of a diocese. Bishops expected to receive support from their other estates, particularly when they moved about as much as some of them did in the royal service. From the charter evidence one finds many illustrations of separated episcopal lands—references to "all the shires in which Bishop Gundulf of Rochester holds lands," to "all the shires in which the bishop of Worcester

63. Feine, pp. 213 f., 366 ff.

64. See, for example, the terms of the synod of 670 (at Hertford, under Theodore) and the reference to the canons' prohibiting a bishop to "intrude into the diocese of another bishop, but [to] be content with governing the people entrusted to him" (*EHD*, I, 651).

65. *Lanfranci Opera*, ed. J. Giles (2 vols.; London, 1884), I, 50.

holds lands," and there are similar indications for Ely, Durham, and Canterbury.[66] In addition to Chichester, Canterbury had peculiar jurisdiction in Winchester, London, Norwich, Lincoln, and Rochester. Rochester controlled only a few diocesan areas, most of them in Norwich. The well-known franchise of Hexham in the diocese of Durham belonged to the archbishop of York, who enjoyed complete authority there, so that "his liberty of Hexham was, as it were, an island in the diocese of Durham." (The Durham franchise in York and Lothian have been examined and discussed in detail in other works.[67]) Diocesan authority, then, should be thought of as broken up among the shires of England and as affecting areas that might be a long way geographically from the parent see.

Within his own diocese, however, a bishop functioned as *iudex ordinarius*, hopefully gathering under his jurisdiction and discipline the cathedral and parochial clergy.[68] Although originally he was assisted by members of his chapter in carrying out the administrative duties of his diocese, by the twelfth century the growth of the institutionalized church and the increased complexity of its organization necessitated a division of labor in which the bishop's work was assigned to specially appointed archdeacons and rural deans, each operating under supervision (more or less strict) in his particular district, while the members of the chapter assumed the task of caring for the cathedral church. It must be borne in mind, of course, that the arrangements by which the lives of the ecclesiastical hierarchy were ordered were never entirely fixed or stable, and the rules and regulations, even the conventions, affecting them were always subject to reexamination and redefinition, dependent upon the persons concerned and the needs of the time. This is particularly true of the status of the bishop in his church, for one of the most important changes during the course of the twelfth century (which, indeed, had begun earlier, and was to continue into the thirteenth) was the gradual estrangement of the bishop from his capitular clergy.[69] The bishop tended to take a smaller and smaller part in routine cathedral life, and, although he retained rights of visitation and appointment, the body of the clergy became more

66. *Regesta*, II, 882, 976, 930, 840.

67. A. H. Thompson, *York Minster Historical Tracts* (London, 1927); F. Barlow, *Durham Jurisdictional Peculiars* (Oxford, 1950).

68. Feine, *loc. cit.*; see I Timothy, 3:4.

69. An important aspect of this estrangement was the separation of lands and revenues between bishop and chapter, which will be treated in my forthcoming article: "*Mensa episcopalis* and *mensa conventualis* in twelfth-century England."

and more a closed corporation, functioning autonomously and increasingly aware of its privileges. This process affected the monastic as well as the secular cathedrals, but the degree of separation varied from see to see.[70] To facilitate our discussion, the English bishoprics may be divided into two groups, each based on the differences between secular and monastic chapters: (1) cathedral churches with chapters of secular canons, at the head of which was a bishop who was usually a secular, and (2) cathedral churches of monastic foundation, with a secular or a monastic bishop.

Distribution of Secular and Monastic Bishops among the English Cathedral Churches

SECULAR CHAPTERS AND SECULAR BISHOPS		MONASTIC CHAPTERS AND SECULAR BISHOPS	
Chester	*Lincoln*	*Bath*	*Rochester*
Robert Limesey	Robert	John	John
Robert Pecce	Alexander	Godfrey	*Winchester*
Roger	*London*	*Durham*	William
Chichester	Maurice	Ranulf	*Worcester*
Ralph	Richard	Geoffrey	Samson
Exeter	Gilbert	*Ely*	Theulf
Osbern	*Salisbury*	Hervey	Simon
William	Roger	Nigel	
Hereford	*York*	*Norwich*	
Gerard	Gerard	Everard	
Regenhelm	Thomas II		
Geoffrey	Turstin		
Richard		MONASTIC CHAPTERS AND MONASTIC BISHOPS	
		Canterbury	*Rochester*
		Anselm	Gundulf
SECULAR CHAPTERS AND MONASTIC BISHOPS		Ralph	Ralph
		William	Ernulf
		Carlisle	*Winchester*
		Adelulf	Henry
Chichester	*Hereford*	*Norwich*	
Seefrid	Robert	Herbert	

70. The development of the chapter as an independent group is directly related to the growing feeling of the corporate nature of society in medieval Europe during the twelfth century.

There was, of course, no legal distinction between a secular and monastic bishop; this difference existed only in practice.

In an age when the *curia regis* was the most important source of episcopal appointments, it is not surprising that secular bishops in churches that possessed chapters of canons formed the largest group, followed by secular bishops in monastic churches; the monastic bishops of course predominated in cathedral abbeys, and the least representative group was that of monastic bishops with secular chapters. Evidence supports the view that the combination of a monastic bishop and a monastic church produced the closest if not the most amicable working relationships, but complete independence was never achieved by a chapter in the sense that a bishop had no contact in his church or diocese. To be sure, the extent he was admitted *in chorum et capitulum* depended on the particular arrangements in each case, but the bishop was married to his see, from which only death could part him, and if the church was the Bride of Christ, to the bishop was given the work of her earthly support.[71] No chapter, however much it may have opposed a bishop in daily practice, thought to deny him the rights of his authority, such as participation in ecclesiastical ceremonies, approval of various chapter acts, and appointments to offices. Furthermore, because a bishop often held his court at episcopal synods, this made the clergy aware of the bishop's ideas and proposals and prompted them to submit their own (as in the division of prebends). Then too, a bishop of the early twelfth century often employed members of the chapter in his personal service, and this practice ensured closer contact.[72] An examination of the bishoprics that existed in the time of Henry I, considered in the order of monastic foundations with monastic bishops, monastic foundations with secular bishops, secular foundations with monastic bishops, and secular foundations with secular bishops, reveals the presence or lack of compatibility that was maintained between bishop and chapter.

At Canterbury, Anselm, despite his prolonged absences, carried on the tradition that enjoined the bishop *in loco abbatis* to live among his monks as a spiritual father, and in the pages of his biographer as well as in his own letters he is found acting as a shepherd to his sheep—guiding,

71. During the vacancy at Canterbury (in the time of William II), Eadmer wrote of the mother church as fallen into widowhood: "Interea regi a bonis quibusque suadetur quatinus communem totius regni matrem instituendo illi pastorem solvat a pristina viduitate"; and "... quae viris suis episcopis scilicet seu abbatibus decidentibus, in viduitatem ea tempestate cadebunt" (*Historia Novorum*, RS 81, pp. 32, 26–27).

72. See below pp. 52 ff.

counseling, reproving, and encouraging them.[73] His successor at Christ Church, Ralph, was of much the same spirit, although his long dispute with the archbishop of York over canonical profession of obedience also made it necessary for him to be away from his see for long periods of time. It may be recalled that his election was disputed by the monks who wanted Faritius, abbot of Abingdon, and the fact that their wishes were not met may have dampened their enthusiasm for Ralph. William of Corbeil, the last archbishop under Henry I and a regular canon of the Augustinian order, was the first to break with the Bec tradition. William of Malmesbury speaks well of him, but Henry of Huntingdon is a good deal less complimentary;[74] in the *Gesta Stephani* he is described as having a bearing befitting an archbishop but without the character to complement it.[75] He seems to have made no lasting impression as archbishop-abbot. "At Canterbury, the best was over with Anselm's death, though his successor, and perhaps Theobald a little later, were in the same tradition."[76]

The three bishops of Rochester, Gundulf, Ralph (later translated to Canterbury), and Ernulf, were monks and seem to have taken to heart the prescriptions of the *Regularis Concordia.* Gundulf, particularly, is portrayed as a diocesan of great spirituality, *sciens et efficax*, much concerned with the welfare of his cathedral family; and he was a remarkable builder of churches within the bishopric.[77]

73. This conception of the role of the diocesan can be traced from a letter of Gregory the Great to Augustine in which Gregory assumed that bishops would live with their clergy (Bede, *Historia Ecclesiastica,* ed. J. E. King [London, 1930], I, xxvii). It was also incorporated into the Winchester consuetudinary (c. 970), *Regularis Concordia* (ed. Symons [London, 1953], Proem). In the *Decreta* of Lanfranc, written for the community at Christ Church, the author intentionally equated abbot with bishop (*Decreta Lanfranci,* ed. D. Knowles [London, 1951], pp. 2–3). For treatment of the status of the bishop-abbot see D. Knowles, *Monastic Order,* pp. 406 ff., 619 ff., and R. W. Southern, *Saint Anselm and His Biographer* (Cambridge, 1963), pp. 246 ff.

74. "Erat enim religionis multae affabilitalis nonullae ceterum nec iners nec imprudens" (William of Malmesbury, *GP,* RS 52, II, 73). "Postea vero sedit Cantuariae Willelmus cujus laudes dici nequeunt quia non sunt" (Henry of Huntingdon, RS 74, 15).

75. "Vir vultu columbinus habituque vere religiosus, sed pecuniarum adquisitarum possessor avidior quam erogantior" (*Gesta Stephani,* ed. K. Potter [London, 1955], p. 6).

76. D. Knowles, *Monastic Order,* p. 623.

77. See R. A. L. Smith, "The Place of Gundulf in the Anglo-Norman Church," *EHR,* LVIII (1943), 272. It was said that on his deathbed he desired to be carried into the presence of his clergy *ut inter monachorum manus spiritum redderet.* For Ernulf, see R. W. Southern, *St. Anselm and His Biographer,* pp. 269 ff., and the reference to the passage in the Peterborough Chronicle for the year 1114 in regard to Ernulf's activity in his church.

Herbert, bishop of Norwich, as he appears in the documents of the Norwich Register and in his letters, also chose to spend a good deal of time, thought, and money on the care of his church and his clergy, and, despite his connections with the royal administration, he emerges clearly as an estimable *almus pater*. Aware of his shortcomings as a shepherd in a savage world, he nevertheless tried to correct and improve the habits of the brethren.[78] Again, the conception of the bishop who is rightfully and sacredly wedded to his church is emphasized; in a letter to the chapter, Herbert urged them to recognize that

> the law which God established corporeally between husband and wife, has Christ proclaimed spiritually between the bishop and his people; and of greater consequence, because whereas the former is a union of the flesh, the latter is a foundation of the spirit. And I recall this to you in order that you may truly reflect on the labors of the service by which I serve you every day, offering the body and blood of Christ on your behalf, and on the loving obedience with which you should respond to my ministry.[79]

Herbert was not unfaithful to his charge, and has left us other letters in which he alternately scolded and encouraged his monks, sometimes apologizing for the use of discipline, often setting forth examples by which they were to order their lives, "perfect in faith, truth, charity and poverty."[80] He cautioned a wayward brother by reminding him it is not possible to reap a harvest in the world and afterwards reign with Christ; at another time he refused to sanction the marriage of the sister of his chaplain because her first husband had not died.[81] As for the separation of episcopal and conventual possessions, the cartulary states that Herbert insisted upon it in order to avoid descending upon the church with his large entourage, and he kept Thorpe manor in his own hands so that he would have a place to stay when he came to Norwich and would not

78. *Primum Registrum Norwicense,* ed. H. W. Saunders (Norfolk: Norfolk Record Society, 1939), Vol. XI, fols. 4 and *passim.* "Obiit autem dictus Herbertus episcopus vir per omnia catholicus eternam sui nominis suis in operibus memoriam derelinquens, multoque omnium comprovincialium dolore, sepultus est in ipsa episcopali ecclesia quam ipse stabilierat possessionibus, libris et diversi generis ornamentis ditaverat ante dominicum altare[m] in sarcofago tanti viri humatione digno." (fol. 9*d*).

79. *Herberti de Losinga Primi Episcopi Norwicensis Epistolae,* ed. R. Anstruther (Brussels, 1846), Letter xxxv.

80. *Ibid.*, Letter lvii. He even found support for his efforts in Rome, from Paschal II (*PL,* CLXIII, col. 432).

81. *Herberti . . . Epistolae,* Letters iii, xiii.

have to disturb the convent.[82] Herbert, however, like other bishops, was acutely aware of the need for increased funds with which to meet the expenses of his new church, the first stone of which he laid in the last years of the eleventh century. There is on record an unusual ad hoc tax that was levied by the bishop on each messuage of his diocese to help defray construction costs,[83] and further evidence of the lack of funds is found in one of Herbert's letters to his prior, Ingulf.

> I am going to court, with few horses and little money, but God will be my protector. To you I leave the cathedral of Norwich, as well as the work of the church and my own; and you I leave in God's care. If there be something wanting, you are to get it on loan and on my return I shall repay everything to your creditors. Peace be with you and all the brethren who with humility and truth preserve the way of our rule in our house.[84]

Compared with the substantial gifts Henry I made to other bishops, particularly to Roger at Salisbury and his nephew, Alexander at Lincoln, and Nigel at Ely, the royal patronage of Norwich was not extravagant, and it seems that much financial support depended on successful solicitation of lay magnates, such as Alan of Flaald, who gave the manor of Eton, and Herbert de Rya, who generously bestowed tithes. The building of the church, moreover, raised other problems, which from time to time resulted in strained relations between Herbert and his monks. Although as he said it was their church, Herbert seems to have thought the monks did not share his enthusiasm for the work. He found them lazy and apathetic, and this caused him no little anxiety. In another letter we find a list of their faults and a gentle reprimand.

> The work does not advance and you are not eager to provide the necessary materials . . . but as I cherish you, I endeavor to deliver [you] from the hands of divine punishment, into which your indolence has led you.[85]

82. *Primum Registrum*, fols. 1*d*, 7*d*. Herbert, nevertheless, was not without ambition in other places, such as Bury St. Edmunds (see n. 44: V. Galbraith).

83. *Ibid.*, fol. 8. Another means of securing aid was that used by Archbishop Thomas II of York, who, needing money to continue work in the nave at Southwell minster, directed the men of Nottinghamshire to pay parish dues at Southwell rather than at York. (*Visitations and Memorials of Southwell Minster*, ed. A. F. Leach [Camden Society], n.s., XLVIII [1891]).

84. *Herberti . . . Epistolae*, Letter xv. The *curia* in this case may be the *curia regis*.

85. *Ibid.*, Letter xiv.

The last in the group of monastic foundations with a monastic bishop was Winchester, where Henry of Blois, the royal nephew and the most powerful churchman in the country, was so concerned with the affairs of the realm that he was unable to establish an intimate relationship with the cathedral clergy.[86]

The monastic churches with secular bishops had even less of the spirit of paternal concern that was infused into the lives of the brethren at Canterbury and Rochester. William Giffard at Winchester, Hervey and Nigel at Ely, John at Rochester, Samson and Simon at Worcester, and John at Bath pursued other interests that drew them away from their abbeys, and although conflicts with their convents were often reconciled so far as the monks were concerned, the bishops stood somewhat apart from the daily life of the community.[87] John of Rochester (1125–1137), the fourth bishop during Henry's reign, appears to have been much less successful than his predecessors in maintaining peaceful concord. Disputes over possessions which he had alienated contributed to an uneasy relationship with his monks, and it was not until after his death, in 1145, that a settlement was reached (in the court of the papal legate).[88] According to charter evidence in the Worcester cartulary, Bishop Simon (1125–1150) made an astonishing number of grants to the Worcester convent and church, but it is known from other sources that disputed property rights were the cause of a long controversy.[89] At Winchester, an agreement was made between Bishop William (1107–1129) and his clergy in 1124, after the intercession of the king and inspiring acts of humility on both sides

86. "Es kann keinem Zweifel unterliegen, dass der zum Regieren fähigere von den beiden Brüdern der Bischof war. Stephans leichtes, liebenswürdiges, aber schwankendes Temperament brachte die feste Energie nicht auf, die nötig war, um sich in seiner Lage durchzusetzen. Heinrich geriet denn auch in den kommenden Jahren immer mehr in die Rolle des Politikers und Staatsmanns hinein, und bei mehr als einer Gelegenheit zeigte es sich, wie sehr der König der besseren Einsicht und der eisernen Willenskraft seines Bruders bedurfte." (Lena Voss, *Heinrich von Blois, Bischof von Winchester* [Berlin, 1932], p. 15). See D. Knowles, *The Episcopal Colleagues of Archbishop Thomas Becket* (Cambridge, 1951), p. 34, for a character sketch.

87. For Winchester, see *Annales Monasterii de Wintonia*, RS 36, *anno* 1126; for Ely, see *Anglia Sacra*, ed. H. Wharton (2 vols.; London, 1691), I, p. 617; for Rochester, see D. Knowles, *Monastic Order*, p. 630; for Bath, see *Historiola . . . Somersetensis*, ed. J. Hunter, p. 22.

88. D. Knowles, *Monastic Order*, p. 630.

89. *Cartularium . . . Hemingi, Ep. Jun.*, ed. T. Hearne (Oxford, 1723) p. 533; D. Knowles, *op. cit.*, p. 630, n. 4; of Samson, Simon's predecessor, William of Malmesbury is non-committal: . . . monachos aliquando liberaliter et honeste tractare, aliquando more praedonis insectari. (*GP*, RS 52, p. 290).

(the report of the agreement, however, because it is part of the Winchester chronicle, may have exaggerated the role of the foundation).[90] The exception among these men was Everard, the successor of Herbert Losinga at Norwich, who evidently patterned his actions upon Herbert's, and so earned the gratitude of the monks.[91]

In the two groups of secular cathedrals we have the unusual cases of two monastic bishops, Seefrid, a "black monk" at Chichester, and Robert de Betun, an Augustinian canon at Hereford, who enjoyed long terms in office until late in the decade of 1140. Seefrid for twenty-one years and Robert for eighteen years. Little is known of Seefrid, although he has been described as a time-server, and was deposed in 1145 for reasons that are at present unclear.[92] Robert de Betun, on the other hand, had a strong influence on the religious life of his clergy and set an example of benevolent spiritual leadership, his various duties outside the diocese notwithstanding. A contemporary chronicler said of him:

> . . . by strict adherence to canonical discipline [he] made his foundation a model to be imitated by others; and . . . with a true bishop's care watched over episcopal affairs in his see, and earned an extraordinary influence and respect in the kingdomfor his sacred work.[93]

In 1143 Robert courageously defended his church and lands against the claims of the earl of Hereford.[94]

The fourth group of churches excluded the monastic element entirely; and where the daily ordering of the life and service of the church lacked strong direction or the relationship of bishop to clergy lacked precise definition, a bishop was, at best, *patrocinator* rather than *pater spiritualis*—patron and protector rather than guiding father. At the worst, he was a despoiler of his cathedral church, an unwelcome visitor to his chapter, and even a stranger to his diocese. In several cases the canons were more guilty of irregularities than their bishop; nevertheless, the widespread division of lands and goods associated with the separation of the *mensa episcopalis* implied a complementary separation in ecclesiastical jurisdiction between

90. *Annales Wintoniensis*, RS 36, *anno* 1124.

91. *Primum Registrum Norwicense*, fol. 9*d*.

92. A. Saltman, *Theobald*, pp. 14, 101. Seefrid may well have been promoted to the episcopacy from Glastonbury with the help of Ralph of Canterbury, whom the Godwin catalogue describes as his brother.

93. John of Hexham, *Chronicle*, in *Scriptores Decem*, ed. R. Twysden (London, 1652), col. 257.

94. *Gesta Stephani*, pp. 104–6.

bishop and chapter, and the assumption of privileges by the capitular authority can be seen in most of the secular cathedrals by the end of the twelfth century.[95]

At York, for example, the archbishop gradually lost control over the canons, retaining only his right of appointment to prebends, but, even then, *nec tamen sine consilio et assensu capituli.*[96] In a charter (1137 X 1140), Archbishop Turstin, "at the prayer and with the consent of the chapter," responded to their wishes by confirming various rights of prebends at the departure or death of a canon, but despite these *ex officio* duties he was denied entrance to the chapter.[97] Between 1109 and 1112, Archbishop Thomas II confirmed to the abbey church of Selby (a proprietary church of York) all the gifts of his predecessors, Thomas I and Gerard—as would be natural—while at precisely the same time a reconfirmation was made independently by the chapter of St. Peter's, York.[98]

From the time of the reconstitution by Thomas I, various difficulties had been encountered. In a letter to Anselm (*c.* 1103), Archbishop Gerard, Thomas's successor, complained of difficulty in convincing his clergy to adhere to the decrees on celibacy that had recently been promulgated. He called the canons *sophistici disputatores*, for they had argued that although the church council had forbidden them from keeping women in their dwellings, there was no ruling against living quietly and unobserved with ladies in a neighbor's house, and they saw no reason for denying themselves the pleasures of such moderate license.[99] Other irregularities plagued the church at York, and Gerard implored Anselm to admonish and correct his canons, making it clear that these abuses were to end, that a canon should not enjoy the fruits of his benefice while he found someone else to perform his duties, and that canons should not ask to be ordained priest or deacon without making profession of obedience.[100] Anselm

95. This kind of authority is defined in the group of privileges supposedly given to the church of Salisbury by Bishop Osmund (*De Officiis Ecclesiasticis Tractatus*, RS 78, I, 14). Whether or not they were in force by the end of the eleventh century, they certainly were by the end of the twelfth, and, as Kathleen Edwards has remarked, the same kind of privilege "was copied into the statute and custom books of practically every English secular cathedral" (K. Edwards, *The English Secular Cathedrals in the Middle Ages* [Manchester, 1949], Introduction).

96. *Visitations . . . of Southwell Minster* (*Liber Albus*), p. 193.

97. *Early Yorkshire Charters*, ed. W. Farrer (London, 1914), I, No. 150 (cf. with No. 149).

98. *Ibid.*, Nos. 43, 44.

99. *Historians of the Church of York*, RS 71, III, 23 ff.

100. *Ibid.*

offered encouragement through his letters, and promised to discuss the matter at a future synod. However the history of Hugh the Chantor indicates that the archbishop and the chapter could support each other in adversity and reduce friction to a minimum, and the chronicler of the Canterbury-York dispute constantly emphasized the cooperation that existed in the face of archiepiscopal and royal threats.[101] But later, during the reign of Henry II, things reached the point that the canons locked the door between the nave and the archbishop's mansion when disagreement arose over the appointment of a dean, and in 1189 the treasurer is reported to have had all the candles put out because Archbishop Geoffrey arrived late for a service and demanded that the chapter begin again.[102]

In London, it seems that Bishop Maurice had appropriated rights and customs that belonged to the dean and chapter, for which he made a general restitution, at the urging of Herbert of Norwich.[103] Maurice, a rather worldly bishop (according to William of Malmesbury), had begun an extravagant building program at St. Paul's, and the need for additional funds may have tempted him to increase his income from capitular sources.[104] The *Liber Pilosus* of the dean and chapter records a series of violent quarrels during the administrations of Maurice and Richard, but more often than not it is impossible to determine the motives behind them or to assign the fault to the bishop or to the canons.[105] (It may have been Richard I, however, who brought about a settlement between episcopal and capitular jurisdictions, particularly on appointments to livings.[106]) Maurice, still intent upon building his church, soon found that his enthusiasm exceeded his exchequer; not only were the rents insufficient, he exhausted his other resources and lost the vigor that had characterized the beginning of his episcopate.[107]

Ranulf Flambard, the controversial minister and bishop of Durham, was accorded varied treatment by contemporaries on the relationship

101. Hugh the Chantor, *History*, ed. C. Johnson (London, 1961), pp. 43–44, 45–46, 52.

102. K. Edwards, *op. cit.*, from Roger of Howden, RS 51, III, 223.

103. *Early Charters of . . . St. Paul*, ed. M. Gibbs, Camden Society, 3d ser., LVIII, No. 59 (London, 1939).

104. William of Malmesbury, *GP*, RS 52, pp. 145–46; Ordericus Vitalis, *Historiae Ecclesiasticae*, ed. A. le Prévost (Paris, 1840), IV, 275.

105. When Richard was accused (among other things) of making a park out of some Essex woodland, he averred he did it "bona intentione scilicet ut canonicis melius custodiretur" (H. W. C. Davis, "London Lands and Liberties of St. Paul's: 1066–1135," in *Essays . . . to T. F. Tout* (Manchester, 1925), p. 54.

106. *Early Charters*, ed. M. Gibbs, pp. xxiv–xxxii.

107. William of Malmesbury, *GP*, RS 52, p. 142.

between bishop and cathedral chapter.[108] We know of the grants he made to the chapter and of his illustrious treatment by a later Durham writer.[109] William of Malmesbury comments on Ranulf's help in the building of Durham cathedral and in the translation of the body of St. Cuthbert, but William does not consider it unworthy (though perhaps in poor taste) to report the bishop's questionable morals.[110] Particularly intriguing is the account of wild parties, to which the monks were invited, where forbidden foods and alluring girls were provided when the abbey of Durham was momentarily transformed into a Paphian temple on the Wear. Roguish stories aside, there is reason to believe that Ranulf exercised tight control over his cathedral clergy. It has been suggested that he applied the techniques of administrative organization he had practiced under Rufus to Durham, and if he was able to provide himself with a source of income by the seizure of monastic property, it is no wonder that some writers treated him severely.[111]

Robert de Limesey, at Chester (at Coventry after 1102), evidently exploited the chapter for his financial advantage, as did Alexander at Lincoln;[112] Bernard, at St. David's, if we believe the chronicler, pursued a policy that forced the canons to live "more like soldiers than clerics";[113] and one can conclude that where such conflicts are found the relationship between bishop and chapter must have been strained, if not hostile. The picture, however, is not wholly black in this respect, for curial bishops (such as Robert of Lincoln) often made significant contributions to the fabric, if not to the spirit, of their church.

These glimpses into the life and work of a diocese reveal only a small

108. For a brief appraisal of some writers and the reasons for their differences, see R. W. Southern "Ranulf Flambard and Early Anglo-Norman Administration," *TRHS*, 4th ser., XVI (1933), 125. The anonymous Durham continuation comments on Flambard's kindness and generosity toward his monks (RS 75, I, 135).

109. *Dialogi Laurentii Dunelmensis Monachi ac Prioris*, ed. J. Raine [Surtees Society], LXX (1880), 233 ff.

110. William of Malmesbury, *GP*, RS 52, pp. 274–75. The description of the alleged incident appears after an erasure in the alternate manuscript. In the *Life of Christina of Markyate* (ed. C. H. Talbot [Oxford, 1959]), Flambard, after he became bishop, is pictured as one of the villains of the story, who, inspired by Satan, attempted to deprive Christina of her virginity (pp. 41–55).

111. R. W. Southern, *op. cit.*, p. 127. The fact that the prior does not appear in any writ or charter of the bishop suggests that he had things his own way (see G. V. Scammell, *Hugh de Puiset* [Cambridge, 1956], p. 141).

112. William of Malmesbury, *GP*, p. 309; Giraldus Cambrensis, *Vita S. Remigi*, RS 21, p. xxii.

113. Giraldus Cambrensis, *De Jure*, RS 21, III, 153.

part of the problem, and it is impossible from such fragmentary evidence to argue that the cited cases faithfully reflect a relationship that prevailed for several years. At best, the evidence indicates tendencies that we can assume were characteristic of the various episcopal administrations, and we should avoid the temptation of thinking that a corner of the canvas reveals the whole picture.

Although a period of training in the royal household might have been of help to a bishop in the government of his see, the fact that his chief interest usually was his service to his lord meant that curial bishops were apt to be estranged from their cathedral clergy. This group of bishops had the most extensive itineraries, and men like Roger of Salisbury, Henry of Winchester, and Robert of Lincoln were absent from their sees so much of the time that the chapters, left to run their own affairs, hardened the lines of their corporate identity.[114] Indeed, as a recent historian has observed, "the dean and chapter came to be regarded as the rulers of a kind of autonomous ecclesiastical republic within the diocese."[115] It is noteworthy that in almost all the secular cathedrals during the reign of Henry I there were deans who could have performed the duties of the absent diocesan.

At London in the time of Maurice, there was a dean and a well-organized chapter.[116] At York, notice of a dean comes early in the twelfth century. At the beginning of his reign, Henry I issued a writ that Gerard should hold pleas in his own baronial court (*in curia sua*), in the lands of his churches (*in terris ecclesiarum suarum*), and in the lands of his archbishopric (*in omnibus terris Eboracensis archiepiscopatus*)—as Thomas, the archbishop, had held them. Gerard also was to execute the king's *nova statuta* in judgments and pleas of false coiners and thieves by his own justice in his own court, exercising authority through his bailiff that would otherwise have been carried out by the sheriff.[117] After a few years, Gerard complained to the king that the church of York was being despoiled by the sheriff; after an investigation, the canons' prebends were confirmed and declared inviolate. No one was to levy a distress there

114. See the lists of episcopal itineraries in Appendix III.

115. K. Edwards, *op. cit.*, p. 100.

116. *Early Charters*, Gibbs, No. 59; *HMCR*, IX, 61; Le Neve, in *Fasti*, lists Ulstanus, 1086–1107, and William, 1111 (p. 182).

117. *Early Yorkshire Charters*, Vol. I, No. 14 (1101 X 1108); see also N. Hunard, "The Anglo-Norman Franchises," *EHR*, LXIV (1949), 315–16, and *Regesta*, II, 501, 518.

until the canon of the affected prebend had been asked to do right; if he refused, the dean of York was responsible and was obliged to set a day to hear the case before the door of the church.[118] A later charter of the king confirmed to Hugh, the dean, all rights in the tithes from certain manors and in the lands of certain churches Henry had given St. Peter's. Archbishop Turstin, during the period 1119–1130, had trouble with a dean who was reluctant to reside in the church and perform his relevant duties.[119]

At Lincoln, Simon, the dean, is mentioned in two royal charters (1107 X 1116 and 1120 X 1123), and by the end of Henry's reign there is notice of a subdean.[120] About 1122 a man named Azo is mentioned as dean at Salisbury, and Le Neve lists five others.[121] Two deans, Richard and Matthew, are noted at Chichester between 1115 and 1125. Exeter, however, seems not to have had a dean, which has been considered surprising, but this has been ascribed to the influence of the rule of Chrodegang upon the canons.[122] Similarly, Hereford probably did not have a dean during this period,[123] and this could have been due to the lack of organization during the relatively short terms of the five bishops who occupied the see and to the thirteen years the bishopric was vacant when the development of a more efficient chapter might have been discouraged. The strong-minded Robert de Betun (appointed in 1131) may have felt no need for a home government in his see.

Despite frequent difficulties in maintaining harmonious relations between bishop and chapter and the gradual separation of interests, early twelfth-century bishops still drew upon the members of their chapter for help and counsel. Although their tasks had grown in complexity by the time of Henry I and one can see an emerging group of

118. *Visitations . . . of Southwell Minster*, pp. 191 ff.; see also *Regesta*, II, 686, 852.

119. *Regesta*, II, 1336 (in a precept issued probably in the year 1122). In *Historians of the Church of York* (RS 71, III, 53), the dating is 1125 X 1130. Le Neve in *Fasti* lists Hugh for 1090–1109, Aldred for 1113, and Hugh for 1130 (p. 312).

120. *Regesta*, II, 1032, 1389; see also F. M. Stenton, *First Century of English Feudalism* (Oxford, 1932), p. 34. Le Neve in *Fasti* lists Simon Bloet for 1110 and Nigellus for 1123–1147 (p. 144).

121. *Regesta*, II, 1324. Le Neve in *Fasti* (pp. 261–62) lists Roger, Osbert, Serlo (no dates), Robert I (d. 1111), and Robert of Chichester(?) (to Exeter c. 1140).

122. A. Morey, *Bartholomew of Exeter* (Cambridge, 1937), p. 88.

123. Arthur T. Bannister, *Cathedral Church of Hereford* (London, 1924), p. 31; his evidence is negative in that the canons issued a conveyance of property (c. 1132) without mention of a dean. Le Neve in *Fasti* (p. 113) lists John Middleton and Hugh de Breusa (no dates), and Ralph (c. 1140). See also Z. N. Brooke, "Hereford Cathedral Dignitaries," *CHJ*, VIII (1944–46), 6–7.

officials who made attendance upon the bishop their primary concern, the episcopal *familia* was still developing; it was not, however, a fully defined element in ecclesiastical administration and therefore was not entirely separated from the capitular clergy.[124] The employment of cathedral canons in the bishop's service was thought natural, as is indicated by the provisions in the Salisbury *tractatus*, which stated that canons must reside in the cathedral church *nisi causa scolarum*, or unless they are in the service of the king, who may have one in his chapel, or of the archbishop who may have one, or of the bishop who may have three.[125] Service away from the see must have been common enough to require written conditions so that the residency requirement could be waived. That this service continued is shown by articles in thirteenth-century canon law, whereby two canons of a cathedral church who were absent with the bishop or in his employment might receive the fruits of their prebends as if resident, contrary customs of the chapter notwithstanding.[126] Although canons and monks helped with household duties, there were episcopal councillors who apparently had no connection with the chapter; the *familia*, therefore, must be defined in terms of its function rather than in terms of its membership which, as will be shown, was apt to vary tremendously.

Toward the middle of the twelfth century witnesses to a confirmation by Archbishop Theobald to the priory of Stoke-by-Clare in Suffolk included a butler, a dispenser, a chamberlain, a steward or seneschal, a chief cook, a doorkeeper or usher, a porter, and a marshal (in that order), as well as the nephews of Theobald, archiepiscopal clerks, a chancellor, and at least two "monks" and "chaplains" of the archbishop.[127] As in many confirmations of this kind, unless there are such qualifications as "of the bishop," "of the archbishop," "our men," "our clerks," etc., it is not always possible to be sure that the witnesses were primarily episcopal

124. C. R. Cheney, *English Bishops' Chanceries: 1100–1250* (Manchester, 1950), pp. 1–21. A charter issued by the dean and chapter of St. Paul's (1111 X 1138) was attested by William, the dean; William, archdeacon; Nicolaus, canon; Walter, son of the bishop; Walter, alderman; Robert, priest; and Gilbert, physician (*Early Charters*, No. 128). The group that attested for the chapter is not radically different from groups that attested for the bishop, and the fact that individuals of the same dignity appear in both groups argues against a formal distinction between the two in the early twelfth century.

125. *De Officiis Ecclesiasticis Tractatus*, RS 78, I, p. 18; and pp. 212–13 for the same statement in the copy of 1091.

126. K. Edwards, *op. cit.*, p. 90.

127. This is discussed by F. M. Stenton in *First Century of English Feudalism*, pp. 266–67, No. 16; see also the comments in C. R. Cheney, *op. cit.*, p. 29.

or conventual servants;[128] and little can be gained by trying to clarify what probably was perfectly clear in the twelfth century. It can be assumed that the household departments of the great magnates gradually became more distinct, probably with separate staffs. For example, a final concord of the early thirteenth century, between the abbot of Westminster and Ivo of Deene, tells us of the abbot's household and the seven officers who were in charge of its chief departments (*officia*): the seneschal, the chamberlain, the pantler, the butler, the usher, the cook, and the marshal. These men are referred to as the abbot's servants, their duties are specified, and they obviously formed part of the itinerant household[129] and handled jobs that were necessary and important. It is not surprising that all of them were included in the earlier confirmation of Archbishop Theobald, although their ranking was different.[130]

An interesting charter of Bishop Hervey of Ely (1109 X 1131), which allows a closer look at household management in this early period of bureaucratic development, records the grant of the office of baker to a certain Haldewyn, along with a messuage (*mansura*) and eighteen acres of arable land in Ely.[131] Having served in the bakehouse (*pistrinum*), Haldewyn and his successors were given charge of the grain (*brennum*), and as members of the episcopal household (*familia nostra*) they were to receive livery and two horses and two grooms on the bishop's allowance; also, they were to engage four faithful bakers, whom the bishop would pay with food, drink, and wages—as others of the household (*de hospicio nostro*). Haldewyn also was responsible for supplying the horses with fodder (*brennum*) when they were bled or were sick, according to the disposition of the bishop's marshal, but only for the first night; after that, the bishop would buy fodder at a lower price. Haldewyn was to hold the land and office for four gifts of bread each year. These terms are the conditions of the charter which is an illustration of hereditary tenure by serjeantry and of a division of labor for the duties of baker and marshal.

Haldewyn's holding can be compared with that of Alfric, the bishop's reeve (*prepositus*), who, in a charter of the same period, was granted a tenement of three virgates with three dwellings and nine acres of wasteland that he and his successors were to hold at an annual rent of one

128. There also is evidence, by the middle of the twelfth century, for the establishment of the prior's household; see R. A. L. Smith, *Canterbury Cathedral Priory* (Cambridge, 1943), pp. 30–31.

129. F. M. Stenton, *op. cit.*, No. 17.

130. See n. 194 (below).

131. Printed in Edward Miller, *Abbey and Bishopric of Ely* (Cambridge, 1951), Appendix V, p. 283.

mark of silver to the bishop of Ely and three loads (*summae*) of flour to the monks. On the basis of these holdings, Alfric ranked higher than Haldewyn; on the other hand, Haldewyn was expressly mentioned as a member of the household. Because of the nature of his duties, Haldewyn must have had closer contact than Alfric with affairs of the see, but one cannot say he was more influential.

In especially important grants, a bishop doubtless called on extra witnesses. Turstanus, *forestarius*, is mentioned in a notification of Gilbert Foliot, bishop of London in the time of Henry II, and may not have been connected with the *familia* or the chapter.[132] For witnesses to a document issued either at home or in transit, a bishop might call upon whatever monks, canons, or servants were present; and many charters concluded the attestations with *et multis aliis* or *et aliis quampluribus*. In other cases, witnesses were drawn from other dioceses or from the royal service—a practice that is illustrated in the instrument (June 14, 1133) of William Warelwast, bishop of Exeter (which settled a dispute over the chapel of Combe in his diocese), in which the witness list included an archdeacon of Salisbury and of Bath, a clerk of the bishop of Winchester, the steward of the bishop of Salisbury, and a steward of the earl of Devon.[133] Another example is the charter of Hervey of Ely, in 1128, to which Henry, archdeacon of Huntingdon, was a witness.[134] This practice has been explained as financially expedient, but it is also reasonable to suppose that such individuals might have been present because they happened to be with the bishop or because they had a special interest in the affair.[135] Elsewhere, Henry of Huntingdon described the grand *familia* of Robert, bishop of Lincoln, in which he had been brought up, and which included Richard, the natural son of Henry I, who later perished in the disaster of the *White Ship*. At Lincoln, the household of the princely bishop served as a school for princes.[136]

From the evidence provided by the witness lists and the narrative sources, the individuals who appeared most often at the side of the bishop in this period were the *clerici* and the *capellani*.[137] When these are further

132. C. R. Cheney, *op. cit.*, p. 6.

133. F. M. Stenton, "Acta Episcoporum," *CHJ*, III (1929), 9. See also the Ely charter of Bishop Hervey (1128).

134. E. Miller, *op. cit.*, Appendix VI; see also n. 166 (below).

135. C. R. Cheney, *op. cit.*, p. 9.

136. "Ricardus quoque filius regis nothus ab episcopo nostro Roberto festive nutritus et in eadem qua degebam familia a me et aliis celebriter honoratus . . ." (in RS 74, p. 304).

137. A distinction between the two is made by Cheney, *op. cit.*, p. 9.

described as *clerici episcopi* or *capellani episcopi*, it may be inferred that they were members of an episcopal household.[138] Sometimes they enjoyed revenues provided by the bishop, as at Norwich, where Bishop Herbert gave various tithes from the episcopal manors to his chaplain and the remainder to the monks of Norwich;[139] or at Hereford, where *capellani episcopi* are recorded as holding land of the bishop in Herefordshire.[140] About 1106, at London, attesting for Bishop Maurice in a charter to Eustace, the count of Boulogne, was Roger, *archidiaconus capellanus episcopi*, whose title may indicate that he was appointed to one position without relinquishing another—and that Maurice was saving money.[141]

Besides clerks and chaplains, other individuals appeared as *ministri* and *servientes*,[142] chamberlains,[143] constables,[144] marshal,[145] *medicus*,[146]

138. For Canterbury, see Eadmer, RS 81, p. 67, and Dugdale, I, 168 f. For Rochester, see *Regesta*, II, 845, and *EHD*, II, No. 279. For Bath, see Dugdale, II, 268. For Durham, see *Pipe Roll*, 31 Henry I, p. 131. For Ely, see D. Douglas, *Feudal Documents from the Abbey of Bury St. Edmunds* (London, 1932), No. 52, and E. Miller, *op. cit.*, p. 285. For Norwich, see *Primum Registrum*, fol. 10 f. For Winchester, see Dugdale, VI, i, 172. For York, see *Chartulary of the Priory of St. Bees*, ed. J. Wilson (Surtees Society), CXXVI (1915), 32. For Chester, see *Magnum Registrum Album*, ed. H. E. Savage (William Salt Archaeological Society, 1924), No. 169. For Chichester, see *Chronicon de Bello*, p. 57. For Exeter, see *Monasticon Diocesis Exoniensis*, ed. G. Oliver (Exeter, 1845–54), p. 199. For Salisbury, see *Regesta*, II, 1324. For St. David's, see *Episcopal Acts*, Davies, Vol. I, D.141, D.148. For Llandaff, see *Regesta*, II, 1466, and *Cartae . . . de Glamorgancia*, ed. G. Clark, I, lxxxv.

139. *Primum Registrum*, fol. 4.

140. Henry Ellis, *Introduction to Domesday Book* (2 vols.; London, 1833), II, 301.

141. *Early Charters*, No. 274.

142. For Chichester, see *Chronicon de Bello*, p. 63. For Bath, see Dugdale, II, 268 (a man named Philip, at Bath, was granted four tofts *in perpetuum* by Bishop Everard [*HMCR*, LXII, Marquess of Lothian, (1905) p. 39]). For Ely, see Douglas, *Feudal Documents*, No. 52.

143. For Canterbury, see Eadmer, RS 81, p. 67. For Rochester, see R. A. L. Smith, *EHR*, LVIII (1943), 267. For Durham, see *Feodarium Prioratus Dunelmensis*, ed. W. Greenwell (Surtees Society), LVIII (1872), 112, 145, and G. V. Scammell, *Hugh de Puiset*, p. 219. For Norwich, see *Primum Registrum*, fols. 10 ff. For Worcester, see *Cartularium Hemingi*, II, 527. For Winchester and London, see *Pipe Roll*, 31 Henry I, pp. 39 and 61.

144. For Ely, see E. Miller, *op. cit.*, pp. 249, 283. For Durham, see *Feodarium*, p. 140, and G. T. Lapsley, *County Palatine of Durham*, "Harvard Historical Studies" (New York, 1900), VIII, 78–94. For Norwich, see *Primum Registrum*, fols. 8*d*, 11*d*. For Salisbury, see *Regesta*, II, 1042. As for Winchester, reference to Herbert "Camerarius," Miles "Constabularius," and Robert "Pincerna," who held knights' fees of the bishop before 1135, indicates men who probably were members of the royal household rather than the bishop's (*Regesta*, II, xiii–xvi).

145. See E. Miller, *op. cit.*, pp. 249, 283.

146. *Ibid.*, p. 285. For York, see *Early Yorkshire Charters*, eds. W. Farrer and C. T. Clay [Yorkshire Arch. Society], III, 1470.

hostilarius,[147] and *scriptor*.[148] Those who bore such titles as cellarer,[149] cantor,[150] almoner,[151] precentor,[152] treasurer,[153] and *secretarius*[154] can safely be considered members of the capitular rather than the episcopal household.[155] Men of academic training, *magistri scolarum*, appear in several of the witness lists, and, because of the tradition of instruction peculiar to the episcopal *familia*, their presence is not surprising in the developing literate climate of the early twelfth century.[156] At Ely, under Bishop Nigel (1133–1169), there is reference to Ern[ulf], Rogerus, Henricus, and Willelmus, all *magistri*.[157] There was a Willelmus *magister* at Norwich during the episcopate of Everard,[158] and there is evidence

147. *Primum Registrum*, fol. 11.

148. Attesting for the bishop of London (in 1106) in a charter of Eustace, Count of Boulogne, was *Simon scriptor qui breum* [sic] *fecit* (*Early Charters*, No. 198); however, the writer who is mentioned in a confirmation of Bishop Wulfstan (at Worcester in 1092) and who attested with the prior, the chantor, and others, may have been attached to the convent rather than to the bishop (*Chartularium . . . Hemingi*, II, 527).

149. For the cellarer at Rochester, see Dugdale, pp. 169 ff.

150. For the cantor at York, see *Early Yorkshire Charters*, II, 357, and III, 1367; see also *Historians of the Church of York*, RS 71, III, 6 ff. For Worcester, see *Chartularium . . . Hemingi*, *loc. cit.*

151. For the almoner at York, see the references above in *Early Yorkshire Charters*.

152. For the precentor at Wells, see *Red Book of the Exchequer*, p. 220.

153. For the treasurer at York, see C. T. Clay (*York Archaeological Journal*, XXXV [1941], 7 ff.), who gives notice of one Ranulf (c. 1090). Then the celebrated William Fitz-Herbert appears, who is mentioned as treasurer in a confirmation of his brother, Herbert, to the canons of Nostell priory (Yorkshire) between 1114 and 1121 (*Early Yorkshire Charters*, I, 26). These brothers were sons of Herbert, a chamberlain to Henry I, who died about 1130 (*Pipe Roll*, 31 Henry I, p. 37 [Herbert, the son, paid relief for the lands of his father]). William Fitz-Herbert, who was chaplain under Stephen, eventually obtained the archbishopric of York, in 1143 (*Early Yorkshire Charters*, 28, 31). His ponficate was not a happy one; for an account of his troubles, see D. Knowles, *CHJ*, V (1936), pp. 162 ff. and A. Saltman, *Theobald*, p. 161.

154. A *secretarius* (sacrist) was mentioned at Rochester in the time of Ernulf, who was charged with giving ten shillings worth of bread to the poor and putting twenty shillings into the monks' refectory (Dugdale, pp. 169 ff.). At Norwich, the *secretarius* was charged with the distribution of chrismal allowances (*Primum Registrum*, fol. 12*d*).

155. A constitution with the four *personae* had been established at Chichester by 1114 (M. E. C. Walcott, *Archaeologia*, XLV [1878], 159). Hugh the Chantor described the appointment of dean, treasurer, precentor, and chancellor under Archbishop Thomas I at York (Hugh the Chantor, *op. cit.*, p. 11).

156. For a discussion of the *magistri* and the chancery, see C. R. Cheney, *op. cit.*, Chaps. 1 and 2.

157. E. Miller, *op. cit.*, p. 285.

158. *Primum Registrum*, fol. 10–10*d*.

for a *magister scolarum* at York from the time of Thomas I.[159] There was a succession of *magistri* at London from Bishop Richard I onwards;[160] a *magister* Radulphus attested a charter of Robert of Lincoln;[161] Bishop Roger had such an individual at Salisbury;[162] and Bernard of St. David's, the leading figure in the ecclesiastical organization in Wales, had a "master John" as witness to one of his charters.[163] (The presence of the related figure, the *cancellarius*, at Canterbury, Norwich, Winchester, and Worcester has been discussed elsewhere, as far as the evidence will allow.[164])

Other dignitaries who appeared often and who are known to have been part of the household in most dioceses are the steward, *dapifer*, and the butler, *pincerna*. At Norwich, in the time of Bishop Herbert, a steward, Godefridus, who was married to Nigreda, gave the land of Newton to the convent; this gift was confirmed *in perpetuum* by the son, Ralph, who donated ten pounds to maintain it.[165] In another charter concerning a settlement of lands in which the abbey of Ramsey had an interest the witnesses include Gwido (Wido), *dapifer* (who also appears in the witness list of two royal charters [1107 and 1111] addressed to Robert, bishop of Lincoln, Simon, the earl of Huntingdon, and Gilbert, the sheriff).[166] The Ramsey charter is early evidence for the close connection between royal and episcopal households that one finds fairly often in this period, although it would be going too far to assert that Gwido was a member of each.[167] Gwido evidently had a son, John, who seems also to have held the office of *dapifer* under Everard. A pair of charters that confirmed grants of lands to the Ramsey convent was attested by *Johannes dapifer*, and, again, by *Johannes filius Wydonis dapifer*.[168]

It would appear that the office of steward was often hereditary in an episcopal household, as it has been shown to have been in the royal

159. Hugh the Chantor, *op. cit.*, p. 11.
160. *Early Charters*, Nos. 237, 274, 275.
161. Dugdale, III, p. 19.
162. K. Edwards, *op. cit.*, pp. 185–86.
163. *Episcopal Acts.*, I, D.145.
164. C. R. Cheney, *op. cit.*, pp. 22 ff.
165. *Primum Registrum*, fol. 4.
166. *Ibid.*, fol. 8*d*; see also *Regesta*, II, 966, 967.
167. It was doubtless desirable to have witnesses of notable standing, and the fact that Gwido held a position of importance in the episcopal household may have been the reason he was called; it also is possible that he had a permanent post in the royal service, but this cannot be verified.
168. *Primum Registrum*, fols. 11–12*d*.

household, as in the case of the Bigod and de Courcy families.[169] *Joannes dapifer episcopi* can be found in confirmations of 1130 and 1135 X 1145, when John attested (with Adam, *dapifer*, and Galfridus, *dapifer*, who held five knights' fees of the bishop before 1135), although whether he is the same Godefridus, husband of Nigreda mentioned earlier, is uncertain.[170] At Salisbury, in a charter granted by Bishop Roger in 1114, Osmund, *dapifer*, Robert, *vetus dapifer*, and Robert, the latter's son, attested; however, there is no evidence that young Robert succeeded his father in the office.[171] The same problem occurred at London, where, in the time of Bishop Maurice, we find a Willelmus de Ochendon and Willelmus, *dapifer*,[172] and a few years later (early in the episcopate of Richard I) a Willelmus Briton, *dapifer*, and Willelmus de Vocchend are found.[173] Later, about 1127, a Willelmus de Occhedon is addressed in a charter of the bishop as "his *dapifer*," and de Occhedon attested the instrument as *dapifer*.[174] Still later, in a charter of Bishop Robert de Sigillo (c. 1142), a Willelmus de Hochedona appears, but without his title, in the company of his son and Rogerus Brunus, *dapifer*.[175] Unfortunately there is not enough information to say whether there might have been more than one *dapifer* at a time, or whether William continued in the office through three episcopates, or whether the hereditary principle was established.

The importance of the office is denoted by Hugh, at Winchester, in his accounting of one mark of gold for the stewardship (*dapiferia*) of the bishop. There evidently was income to be had from the exercise of this authority, although in this particular case it is difficult to say whether Hugh was buying or redeeming his post.[176] Members of the *familia* at Canterbury in this period included several *dapiferi*, one of whom, Ansfrid, attested a notification of Henry I (1130 X 1133) that was issued at London in favor of the bishop of Rochester.[177] Ansfrid is called the steward of the archbishop and is listed after Hugh Bigod, *dapifer* of the royal household. Here, as at Norwich, a member of the episcopal *familia* is closely

169. The hereditary reeveship at Ely has been noted, see also E. Miller, *op. cit.*, p. 124.

170. *Primum Registrum, loc. cit.*; *Red Book of the Exchequer*, I, 391.

171. *Regesta*, II, 1042; Dugdale, IV, 64–65; *Vetus Registrum*, RS 78, p. 215.

172. *Early Charters*, No. 198.

173. *Ibid.*, No. 63.

174. *Ibid.*, No. 274.

175. *Ibid.*, No. 219.

176. *Pipe Roll*, 31 Henry I, Hugo de Fiscapo (or Fiscano), p. 39. A Hugo de Fiscano held four knights' fees of the bishop of Winchester in 1166.

177. *Regesta*, II, 1867.

connected with the royal service; on this occasion, however, he is in the company of William, the archbishop, which may mean only that Ansfrid was with William when he attested the document.

There can be no doubt that the stewardship was one of the chief offices of the episcopal household; the *dapifer* is usually cited at the beginning of witness lists, and in at least two cases he enjoyed important tenurial status. This dignity corresponds with the steward's position in the administrative organization of the twelfth-century lay baronial household;[178] at York, for example, the archbishop's *dapifer* was able to relieve all the manorial reeves of representation in the shire court when he was present.[179] This would indicate that the *dapifer* acted on authority delegated to him by his lord in much the same way as *dapiferi* of the great lay magnates represented theirs, with an interest in the profits of justice.

The last group of importance connected with the episcopal *familia* was the archidiaconal,[180] an office that was known in the Anglo-Saxon church and that became increasingly important as ecclesiastical organization developed.[181] The primary pre-Conquest evidence comes from the diocese of Worcester and from the north, where, in the law of the Northumbrian priests, the archdeacon functioned as the bishop's deputy (the priest who "neglects the bishop's own summons is to pay 20 ores, and

178. See F. M. Stenton, *First Century of English Feudalism*, pp. 73–82, and especially pp. 76–78, where the duties of the *dapifer* in the household of the honorial baronage are described.

179. "Et dapifer archiepiscopi si sit in comitatu potest acquietare omnes praepositos maneriorum faciendo id quod facerent praepositi si adessent" (*Visitations of Southwell Minster*, p. 196). See *Leges Henrici*, VII, 7: "Si quis baronum regis vel aliorum comitatui secundum legem interfuerit, totam terram quam illic in dominio suo habet, acquietare poterit. Eodem modo est si dapifer ejus legitime fuerit. Si uterque necessario desit, praepositus et sacerdos et quatuor de melioribus villae assint pro omnibus qui nominatim non erunt ad placitum submoniti." (in Stubbs, *Select Charters*, p. 124).

180. In the Salisbury register the archdeacon's traditional charge was: *Archidiaconi in sollicitudine parochiarum et in cura pollent animarum*; and, in the *Tractatus: Archidiaconi officiales sunt domini episcopi quorum officium in exterioribus administrationibus consistit* (RS 78, p. 214, and I, 12). Although this is probably descriptive of the early thirteenth century, it also is relevant to twelfth-century conditions (see n. 184). By the thirteenth century, archdeacons occupied so important a place in the diocesan hierarchy that—for Canterbury, at least—"administration of the diocese . . . was largely in the hands of the archdeacons and the rural deans" (Brian L. Woodcock, *Medieval Ecclesiastical Courts in the Diocese of Canterbury* [Oxford, 1952], p. 103).

181. F. M. Stenton, *Anglo-Saxon England*, p. 434; J. Godfrey, *The Church in Anglo-Saxon England* (Cambridge, 1962), p. 391. See the remarks by C. R. Cheney, *op. cit.*, pp. 7–9.

12 ores if he neglects the archdeacon's summons").[182] As the bishops' work grew in complexity, it was mainly through the archdeacons that a bishop fulfilled his diocesan responsibilities; consequently, the archdeacon was often—but not always—a member of the *familia* and a frequent witness to episcopal *acta*.

During the reign of Henry I these officials are found in every English and Welsh see.[183] As episcopal appointees, their duties were various, but in the few documents of this period that show them at work they usually seem to be involved in administrative tasks and the enforcement of episcopal decisions.[184] At Bath, two archdeacons were present at what probably was the bishop's court.[185] Exemptions from archidiaconal visitations and from demands for hospitality have already been noted (in connection with Godstow and Burton abbeys), and later accounts show that such visitations could be ruinous, and the exemption highly prized.[186] Interference by archdeacons in a peculiar jurisdiction within the area of their overall supervision also has been noted (the Canterbury-Chichester dispute), and, in addition, several *acta* of Archbishop Theobald shortly after the reign of Henry I charged various archdeacons and their rural deans with implementing the excommunications of persons who annoyed pilgrims to Bury St. Edmunds and of the burgesses of Colchester if they continued their oppression of the abbey by compelling the monks to hold the farm of the town. The *acta* also obliged defaulters to pay tithes to the canons of Oseney abbey and to the monks

182. *EHD*, Vol. I; F. Barlow, *The English Church*, pp. 247–49. By the writ of William I, the jurisdiction of the archdeacon and his bishop was restricted to hearing pleas in the spiritual court; excommunication was to be pronounced on anyone who refused to attend the episcopal court after three summonses.

183. See Appendix II.

184. Wilkins, *Concilia*, I, 363; Feine, pp. 201–2. A charter of Henry I to Almod, archdeacon in Lincoln, ordered him to restore to the abbot of Thorney the abbot's manor of Sawbridge as Almod had received it. The editors indicate that Almod probably took possession of the estate upon the death of the previous abbot (*Regesta*, II, 1033). At Lincoln, Gilbert of Sempringham refused an archdeaconry that was offered him by Bishop Robert, "for he wold sey sum-tyme [th]at [th]ese benefices of grete expense be often-tyme a redy wey to losse of a mannes soule." (*Vita Gilberti*, *EETS*, o.s., CXL, 65.)

185. *Two Cartularies of Bath Abbey*, ed. W. Hunt (*Somerset Record Society*, 1893), I, 53. An episcopal court at Bath as early as 1111 is indicated in two royal precepts (*Regesta*, II, 988, 1302).

186. The third Lateran Council (1179) ordered that archbishops be limited to forty or fifty horses on visitations, bishops to twenty or thirty, archdeacons to five or seven, and deans to two.

of Stoke-by-Clare.[187] Although these documents fall within the period 1139–1161, it seems reasonable to assume that this kind of activity was typical of archdeacons ten or twenty years earlier. Theobald also abolished the jurisdiction of the archdeacon of Canterbury in the monastic chapter and excluded the archdeacons from adjudicating crimes committed within the cathedral precincts, reserving this right to himself and the convent which would seem to be a gesture that emphasized the archbishop's desire to reconcile his differences with the monks.

Sometimes, as at Durham in the early years of the episcopate of Ranulf Flambard, monks filled the office of archdeacon, but secular officers usually were appointed in the monastic cathedrals. Secular appointments, of course, were another source of hostility and discord, and the extent to which a convent succeeded in defending its independence from archidiaconal-episcopal supervision was a measure of its success toward becoming an autonomous group.[188] Although this antagonism did not obtain in the secular cathedral churches, there were protracted disputes over an archdeacon's right to sit in the chapter as at London in the time of Bishop Richard I, when archdeacons were excluded from interfering with the chapter's land, churches, priests, or its men on the manors unless they held a prebend.[189] At Ely, Bishop Hervey conferred the two manors of Pampisford and Little Thetford upon his nephew, William, archdeacon of Ely and a chaplain of Henry I, which were to be held by hereditary right.[190] Hervey's grant was confirmed by the king in 1127, and Pampisford was to be held for the service of one knight and Little Thetford for the payment of five shillings, rendered annually to the monks of Ely (although it appears that Pampisford was soon recovered for the church).[191] Assuming that William was a member of the royal household, this would be another indication of the close connection between the royal and episcopal *familiae* spoken of earlier, and it would suggest

187. A. Saltman, *Theobald*, Nos. 26, 75, 196, 258.

188. *Ibid.*, Nos. 30, 50, 171; see also D. Knowles, *Monastic Order*, pp. 629–30. At Canterbury (c. 1150) it was decided that the archdeacon, having had no traditional right to enter the chapter unless called by the monks, was not to do so in the future. The archdeacon, if he was permitted to be present, had to sit on the archbishop's footstool (Saltman, *op. cit.*, No. 30).

189. *Early Charters*, p. xxx and No. 63.

190. E. Miller, *op. cit.*, p. 280. A charter of Henry I (1100 X 1135) granted the church at Barnwell to the monks at St. Neots, which Nigel, archdeacon of Lincoln, held of Henry and of William II, and which Nigel's son, Michael, held after him. Michael became a monk and the grant in alms was made (*Regesta*, II, 1969). There is no evidence, however, that Michael succeeded his father as archdeacon.

191. *Regesta*, II, 1502. See E. Miller, *op. cit.*, pp. 166–69, for the descent of Pampisford.

that the archdeacon, as an absentee official, may have had a deputy who carried out his duties.

The important place archdeacons may have had in their dioceses is illustrated in a letter of Herbert, bishop of Norwich, in which he considered the presence of one of his archdeacons so vital to his interests that he refused to attend a synod unless he could be sure that this dignitary also would be present.[192] Archdeacons also functioned outside the limits of their *provincia*. During the controversy between Canterbury and York over the primacy, one of the archdeacons of Canterbury who was present at the consecration of Turstin—at Reims, in 1119—threatened not only Turstin but also the pope on behalf of the king if the ceremony were performed.[193]

It is evident from this investigation that early twelfth-century episcopal households comprised a number of different individuals of no precise membership, although several officials were common to all. In the absence of a *constitutio domus episcopi*, there is no acceptable way of ranking the members of a *familia* in order of household status or importance,[194] but such dignitaries as the archdeacon, the chancellor, and the *magister* usually appear first in witness lists, and individuals who were concerned mainly with the daily supply—such as the butler, the cook, and the marshal—appear last. The *dapifer* is an exception, but in the households of the greater bishops he may have performed his duties only on ceremonial occasions. That many *familiae* contained an inner group that was close to the bishop can be argued *a priori* and can be inferred from such statements as that of Hugh the Chantor, who told how King Henry ordered the archbishop of York to meet him in council with the dignitaries of his church and his "elder and wiser clerks"—or from Eadmer, who reported that Anselm, in exile after the council at Rockingham, was accompanied by his "chief councillor," the monk Baldwin.[195] Aside from those who were primarily associated with the church, laymen also were attached to episcopal households, but they may have been interested only in their personal holdings within the diocese.[196]

192. *Herberti . . . Epistolae*, I, xxi.

193. Hugh the Chantor, *op. cit.*, p. 72.

194. C. R. Cheney, *op. cit.*, p. 4. See T. A. M. Bishop, *Scriptores Regis* (Oxford, 1961), p. 19, for the ranking of witnesses to royal chancery charters.

195. See R. W. Southern, *St. Anselm and His Biographer*, pp. 194–203.

196. Late in the twelfth century (c. 1183), at Durham, individuals are mentioned, probably villeins, who went about on the bishop's errands: "Willelmus Coupem . . . et vadit in legationibus episcopi" (*Boldon Book*, ed. W. Greenwell [Surtees Society, VIII, 1852], p. 25), but there is no basis for attaching them to the household.

In an age when prestige was built on the size of one's entourage, it must be assumed that the great curial bishops were accompanied by a large and noisy group. In this period the household usually was personal and informal, with only the beginnings of the professionalism of later years, which suggests that several functions were sometimes combined in one man. This practice would have made use of the most competent or loyal individuals, and would have served, as we have noted, to reduce a bishop's expenses.

The scattered and incomplete evidence at hand should not induce us to oversimplify the episcopal household.[197] In the time of Henry I, the bishop's administrative group was only a part of the whole *familia*; and if we can judge by the rapid bureaucratic development during the decades after 1135, it would appear to have been already a complex if not an entirely differentiated group at the beginning of the twelfth century.

197. F. M. Stenton, *First Century of English Feudalism*, p. 65.

APPENDIX I—THE BISHOPS OF HENRY I

1. Bath	John	1088–1122
	Godfrey	1123–1135
2. Canterbury	Anselm	1093–1109
	Ralph	1114–1122
	William	1123–1136
3. Carlisle	Adelulf	1133–1157
4. Chichester	Ralph	1091–1123
	Seefrid	1125–1145
5. Chester	Robert de Limesey	1086–1117
	Robert Pecce	1121–1127
	Roger	1129–1148
6. Durham	Ranulf Flambard	1099–1128
	Geoffrey	1133–1140
7. Ely	Hervey	1109–1131
	Nigel	1133–1169
8. Exeter	Osbern	1072–1103
	William	1107–1137
9. Hereford	Gerard	1096–1101
	Regenhelm	1107–1115
	Geoffrey	1115–1120
	Richard	1121–1127
	Robert	1131–1148
10. Lincoln	Robert	1094–1123
	Alexander	1123–1148
11. London	Maurice	1086–1107
	Richard	1108–1127
	Gilbert	1128–1134
12. Norwich	Herbert	1091–1119
	Everard	1121–1145
13. Rochester	Gundulf	1077–1108
	Ralph	1108–1114
	Ernulf	1115–1124
	John	1125–1137
14. Salisbury	Roger	1107–1139
15. Winchester	William	1107–1129
	Henry	1129–1171
16. Worcester	Samson	1096–1112
	Theulf	1115–1123
	Simon	1125–1150
17. York	Gerard	1101–1108
	Thomas	1109–1114
	Turstin	1119–1140
18. Bangor	Hervey	1092–1109
	David	1120–1139
19. Llandaff	Herewald	1056–1104
	Urban	1107–1133(?)
20. St. David's	Wilfrid	1085–1115
	Bernard	1115–1148

LIST OF SOURCES CITED IN APPENDICES II AND III

Ancient Charters, ed. J. H. Round, Pipe Roll Society (London, 1888) X.
Book of Llan Dâv, ed. E. D. Jones (National Library of Wales, 1946).
Brut y Tywysogion, RS 17.
Cartae . . . quae ad dominum de Glamorgancia pertinent, ed. G. T. Clark (Cardiff, 1910) I.
Christina of Markyate, ed. C. H. Talbot (Oxford, 1959).
Crawford Collection of Early Charters . . ., ed. A. S. Napier and W. H. Stevenson (Oxford, 1895).
Eadmer, *Historia Novorum*, RS 81.
Early Charters of the Cathedral Church of St. Paul, ed. M. Gibbs (London, 1939).
Early Yorkshire Charters, ed. W. Farrer and C. T. Clay (London, 1914, 1937).
Ellis, H. A., *A General Introduction to Domesday Book* (London, 1833).
Episcopal Acts . . . relating to Welsh Dioceses, ed. J. C. Davies (Cardiff, 1946).
Eyton, R. W., *Antiquities of Shropshire* (London, 1854–1860).
Farrer, W., *An Outline Itinerary of King Henry I* (Oxford, 1919).
Feodarium Prioratus Dunelmensis, ed. W. Greenwell (Surtees Society, 1872).
Florence of Worcester, *EHS* (London, 1848–1849).
Gesta Stephani, ed. K. R. Potter (London, 1955).
Gloucester Cartulary, RS 33, I.
Hatton, Sir Christopher, *Book of Seals*, ed. D. Stenton and L. C. Loyd (Oxford, 1950).
Herberti de Losinga . . . *Epistolae*, ed. R. Anstruther (Brussels, 1846).
Historiola de Primordiis Episcopatus Somersetensis, ed. J. Hunter (London, 1840).
Holtzmann, W., *Papsturkunden in England* (Berlin and Göttingen, 1930 et seqq).
Hugh the Chantor, ed. C. Johnson (London, 1961).
Knowles, D., *The Monastic Order in England* (Cambridge, 1950).
Liber Vitae Dunelmensis, ed. A. H. Thompson (Surtees Society, 1923).
Matthew Paris, RS 44.
Merton Cartulary, ed. A. Heales (London, 1898).
Miller, E., *The Abbey and Bishopric of Ely* (Cambridge, 1951).
Monasticon . . . Exoniensis, ed. J. Oliver (Exeter, 1845–1854).
Morey, A., *Bartholomew of Exeter* (Cambridge, 1937).
Primum Registrum Norwicense, ed. H. W. Saunders (Norfolk Record Society, 1939).
Ralph de Diceto, RS 68.
Sancti Anselmi Opera, ed. F. Schmitt (Rome and Edinburgh, 1938–1951).
Symeon of Durham, RS 75.
Vetus Registrum Sarisberiense, RS 78, I.
Walter of Coventry, RS 58.
William of Malmesbury, *Historia Novella*, ed. K. R. Potter (London, 1955).
Whitby Cartulary, ed. J. C. Atkinson (Surtees Society, 1878).

APPENDIX II
ARCHIDIACONAL LISTS FOR THE REIGN OF HENRY I

Archdeacon	*Years*	*Source*
	Bath–Wells	
Walkerius	c. 1106	Dugdale, II, 268
		Le Neve, p. 43
Robertus	c. 1106	Le Neve, *loc. cit.*
Girbertus or Gisbert	c. 1106	Le Neve, p. 45
John	c. 1120	*Historiola*, p. 22
	1125	Le Neve, p. 43
Herald	1133	MS BM. Cott. Vesp. F, XV, fol. 171
		Le Neve, p. 45
	Canterbury	
Anschitil	c. 1087	Ellis, II, 287
Asketin	(?)	Le Neve, p. 11
Stephen	c. 1100	*PL*, CLIX, col. 82
William	1102–1109	*Ibid.*, cols. 94, 150, 234
	1107	*Regesta*, II, 845; Le Neve, p. 11
John (later bishop of Rochester)	1115–1125	Eadmer, p. 231
		Ancient Charters, p. 11; Le Neve, p. 11
	Carlisle	
Elya	after 1133	*Whitby Cartulary*, p. 38
	Chichester	
Notice of an archdeacon	1093 X 1109	*Sancti Anselmi Opera*, V, 469
Henry	before 1123	*Chronicon de Bello*, p. 57
	1120	Le Neve, p. 65
	Durham	
Turgot	c. 1093–c. 1104	Symeon of Durham, I, 129
Michael	1099 X 1128	Dugdale, IV, 331
Robert	c. 1128–c. 1131	*Feodarium*, p. 56, 112, 145
		Symeon of Durham, II, 312
Ranulf	before 1128	*Ibid.*
William(?)	before 1140	*Ibid.*, I, 143; II, 314
	Ely	
William	1109 X 1131	*Regesta*, II, 1502
William de Laventona	1125	Le Neve, p. 73

Archdeacon	*Years*	*Source*
	Exeter	
Rolamnus................	d. 1104	Le Neve, p. 92; *Monasticon . . . Exoniensis,* pp. 137, 199
Ascelinus.................	1107–1137	*Ibid.*
Ernaldus.................	1110 1136	Le Neve, p. 94 *Ibid.*, p. 92
Robert...................	c. 1113–1135	*Regesta,* II, 1909 J. Tatlock, *Speculum,* VIII (1933), p. 461
Hugh de Ang.............	c. 1135	Le Neve, p. 94
Notice of four archdeacons..	1133	Morey, p. 115
Ralph de Len............. (subarchdeacon) (?)		*Crawford Collection,* XIII
	Hereford	
Humphrey................	c. 1085	*EHD,* II, No. 221
Geoffrey..................	d. 1120	Le Neve, p. 118
Peter.....................	c. 1139	Eyton, I, 207
	Lichfield–Coventry–Chester	
Gilbert...................	c. 1105	Le Neve, p. 134
Godfrey (Derby)...........	1102 X 1127	*Regesta,* II, 1361
Richard Pecce (Chester)....	1125	Le Neve, p. 131
Roger (Shropshire).........	c. 1130	*Ibid.*, p. 134
Robert (Stafford)..........	1130 X 1132	Hatton, No. 130
	Lincoln	
Richard..................	1092	Le Neve, p. 155
Nigel (Northampton[?])....	1092–1109	*Ibid.*, p. 160; *Regesta,* II, 1969
Nicholas (Huntingdon)..... (Bedford).........	1092	Le Neve, p. 158 Henry of Huntingdon, pp. 302 f.
Osbert (Bedford)..........	1092	Le Neve, p. 169
Ralph (Leicester).......... (Bedford)...........	1092 1105	*Ibid.*, p. 163 *Ibid.*, p. 169 Henry of Huntingdon, *loc. cit.*
David (Buckingham....... and nephew of Bishop Alexander)	1094 X 1123	Dugdale, III, 19 Henry of Huntingdon, *loc. cit.*
Robert (Oxford).......... (Buckingham)......	1094 X 1123	Dugdale, *loc. cit.* Henry of Huntingdon, *loc. cit.*
Robert de Merceto........ (Leicester)		*Ibid.*
Robert (Northampton).....	1115–1120	Le Neve, p. 160
Robert de Burham......... (Buckingham)	1131	*Ibid.*, p. 167
Gislebert (Buckingham)....	1100	*Ibid.*

Archdeacon	*Years*	*Source*
Albertus Longobardus......	1100	*Ibid.*, p. 155
Godfrey (Leicester)........	c. 1100	*Ibid.*, p. 163
Walter (Oxford)...........	1104	*Regesta*, II, 1000, 1836
		EETS, o.s., Vol. 130, 644
		Le Neve, p. 165
(Leicester).........	c. 1120	Le Neve, p. 163
Henry (Huntingdon).......	1110(?)	*Ibid.*, p. 158
		Henry of Huntingdon, *loc. cit.*
		EHD, II, 831
Hugh (Bedford)...........	1110	Le Neve, p. 169
Almod..................	1112 X 1113(?)	*Regesta*, II, 1033
William (Northampton.... and nephew of Bishop Alexander)		Henry of Huntingdon, *loc. cit.*
William Bajocensis.........	1115	Le Neve, p. 155
Alexander................	c. 1121	*Regesta*, II, 1301
		Merton Cartulary, Appen. IX
Roger de Clinton.......... (Buckingham)	before 1129	Le Neve, p. 167
		Matthew Paris, II, 158
Richard (Buckingham).....	1129	Le Neve, p. 167

London

Archdeacon	*Years*	*Source*
Walter....................	1102	*Early Charters*, Nos. 63, 178
Reingerus................	1102	*Ibid.*
Quintillianus..............	1102	*Ibid.*
	c. 1115	*HMCR*, IX, p. 61
Robert...................	1102	*Early Charters*, No. 178
Roger....................	1106	*Ibid.*, No. 198
Roger (Middlesex).........	before 1138	Le Neve, p. 192
William..................	1111 X 1138	*Early Charters*, No. 218
		Le Neve, p. 186
		HMCR, IX, p. 65
Alvinus...................	c. 1123	*Ibid.*, fol. 42b
Richard (Essex)...........	c. 1132	*Red Book of the Exchequer*, I, 187
(Colchester).......	1132	Le Neve, p. 195

Norwich

Archdeacon	*Years*	*Source*
Gonfridus.................	c. 1087	Ellis, II, 330
Geoffrey(?)...............	1107(?)	*Regesta*, II, 834
Alvred(?).................	1107(?)	*Ibid.*
Walter...................	c. 1111	*Ibid.*, 987
		Primum Registrum, fol. 8*d*
	1115	*Regesta*, II, 1089
		Herberti . . . Epistolae, XXI
Everard..................	1115	*Regesta*, II, 1089

Archdeacon	*Years*	*Source*
William (Fitz-Humphrey) . .	1121 X 1145	*Primum Registrum*, fol. 10
	1126	Le Neve, pp. 222, 217
	1127 X 1134	Hatton, No. 407
Richard (Suffolk)	1121–1127	Le Neve, p. 220
	1108 X 1133	*Regesta*, II, 1219, 1783, 1855
Walkeline (Suffolk)	1127	Le Neve, p. 220
Roger	1135 X 1145	*Red Book of the Exchequer*, I, 391
		HMCR, Marquess of Lothian, p. 39
	Rochester	
Anschitillus	1089	Le Neve, p. 253
Aschetil	c. 1107	*Regesta*, II, 845
William	1108	Eadmer, pp. 196 f.
	Salisbury	
Robert	1088	Le Neve, p. 273
Azo	c. 1098	*Vetus Registrum*, I, 215
Arnaldus	c. 1098	*Ibid.*
	1122(?)	*Regesta*, II, 1324
Humbald	1100	Le Neve, p. 273
Eborard or Everard . . . . (later bishop of Norwich)	1121	*Ibid.*
John (Dorset[?])	1121	*Ibid.*, p. 280
Athelhelm	1122(?)	*Regesta*, II, 1324
Roger (Wiltshire?)	1122(?)	*Ibid.*
		Vetus Registrum, I, p. 232
Alexander . . . . (later bishop of Lincoln)	1123	Le Neve, p. 273
Aaron		*Ibid.*, p. 280
	Winchester	
Henry	1114	Le Neve, p. 289
Stephen (Surrey)	1120	*Ibid.*, p. 291
	1121	*Regesta*, II, 1301
Alexander	1121	*Ibid.*
Richerus	1124	Le Neve, p. 289
Ralph (Hampshire)	1130	*Ibid.*
Robert (Surrey)	1130–1171	*Ibid.*
Joceline	1139	*Ibid.*
	Worcester	
Agelric	1092	Le Neve, p. 302
		EHD, II, p. 624
Hugh	d. 1125	Le Neve, p. 302
Robert (Gloucester)	1132	*Ibid.*, p. 303
Richard (Gloucester)	1134	*Regesta*, II, 1902

Archdeacon	*Years*	*Source*
Gervase..................	c. 1134	Le Neve, p. 302
William Commin.......... (Gloucester)	before 1140	*Ibid.*, p. 303
	York	
Conanus (Richmond)......	1088	Le Neve, p. 323
Durandus (W. Riding).....	1093–1113	*Ibid.*, p. 322
William (W. Riding).......	1114–1140	*Ibid.*
William Fitz-Tole..........	1123 X 1133	*Regesta,* II, 1851
William filius Durandi..... (E. Riding)	1130	Le Neve, p. 326
Turstin (Richmond)........	1114 X 1129	*Regesta,* II, 1332
	1130	Le Neve, p. 323
Osbert (Richmond........ and nephew of Turstin)	1138 X 1145	C. Brooke, *CHJ*, XII (1956), 16
		Early Yorkshire Charters, III, 1470
	1140	Le Neve, p. 322
Hugh (the Chantor).......	1133	Hugh the Chantor, p. viii
		Knowles, p. 235
	Bangor	
Symeon..................	1137	*Episcopal Acts,* II, B.37
	Llandaff	
Abraham (Gwent).........	1056 X 1104	*Ibid.*, I, L.9
Lifris (Glamorgan......... and son of Bishop Urban)		*Ibid.*, L.6
Urban..................	1107	*Cartae . . . de Glamorgancia,* I, xxxix
	1108	Le Neve, p. 524
Uchtred..................	1126	*Ibid.*
		Brut y Tywysogion, p. 213
	St. David's	
William..................	1115 X 1125	*Gloucester Cartulary,* I, No. 128
William (Kermerdin)......	c. 1120	*Episcopal Acts,* Davies, I, D.43
(St. David's)......	1128	Le Neve, p. 517
	1129	*Cartae . . . de Glamorgancia,* I, lxvi
Elias (Brecon).............	1115 X 1120(?)	*Episcopal Acts, loc. cit.*
Robert..................	1115 X 1125(?)	*Gloucester Cartulary,* I, lxvi
Daniel (Powys............ and son of Bishop Sulien)	d. 1127	*Episcopal Acts,* pp. 165 f.
Cardifor (Cardigan........ and son of Daniel)		*Ibid.*
Jordan..................	1135 X 1148	*Ibid.*, D.148

APPENDIX III
EPISCOPAL ITINERARIES FOR THE REIGN OF HENRY I

These episcopal itineraries are based largely on the witness lists to the royal charters in Volume II of the *Regesta Regum Anglo-Normannorum* (Oxford, 1956). Although there is hesitation on the part of some scholars in accepting the date of a charter as the date when its witnesses appeared at the place of issue, there is no strong argument to show that they did not do so—at least not in the early twelfth century. (On this problem see F. M. Stenton, *Transcripts of Charters Relating to Gilbertine Houses* [Lincoln Record Society, 1922], Introduction, and *Regesta Regum Anglo-Normannorum*, II, xxviii.) Citations from other sources support the evidence in the *Regesta*—except for No. 1391, tentatively dated April 15, 1123, at Winchester, and No. 1430, tentatively dated October, 1125, at Rouen. (In the first case the witnesses included Archbishop Turstin of York and Bishop Bernard of St. David's. Turstin, however—according to Hugh the Chantor—was in Rome late in March of 1123 and did not reach Normandy until late June or early July; and Bernard, although perhaps at Canterbury in February, also was in Rome—with Turstin. In the second case Bernard was back in England on September 8, 1125, and—unless he immediately went abroad again—it seems unlikely that he was in Rouen in October.

In any event, the dating of the documents in the *Regesta* is uncertain and it would appear that the dates might sometimes have to be adjusted to conform with the chronology given in the narrative. Accurate dating is the chief problem in all the charters. Where the editors of the *Regesta* have been fairly certain of the dates I have used them without comment; where only terminal dates have been established the suggested year has been indicated with a question mark.

John, Bishop of Bath

1100		Westminster	*Regesta*, II, 512
1101	September 3	Windsor	*Ibid.*, 547
1102		Westminster	Eadmer, pp. 132–33
1103	January 13	Salisbury	*Regesta*, II, 626
1105	February	Romsey	*Ibid.*, 684

1107	August 11	Canterbury	Haddan and Stubbs, I, 303 *Cartae . . . de Glamorgancia*, I, 39
1109	Pentecost	London	Eadmer, p. 207
1110(?)	Easter	Marlborough	*Regesta*, II, 939
1110	May 29	Windsor	*Ibid.*, 945
1110		Woodstock	*Ibid.*, 958
1114	September 13	Westbourne	*Ibid.*, 1070
1121	January 7	Westminster	*Ibid.*, 1243

Godfrey, Bishop of Bath

1123	March 25	Woodstock	Anglo-Saxon Chronicle, *anno* 1123
1123	April 15(?)	Winchester	*Regesta*, II, 1391
1127	August	Eling	*Ibid.*, 1507
1130	May 4	Canterbury	Anglo-Saxon Chronicle (I, 380)
1130	May 8	Rochester	*Ibid.*, II, 227
1132	April 29	Westminster	*Regesta*, II, 1736

Anselm, Archbishop of Canterbury

1100	September 23	Dover	Eadmer, p. 118
1100	November 11	Westminster	Anglo-Saxon Chronicle, *anno* 1100
1101	Summer	Alton	Farrer, *Itinerary*, No. 69
1101	September 3	Windsor	*Regesta*, II, 544
1102	May 25	Westminster	*Ibid.*, 570
1102	Michaelmas	Westminster	Anglo-Saxon Chronicle, *anno* 1102
1103	After Easter	Left England	Farrer, *op. cit.*, No. 69
1103	April 27	Wissant	Eadmer, p. 149
1103	Pentecost	Chartres	*Ibid.*, p. 151
1103	Mid-August	Rome	*Ibid.*
1103	Mid-November	Lyon	*Ibid.*, p. 157
1105	After March 25	Blois to Chartres	*Ibid.*, pp. 163 f.
1105	July 22	Castle of Aquila	*Ibid.*
1106	Spring(?)	Rouen	*Ibid.*, p. 177
1106	Summer	Jumièges	*Ibid.*, p. 182
1106	August 15	Bec	*Ibid.*
1107	August 1	Westminster	*Regesta*, II, 825
1107	August 11	Canterbury	Eadmer, p. 187
1108	February 27	Lambeth	*Ibid.*, p. 190
1108	May 24	Westminster	*Regesta*, II, 881
1108	July 26	Pagaham	Eadmer, p. 197
1108	August 9	Canterbury	*Ibid.*, p. 198

Ralph, Archbishop of Canterbury

1114	May	Canterbury	Eadmer, p. 223
1114	September 13	Westbourne	*Regesta*, II, 1062
1115	June 27	Canterbury	Eadmer, p. 230
1115	September 16	Westminster	*Regesta*, II, 1091
1115	September 19	Westminster	Eadmer, p. 235
1116	March 20	Salisbury	*Ibid.*, p. 237
1116		Castle of Feritas	*Ibid.*, p. 239
1116(?)	April 2	Odiham	*Regesta*, II, 1131
1117	Before March 24	Rome	Hugh the Chantor, p. 50
1117	Spring	Sutria	Eadmer, p. 242

1117	Spring	Rouen	*Ibid.*
1118	October 7	Rouen	*Regesta*, II, 1182
1119	May(?)	Rouen	*Ibid.*, 1203
1119	June	Rouen	*Ibid.*, 1205
1119	October 17(?)	Reims(?)	Hugh the Chantor, p. 73
1120	January 4	Canterbury	Eadmer, p. 259
1120	Before Easter	Reims	Hugh the Chantor, p. 92
1121(?)	January 7	Westminster	*Regesta*, II, 1242
1121	January 30	Windsor	*Ibid.*, 1247
1121	March 13	Abendoniam	Eadmer, p. 293
1121	October 2	Lambeth	*Ibid.*, p. 298
1122(?)	May 17–20	London	*Regesta*, II, 1325
1122	October 20	Canterbury	Eadmer, p. 302

William, Archbishop of Canterbury

1123	March 11	Woodstock	Hugh the Chantor, p. 111
1123	March 16 (?)	Rome	Symeon of Durham, II, 269
1123	April	Rome	Hugh the Chantor, p. 112
1123	April 15 (?)	Winchester	*Regesta*, II, 1391
1123	Summer (?)	Normandy	Hugh the Chantor, p. 119
1125	January–March	Normandy	*Regesta*, II, 1424
1125	September 8–10	Westminster	Hugh the Chantor, p. 121
1125	After Michaelmas	Rome	Anglo-Saxon Chronicle, *anno* 1125
1125	October (?)	Rouen	*Regesta*, II, 1426
1126	Spring	Canterbury	Hugh the Chantor, p. 128
1126	September 11(?)	Portsmouth	*Regesta*, II, 1448
1126		Woodstock	*Ibid.*, 1466
1126	Christmas	Windsor	Hugh the Chantor, p. 129
1126	After Christmas	London	*Ibid.*
1127(?)	January 1(?)	Westminster	*Regesta*, II, 1474
1127	May 22	Winchester	*Ibid.*, 1485
1127	May	London	Hugh the Chantor, p. 130
1127	August 26(?)	Eling	*Regesta*, II, 1507
1127	September(?)	To England	Symeon of Durham, p. 281
1129	Michaelmas	London	Anglo-Saxon Chronicle, *anno* 1129
1130	May 4	Canterbury	*Ibid., anno* 1130
1130(?)		Westminster	*Regesta*, II, 1649
1131	August(?)	Waltham	*Ibid.*, 1711
1131(?)	September 8	Northampton	*Ibid.*, 1712
1131(?)		London	*Ibid.*, 1719
1131(?)		Woodstock	*Ibid.*, 1724
1132(?)	April 29	Westminster	*Regesta*, II, 1737
1132(?)	Christmas	Windsor	*Ibid.*, p. 1740
1133	June (?)	Winchester	*Ibid.*, 1765
1134(?)		Rouen	*Ibid.*, 1896
1135	December 22	London	*Gesta Stephani*, p. 8

Adelulf, Bishop of Carlisle

1133	June (?)	Winchester	*Regesta*, II, 1764
1134		Rouen	*Ibid.*, 1902
1135(?)		Falaise	*Ibid.*, 1913

Ralph, Bishop of Chichester

1101	September 3	Windsor	*Regesta*, II, 544
1102		Westminster	Eadmer, p. 132
1105	February	Romsey	*Regesta*, II, 684
1107	August 1	Westminster	*Ibid.*, 825
1107	August 11	Canterbury	Haddan and Stubbs, p. 303
1108		London	Walter of Coventry, *anno* 1108
1108	July 26	Pagaham	Eadmer, p. 197
1108	August 9	Canterbury	*Ibid.*
1109	June 26	London	Ralph de Diceto, *anno* 1109 Eadmer, p. 207
1115	December 26	Canterbury	*Ibid.*, p. 237
1121	January 7	Westminster	*Regesta*, II, 1243
1123	April 15(?)	Winchester	*Ibid.*, 1391

Seefrid, Bishop of Chichester

1125	January–March	Rouen	*Regesta*, II, 1425
1126/27(?)		Reading	*Regesta*, II, 1536
1127(?)	January 1	Westminster	*Ibid.*, 1474
1127(?)	May	Westminster	*Ibid.*, 1483
1127(?)	August 26	Eling	*Ibid.*, 1507
1130	May 4	Canterbury	Anglo-Saxon Chronicle, RS 23, I, p. 380
1130	May 8	Rochester	*Ibid.*, II, p. 227
1131(?)	August	Westbourne	*Regesta*, II, 1710
1131	September 8	Northampton	*Ibid.*, 1715
1134(?)		Rouen	*Ibid.*, 1900

Ranulf Flambard, Bishop of Durham

1100	August 13	London (Tower)	Anglo-Saxon Chronicle, *anno* 1100
1101	February 2	To Normandy	*Ibid.*, *anno* 1101
1101	September 3	Windsor	*Regesta*, II, 544
1101(?)		Winchester	*Ibid.*, 559
1102	September 29(?)	Sutton	*Ibid.*, 595
1105	February	Romsey	*Ibid.*, 683
1105	October 18	Cornbury	*Ibid.*, 699–701
1106	November 7	Rouen	*Ibid.*, 790
1107	August 1(?)	Westminster	*Ibid.*, 826
1107/8(?)	May	Winchester	*Ibid.*, 887
1107	August 11	Canterbury	Haddan and Stubbs, p. 303
1109	June 26	London	Ralph de Diceto, *anno* 1109
1109	October 17	Nottingham	*Regesta*, II, 919
1109(?)	Christmas	Westminster	*Ibid.*, 929
1110(?)		Westminster	*Ibid.*, 962
1111	August 13	Portsmouth	*Ibid.*, 995
1113(?)		Trumpington	*Ibid.*, 1030
1113		Ditton	*Ibid.*, 1027
1114	September 13	Westbourne	*Ibid.*, 1070
1115	September(?)	Winchester	*Ibid.*, 1097
1116	February 2	Windsor	*Ibid.*, 1127
1116		St. Albans	Matthew Paris, p. 142
1118(?)		Caen	*Regesta*, II, 1215
1119	June	Rouen	*Ibid.*, 1205

1119		Bonneville	*Ibid.*, 1217
1119	October 20(?)	Reims	Hugh the Chantor, p. 74 Eadmer, p. 255
1121	January 7	Westminster	*Regesta*, II, 1243
1121	March(?)	Waterperry(?)	*Ibid.*, 1255
1121	April(?)	Clarendon	*Ibid.*, 1272
1122	October–December	York	*Ibid.*, 1335
1123	April 15	Winchester	*Ibid.*, 1391
1126(?)	Autumn	Rockingham	*Ibid.*, 1463
1126		Woodstock	*Ibid.*, 1466
1127	July 16(?)	Rochester	*Liber Vitae Dunel.*, p. 59

Geoffrey, Bishop of Durham

1133	July	Fareham	*Regesta*, II, 1777
1133	July	Westbourne	*Ibid.*, 1787
1133	August 15	York	Symeon of Durham, p. 285

Hervey, Bishop of Ely

1109	October 17	Nottingham	*Regesta*, II, 918
1111	August 8	Waltham	*Ibid.*, 988
1114		Oxford	*Ibid.*, 1038
1121	January(?)	London	*Ibid.*, 1046
1121	August(?)	Westminster(?)	*Ibid.*, 1301
1122(?)	March 26	Northampton	*Ibid.*, 1317
1123	April 15	Winchester	*Ibid.*, 1391
1128		Thorney(?)	E. Miller, *Abbey and Bishopric of Ely*, p. 284

Nigel, Bishop of Ely

1133	June	Woodstock	*Regesta*, II, 1757
1133	June(?)	Westminster	*Ibid.*, 1759
1133	July	Fareham	*Ibid.*, 1777
1133	July(?)	Westbourne	*Ibid.*, 1784
1134		Rouen	*Ibid.*, 1902
1135		Rouen	*Ibid.*, 1908
1135		Caen	*Ibid.*, 1909

Osbern, Bishop of Exeter

1101	September 3	Windsor	*Regesta*, II, 544

William Warelwast, Bishop of Exeter

1094/95		Rome	Eadmer, p. 68
1106		Rome	*Regesta*, II, 737
1107	August 1	Westminster	*Ibid.*, 825
1107	August 11	Canterbury	Eadmer, p. 187
1108(?)	April 5	Winchester	*Regesta*, II, 873
1108(?)	May	Fishley	*Ibid.*, 877
1108	May 24	Westminster	*Ibid.*, 878
1108	After Whitsuntide	Windsor	*Ibid.*, 879

1108(?)		Nottingham	*Ibid.*, 886
1108	May–July	Windsor	*Ibid.*, 899
1108	July 26	Pagaham	Eadmer, p. 197
1109	Pentecost	London	*Ibid.*, 207
1109	October 17	Nottingham	*Regesta*, II, 918
1110(?)	Easter	Marlborough	*Ibid.*, 937–39
1110	May 29	Windsor	*Ibid.*, 945
1111	August 8	Waltham	*Ibid.*, 988
1111(?)	August 13(?)	Portsmouth	*Ibid.*, 995
1114(?)		Tamworth	*Ibid.*, 1054
1114	September 13	Westbourne	*Ibid.*, 1070
1115	September 16	Westminster	*Ibid.*, 1092
1116(?)	February 2	Windsor	*Ibid.*, 1125
1119	May 7	Clermont	Hugh the Chantor, p. 68
1119	June(?)	Rouen	*Regesta*, II, 1204
1119	October 18–20	Reims	Hugh the Chantor, p. 73
1120	February	Valence	Hugh the Chantor, p. 85
1121	January 7	Westminster	*Regesta*, II, 1243
1121(?)	March	Woodstock	*Ibid.*, 1261
1121	March 13	Abingdon	Eadmer, p. 293
1123(?)	April 15	Winchester	*Regesta*, II, 1393
1125	January–March(?)	Rouen	*Ibid.*, 1425
1127	May 22	Winchester	*Ibid.*, 1485
1131	September 8	Northampton	*Ibid.*, 1715
1132	April 29	Westminster	*Ibid.*, 1736

Gerard, Bishop of Hereford

1094/95		Rome	Eadmer, p. 68
1100	July 15(?)	Gloucester	Symeon of Durham, p. 250
1100	August 5	Westminster	*Regesta*, II, 488
1107	August 1	London	Eadmer, p. 186

Regenhelm, Bishop of Hereford

1107	August 11	Canterbury	Eadmer, p. 187
1109	Pentecost	London	*Ibid.*, pp. 207–8
1109	October 17	Nottingham	*Regesta*, II, 919
1111	August 8	Waltham	*Ibid.*, 988

Geoffrey, Bishop of Hereford

1115	Christmas	Canterbury	Eadmer, p. 237

Richard, Bishop of Hereford

1121(?)	January 7	Westminster	*Regesta*, II, 1245
1121	January 16	Lambeth	Eadmer, p. 291
1121	June 12	Canterbury	*Ibid.*, p. 294
1121(?)	Summer	Hereford	*Regesta*, II, 1294
1123	April 15	Winchester	*Ibid.*, 1391
1123	October 24	Tewkesbury	Florence of Worcester, II, 77
1127(?)	May–August	Hereford	*Regesta*, II, 1490

Robert, Bishop of Hereford

1131(?)	August	Westbourne	*Regesta*, II, 1710
1131	September 8	Northampton	*Ibid.*, 1715
1132	April 29	Westminster	*Ibid.*, 1736
1132(?)	Christmas	Windsor	*Ibid.*, 1740
1133	June(?)	Winchester	*Ibid.*, 1765
1134–35		Rome	*Holtzmann*, II, 15

Robert de Limesey, Bishop of Chester, Coventry

1100	September 14	Westminster	*Regesta*, II, 492
1101	March 10	Dover	*Ibid.*, 515
1101	Easter	Winchester	*Ibid.*, 518
1101	September 3	Windsor	*Ibid.*, 544
1102		Westminster	Eadmer, p. 132
1102		Rome	*Ibid.*
1107	August 11	Canterbury	Haddan and Stubbs, 303
1107–8		Nottingham	*Regesta*, II, 886
1109	Pentecost	London	Eadmer, p. 207
1109	October 17	Nottingham	*Regesta*, II, 918
1110	May 29	Windsor	*Ibid.*, 945

Robert Pecce, Bishop of Coventry

1121(?)	January 7	Westminster	*Regesta*, II, 1245
1121	March 13	Abingdon	Eadmer, p. 293
1121	June 12	Canterbury	*Ibid.*, p. 294
1121(?)	Summer	Condover	*Regesta*, II, 1297
1122(?)	March 26	Northampton	*Ibid.*, 1317
1123	January(?)	Lincoln	Anglo-Saxon Chronicle, *anno* 1123
1123	April 15	Winchester	*Regesta*, II, 1391

Roger de Clinton, Bishop of Coventry

1130	May 4	Canterbury	Anglo-Saxon Chronicle, I, 380
1130	May 8	Rochester	*Ibid.*, II, 227
1131	September 8	Northampton	*Regesta*, II, 1715
1132(?)		Beckenham	*Ibid.*, 1744

Robert, Bishop of Lincoln

1100	September 29(?)	Salisbury	*Regesta*, II, 495
1100	Christmas	Westminster	*Ibid.*, 506
1101	March 10	Dover	*Ibid.*, 515
1101	March 12	Rochester	*Ibid.*, 516
1101(?)	Easter	Winchester	*Ibid.*, 527
1101(?)	May(?)	Cambridge	*Ibid.*, 528*a*
1101	August	London	*Ibid.*, 539
1101	September 3	Windsor	*Ibid.*, 544
1101	Christmas	Westminster	*Ibid.*, 552
1101–2	November–February	Westminster	*Ibid.*, 568
1102(?)	June 24	Cirencester	*Ibid.*, 572
1102(?)	June 29	Geddington	*Ibid.*, 573

1102(?)	July(?)	Wolverhampton	*Ibid.*, 576
1102	July(?)	Northampton	*Ibid.*, 577
1102	October	Reading	*Ibid.*, 607
1103	January 13	Salisbury	*Ibid.*, 626
1103(?)	March 8	Canterbury	*Ibid.*, 634
1103(?)	March 29(?)	Winchester	*Ibid.*, 639
1103	May 24	Windsor	*Ibid.*, 650
1103(?)		Norwich	*Ibid.*, 659
1105	February 13	Romsey	*Ibid.*, 682
1105(?)	February	New Forest	*Ibid.*, 687
1105(?)	October(?)	Brill	*Ibid.*, 696
1105(?)	October(?)	Hanborough	*Ibid.*, 698
1105(?)	October 18	Cornbury	*Ibid.*, 701
1105(?)	Autumn(?)	York	*Ibid.*, 713
1106(?)	February(?)	Northampton	*Ibid.*, 740
1106(?)	February(?)	Rockingham	*Ibid.*, 741
1106(?)	May(?)	Marlborough	*Ibid.*, 753
1106(?)		King's Cliff	*Ibid.*, 767
1106	July(?)	Winchester	*Ibid.*, 779
1106(?)		Norwich(?)	*Ibid.*, 786
1107(?)	May(?)	Westminster	*Ibid.*, 812
1107	June 2	Westminster	*Ibid.*, 816
1107	August 1	Westminster	*Ibid.*, 825
1107	August 11	Canterbury	Haddan and Stubbs, 303
1107	September(?)	Thetford	*Regesta*, II, 834
1107(?)		Bushley	*Ibid.*, 852
1108	March(?)	Windsor	*Ibid.*, 871
1108	May–July 31	Windsor	*Ibid.*, 899
1109(?)	June 13(?)	Westminster	*Ibid.*, 915
1109	Pentecost	London	Eadmer, p. 207
1109	October 17	Nottingham	*Regesta*, II, 919
1109(?)		York	*Ibid.*, 925
1109(?)		Lincoln	*Ibid.*, 934
1110	May 17	Dover	*Ibid.*, 941
1110	May 29	Windsor	*Ibid.*, 944
1110	May 29(?)	Reading	*Ibid.*, 949
1110	July 5	Stamford	*Ibid.*, 950
1110		Brampton	*Ibid.*, 953
1111	March–August(?)	Reading	*Ibid.*, 981
1111	Before August 8	Newbury	*Ibid.*, 985
1111	Before August 8	Winchester	*Ibid.*, 987
1111	August 8	Waltham	*Ibid.*, 988
1111(?)	August 13(?)	Portsmouth	*Ibid.*, 994
1113		Ditton	*Ibid.*, 1027
1114	February–March	Woodstock	*Ibid.*, 1034
1114		Oxford	*Ibid.*, 1038
1114		Tamworth	*Ibid.*, 1054
1114	September 13	Westbourne	*Ibid.*, 1062
1114	Christmas	Rouen	*Ibid.*, 1074
1115	September 16	Westminster	*Ibid.*, 1091
1115	After September 18	Winchester	*Ibid.*, 1097
1115(?)		Buckden	*Christina of Markyate*, p. 65

1116	February 2	Windsor	*Regesta*, II, 1124
1116–17(?)		Westminster	*Ibid.*, 1180
1116–18(?)		Oxford	*Ibid.*, 1198
1121(?)	January 7(?)	Westminster	*Ibid.*, 1242
1121	January 30	Windsor	*Ibid.*, 1247
1121(?)	March(?)	Waterperry(?)	*Ibid.*, 1255
1121	April 10–May 29	Winchester	*Ibid.*, 1280
1121	October 2	Lambeth	Eadmer, p. 291
1123	January 10	Woodstock	Anglo-Saxon Chronicle, *anno* 1123

Alexander, Bishop of Lincoln

1123	April 15(?)	Winchester	*Regesta*, II, 1391
1125	October	Rouen	*Ibid.*, 1426 Hugh the Chantor, p. 122
1125	After Michaelmas	Rome	Anglo-Saxon Chronicle, *anno* 1125
1126(?)		Brampton	*Regesta*, II, 1449
1126(?)	Autumn	Rockingham	*Ibid.*, 1459
1127(?)	May 13–16(?)	London	*Ibid.*, 1477
1127	August 26	Eling	*Ibid.*, 1502
1128(?)		Rouen	*Ibid.*, 1552
1130	May 4	Canterbury	Anglo-Saxon Chronicle, I, 380
1130	May 8	Rochester	*Ibid.*, II, 227
1130(?)		Windsor	*Regesta*, II, 1656
1130		Waltham	*Ibid.*, 1668
1131(?)	August	Westbourne	*Ibid.*, 1710
1131	September 8	Northampton	*Ibid.*, 1716
1132	April 29	Westminster	*Ibid.*, 1736
1132(?)	Christmas	Windsor	*Ibid.*, 1740
1132		Marden	*Ibid.*, 1742
1133	June(?)	Winchester	*Ibid.*, 1765
1134	September	Verneuil	*Ibid.*, 1895
1135(?)		Godstow Abbey	*EETS*, 129 (o.s.), 27

Maurice, Bishop of London

1100	August 5	Westminster	*Regesta*, II, 488
1101	September 3	Windsor	*Ibid.*, 544
1102		Westminster	Eadmer, p. 132
1102–3(?)	April 3	Westminster	*Regesta*, II, 644
1102(?)	June 29	Geddington	*Ibid.*, 573
1107	August 1–5	London(?)	*Ibid.*, 828–32
1107	August 11	Canterbury	Haddan and Stubbs, 303

Richard, Bishop of London

1108	May–July	Reading	*Regesta*, II, 892
1108	July 26	Pagaham	Eadmer, p. 197
1108	August 9	Canterbury	*Ibid.*, p. 198
1109	June 26	London	Ralph de Diceto, *anno* 1109
1109	October 17	Nottingham	*Regesta*, II, 918
1109	Christmas	London	Eadmer, p. 212
1111	August 8	Waltham	*Regesta*, II, 988
1114(?)		Holdgate Castle(?)	*Ibid.*, 1061
1114	September 13	Westbourne	*Ibid.*, 1062

1115	September 16	Westminster	*Ibid.*, 1091
1116		St. Albans	Matthew Paris, 142
1121(?)	January 7	Westminster	*Regesta*, II, 1242
1121	January(?)	London	*Ibid.*, 1246
1121	January 16	Lambeth	Eadmer, p. 291
1121	January 30	Windsor	*Regesta*, II, 1247
1121(?)	March	Woodstock	*Ibid.*, 1262
1121(?)	April–May	Winchester	*Ibid.*, 1283
1121(?)	Summer	Condover	*Ibid.*, 1297
1121(?)	Summer	Shrewsbury	*Ibid.*, 1299
1121	October 2(?)	Canterbury	Walter of Coventry, *anno* 1121
1123	February 3	Gloucester	Hugh the Chantor, p. 109
1123	April 15(?)	Winchester	*Regesta*, II, 1391

Gilbert, Bishop of London

1130	May 3	Canterbury	Walter of Coventry, *anno* 1130
1130	May 8	Rochester	Anglo-Saxon Chronicle, II, 227
1131	August(?)	Waltham	*Regesta*, II, 1711
1131	September 8(?)	Northampton	*Ibid.*, 1713–15
1131(?)		London	*Ibid.*, 1728
1132	April 29	Westminster	*Ibid.*, 1736

Herbert, Bishop of Norwich

1101	September 3	Windsor	*Regesta*, II, 544
1102		Rome	Eadmer, p. 132
1102		Westminster	*Ibid.*
1107	August 1	Westminster	*Regesta*, II, 825
1107	August 11	Canterbury	Haddan and Stubbs, 303
1107	Before September 15	Thetford	*Regesta*, II, 834
1109	June 26	London	Ralph de Diceto, *anno* 1109
1109	October 17	Northampton	*Regesta*, II, 918
1114		Thetford	*Ibid.*, 1057*a*
1115(?)	September 16	Westminster(?)	*Ibid.*, 1094
1116		France and Lombardy	Hugh the Chantor, p. 50

Everard, Bishop of Norwich

1121	June 12	Canterbury	Eadmer, p. 294
1121	October 2(?)	Canterbury	Walter of Coventry, *anno* 1121
1123	April 15(?)	Winchester	*Regesta*, II, 1391
1126(?)	Autumn(?)	Rockingham	*Ibid.*, 1461
1130	May 8	Rochester	Anglo-Saxon Chronicle, II, 227
1131	September 8(?)	Northampton	*Regesta*, II, 1715
1131(?)		London	*Ibid.*, 1719
1132	April 29	Westminster	*Ibid.*, 1736

Gundulf, Bishop of Rochester

1100	July 15(?)	Gloucester	Symeon of Durham, p. 250
1100	August 5	Westminster	*Regesta*, II, 488
1101	September 3	Windsor	*Ibid.*, 544
1102		Westminster	Eadmer, p. 132

1107	August(?)	London	*Regesta*, II, 832
1107	August 11	Canterbury	Haddan and Stubbs, 303
1107	Before September 15	Thetford	*Regesta*, II, 834
		Ralph, Bishop of Rochester	
1108	June 29	Canterbury	Eadmer, p. 196
1108	August 9	Canterbury	*Ibid.*
1109	June 26	London	Ralph de Diceto, *anno* 1109
1109	October 17	Nottingham	*Regesta*, II, 919
1110	May 29	Windsor	*Ibid.*, 945
		Ernulf, Bishop of Rochester	
1114	September 28	Canterbury	Eadmer, p. 225
1114	October 10	Rochester	*Ibid.*
1115	December 26	Canterbury	*Ibid.*, p. 237
1121	January 7	Westminster	*Regesta*, II, 1243
1121	January 16	Lambeth	Eadmer, p. 291
1123	February(?)	Canterbury	Anglo-Saxon Chronicle, *anno* 1123
		John, Bishop of Rochester	
1127	May 13–16	Westminster	*Regesta*, II, 1484
1130	May 4	Canterbury	Anglo-Saxon Chronicle, I, 380
1130	May 8	Rochester	*Ibid.*, II, 227
1131	September 8	Northampton	*Regesta*, II, 1715
1132(?)	Christmas	Windsor	*Ibid.*, 1740

		Roger, Bishop of Salisbury	
1101	September 3	Windsor	*Regesta*, II, 549
1102	September 24	Sutton	*Ibid.*, 596
1102	Christmas	Westminster	*Ibid.*, 613
1103	January 13	Sarum	*Ibid.*, 626
1103(?)	April 3	Westminster	*Ibid.*, 644
1103	May 17	Windsor	*Ibid.*, 649
1103	September 25	Westminster	*Ibid.*, 653
1105	February 13	Romsey	*Ibid.*, 682
1106(?)	May 13	Sarum	*Ibid.*, 755
1106(?)		Bury St. Edmunds	*Ibid.*, 762
1106	Before July 31	Winchester	*Ibid.*, 779
1107(?)	After May 1	Westminster	*Ibid.*, 812
1107	June 2	Westminster	*Ibid.*, 813
1107	August 1	Westminster	*Ibid.*, 825
1107	August 11	Canterbury	Eadmer, p. 187
1107(?)	Christmas	Westminster	*Regesta*, II, 839
1108	March(?)	Windsor	*Ibid.*, 871
1108(?)	April 5	Winchester	*Ibid.*, 873
1108(?)	May 9	Norwich	*Ibid.*, 875
1108	May 24	Westminster	*Ibid.*, 878
1108	May–July	Reading	*Ibid.*, 892
1108	May–July	Dunstable	*Ibid.*, 897
1108(?)		Newenham(?)	*Ibid.*, 898
1108	May–July	Windsor	*Ibid.*, 899
1108	July 26	Pagaham	Eadmer, p.197

1109(?)	June 13	Westminster	*Regesta*, II, 915
1109	October 17	Nottingham	*Ibid.*, 919
1110(?)	April	Clarendon	*Ibid.*, 940
1110	May 29	Windsor	*Ibid.*, 945
1110	May 29(?)	Reading	*Ibid.*, 949
1110(?)		Romsey	*Ibid.*, 957
1110(?)		Westminster	*Ibid.*, 963
1111(?)	Before April 2(?)	Woodstock	*Ibid.*, 975
1111	August 8	Waltham	*Ibid.*, 988
1111	August 13	Portsmouth	*Ibid.*, 991
1111	September 30(?)	Winchester	*Ibid.*, 1000
1113		Ditton	*Ibid.*, 1027
1114	February–March	Woodstock	*Ibid.*, 1034
1114	May	Gloucester	*Ibid.*, 1041
1114(?)		Cannock	*Ibid.*, 1053
1114(?)		Tamworth	*Ibid.*, 1054
1114(?)		Thetford	*Ibid.*, 1057
1114(?)		Eye Castle	*Ibid.*, 1059
1114(?)	September 21(?)	Portsmouth	*Ibid.*, 1056
1115(?)	September 13	Westminster	*Ibid.*, 1090
1115	September 16	Westminster	*Ibid.*, 1091
1115(?)	After September 15	Winchester	*Ibid.*, 1098*a*
1116	February 2	Windsor	*Ibid.*, 1124
1116		St. Albans	Matthew Paris, p. 142
1120	November–December	Portsmouth	*Regesta*, II, 1238
1121(?)	January 7	Westminster	*Ibid.*, 1242
1121	January 30	Windsor	*Ibid.*, 1247
1121	March	Woodstock	*Ibid.*, 1259
1121	Easter	Berkeley	*Ibid.*, 1265
1121(?)	April	Alveston	*Ibid.*, 1267
1121	April	Cheddar	*Ibid.*, 1268
1121	April–May	Winchester	*Ibid.*, 1280
1121(?)	Summer	Hereford	*Ibid.*, 1294
1121	October 2(?)	Lambeth	Eadmer, p. 298
1122	March 26	Northampton	*Regesta*, II, 1313
1122		Eling(?)	*Ibid.*, 1347
1122(?)		Oxford	*Ibid.*, 1346
1123	January	Woodstock	Anglo-Saxon Chronicle, *anno* 1123
1123	February	Canterbury	*Ibid.*
1123	April 15	Winchester	*Regesta*, II, 1391
1123(?)	June 1	Winchester	*Ibid.*, 1394
1123(?)	June 3–10	Portsmouth	*Ibid.*, 1397
1125	Christmas	Winchester	Anglo-Saxon Chronicle, *anno* 1125
1126(?)	Autumn	Rockingham	*Regesta*, II, 1459
1126		Woodstock	*Ibid.*, 1466
1127	January	Winchester	*Ibid.*, 1475
1127(?)	May 13–16	London	*Ibid.*, 1476–83
1127	May 22(?)	Winchester	*Ibid.*, 1486
1127	August	Eling	*Ibid.*, 1499
1129		Rouen	*Ibid.*, 1576
1129		Normandy	*Ibid.*, 1575

1129	July 15	Portsmouth	*Ibid.*, 1603
1130	May 4	Canterbury	Anglo-Saxon Chronicle, I, 380
1130	May 8	Rochester	*Ibid.*, II, 227
1130	March–September	Winchester	*Regesta*, II, 1641
1130(?)	August(?)	Waltham	*Ibid.*, 1668
1131(?)	August(?)	Westbourne	*Ibid.*, 1710
1131	September 8(?)	Northampton	*Ibid.*, 1713
1132	April 29	Westminster	*Ibid.*, 1736
1132(?)	Christmas	Windsor	*Ibid.*, 1740
1132		Gillingham	*Ibid.*, 1746
1133	June	Woodstock	*Ibid.*, 1757
1133	June(?)	Westminster	*Ibid.*, 1759
1133	June(?)	Winchester	*Ibid.*, 1764
1133	July(?)	Fareham	*Ibid.*, 1770
1133(?)		Blackmoor(?)	*Ibid.*, 1791
1135	December 22	London	William Malmesbury, *HN*, p. 16

William, Bishop of Winchester

1100	August 5	Westminster	*Regesta*, II, 488
1100	September 14	Westminster	*Ibid.*, 492
1101	March 10	Dover	*Ibid.*, 515
1101	March 12	Rochester	*Ibid.*, 516
1101	September 3	Windsor	*Ibid.*, 544
1101	Christmas	Westminster	*Ibid.*, 552
1102(?)	January(?)	Gillingham	*Ibid.*, 560
1102	June–July(?)	Northampton	*Ibid.*, 577
1102	September 29	Sutton	*Ibid.*, 595
1102(?)		Westminster	*Ibid.*, 600
1105	February	Romsey	*Ibid.*, 684
1106(?)	May(?)	Marlborough	*Ibid.*, 753
1106	November 7	Rouen	*Ibid.*, 790
1107	June 2	Westminster	*Ibid.*, 813
1107	August 1	Westminster	*Ibid.*, 825
1107	August 11	Canterbury	Eadmer, p. 187
1108	May 24	Westminster	*Regesta*, II, 885
1108(?)		Nottingham	*Ibid.*, 886
1108(?)		Westminster	*Ibid.*, 906
1108	July 26	Pagaham	Eadmer, p. 197
1108	August 9	Canterbury	*Ibid.*, p. 198
1109	Pentecost	London	*Ibid.*, p. 207
1110	May 29	Windsor	*Regesta*, II, 945
1111	August 8	Waltham	*Ibid.*, 988
1114	May	Gloucester	*Ibid.*, 1041
1114	May 13	Westbourne	*Ibid.*, 1063
1115	September 16(?)	Westminster(?)	*Ibid.*, 1092
1115	Christmas	Canterbury	Eadmer, p. 237
1121	January 7	Westminster	*Regesta*, II, 1243
1121	January 30	Windsor	*Ibid.*, 1247
1121	March 13	Abingdon	Eadmer, p. 293
1121(?)	March(?)	Woodstock	*Regesta*, II, 1262
1121(?)	April–May(?)	Winchester	*Ibid.*, 1281

1122(?)	May 17–20	London	*Ibid.*, 1325
1123	February(?)	Canterbury	Anglo-Saxon Chronicle, *anno* 1123
1123	April 15(?)	Winchester	*Regesta*, II, 1391
1125	January–March	Rouen	*Ibid.*, 1424
1126		Woodstock	*Ibid.*, 1466
1127(?)	January 1	Westminster	*Ibid.*, 1474
1127(?)	May 13–16(?)	Westminster	*Ibid.*, 1483
1127	May 22	Winchester	*Ibid.*, 1485

Henry, Bishop of Winchester

1130	May 4	Canterbury	Anglo-Saxon Chronicle, I, 380
1130	May 8	Rochester	*Ibid.*, II, 227
1130	March–September	Winchester	*Regesta*, II, 1641
1131	August(?)	Waltham	*Ibid.*, 1711
1131(?)	August	Westbourne	*Ibid.*, 1710
1131	September 8	Northampton	*Ibid.*, 1715
1131(?)		Woodstock	*Ibid.*, 1721
1132	April 29	Westminster	*Ibid.*, 1736
1132(?)	Christmas	Windsor	*Ibid.*, 1740
1132		Marden(?)	*Ibid.*, 1742
1133	June	Woodstock	*Ibid.*, 1757
1133	July	Westbourne	*Ibid.*, 1787
1133		Westminster	*Ibid.*, 1795
1135	December 22	London	William Malmesbury, *HN*, p. 16

Samson, Bishop of Worcester

1100	July 15(?)	Gloucester	Symeon of Durham, p. 230
1101	September 3	Windsor	*Regesta*, II, 544
1102		Westminster	Eadmer, p. 132
1102(?)	June 29	Geddington	*Regesta*, II, 573
1107	August 1	Westminster	*Ibid.*, 825
1107	August 5(?)	London(?)	*Ibid.*, 832
1108	May 24	Westminster	*Ibid.*, 885

Theulf, Bishop of Worcester

1115	June 27	Canterbury	Eadmer, p. 230
1115	September(?)	Westminster(?)	*Regesta*, II, 1092
1121	January 7	Westminster(?)	*Ibid.*, 1243
1121	April 10	Berkeley	*Ibid.*, 1265
1123	April 15(?)	Winchester	*Ibid.*, 1391
1123	October 24	Tewkesbury	Florence of Worcester, II, 77

Simon, Bishop of Worcester

1125	October(?)	Rouen	*Regesta*, II, 1427
1126	September–October(?)	Portsmouth	*Ibid.*, 1448
1127(?)	May–August	Hereford	*Ibid.*, 1490
1130	May 4	Canterbury	Anglo-Saxon Chronicle, I, 380
1130	May 8	Rochester	*Ibid.*, II, 227
1131	September 8	Northampton	*Regesta*, II, 1715

1131(?)		Woodstock	*Ibid.*, 1726
1131–33(?)		Combe	*Ibid.*, 1827
1132	April 29	Westminster	*Ibid.*, 1736

Gerard, Archbishop of York

1094–95		Rome	Eadmer, p. 68
1101	March 10	Dover	*Regesta*, II, 515
1101	September 3	Windsor	*Ibid.*, 544
1102	Early October	Reading	*Ibid.*, 607
1102		Sicily	*Quadripartitus*, p. 159
1102		Rome	Eadmer, p. 132
1102		Westminster	*Ibid.*
1107(?)	August 1	Westminster	*Regesta*, II, 831
1107	August 11	Canterbury	Haddan and Stubbs, I, 303
1108	March	Windsor	*Regesta*, II, 871
1109	October 12	Nottingham	*Ibid.*, 918

Thomas II, Archbishop of York

1109	June 13	Westminster	Hugh the Chantor, p. 24
1109	June 27	London	*Ibid.*, p. 29
1109	August 1	York	*Ibid.*, p. 31
1114	September 13	Westbourne	*Regesta*, II, 1063

Turstin, Archbishop of York

1115	September 16	Westminster	*Regesta*, II, 1091
1116	April(?)	Normandy	Hugh the Chantor, p. 46
1118	Autumn	London and Dover	*Ibid.*, p. 51
1118	Autumn	Rouen	Eadmer, p. 249
1119	February–March	France	Hugh the Chantor, p. 65
1119	June(?)	Rouen	*Regesta*, II, 1204
1119	Summer	Chartres	Hugh the Chantor, p. 69
1119	September 22	Tours	*Ibid.*
1119	October 1–5	Paris	*Ibid.*, p. 70
1119	October 16	Reims	*Ibid.*, p. 71
1119	Late November	near Gisors	*Ibid.*, p. 76
1119	November 30	Ferrières	*Ibid.*, p. 82
1119	December	Sens	*Ibid.*, p. 83
1119	December	Auxerre	*Ibid.*
1119	Christmas	Autun	*Ibid.*, p. 84
1120	January 6	Cluny	*Ibid.*
1120	February 2	Vienne	*Ibid.*
1120	February	Valence(?)	*Ibid.*, p. 87
1120	March 6	Gap	*Ibid.*, p. 88
1120	March	Reims	*Ibid.*, p. 92
1120	Before Easter	Soissons	*Ibid.*
1120	April 18	Colombes	*Ibid.*
1120	April 20	Dammartin Castle	*Ibid.*
1120	Late April	Marcigny	*Ibid.*, p. 93
1120	May 30	near Vernon	*Ibid.*, p. 97
1120	November 25(?)	near Barfleur	*Ibid.*, p. 99
1121	January 29	crossed Channel	*Ibid.*, p. 100

1121	January 30(?)	Windsor	*Ibid.*
1121	February 20	York	*Ibid.*
1121(?)	April	Clarendon	*Regesta*, II, 1272
1122(?)	March	Rockingham	*Ibid.*, 1320
1122(?)	October–December	York	*Ibid.*, 1334
1122	December 6	York	*Ibid.*, 1337
1122(?)		Nottingham	*Ibid.*, 1327
1123	February 2	Gloucester	Hugh the Chantor, p. 108
1123	March 11	Woodstock	*Ibid.*, p. 111
1123	March	Sutri	*Ibid.*
1123	March 16(?)	Rome	Anglo-Saxon Chronicle, *anno* 1123
1123	late June or July	Normandy	Hugh the Chantor, p. 119
1125	January–March(?)	Rouen	*Regesta*, II, 1425
1125	September 8–10	Westminster	Hugh the Chantor, p. 121
1125	Autumn	Normandy	*Ibid.*, p. 122
1125	October(?)	Evreux	*Regesta*, II, 1433
1125	After Michaelmas	Rome	Anglo-Saxon Chronicle, *anno* 1125
1126	Spring	Normandy	Hugh the Chantor, p. 128
1126	Spring	Wissant	*Ibid.*
1126	Spring	Canterbury	*Ibid.*
1126	June 29	York	*Ibid.*
1126(?)	Autumn	Rockingham	*Regesta*, II, 1459
1126	Christmas	Windsor and London	Hugh the Chantor, p. 129
1127	January 1(?)	Westminster	*Regesta*, II, 1474
1127	July 16(?)	Rochester	*Liber Vitae D.*, p. 59
1127	September(?)	Rouen	*Regesta*, II, 1547
1128(?)	December(?)	Touques(?)	*Ibid.*, 1554
1129		Rouen	*Ibid.*, 1580
1130(?)		Winchester	*Ibid.*, 1654
1131(?)	July–August	Arques	*Ibid.*, 1692
1131(?)	August	Westbourne	*Ibid.*, 1710
1131(?)	August	Waltham	*Ibid.*, 1711
1131	September 8(?)	Northampton	*Ibid.*, 1716
1131(?)		Woodstock	*Ibid.*, 1721
1131(?)		London	*Ibid.*, 1719
1132(?)	April 29	Westminster	*Ibid.*, 1736
1133(?)	June	Westminster	*Ibid.*, 1759

Hervey, Bishop of Bangor

1102		Westminster	Eadmer, p. 132
1104(?)		Evreux	*Regesta*, II, 675
1105	February	Romsey	*Ibid.*, 683
1107	August 1	London(?)	*Ibid.*, 828
1109	June 26	London	Ralph de Diceto, *anno* 1109

David, Bishop of Bangor

1120	April 4	Westminster	Eadmer, p. 260
1121	January 7	Westminster	*Regesta*, II, 1243
1121	October 2	Lambeth	Eadmer, p. 298

Urban, Bishop of Llandaff

1107	August 11	Canterbury	Eadmer, p. 187
1115	September 16	Westminster	*Regesta*, II, 1091
1119	After May 16	Rouen	*Ibid.*, 1203
1119	October 20	Reims	Eadmer, p. 255
1119(?)	October(?)	Rome(?)	*Book of Llan Dâv*, p. 92
1121	January 7	Westminster	*Regesta*, II, 1243
1121	March 13	Abingdon	Eadmer, p. 293
1123	October 24	Tewkesbury	Florence of Worcester, II, 77
1127	May 22	Winchester	*Regesta*, II, 1485

Bernard, Bishop of St. David's

1115	September 19	Westminster	Eadmer, p. 235
1115	After September 18	Winchester	*Regesta*, II, 1097
1115	Christmas	Canterbury	Eadmer, p. 237
1119	June	Rouen	*Regesta*, II, 1205
1119	October 20	Reims	Eadmer, p. 255
1120	March 6	Gap	Hugh the Chantor, p. 90
1121	January 7	Westminster	*Regesta*, II, 1243
1121	January 16	Lambeth	Eadmer, p. 291
1121	March 13	Abingdon	*Ibid.*, p. 293
1121(?)	March	Woodstock	*Regesta*, II, 1261
1121(?)	April	Clarendon	*Ibid.*, 1270
1121(?)	April–May	Winchester	*Ibid.*, 1281
1121(?)	Summer	Bridgenorth	*Ibid.*, 1296
1121(?)	Summer	Condover	*Ibid.*, 1297
1121(?)		Norton	*Ibid.*, 1300
1123	February(?)	Canterbury	Anglo-Saxon Chronicle, *anno* 1123
1123	Late March or Early April	Rome	Hugh the Chantor, p. 111
1125	January–March	Rouen	*Regesta*, II, 1425
1125	September 8	London	Hugh the Chantor, p. 121
1126		Ste Vaubourg (Rouen)	*Regesta*, II, 1439
1127(?)	May	Westminster	*Ibid.*, 1483
1127	May 22	Winchester	*Ibid.*, 1485
1127(?)	May–August	Hereford	*Ibid.*, 1490
1127	August 26(?)	Eling	*Ibid.*, 1507
1127	September(?)	Rouen	*Ibid.*, 1547
1129		Rouen	*Ibid.*, 1578
1130	May 4	Canterbury	Anglo-Saxon Chronicle, I, 380
1130	May 8	Rochester	*Ibid.*, II, 227
1130	March–September	Winchester	*Regesta*, II, 1642
1131(?)	August	Westbourne	*Ibid.*, 1710
1131(?)		Woodstock	*Ibid.*, 1721
1132(?)	Christmas(?)	Windsor	*Ibid.*, 1740
1133	June	Woodstock	*Ibid.*, 1757
1133	June(?)	Westminster	*Ibid.*, 1761
1133	June(?)	Winchester	*Ibid.*, 1765
1133(?)	July	Westbourne	*Ibid.*, 1786
1134(?)		Rouen	*Ibid.*, 1896

THE ENGLISH HOSPITALLERS DURING THE GREAT SCHISM

Charles L. Tipton

Lehigh University

THE ENGLISH HOSPITALLERS DURING THE GREAT SCHISM

I. Introduction

Modern historians have generally adopted the view that the Great Schism had a divisive effect upon the Order of the Knights of the Hospital of St. John of Jerusalem. There, as in other international orders, we are told, national loyalty was stronger than religious vows, and the members of each *langue* naturally sided with the pope chosen by the monarch of their particular country. The obvious result was schism within the ranks. The grand master of the order, whose headquarters was then at Rhodes, and who adhered to the Avignon pope, Clement VII, was deserted by the Knights of those countries whose rulers regarded the Roman claimant as legitimate. Inasmuch as the English king, parliament, and clergy declared their allegiance to Urban VI, the Roman pontiff, it necessarily follows that the Hospitallers of this nation should be found among the list of those who abandoned the grand master. And so they are, for again historians have almost universally agreed that, faced with the alternative of siding with their king and people or with their superior in the order, the English Knights stood firmly with their nation. Having gone this far, these same historians, with only an occasional qualification, then go on to tell us that all cooperation between the Roman and Avignon factions of the order was impossible so long as they regarded each other as "schismatic." Thus, we are left with the impression that the order remained internally divided and that the English Knights refused to recognize the authority of the grand master until, in 1409, the Council of Pisa elected Alexander V. With this election the schism among the Hospitallers came to an end as all *langues* and the grand master recognized the new pope as the sole head of the church.[1]

1. J. Bosio, *Dell'Istoria della Sacra Religione et Illustrissima Militia de San Giovanni Gerosolimitano* (Rome, 1594–1602), I, i, 89; R. de Vertot, *Histoire des Chevaliers de St. Jean de Jérusalem* (Paris, 1726), II, 104; A. Sutherland, *The Achievements of the Knights of Malta* (Edinburgh, 1830–31), I, 325; K. Falkenstein, *Geschichte des Johanniter Ordens* (Dresden, 1833), p. 137; A. Winterfield, *Geschichte des Ritterlichen Ordens St. Johannis vom Spital zu Jerusalem* (Berlin, 1859), p. 168; E. Flandin, *Histoire des Chevaliers de Rhodes* (Tours, 1867), pp. 160–61; K. Herquet, *Juan Fernandez de Heredia, Grossmeister des Johanniterordens, 1377–1396* (Mulhouse, 1878), pp. 74–76; F. C. Woodhouse, *The Military Religious Orders of the Middle Ages* (London, 1879), p. 61; W. Porter, *History of the Knights of Malta* (rev ed.;

The prevalence of this hypothesis regarding the English *langue* is the result of a combination of factors. First, there has been a definite shortage of research. Comprehensive studies based upon original records are non-existent for the English Hospitallers. The small body of literature that we possess comes chiefly from members of the revived Order of St. John of Jerusalem in the British Realm—and members of this group have not always investigated their subject as thoroughly as the sources permit.[2] Consequently, the factual framework upon which sound conclusions must rest is incomplete and traditional interpretations hold the field without challenge. The general history of the Rhodian era of the Knights, moreover, has fared only slightly better; with the exception of some fine articles by Anthony Luttrell,[3] one still must turn to the fifty-year-old work of Joseph Delaville le Roulx to find scholarly coverage of their history in the fourteenth century. Besides Delaville le Roulx's, the most reliable study of any length is that of Jacomo Bosio, written at the end of the sixteenth century.[4]

London, 1883), pp. 195–97; N. Valois, *La France et le grand schisme d'Occident* (Paris, 1896–1902), II, 222–24; J. Edwards, "The Hospitallers in Scotland in the Fifteenth Century," *Scottish Historical Review*, IX (1911–12), 56; J. Delaville le Roulx, *Les Hospitaliers à Rhodes jusqu'à la morte de Philibert de Nailhac, 1310–1421* (Paris, 1913), pp. 248–50; H. Workman, *John Wyclif: A Study of the English Medieval Church* (Oxford, 1926), II, 61; M. Barbaro di San Giorgio, *Storia della Costituzione del Sovrano Militare Ordine di Malta* (Rome, 1927), p. 34; E. Perroy, *L'Angleterre et le grand schisme d'Occident* (Paris, 1933), pp. 93–94; E. J. King, *The Knights of St. John in the British Empire* (London, 1934), pp. 64–65; G. Bottarelli, *Storia Politica e Militare del Sovrano Ordine di S. Giovanni di Gerusalemme detto di Malta* (Milan, 1940), pp. 160–61; W. Rees, *A History of the Order of St. John of Jerusalem in Wales and on the Welsh Border* (Cardiff, 1947), p. 76.

2. The standard English histories are Porter, *op. cit.*; King, *op. cit.*; W. K. R. Bedford and R. Holbeche, *The Order of the Hospital of St. John of Jerusalem* (London, 1902); and H. W. Fincham, *The Order of the Hospital of St. John of Jerusalem and Its Grand Priory of England* (2d ed.; London, 1933).

3. "Venice and the Knights Hospitallers of Rhodes in the Fourteenth Century," *Papers of the British School at Rome*, XXVI (1958); "The Knights Hospitallers of Rhodes and Their Achievements in the Fourteenth Century," *Revue de l'Ordre souverain militaire de Malte*, XVI (1958); "Greek Histories Translated and Compiled for Juan Fernández de Heredia, Master of Rhodes, 1377–1396," *Speculum*, XXXV (1960); "The Aragonese Crown and the Knights Hospitallers of Rhodes, 1291–1350," *English Historical Review*, LXXVI (1961); "Emmanuele Piloti and Criticism of the Knights Hospitallers of Rhodes: 1306–1444," *Annales de l'Ordre souverain militaire de Malte*, XX (1962); "Intrigue, Schism, and Violence among the Hospitallers of Rhodes: 1377–1384," *Speculum*, XLI (1966).

4. H. A. Balbi, "On the Study of the History of the Order of St. John of Jerusalem," *Archivum Melitense*, VI (1927), 188. For Delaville le Roulx as a historian, see A. Dezarrois,

The paucity of research may well stem from inadequate information concerning the archives of the order. Published catalogues of this vast collection,[5] now housed at the Royal Malta Library, quite often convey an erroneous impression of the amount of material available for individual *langues*. For example, all report that the archival section devoted exclusively to records of the English priory consists of only six small volumes. It is therefore possible to assume—as one writer has—that "at Malta scarcely anything relating to English members of the order has been preserved."[6] This assumption apparently has discouraged subsequent investigation of the Malta manuscripts.

If nothing else, this study should illustrate the value of Malta's documents for those interested in the English Knights. Though the topic treats only a thirty-year period in the history of the *langue*, the archives contain more information than can be used. Thus many details about finance, personnel, and property have been omitted because they would not materially strengthen the present thesis. This does not mean that such items are unimportant. On the contrary, until these particulars are widely known—and others that exist for the periods before and after the Schism—we can neither eliminate obvious gaps in our standard sources nor create a fabric of fact that will support a historically sound account of the Hospitallers in England.

The final explanation for widespread acceptance of the notion that the English Knights refused obedience to their Clementine grand masters is the equally widespread nationalistic interpretation of the Great Schism. Because most writers have stressed the role of nationalism as a factor in dividing the church, it has been assumed that the various religious orders would be similarly affected. In some orders, indeed, there was discord and division, perhaps even nationalism, as the studies of Valois, Perroy, Rose

---

"Joseph De La Ville Le Roulx," *Annales de l'Ordre souverain militaire de Malte*, XIX (1961), 131–39. Cf. Luttrell, "Intrigue, Schism, and Violence," p. 31, n. 1. For Bosio, see P. Falcone, "Il valore documentario della Storia dell'Ordine Gerosolimitano di Giacomo Bosio," *Archivio Storico di Malta*, X (1939), 93–135.

5. L. de Mas Latrie, *Archives, Bibliothèque, et Inscriptions de Malte* (Paris, 1857); J. Delaville le Roulx, *Les archives, la bibliothèque et le trésor de l'Ordre de Saint-Jean de Jérusalem à Malte* (Paris, 1883); H. P. Scicluna, "Some Important Documents of the Archives of the Sovereign Military Order of St. John of Jerusalem," *Archivum Melitense*, I (1910), 151–76. A new catalogue (*Catalogue of the Records of the Order of St. John of Jerusalem in the Royal Malta Library*), compiled by A. Zammit Gabarretta and J. Mizzi, is in progress. Portions of this catalogue were published by the Malta University Press in 1964 and 1965.

6. Bedford and Holbeche, *op. cit.*, p. 32.

Graham,[7] and E. Margaret Thompson[8] have shown. It does not follow, however, that all behaved the same and we should resist the presumption that they did until sufficient evidence is presented.

The unique organization of the Knights of St. John has also made them easy prey for those historians who have emphasized nationalism. Though most were well aware that the *langues* were not representative of what we think of today as nation-states, they have often equated the two, endowing the former with national characteristics and forcing upon them a very modern type of patriotism. Thus the English *langue* often appears to be synonymous with England, the Spanish with Spain, and so on.[9] Add to this the opinion that the Hospitallers "in taking the habit did not abdicate their nationality"[10] and it follows that the *langues* would support the "national policy" of their respective countries.

In contrast to the traditional interpretation, it is here the thesis that the Great Schism had no pronounced effect upon the English Hospitallers. A careful study of the documents in the order's archives reveals that they recognized the authority of their Clementine grand master throughout the period, received appointments at his hands, performed garrison duty at Rhodes, met their financial obligations to the convent, and in general behaved as they had for more than two centuries. Since the rules and statutes of the Hospital made no provision for such problems as those created by a dual papacy the brethren simply refused to admit that any existed. By dealing only with their immediate superior, the grand master, and by ignoring all other issues they were able to avoid an open declaration for or against either pope.

7. R. Graham, "The Papal Schism of 1378 and the English Province of the Order of Cluny," *English Historical Review*, XXXVIII (1925), 481–95; "The Great Schism and the English Monasteries of the Cistercian Order," *EHR*, XLIV (1929), 373–87. The best summary of the effects of the Schism upon the religious orders (except the Hospitallers) in England is found in David Knowles, *The Religious Orders in England* (Cambridge, 1950–55), II, 167–70.

8. *The Carthusian Order in England* (London, 1930), pp. 259–62.

9. It is hardly necessary to state that this is a gross oversimplification. In the fourteenth century the *langues* included several independent countries, each of which had its "national policy." For example, the English *langue* was made up of England, Ireland, and Scotland. During the Schism Scotland not only recognized the Avignon pope but usually was at war with England. Neither the war nor the divided papacy, however, disturbed the internal harmony of the *langue*; the Scottish and English members ignored both events. This aspect of the Schism has been treated separately in my "The Scottish and English Hospitallers During the Great Schism," *Catholic Historical Review*, LII (1966), 240–45.

10. Delaville le Roulx, *Hospitaliers*, p. 248. He continues: "Leur attitude fut partout conformé à celle des états qu'ils habitaient, et se modifa avec celle-ci."

Although interesting and informative in itself, the behavior of the English Knights in this era is also valuable for its illumination of a larger historical issue. The extent to which their attitude and activity paralleled those of the government impinges directly upon the complex and often debated question of the role of nationalism during the Schism. If they thought of themselves as Hospitallers first and Englishmen second, they subordinated nationality to religious vows. If they were not berated or bedeviled by other Englishmen for holding such a view, the strength of national feeling was less than generally believed. If England's monarchs did nothing to prevent them from consorting with "schismatics," even intervened to protect them from papal control, English "national interests" were not always consistent with a strict pro-Roman policy. This being the case, the present study cannot avoid a secondary thesis on the subject of nationalism in the fourteenth century. Briefly stated, this thesis is that the Hospitallers were not nationalistic, that English kings knew this but did not care, that these same rulers realized that the interests of the Knights—and, indirectly, those of the king—were best served by allowing them to obey a Clementine grand master, and, finally, that the Schism was more complicated than those who stress the division of Europe into national blocs would have us believe.

II. Prior Robert Hales (1378–1381)

During the early years of the Schism the Knights of St. John were supposedly saved from committing themselves either to Avignon or to Rome because of the absence of their grand master. According to a tale originated by Bosio and reported by almost all students of Hospitaller history, Juan Fernández de Heredia, head of the order, sailed for the Morea in 1378 for a campaign against the Turks, was captured, and held for ransom. The priors of England, Rome, and St. Giles, who accompanied the expedition, gallantly offered themselves as hostages if the Turks would free Fernández de Heredia to raise the necessary money. This chivalrous offer was declined, not by the enemy, but by the grand master, who wisely remarked that three young fighting men were more valuable to the order than a single old one. Thus the three priors sadly made their way to Rhodes, and then back to their priories, leaving Fernández de Heredia in captivity. There he remained for three years—until his family was able to raise sufficient funds for his liberation.[11]

11. Bosio, *op. cit.*, I, i, 87–88; Sutherland, *op. cit.*, I, 298; Porter, *op. cit.*, p. 195; King, *op. cit.*, pp. 63–64; Bottarelli, *op. cit.*, p. 159.

The falseness of this hoary myth was partially exposed by Delaville le Roulx—though no one seems to have paid the slightest attention to his relation of what actually occurred.[12] While it is true that Fernández de Heredia was captured by the Turks in the summer of 1378, it is not true that he remained captive for three years. Actually, his imprisonment lasted less than a year. As early as July, 1379, he was back at the convent of Rhodes, issuing orders, making appointments, and renewing his communications with the far-flung possessions of the order in the west.[13] There he remained until the spring of 1382 when he set out for Avignon to take up residence at the court of Clement VII.[14]

As for the prior of England accompanying the grand master to Greece, this too is fiction. Sir Robert Hales, who occupied this position, had long since forsaken the saddle for a more rewarding career in the corrupt court politics that marked the later years of Edward III and the minority of Richard II. With prospects for advancement and privileges continually increasing, the prior was hardly the man to go crusading. Though historians cling to the story that he offered himself as hostage for Fernández de Heredia, and one even relates that the offer was accepted and Hales imprisoned until 1381,[15] he was in England all of the time. Evidence for this is found in the records of the parliaments of 1378 and 1379, the former, incidentally, being that in which Urban VI was declared by England to be the rightful pope. In the first of these the prior was appointed a member of the "continual council" to govern during the king's minority, and in both was a trier of petitions.[16] This precludes any possibility that he participated in the grand master's campaign.

The English Hospitaller who accompanied Fernández de Heredia to the Morea was Richard Overton, Turcopolier of Rhodes, the highest

12. Delaville le Roulx, *Hospitaliers*, p. 206.

13. Luttrell, "Intrigue, Schism, and Violence," p. 34.

14. There are six original bulls of Fernández de Heredia, three with seals appended, that cover the period September 23, 1379, to October, 1380, in the Archives of the Knights of the Hospital of St. John of Jerusalem, Royal Library of Malta, Valletta (hereafter cited as Malta Archives): Vol. 16, fols. 57–62. Other bulls, which cover the period to March, 1382, are in Vol. 24, fols. 18–21, 24. The earliest extant bull from Avignon, dated August 8, 1382, is in Vol. 24, fol. 2.

15. Porter, *op. cit.*, p. 195.

16. *Rotuli Parliamentorum* (hereafter *Rot. Parl.*) (London, 1767–77), III, 34, 55–56. In 1380 the prior was a commissioner in negotiating Scottish debts; see *Rotuli Scotiae in Turri Londinensi et in Domo Capitulari Westmonasteriensi Asservati* (London, 1814–19), II, 27, 29.

officer of the English *langue*.[17] He had come to England in 1371 as a visitor-general of the grand master,[18] and it was during his prolonged stay that Gregory XI decided to raise a great army of Knights and wrest the Morea from the Turks. The English quota for this crusade was set at thirty-eight Hospitallers, who should choose their esquires and hold themselves in readiness to depart for the East in 1378.[19] At the head of this contingent, the turcopolier left the island in late 1377 to join Fernández de Heredia.[20] What role Overton played in the numerous battles remains unknown. It seems, however, that he did not survive them but fell somewhere in Greece, the victim of a Turkish arrow or lance.[21]

At first glance it may seem that all of this information shows only the errors of historians about the grand master's campaign and has no bearing upon the Great Schism. But there is more to the story. Showing that Fernández de Heredia returned to Rhodes in the fall of 1379 creates another problem: When and how did he choose between the two rival popes? For those historians who have accepted Bosio's relation of a three-year captivity, the decision necessarily came after 1381, while Delaville le Roulx refuses to commit himself one way or the other. But this date is much too late and implies a three-year period of inactivity by the grand master which is quite impossible to accept. As the head of an organization that recognized no superior except the pope, Fernández de Heredia could hardly have been ignorant of the fact that there were two popes to choose from and that a decision must be made. How or precisely when he made his choice must forever remain a mystery, as the records of the council meetings of this era have long since perished. But make it he did. As early as October 10, 1379, he committed himself to the Avignon papacy by appointing Peter Brecii, Commander of Montpellier, as procurator-

17. The office of turcopolier, one of eight conventual bailiwicks in the fourteenth century, was held by Englishmen from 1330 until the dissolution of the order in 1540. In the field, the turcopolier commanded the light cavalry; in garrison, he was in charge of coastal defenses.

18. *Calendar of Patent Rolls* (*CPR*), *1370–74*, p. 92.

19. *Calendar of Entries in the Papal Registers relating to Great Britain and Ireland: Letters* (*Papal Registers*), IV, 111.

20. Overton received license to leave England in March, 1376 (*Calendar of Close Rolls* [*CCR*], *1374–77*, pp. 297–98), but was still in England in 1377, residing at the preceptory of Eagle (Thomas Hugo, *The History of Eagle in the County of Lincoln* [London, 1876], p. 20). He left before February, 1378, however, because his position as receiver was filled by a procurator (Malta Archives, Vol. 48, fol. 16*v*.)

21. Delaville le Roulx, *Mélanges sur l'Ordre de S. Jean de Jérusalem* (Paris, 1910), XVI, 8.

general at the court of Clement VII.[22] More than this, Fernández de Heredia selected three of the Avignon cardinals as "protectors" of the order's interests, assigning to each an annual stipend of three hundred florins.[23] Thus by the end of the first year of the Schism the position of the Knights of St. John was known to all who might care to inquire. At the court of Clement resided the three "protectors," the procurator-general, and probably a fifth individual, the receiver-general. This latter official, Peter de Provins, of the *langue* of France, was forced by the nature of his position to move about in Western Europe a great deal. But when he did remain stationary it was at the court of Clement VII, and he was as early as 1379 keeping his accounts in florins, "court money of Avignon."[24]

In 1380 contacts between the Knights and Clement VII were numerous. The receiver-general made the first payment of the "protectors'" stipends and advanced small sums of money to the papal chancery in connection with bulls being sent to Rhodes.[25] At the convent these bulls, confirming the order in its privileges and ratifying the grand master's administrative changes, were freely accepted and made a part of the order's archives, as was the custom.

The most important event of 1380, however, was the convocation at Valenciennes, on February 1, of a chapter-general of the order. Who presided in the absence of Fernández de Heredia, who was then at Rhodes, is impossible to say. Nor do we know who attended or, with one exception, what matters were deliberated. The only thing that can be said for certain is that the assembly decided to raise a part of the ransom still owed the Turks by the grand master by means of a *taille* upon certain priories. Among the priories that were to contribute to the ransom fund were those of England and Ireland, each of which was assessed 1,000 florins.[26]

Can we assume that Prior Hales remained blissfully unaware of all the events that took place between the departure of Overton in 1377 and the end of 1380? No, we cannot, for it has previously been shown that he

22. Malta Archives, Vol. 24, fol. 5. During Fernández de Heredia's captivity a chapter-general was held at Rhodes under the presidency of the grand preceptor. The statutes of this assembly were confirmed—with reservations—by Clement VII in early August, 1379 (Luttrell, "Intrigue, Schism, and Violence," p. 34).

23. Malta Archives, Vol. 48, fol. 18*v*.

24. *Ibid.*, fols. 1–11.

25. *Ibid.*, fols. 18*v*, 21–22*r*. For other contacts see Luttrell, "Intrigue, Schism, and Violence," pp. 34–35 and *passim*.

26. Malta Archives, Vol. 48, fols. 34*v*–35*r*.

participated in the parliament that chose Urban VI. We also know that Hales was in England in 1379, the year in which the bull that excommunicated Clement VII and all of his followers was published by the English clergy.[27] Later events also prove that he was aware of the death of Overton and of the chapter-general of 1380, as he had the sums of money connected with those events ready for the receiver-general. We must therefore conclude that Hales knew of the decision of Fernández de Heredia and the convent of Rhodes to support Avignon against Rome; any other interpretation must assume that a man so high in his own order as well as in English government circles completely ignored all political and ecclesiastical affairs.

If there was any doubt in the prior's mind, it must certainly have been removed in January, 1381, when Peter de Provins, the receiver-general, visited England to collect the *taille* and the mortuaries of the priory.[28] Hales and the English receiver, Robert Normanton, promptly turned over 300 marks sterling, equal to 1,500 florins of Avignon. Of this sum, 500 florins represented Richard Overton's mortuary and the remaining 1,000 florins the amount levied at Valenciennes.[29] In addition, the two English officers paid the 1,000 florins the chapter-general had ordered the priory of Ireland to pay.[30] Four months later Provins was back again, this time to collect the dues, known to the order as *responsions*, periodically paid by each priory. On this occasion the sum turned over by Hales and Normanton was 5,000 florins.[31] Thus in less than six months the English *langue* paid 7,500 florins to an excommunicated person who resided at the court of Avignon and who was a known adherent of Clement VII.[32]

In the interval between the visits of the collector from Avignon, the English prior crowned his political career with an appointment as

27. Odericus Raynaldi, *Annales Ecclesiastici ab anno MCXCVIII ubi desinit Cardinalis Baronius* (Paris, 1864–83), XXVI, 262–66.

28. Mortuaries were sums due to the treasury of the order upon the death of one of its members. These comprised the revenues of the deceased's preceptories until a new appointment was made and also the money received from the sale of his personal effects.

29. Malta Archives, Vol. 48, fol. 34*v*.

30. *Ibid.*, fol. 35*v*.

31. *Ibid.*, fol., 35*r*.

32. This money was sent to the convent of Rhodes in March, 1382, where a duplicate set of records was kept. The figures balance with those in Provins' account book, though the Rhodes records reveal additional miscellaneous information. Thus we learn that John Dayton, preceptor of Shingay, and John Dingley, preceptor of Dalby and Beverly, had died in the previous year and that Provins had collected but not itemized their mortuaries (*ibid.*, Vol. 322, fols. 333*r*–334*r*).

Treasurer of England. The new post, however, soon turned out to be a most unenviable one. In attempting to collect a heavy poll tax that had been levied by parliament, Hales touched off the bloody Peasants' Rebellion of 1381, an uprising that cost him his life. On June 14 the prior, who had taken refuge in the Tower of London, was dragged forth by a mob under the leadership of Wat Tyler, kicked and cuffed to nearby Tower Hill and immediately beheaded upon a fallen log.

By the time of Hales' death the attitude of the English Hospitallers toward the Schism had been shaped. A firm opponent of papal interference in the order's affairs,[33] the prior was shrewd enough to realize that the Hospitallers' independence could only be weakened by participation in papal politics. His strategy, therefore, was largely a matter of ignoring rival popes and their claims while maintaining normal relations with his superiors in the order. The continuity of this policy by his successors, and the absence of records indicating dissent from or dissatisfaction with such behavior by English brethren, make it clear that it enjoyed general support. This is precisely what one would expect of the Knights of St. John; their interests were not theological disputes or schisms but weapons and crusades.

The opportunity for Hales to renounce Fernández de Heredia as a schismatic was there after 1379, but he did not. Nor did he fail to meet the financial obligations of the English *langue* to the convent. Here was a temptation, if ever there was one. The 7,500 florins Hales paid to Provins in 1381 would have remained at home had he gone to the king—whose ear he had—and asked that the moneys be arrested. He made no such move. It was clear from his actions that the dispute within the church was not going to affect his order unless some outside force intervened.

III. PRIOR JOHN RADYINGTON (1381–1396)

By the time of Prior Hales' murder, Urban VI had pinpointed his major enemies and was looking about for minor ones. His eye fell upon the Knights of St. John. In April, 1381, he ordered the Archbishop of Venice to conduct an inquiry into the behavior of Fernández de Heredia, and,

33. In 1374 the prior and Gregory XI had a lengthy dispute over the disposition of lands subject to the English *langue*. Hales appealed to Edward III, who arrested the *responsions* until the pope and grand master could reach a compromise with Hales (Thomas Rymer, *Foedera* [3d ed.; London, 1739–45], III, iii, 38, 40, and *Papal Registers*, IV, 140–42).

should it be found that he was loyal to Avignon, to depose and excommunicate him by name.[34] The records of this investigation have not survived but its results are plain: before the death of Hales—presumably in May or June—the grand master was declared deposed by the Roman pontiff. This outcome is indicated by the actions of Richard II. Immediately following the death of the English prior the king issued an order forbidding any member of the *langue* going to Rome or attempting in any way to secure the vacant office from Urban.[35] In ordinary circumstances no such order would have been necessary; the pope had no authority to appoint officials within the ranks of the Knights, and no English member of the order would have thought of soliciting an office from him. All privileges of nomination, appointment, and confirmation to all positions rested with the grand master and the conventual bailiffs of Rhodes. Thus the king's order revealed that he knew the Knights were, theoretically, without a head for their organization. It shows, moreover, that Richard was determined to sever communications between Rome and the English Hospitallers—under his special protection since the murder of Hales[36]—lest some ambitious fellow upset tradition by dragging the pope into the affairs of the order. This policy, best summed up by the old adage "let sleeping dogs lie," was to be a characteristic feature of the posture taken by Richard II and Henry IV vis-à-vis the English Knights of St. John. Throughout the Great Schism the two monarchs allowed the order to go its own way; they carefully avoided direct intervention in its affairs, unless compelled by unusual circumstances.

No better example of this royal policy of non-interference could be found than that offered by the selection of a successor to Hales. No attempt was made to influence the outcome, nor any reference made to the fact that the convent and grand master were schismatics. Events moved precisely as they should have under the statutes of the order. These rules provided that when a prior died in his priory the preceptor of the house nearest the place of death should summon the twelve closest preceptors and elect a "president" or prior *ad interim*.[37] It would be the duty of this

34. Valois, *op. cit.*, II, 222–23. Cf. Luttrell, "Intrigue, Schism, and Violence," p. 35.

35. *CPR*, 1381–85, p. 75; *CCR*, 1381–85, p. 12.

36. After the Peasants' Rebellion, Richard II had taken the Hospitallers under his special protection for one year (*CPR*, 1381–85, p. 32). That Richard was much interested in their welfare is indicated by his cooperation with the "president" and by his order forbidding assemblies, associations, and "things" that might hurt the order (*CCR*, 1381–85, pp. 3, 5, 9).

37. *The Rule Statutes and Customs of the Hospitallers, 1099–1310*, ed. E. J. King (London, 1934), pp. 61–62.

individual to notify the grand master that a vacancy existed. At the convent the conventual bailiff of the *langue* concerned would, by virtue of his position, have priority upon such a post. And, though it was actually a step down in prestige and authority it was customary for all conventual bailiffs to take appointments as priors to avoid continuous residence in the East.

With a single and unimportant exception, each point in the preceding hypothetical situation can be documented in the "real-life" case presented by Hales' murder. The "president" elected by the brethren in England was one Hildebrand Inge, Preceptor of Buckland, who served in that capacity until a new prior arrived to assume command.[38] When Inge notified the convent of the prior's death we cannot say as incoming correspondence from the various priories was not registered. But we know that it was informed, for on November 18, 1381 Fernández de Heredia appointed the turcopolier, John Radyington, Prior of England.[39] In February of 1382 the new prior received permission from the grand master to receive six members into the Hospital, and the next month license to leave the convent for his priory.[40] It seems likely that he was accompanied on his journey as far as Avignon by Fernández de Heredia himself; their itineraries are almost identical.[41] At any rate, Radyington was there in July, 1382, and received from Peter de Provins a safe-conduct for himself and fifteen men to cross France.[42] By September he had reached England, where, on the twenty-third of that month, he gave the oath of fealty to Richard II, protesting that his oath should not prejudice the rights of his order in time to come.[43]

Before taking up the events that followed Fernández de Heredia's residence at Avignon and Radyington's in England, we should note several events of importance that occurred prior to their departure from Rhodes. First, the grand master made several appointments to English preceptories left vacant by members of the order who had died or—as in the case of Radyington—had resigned. One of the new appointees, John

38. *CPR*, 1381–85, pp. 32, 46, 84; *Calendar of Miscellaneous Inquisitions*, IV, 104.

39. Malta Archives, Vol. 321, fol. 136. Although authorities never list Radyington as a turcopolier of the English *langue*, he acted in that capacity at a council meeting at Rhodes on April 19, 1381 (*ibid.*, fol. 211*v*).

40. *Ibid.*, fols. 137*v*–138*r*.

41. For Fernández de Heredia's itinerary, see Delaville le Roulx, *Hospitaliers*, p. 215. Radyington's permission to leave was granted only a month before the departure of the grand master. Both men arrived at Avignon in July.

42. Malta Archives, Vol. 48, fol. 71*r*.

43. *CCR*, 1381–85, p. 208.

Brynkyl, almost certainly accompanied the new prior to England,[44] and others—such as John Brunston, Thomas Skipwyth, James Sylvester, and Walter Grendon—may also have done so.[45] Although we have no recorded license for their departure from the convent, we know that Radyington was accompanied by fifteen men, a retinue too large to be composed solely of servants. Even if this was not the case, we can safely assume that the official papers for the appointments were carried, along with several others, in the saddlebags of the prior.[46]

Also, there had been a council meeting at the convent shortly before Fernández de Heredia's departure. The Knights on Rhodes were concerned about the grand master's decision to reside at Avignon. In order to ensure that while there he did nothing prejudicial to the order, the conventual bailiffs decided that four members of the garrison should accompany him as "advisors." In this assembly England was represented by a lieutenant-turcopolier, reported by Bosio to have been one Ascanio Gervasio.[47] Delaville le Roulx, believing that the English Hospitallers were deserting the grand master because of his deposition, then concluded, on the basis of the name, that "Gervasio" was probably an Italian.[48] On the contrary, this person was the English Knight Thurstan Gervase, who acted as lieutenant-turcopolier until the successor of Radyington could arrive from England.[49] Thus, the English *langue* at the convent enjoyed perfect continuity under his leadership throughout the year 1382.

44. Appointed to the preceptory of Newland, left vacant by the death of Hales, Brynkyl was given permission to receive one knight into the order and license to leave the convent on the same day as Radyington (Malta Archives, Vol. 321, fol. 137*v*).

45. Brunston was appointed to the preceptory of Ribston, left vacant by the resignation of Radyington, in November, 1381; Skipwyth to the preceptory of Shingay in February, 1382; Sylvester to the preceptory of Yeavely and Barrow in March, 1382; and Grendon to the preceptory of Halston in February, 1382 (*ibid.*, fols. 137*r*–138*r*).

46. In October, 1381, Brian de Grey was appointed preceptor of Beverly, and in February, 1382, he was made receiver of England (the scribe mistakenly called him "Henry de Grey"). In addition, Radyington would have carried the confirmation of John Vilanton to an unspecified preceptory and a letter to Robert Normanton asking for the state of the finances in the priory (*ibid.*, fols. 136*r*–138*r*).

47. Bosio, *op. cit.*, I, ii, 132.

48. Delaville le Roulx, *Hospitaliers*, p. 213, n. 4.

49. The records of this meeting are in Malta Archives, Vol. 322, fols. 279*r*–280*r* (of the first name I make not "Ascanio" but "Trcanio"). In July of 1382, Gervase still acted as lieutenant-turcopolier and was referred to at that time simply as "Thurston." In 1385 he was promoted to the preceptory of Greenham, and before 1400 he was promoted to Yeavely and Barrow. He died in 1408, still in possession of the latter preceptory (*ibid.*, Vol. 48, fols. 215*r*; Vol. 322, fol. 240*r*; Vol. 323, fol. 137*v*; Vol. 330, fol. 80*v*; Vol. 334, fol. 103*v*). On one occasion Gervase acted as an attorney for Radyington in England (*CPR*, 1396–99, p. 273).

One of Fernández de Heredia's first acts in Avignon was the calling of a chapter-general to meet at Valence-sur-Rhone in March, 1383. A mandate summoning Radyington to this assembly was sent from Clement's court in August of the preceding year,[50] and, in the winter of 1382/83, Peter de Provins secured a safe-conduct for the English prior to pass through France.[51] The state of the order and its properties in England, however, prevented Radyington from attending. Nor does it appear that he sent procurators, as Provins subsequently complained that the safe-conduct which he had secured "with great difficulty" had not been used.[52] Perhaps it would have been better had Radyington gone; he might have argued that the state of the English priory was such that it would be exceedingly difficult to raise any special *taille*. But, since he was not present, the chapter-general tallaged England along with the other priories. The sum to be raised by the island's brethren was set at 8,000 florins.[53] All of the actions of this assembly were, of course, carried out under the authority of "our holy father Clement."[54]

The grand master's residence at Avignon and his decision to summon a chapter-general stimulated Urban VI to stronger measures. Though Fernández de Heredia had been deposed, nothing had been done to provide the Knights of those countries siding with Rome a figure around whom they could rally. Consequently, the pope, doubtless informed of the impending meeting by one of the Italian priors, issued an order in December, 1382, forbidding all Hospitallers loyal to Rome from having any contact with such a schismatic as Fernández de Heredia.[55] In April, 1383, Urban took the final step in his plan to divide the order in its allegiance: he appointed Richard Caracciolo, Prior of Capua, the grand master for all priories of Roman obedience.[56] This act, we are told, occasioned the complete defection of the English Knights, who, until then, had been in doubt as to the course of action they should follow.[57]

It would seem, then, that by the spring of 1383 the English prior's course was clear. There was now an anti–grand master to whom he could give his obedience, and no further dealings with Fernández de Heredia

50. Malta Archives, Vol. 322, fol. 180*r*.
51. *Ibid.*, Vol. 48, fol. 101*r*.
52. *Ibid.*, fol. 102*r*.
53. *Ibid.*, Vol. 24, fols. 1, 6, and Vol. 322, fols. 180*r*, 282*v*.
54. *Ibid.*, Vol. 24, fol. 1.
55. Valois, *op. cit.*, II, 223.
56. Bosio, *op. cit.*, I, ii, 94.
57. Delaville le Roulx, *Hospitaliers*, p. 249.

would be necessary. But all of these declarations from Rome meant nothing to Radyington. Once allow a pope to appoint grand masters arbitrarily, instead of having them elected by their fellow Knights and the independence of the order would be badly damaged. For the Italian commanders there was perhaps some excuse, as it would be they who would profit from Urban's appointments. But for an English prior it was only changing the known for the unknown and inviting papal interference in the affairs of the *langue*. There had been no difficulty from Clement, and Fernández de Heredia was under the supervision of "advisors." Loyal to the order's statutes thus far, Radyington and his fellows in England determined to remain so, despite Urban's attempts to bring them under his control.

Ample proof of this is found in the exchanges between the English prior and the Clementine grand master in 1383. In March of that year messages were sent to England and though their contents were not specified it is fairly obvious that Radyington was being informed of the decisions of the chapter-general, and in particular that England was to raise the sum of 8,000 florins.[58] In the same year there was also an exchange of letters over a sum of money Radyington had borrowed from the convent before his departure; the prior was requested to forward the money so that the debt might be canceled.[59] Finally, we have, on April 19, the appointment of Brian de Grey to succeed John Radyington as turcopolier of Rhodes.[60] Two features of this appointment are significant: Grey was in England when he was appointed,[61] and the bull of Fernández de Heredia came from Avignon.[62] As all of this activity came after Urban VI had ordered the English Hospitallers to cease contacts with Fernández de Heredia, it is obvious that his commands carried little weight with them.

In contrast to these contacts between the grand master at Avignon and the English prior in 1383, we have evidence that in the same year Richard II intervened to keep Rome from disturbing the *langue*. In

58. Malta Archives, Vol. 48, fol. 102*r*; see n. 71.

59. *Ibid.*, fol. 203*v*, and Vol. 322, fol. 310*r*.

60. *Ibid.*, fol. 181*r*.

61. Otherwise there would have been no need for the long delay and no explanation of why Thurstan Gervase acted as lieutenant-turcopolier during much of 1382.

62. Porter's list of officials of the English *langue* gives all of Fernández de Heredia's appointments as if they originated from Rhodes—a serious error of scholarship that considerably distorts any interpretation of the Schism. The appointments of Grey—and of all others—between 1382 and 1396 came from Avignon and are so signed in the archives.

October the king received word that certain persons were trying to enter the realm with documents harmful to the "rights and privileges" of the Hospitallers. The Italian merchants who were delivering these papers were ordered at once to surrender them to the royal officials.[63] Though the nature of these damaging documents remains unknown, it is more than likely that they represented a summons to the chapter-general that the anti-grand master had called for March, 1384, or some other attempt by Urban VI or his puppet to enforce their authority upon a priory they supposed loyal. The action of the king undoubtedly was taken at the request of Radyington, who had somehow convinced Richard that it was possible to be a loyal subject while also remaining faithful to the legitimate grand master.[64] Richard's desire to limit papal influence in England would have inclined him to accept Radyington's argument rather than suffer Rome to gain a measure of control by acting through the agency of its appointed grand master.[65] The support given to Rhodes did not harm England, and the money sent to the convent was used for a worthy purpose. But to send money to Rome was another matter. Urban and his small band of Hospitallers had no base of operations, and Richard could well imagine where the money would end: in the papal coffers.

In the spring of 1384 (March 28–April 6), Caracciolo held a chapter-general at Naples for the purpose of organizing the priories of those countries favorable to Rome. This meeting has been proclaimed as proof that England was within the Roman orbit, for Delaville le Roulx makes it appear that Hildebrand Inge and Robert Normanton attended.[66] The records of the meeting, however, show that this is incorrect. The documents reveal only that, among the many things "deliberated and decided," the two Englishmen were appointed joint receivers of the English priory,[67] and this is not proof that they were present. In fact, had they attended the chapter-general their names would have been recorded with those of the forty-five others in attendance.[68] The anti-grand

63. *CCR*, 1381–85, p. 329.

64. Radyington had already served as a trier of petitions, in the parliament of 1383, and was shortly to be appointed admiral of the king's fleet (*Rot. Parl.*, III, 151, and *CCR*, 1381–85, p. 523).

65. For an analysis of ecclesiastical politics under Richard II, see J. Dahmus, "Richard II and the Church," *Catholic Historical Review*, XXXIX (1954), 408–33.

66. Delaville le Roulx, *Hospitaliers*, p. 251.

67. Malta Archives, Vol. 281, fol. 6*r*.

68. *Ibid.*, fol. 1*rv*. Except for one German, all of those present when the meeting opened were Italians. Several influential Italians also were at Fernández de Heredia's 1383 chapter-general (Luttrell, "Intrigue, Schism, and Violence," p. 41). Luttrell

master's appointment of Inge and Normanton was only an empty gesture, made in the hope that England could be tempted to rally to his banner.

As a matter of fact, at the same time that the Knights were in assembly at Naples, Radyington ran up his true colors in England. In the Salisbury Parliament of 1384 the commons petitioned the king that the *responsions* of the Hospitallers be used by the government for the general aid and support of the realm. The thought had apparently occurred to them that these revenues were liable to seizure. As they saw it, the prior had no alternative but to pay them either to a schismatic grand master or to the Roman pope, and neither of these recipients was half so worthwhile as the "poor people" of England. To this plea the prior of St. John entered a counter petition, protesting that the island of Rhodes was a "frontier of Christianity" and that the *responsions* were used to carry on the holy war against the infidels. He begged that the king allow these revenues to be paid to the convent at Rhodes, as "ordained in the foundation of the Hospital and as the progenitors of the king had long suffered the order to do." Richard's answer was affirmative. He ordered that Radyington uphold the financial obligations of the English brethren to the convent for the maintenance of the war on behalf of Christianity. Only, said the king, if the prior did not dispose of the dues in the accustomed manner would the crown interfere in the matter.[69] This is perhaps the most striking document upon the entire question of the relations of the English priory with the "schismatics" of Rhodes. Certainly it is a clear example of the royal policy of noninterference, and should be enough in itself to explode any hypothesis of a rupture in the order so far as England was concerned.

But we do not have to be content merely with what the king and the prior said in the Salisbury Parliament, their words were soon transformed into deeds. At the moment the parliament was sitting, Radyington received word from Peter de Provins to make ready the *responsions*.[70] The next month the receiver-general was in England, where he collected no

---

throws much light on the Italian *langue*, and, in view of his conclusion that Urban "achieved only limited success" with this group, it seems that Italian nationalism also has been overemphasized during the Schism.

69. *Rot. Parl.*, III, 179. The petition of the commons referred to by the prior has been misplaced by the editor of the *Rotuli Parliamentorum* and is entered with the petitions of the parliament of 1385 (*ibid.*, p. 213).

70. Malta Archives, Vol. 48, fol. 123*v*.

less than 25,000 florins, the largest single payment ever recorded for the priory of England.[71] Unfortunately, Provins did not break this sum down into its component parts and only an "educated guess" is possible regarding what the money represented. The records show that the annual payments ran roughly around 2,500–3,000 florins and that no collections had been made since 1381. Thus, approximately 7,500–9,000 florins was the regular yearly installments of the *responsions*. To this we can add the 8,000 florin *taille* levied at Heredia's 1383 chapter-general. The remainder, almost 10,000 florins, must then be classified as *responsions* in arrears, the mortuaries of Hales and other deceased brethren, the rental of the magisterial *camera*, and miscellaneous dues regularly paid to the convent. There may even have been some money from Ireland. Inge and Normanton were collectors for that priory as well, and the Irish prior had been in England on business matters in December, 1383.[72] If so it was the last payment the convent was to see from this source for some time; the Irish had broken with Radyington on the question of recognizing Caracciolo.[73]

England's fidelity to Fernández de Heredia was rewarded in 1385. Aware that Caracciolo was attempting to secure control of the priory by making appointments, the grand master swamped the chancery clerks with a mass of bulls appointing brethren to richer preceptories and confirming others in those they held on a temporary basis. In this battle of appointments the advantage lay with Fernández de Heredia, who possessed the chancery records and knew which of the English Knights might be concerned about their status. The anti–grand master, on the other hand, had little knowledge of England, and thus nothing to offer individual members. All in all, Fernández de Heredia issued appointments and confirmations for thirteen English Hospitallers.[74] Bearing in

71. "Premier. en mois de May lan 1111^{xx} & 1111. Receu a londre de religieux personnes monseigneur le prieur dangleterre et freres Robert de normenton & Mdrebram Inge receveurs de lospital en dit priore en deduction des responcons aurragez dicellez mortuores & autres biens quelconques de uzau tresor de maistre et du convent de Rodez en dit priore dangleterre du temps passe la somme de V^{m} marc de sterllis monneys dangleterre *du temps passe* en pars et valeur de X^{m} nobles pour le valeur de XX^{m} francs quivalent florins court monneys davignon a paison de compte 1111 francs pour v florins . . . XXV^{m} florins." (*Ibid.*, fol. 88*v*.)

72. *CPR*, 1381–85, p. 344.

73. I hope to discuss this rupture in detail in an article on "The Irish Hospitallers During the Great Schism."

74. Richard de Multon was confirmed preceptor of Carbrooke, John de Ichyngton preceptor of Clanfield, Tilmannus Nydek preceptor of Trebeigh, John Brynkyl preceptor of Ossington, Richard Barrow preceptor of Dalby and Dingley, John Maydenston

mind that every bull bore his seal and came from Avignon, we have at least thirteen documents that refute the theory that the English brethren adhered to Rome.

While Fernández de Heredia was ensuring the loyalty of the English Knights, Radyington was making ready for a journey to Rhodes. He had planned to leave early in 1385[75] but had been delayed by Richard II's Scottish invasion in that year and by rumors that the French planned a massive invasion of England.[76] On February 5, 1386, however, Radyington finally secured permission from the king to sail for the convent.[77] At the same time, he was commissioned by Richard to transact "certain business" touching the realms of Cyprus and Rhodes.[78] Edouard Perroy has suggested that the purpose of this trip was to persuade the king of Cyprus and the convent of Rhodes to accept Urban VI.[79] This seems unlikely. We have already seen that Radyington was loyal to the legitimate grand master and that Richard II knew this but did not care. Under these circumstances the prior would have been an extremely poor missionary for converting Rhodes or Cyprus to Urban's cause. Moreover, had Radyington undertaken such a mission his reception at Rhodes would have been a warm one indeed. Less than two years before Fernández de Heredia had stripped the crusader's tunic from a "traitor Knight" and tossed him into a cell for life because he had tried to subvert the English and Germans at the convent by claiming that Caracciolo was the true grand master.[80]

---

preceptor of Maltby and Skirbeck, William Forkesden preceptor of Chibourne. Brian de Grey was appointed preceptor of Eagle for life because of his "efforts on behalf of the faith." Robert Normanton was appointed preceptor of Quennington, Henry Crownhale preceptor of Willoughton, Thurstan Gervase preceptor of Greenham, Thomas Skipwyth preceptor of Hardwick, and Hildebrand Wotton preceptor of Ansty. (Malta Archives, Vol. 323, fols. 135*r*–137*v*.)

75. *CPR*, 1385–89, p. 101.

76. Radyington was one of those appointed by the king to defend southern England during the royal absence (*ibid.*, p. 80).

77. Rymer, *op. cit.*, III, iii, 192.

78. L. de Mas Latrie, *Histoire de l'île de Chypre sous le règne des princes de la maison de Lusignan* (Paris, 1852–61), II, 401.

79. Perroy, *op. cit.*, p. 290. Elsewhere, however (pp. 93–94), Perroy indicates that he believes Radyington did not use this license, or others that were subsequently granted, because Rhodes was Clementine and no Englishman would have dared venture there.

80. Malta Archives, Vol. 24, fol. 10. Extracts from the trial proceedings have been published by Sebastiano Pauli in *Codice Diplomatico del Sacro Militare Ordine Gerosolimitano Oggi di Malta* (Lucca, 1733–37), II, 101. The background and importance of this incident is discussed by Luttrell in "Intrigue, Schism, and Violence" (pp. 42–46).

What Radyington did during his journey is not recorded. We know only that he left in 1386 and spent more than one year abroad. He arrived home again some time early in 1388, in time, one chronicler tells us, to witness the "merciless parliament."[81] For our thesis, however, the most interesting fact is simply that the English prior visited the convent and returned without incident.

During Radyington's journey, Hildebrand Inge supervised the order's affairs,[82] and it fell to him to pay the *responsions*. Like Radyington and Hales before him he had the option of not paying to schismatics. Indeed it might be said that the pressure upon him was somewhat greater, for Caracciolo had appointed a receiver-general for the priories of Roman obedience in 1385, and had sent one Gerard Enschede to England in April of the next year for "certain negotiations."[83] Inge, however, ignored all save his responsibility to the convent. In May, 1386, he paid 2,000 English marks to a Genoese merchant who changed it into 10,000 florins of Avignon and forwarded it to Peter de Provins, Fernández de Heredia's receiver-general.[84] Once again we have dramatic evidence of how little the English Hospitallers were disturbed by the existence of two popes and two grand masters.

Unfortunately, there is a deterioration in the archival material following the year 1388. In part this is due simply to the loss of manuscripts. Provins' account book, for example, terminates in that year and others that he must have kept have not been found. The *Liber Bullarum* for each year also degenerates in quality. Fernández de Heredia seems to have relaxed his supervision of the clerks, and their registration of his bulls—never good at best—came almost to a standstill. Only appointments or correspondence of considerable importance remains for the researcher. References to the numerous preceptors of the *langue*—their deaths, exchanges of estates, and appointments—fade to nothing, leaving us with information for only the leading figures of the priory. The meagerness of the archives for these years notwithstanding, some material does remain. This added to outside sources is more than sufficient to show that England, Avignon, and Rhodes continued their cooperation.

81. Thomas Favent, *Historia Siue Narracio de Modo et Forma Mirabilis Parliamenti apud Westmonasterium anno Domini Millesimo CCCLXXXVI*, ed. May McKisack, *Camden Miscellany*, XIV (London, 1926), p. 21. Radyington was back in England in May of 1388, and in July he served as a member of Richard II's council (*Registrum Johannis Gilbert, Episcopi Herefordensis*, ed. J. H. Parry [London, 1915], p. 121, and *CPR*, 1385–89, p. 502).

82. *CCR*, 1385–89, p. 424, and *Reg. Gilbert*, p. 121.

83. Malta Archives, Vol. 281, fols. 75*r*, 85*v*.

84. *Ibid.*, Vol. 48, fol. 146*r*.

One of the items in the *Liber Bullarum* is Fernández de Heredia's notification to Inge that Brian de Grey, the turcopolier, had died at the convent. In another letter of the same date, the grand master ordered the receiver to determine the possessions the dead man held so that Rhodes could await his mortuary and his preceptories could be distributed to others.[85] These aspects of Grey's demise, however, were of less importance to the *langue* than the problem of filling the high position he left vacant. In this particular instance the process took three years. But at length it was accomplished and Inge found himself called to the highest post his brethren could bestow upon him. On October 20, 1392, he was appointed turcopolier of Rhodes by Fernández de Heredia.[86]

We have evidence from other sources that Radyington traveled to Rhodes three more times after his 1386 voyage. The first of these journeys, in 1390, seems to have been intended only to convey the *responsions* to Rhodes. It is not entirely clear why the method of payment was changed, but thereafter it became the practice to pay directly to the convent rather than to Provins at Avignon. This may well have resulted from the greater ease with which the prior was able to move about in Italy following the death of Urban VI in 1389, for the death of that bellicose pope brought a lessening of tensions within the order. This also seems indicated from the conduct of the Venetians, who remained loyal to Rome and Urban's successors but allowed English marks to be changed into ducats and sent to the convent.[87]

The English prior received license from Richard II to leave England for Rhodes in March, 1390, and to take with him 1,000 English marks.[88] He delayed his departure, however, to coincide with that of the crusaders who were going to Barbary with Louis of Bourbon,[89] and was perhaps persuaded by them to join in their expedition before going on to Rhodes.[90] If this was the case he would have given his letters of exchange to Genoese bankers while the crusaders were gathering in that city preparatory to embarking. These bankers, in turn, would have sent the money via

85. The letter is dated September 29, 1389 (Avignon); Malta Archives, Vol. 324, fols. 96*r*–97*r*.

86. *Ibid.*, Vol. 326, fol. 100*r*.

87. Radyington, in 1389, had sent 7,000 ducats to Rhodes via Venice (Luttrell, "Venice and the Knights Hospitallers," p. 209).

88. *CPR*, 1388–92, p. 205.

89. Monk of Westminster in Ranulph Higden's *Polychronicon* (London, 1865–86), IX, 234.

90. After the crusade, several ships sailed for Rhodes (Jean Froissart, *Oeuvres*, ed. K. de Lettenhove [Brussels, 1867–77], XIV, 274).

Venice, the most direct line of communication with Rhodes. This seems all the more probable since Luttrell discovered in the Venetian archives documents which show that in 1391 the English prior sent via Venice 8,000 ducats, or approximately 1,000 marks.[91]

We do not know that Radyington returned to England in 1391. If he did, it was only for a short time, for in March, 1392, he was campaigning in the Morea.[92] Later in the same year, either at Venice or Vienna, he joined company with Henry, Earl of Derby, who was on his way to the Holy Land,[93] and together the two made their way to Jerusalem, stopping at Rhodes both on the way and on their return. Derby's household accounts even relate that, while at Rhodes, Radyington was sent on an embassy to the king of Cyprus, a court with which he was familiar because of his voyage of 1386–87.[94]

During Radyington's absence with Derby the anti–grand master made an effort to locate the itinerant prior, but was informed by Richard II that he was somewhere in the East performing feats of arms.[95] Although Perroy takes this letter as proof that Radyington should have been on his way to Rome, and believes the king's answer is an indication of rather close relations between the English Knights and Rome,[96] it is easier to argue that the letter is evidence of rather poor relations, for it reveals that Caracciolo had little or no contact with the English priory and did not know the whereabouts of the prior. Had the rapport suggested by Perroy existed between the English Knights and the anti–grand master, the latter could have contacted one of the brethren present in England and asked for information instead of bothering the king. Nor can any importance be attached to the polite nature of Richard's answer; he was merely being diplomatic in an awkward situation. There was no need to tell Caracciolo that Radyington was frequently going to or coming from Rhodes. Certainly, in the face of the massive evidence showing the prior's loyalty to Fernández de Heredia, no great weight can be given to a single piece of correspondence that merely asks questions.

In March, 1394, Fernández de Heredia ordered Radyington to

91. Luttrell, "Venice and the Knights Hospitallers," p. 199.

92. Malta Archives, Vol. 325, fol. 100*r*. There is evidence that Radyington participated in the battle of Nicopolis Minor; see my "The English at Nicopolis," *Speculum*, XXXVII (1962), 536–40.

93. *Expeditions to Prussia and the Holy Land Made by Henry, Earl of Derby*, ed. L. Smith (London, 1894), pp. lviii–lix.

94. *Ibid.*, p. 226.

95. *The Diplomatic Correspondence of Richard II*, ed. E. Perroy (London, 1933), pp. 114–15.

96. Perroy, *op. cit.*, p. 94, n. 1.

Rhodes. A grand campaign was being prepared against the Turks and the grand master was calling together every available man.[97] By July, 1395, the crusading prior was ready to leave, and in that month secured license to travel again to Rhodes.[98] Apparently, however, Radyington did little more than shepherd the English contingent to the convent and pay the *responsions*.[99] By 1396 he was back in England, and in the same year died at Clerkenwell.[100]

In the fifteen years that he was prior, Radyington did not abandon Fernández de Heredia for a moment. Although he had ample opportunity to do so—and, according to a nationalistic interpretation, ought to have done so—he ignored all efforts to bring the English Hospitallers into the Roman fold. His journeys, the payment of the *responsions*, and the acceptance of positions by members of the priory are so numerous that to continue to cling to the belief that England deserted Fernández de Heredia is quite unrealistic.[101] During the period of his rule we also see a continuation of the policy of the government in letting the order handle its own affairs. Although Prior Radyington sat high in the council of the king and served him loyally in many capacities, no effort was made to pressure him into joining the Urbanite Hospitallers.[102] So long as the order did not trouble Richard II, he did not trouble it.

97. Malta Archives, Vol. 328, fol. 118*r*.

98. Rymer, *op. cit.*, III, iv, 109. Attorneys appointed for his absence (*CPR*, 1391–96, p. 622).

99. Radyington took 8,500 ducats through Venice (Luttrell, "Venice and the Knights Hospitallers," p. 199).

100. The date of Radyington's death is given as 1399 in the lists of King and Porter, but his successor was appointed in September, 1396 (Malta Archives, Vol. 330, fol. 76*r*). I also was wrong in my suggestion that Radyington probably died in the East, perhaps at Nicopolis ("English at Nicopolis," p. 539), for his tomb was seen at Clerkenwell shortly before the priory was destroyed (John Stowe, *A Survey of London*, London, 1908 [reprint of 1603 ed.]), II, 85.

101. The sisters of the order of St. John also continued to look to Rhodes. In 1387, Peter Culant, Fernández de Heredia's lieutenant at the convent, ratified actions they had taken relative to various properties in England, and in 1391 he requested that the English Knights elect an "elderly or chaste" Hospitaller to oversee the sisters' house at Buckland (*A Cartulary of Buckland Priory in the County of Somerset*, ed. F. W. Weaver [London, 1909], pp. 16–20).

102. Radyington was a member of the king's council in 1388, 1389, and 1395; in 1394 he was one of those appointed to negotiate a truce with the Scots, and on many occasions he was admiral of the fleet (*Proceedings and Ordinances of the Privy Council* [*1386–1542*], ed. H. N. Nicolas [London, 1834–37], I, 11, 17, and J. F. Baldwin, *The King's Council in England during the Middle Ages* [Oxford, 1913], pp. 504–5; Rymer, *op. cit.*, III, iv, 102; *CCR*, 1381–85, p. 523; *CCR*, 1385–89, pp. 651–52; *CCR*, 1389–92, pp. 88, 485; *CCR*, 1392–96, p. 75).

IV. Prior Walter Grendon (1396–1409)

The man selected to fill Radyington's post was Walter Grendon, who was appointed prior September 25, 1396.[103] With his appearance the drama of the schism moves into its second act; the theme and scenery remain the same but a new cast takes over from the old. Fernández de Heredia, who died in the same year as Radyington, was replaced by Philibert de Nailhac, formerly prior of Aquitaine. Death also had removed Caracciolo, in 1395, and the new pope, Boniface IX, who had succeeded Urban VI in 1389, changed the Roman tactics slightly. Rather than appoint another anti–grand master to oppose the master recognized by Rhodes, Boniface convoked an assembly of Italian Hospitallers and set up a commission to govern the portion of the order that was loyal to Rome. The acts and appointments of Caracciolo were annulled and the office of grand master was declared vacant. Until the vacancy could be filled by a proper election, Bartholomew Carafa, Prior of Rome, was to act as lieutenant–grand master, and, in concert with the commission, supervise the administration of the priories of Roman obedience.[104]

This move by Boniface was interpreted by Delaville le Roulx as an attempt to heal the schism within the order.[105] At first glance such a hypothesis appears to have merit, particularly if the nullification of Caracciolo's appointments is stressed. But subsequent events show that the theory is unjustified and that the pope's motivation must be examined more closely.

The pope was trying to extricate the Roman See from the untenable position into which it had been plunged by Urban's direct appointment of a grand master. That maneuver had gained nothing for the Roman faction; Caracciolo had been ignored by all save a few of his fellow Italians. Thus Boniface skillfully avoided any such direct and high-handed interference with the order. The commission, elected by the Italians and headed by Carafa, was ostensibly managing the Hospital until the Knights could elect their own grand master. With Fernández de Heredia old and ill, the pope gambled upon human nature to drag hopeful candidates toward Rome when he died. The fiction that the grand mastership was vacant was intended to serve as a lure for natural

103. "Allatus supradictum prioratum angleterre nuper per nos ad annos decem de anno nonagesimo sexto die viasima quinta mensis septembris" (Malta Archives, Vol. 330, fol. 76*r*).

104. *Ibid.*, Vol. 1129, fols. 154*rv*. The papal bull is published in Pauli, *op. cit.*, II, 105.

105. Delaville le Roulx, *Hospitaliers*, pp. 261–62.

ambition. Similarly, the setting aside of the acts of Caracciolo was designed to induce defection from the ranks of those loyal to Rhodes. New appointments would have to be made by a new grand master, and the Knights who came to Rome would have an opportunity to share in their distribution.

The strategy of Boniface, imaginative but ineffective, was continued by succeeding Roman popes. Carafa served as lieutenant–grand master during the supposed vacancy, until his death in 1405.[106] Innocent VIII, the next Roman pope, then appointed Nicolas Orsini, Prior of Venice, to the lieutenancy, and he was still serving in that capacity when the Schism came to a close.[107]

In theory, then, it should have been to these lieutenant–grand masters that the English Knights adhered. But they did not. Grendon and the brethren in England remained loyal to Philibert de Nailhac. When it became obvious to Boniface IX that his plan was not going to work, he summoned the English prior to Rome for the purpose of electing a new grand master.[108] It is doubtful, however, if Grendon heard of this summons until it was too late; he spent almost his entire career at Rhodes. His first journey was a short one, in 1398, probably for the purpose of personally acquainting himself with his fellows in garrison there and acknowledging his allegiance to De Nailhac.[109] In May, 1399, he was at Venice, again on his way to the East.[110] He returned from this voyage in December, 1400, in the company of Manuel II, the Byzantine emperor, who was touring the West seeking aid for his beleaguered capital.[111] Immediately thereafter Grendon departed for the convent[112] and remained at Rhodes until the new king of England, Henry IV, summoned him

106. Malta Archives, Vol. 1129, fol. 158*r*, and Vol. 1141, fols. 289*r*, 305*r*. Ugo Orlandini, "Il sepolcro di Bartolomeo Carafa, Gran Priore dell'Ordine di San Giovanni," *Rivista dell Collegio Araldico*, V (1907), 279–81.

107. Malta Archives, Vol. 1129, fol. 164*r*.

108. The summons is dated November 5, 1399; the meeting was to be held November 1, 1400 (*Papal Registers*, V, 249).

109. Rymer, *op. cit.*, III, iv, 141. Attorneys appointed for his absence (*CPR*, 1396–99, p. 273).

110. Archivio di Stato di Venezia: Senato Misti, Vol. XLIV, fol. 99*v*. I am indebted to Professor Donald Queller for this information.

111. E. F. Jacob, *The Fifteenth Century* (Oxford, 1961), p. 77. Grendon's permit to leave the convent is dated October 28, 1400 (Malta Archives, Vol. 330, fol. 134*v*).

112. Grendon was not present in February, 1401, when Peter Holt, Prior of Ireland, presented England's contribution to the Greek emperor (*Royal and Historical Letters of Henry IV*, ed. F. C. Hingeston [London, 1860], I, 56–57). During this absence Robert Normanton acted as lieutenant-prior in England (British Museum, Cotton MSS, Nero E. VI., fol. 275*v*).

home to aid in suppressing the rebellions that plagued the early years of his reign.[113]

It was during these numerous trips that the summons came from Boniface, and, in the absence of the prior, was brought to the attention of the king. Henry, an old friend of Radyington, and favorably disposed toward the order, issued an order in August, 1400, forbidding either the prior of England or the prior of Ireland to travel without the king's express permission.[114] Such interference by the king could hardly have been motivated by anything other than a desire to guard the Hospitallers from Rome. His order protected the two priors from possible charges of disobedience by making the crown responsible for their absence from the pope's intended assembly. It also is obvious that Henry had no intention of prohibiting contacts between the Knights and Rhodes; at the time of his command, Grendon was residing at the convent.[115] Thus from the very beginning of his reign Henry IV indicated that he intended to pursue a policy identical to that of his predecessor.

Grendon's recall by Henry IV in 1401 kept the prior in England only a few months. As soon as affairs were securely in hand, he packed off to Rhodes again, a request for his safe-conduct having been issued on December 5, 1401.[116] It was during this sojourn among his brethren at the convent that he participated, with the grand master, in the expedition of the French marshal, Jean Boucicaut, who was campaigning in the East. Of this there cannot be the slightest doubt; his name appears as a witness to a treaty signed between Boucicaut and the king of Cyprus.[117] It was not until October, 1404, that Grendon asked for and received permission to leave the convent and return to England.[118]

The prior returned home early in 1405 and immediately renewed his permission to go to Rhodes, this time it being specified that the license was good for three years.[119] He may have soon returned to the convent but it seems doubtful as there are no requests for him to leave Rhodes in the years 1405 or 1406.[120] Henry IV apparently had caught him "at home"

113. Rymer, *op. cit.*, III, iv, 188; *CCR*, 1399–1401, p. 248.

114. *CPR*, 1399–1401, p. 354.

115. See n. 111.

116. Rymer, *op. cit.*, IV, i, 19.

117. Mas Latrie, *Chypre*, II, 466–71.

118. Malta Archives, Vol. 333, fol. 73*r*.

119. Rymer, *op. cit.*, IV, i, 78. It is perhaps significant that Grendon also had Henry IV confirm the petition Radyington had made to the parliament of 1384 (*CPR*, 1405–8, p. 15).

120. In June, 1405, Grendon presided over a provincial chapter of the English Knights at Clerkenwell (St. John's Gate MSS, St. John's Gate, London, K2/34).

long enough to assign him to a royal commission that had been appointed to settle trade disputes between England and the Teutonic Knights.[121] Grendon must have returned to Rhodes in late 1406 or early 1407 and renewed his crusading ventures. We know that he was away from England in May of 1407 because the "visitation" appointment of Peter Holt to the English *langue* was not addressed to the prior as it would have been had he been present.[122] Finally, we have evidence that Grendon was at Rhodes in September, 1408, for he was at that time given permission to return to England.[123] In December of the same year Henry IV promised the clergy of Aquitaine that Grendon would be among the English delegation that was being readied for the Council of Pisa.[124] Thus we may assume that the English prior, along with the grand master, stood on the sidelines as the church proceeded to unify itself—at least so far as the Hospitallers were concerned—by electing Alexander V.

During the years of the Schism that fell within Grendon's leadership of the English priory there is massive evidence demonstrating the loyalty of the English Knights to Nailhac and Rhodes. There is, in fact, so much that it is impossible to list it all. Of confirmations, appointments, and promotions there are many, and the same type of detailed evidence is available for the payments of the *responsions*. Between 1400 and 1409 there is almost a complete record of receipts given to the receivers of England for moneys paid into the treasury of the order.[125] Further evidence to support the thesis that the English Hospitallers adhered to the legitimate grand masters can be found in the manner in which they filled their ranks. There was an established routine of long standing and it continued without interruption during the period when two popes and two grand masters vied for the allegiance of men.

The numerical strength of the English *langue* depended upon the property it held, for this was the means by which it sustained its members. By the end of the fourteenth century a decline in numbers had started. The Hospitallers, like other landowners in that age, were caught in the vise of customary rents and rising prices. Still, life was hazardous in an order committed to continual war, and usually there was a need for new men after each season's campaigning. Of recruits there seemed to be no shortage; the order's cross offered adventure and privileges, and—if one survived—security in old age.

121. *CPR*, 1405–8, pp. 153, 234, 237, 301.
122. Malta Archives, Vol. 334, fols. 101*v*–102*r*.
123. *Ibid.*, fol. 105*r*.
124. Rymer, *op. cit.*, IV, i, 146.
125. See table.

PAYMENT OF THE *Responsions*

Date of Receipt	*Sum (Ducats)*	*English Officer*	*Malta Archives Volume & Folio*
September, 1400	6,000	Hildebrand Wotton	330, 133*r*
May, 1402	5,000	Hildebrand Wotton	332, 174*v*
November, 1403	4,400	John de Ichyngton	332, 181*r*
September, 1404	6,000	Hildebrand Wotton	333, 133*r*
1404 (month unknown) . . .	2,500	Walter Grendon	333, 133*r*
November, 1406	5,000	Hildebrand Wotton	333, 137*v*
September, 1407	5,000	Unspecified	334, 145*r*
(In addition to the above payments, Henry Crownhale, the English receiver of the magisterial *camera* (West Peckham, Kent), paid into the treasury of the convent the following sums:)			
July, 1402	600		332, 110*r*
July, 1402	600		332, 175*v*
November, 1403	600		332, 181*v*
October, 1406	1,200		333, 128*r*
September, 1407	600		334, 145*v*
August, 1409	1,200		337, 129*v*

Once admitted into the order, a new member was sent to the convent for a three-year tour of duty; he then was appointed to a preceptory, if one was vacant, or placed on a seniority list to await his turn. Until the end of his life the Knight's service alternated between England and Rhodes, depending upon the needs of the order and his physical ability to undertake the required military service. By gradually moving up the seniority list he could expect to exchange the smaller preceptory with which he had begun his career for richer ones, or perhaps add to it, again depending upon the situation at a particular time.

Throughout the Schism this system continued undisturbed. There are licenses for members of the English priory to bring at least forty new members into the order and we can reasonably assume that at least half as many members were unregistered. These permits to enlist men would have produced ten recruits in the time of John Radyington[126] and thirty in the time of Walter Grendon.[127] That these permits were used is not

126. Radyington received permission to recruit six men and John Brynkyl to recruit one man in 1382 (Malta Archives, Vol. 321, fol. 137*v*). In 1391, Hildebrand Inge received a license to recruit three men (*ibid.*, Vol. 325, fol. 128*r*).

127. In 1400, Grendon was given permission to enlist thirteen brothers; Henry Crownhale three brothers, and Thurstan Gervase two brothers (*ibid.*, Vol. 330, fols. 74*v*, 75*r*, 79*v*). In 1404, Grendon was to enroll four brothers, Peter Holt ten in 1407, and John Seyville two in 1408 (*ibid.*, Vol. 333, fol. 73*v*; Vol. 334, fols. 102*v* and 107*r*).

difficult to demonstrate. In one instance a scribe recorded the entry of a man into "the religion," and in another the receiver-general paid for a habit for a new member.[128] Also, there are many references to the deaths of the brethren in the appointments of new men to the places left vacant; in fact, by 1409 there are few names that definitely predate the outbreak of the Schism. Names found earlier in the records are mentioned no more: Inge, Radyington, Grey, Normanton, Gervase, and others belonged to the past; a new generation had enrolled to fight the Turk. Unless we assume that such men as Richard Paule,[129] William Hulles,[130] and Thomas Launcelure[131] (still active in the third decade of the fifteenth century) entered the ranks during the dual papacy, we must suppose that by 1430 the English *langue* was composed almost entirely of septuagenarians.

Another item of importance during the time of Prior Grendon deserves notice: Peter Holt's difficulty in having his title, Turcopolier of Rhodes and Prior of Ireland, recognized. Appointed turcopolier in August, 1396, and prior of Ireland at an earlier date, Holt, like Grendon, preferred the Eastern clime.[132] His activities, and particularly the fact that he spent most of his time in England or in the East, did not set well with his brethren in Ireland. To remedy this situation and to regain control of the priory of Ireland, a band of dissident Knights, headed by Robert White, entered an appeal at Rome. In February, 1400, Boniface IX answered this appeal by stating that the lieutenant–grand master, Bartholomew Carafa, had confirmed the election of White by the group

128. Henry Crownhale in 1381 and John Kylquyt in 1400 (*ibid.*, Vol. 48, fol. 39*v*, and Vol. 330, fol. 74*v*).

129. First mentioned in 1401 as lieutenant-turcopolier at Rhodes, Paule left the convent in the same year. Paule held the preceptories of Maltby and Skiebeck (before 1408), Dinmore and Garway (1408), Yeavely and Barrow (1408), and Temple Brewer (1415); he held Temple Brewer at the time of his death, in 1431 (*ibid.*, Vol. 331, fols. 111*r*, 188*v*; Vol. 334, fols. 103*v*–104*r*, 107*r*; Vol. 339, fol. 148*v*, and Vol. 350, fol. 112*v*).

130. Hulles was preceptor of Templecombe in 1396 and of Baddesley in 1397 (Winchester College, Muniments, 12843, and British Museum Harleian MSS fol. 72), but he was not mentioned in the archives until 1399, when he was appointed to Swingfield. He was elected prior in 1417 and died in that post in 1433 (Malta Archives, Vol. 330, fol. 74*r*, and Vol. 340, fol. 111*rv*).

131. Launcelure is first mentioned in 1408, when he was given permission to leave the convent. In 1415 he was appointed to the preceptory of Dalby and Rothley, after the death of Peter Holt. Elected turcopolier in 1423, Launcelure held that position until his death, in 1441 (*ibid.*, Vol. 334, fol. 106*v*; Vol. 339, fol 151*r*, and *Official Correspondence of Thomas Bekynton*, ed. G. Williams [London, 1872], I, 211–12).

132. Malta Archives, Vol. 329, fol. 91*r*.

opposed to Holt, and that the latter was deposed for failure to pay the *responsions* as well as for other unspecified delinquencies.[133] Holt, who was then in England, entered an appeal to Henry IV.[134] On November 16, 1400, the king ordered that his lieutenant in Ireland restore Holt, who had been rightfully appointed while he was "by license of the late king at Rhodes in the service of God resisting the unbeliever."[135] Robert White, who had appealed to Rome, was summoned to the royal presence to explain why he had opposed the legitimate prior of Ireland.[136] Evidently his reasons were not deemed valid, for Henry issued a new order—in September, 1401—that again ordered the restoration of Holt.[137]

Royal commands were easy to give but difficult to enforce in medieval Ireland. The prior's continual absence and the political turmoil of the country made effective execution of Henry's order impossible. Though Holt was regarded as prior of Ireland by the English Knights, the grand master and the convent, and the king of England, Robert White continued to be recognized by Boniface IX and the Irish Knights.[138] Most important, White was actually in Ireland and thus in a position to exercise de facto control of the priory, with or without the king's approval. Throughout the period 1402 to 1407, the years of Holt's residence at Rhodes, he lived off the income of English preceptories that had been "lent" him by Walter Grendon.[139] Not until 1407, when he returned to England as a visitor-general, was Holt in a position to press effectively his claim to Ireland.

Before setting out from the convent, Holt took care to have himself confirmed prior of Ireland again.[140] When he arrived home, however, he found the situation slightly changed. Robert White, perhaps aware that Holt was coming with the full weight of the order behind him, quietly

133. *Papal Registers*, V, 323.

134. Holt was given permission to remain in England on the very day that the Knights loyal to Rome were to elect a new grand master (*CPR*, 1399–1401, p. 372, and n. 108).

135. *CCR*, 1399–1401, p. 225.

136. *Ibid.*

137. *Ibid.*, p. 373.

138. Styled "Prior of Ireland" in a brief of the pope in March, 1404 (*Papal Registers*, V, 626).

139. Malta Archives, Vol. 332, fol. 110*r*. For Holt's career, see my "Peter Holt, Turcopolier of Rhodes and Prior of Ireland," *Annales de l'Ordre souverain militaire de Malte*, XXII (1964), 82–85.

140. Malta Archives, Vol. 334, fol. 100*r*.

transferred his claims to the priory to Thomas Boutiller, who promptly began calling himself prior. Holt, of course, did not care what the name of the other claimant was; he was sure that he alone was the rightful prior. So too was Henry IV after he was made aware that his two previous orders had not been carried out. The king immediately issued an order that spelled out quite clearly what had been the attitude of England's monarchs throughout the Schism. It was declared that "all priories, bailiwicks, preceptories . . . pertaining to the master and convent of Rhodes belong to the same master and convent." Furthermore, said the king, no person could hold a title in the order of St. John without appointment from the said "master and convent." Therefore, because Holt held such a title and Robert White and Thomas Boutiller did not, Holt was ordered restored.[141]

Obviously, the wishes of Boniface IX and Bartholomew Carafa had nothing to do with the traditional rights of the grand master of Rhodes over appointments within the order. In so stating the king was doing nothing more than committing to writing and making a matter of official record the recognition that he and Richard II had extended to the acts of the grand master when requested, the Schism within the church notwithstanding. This attitude of the English kings very definitely shows that the government did not reckon the division in the church as having any legal implications for the Knights of St. John.

V. Conclusion

A close examination of the traditional interpretation of the behavior of the English Hospitallers during the Great Schism reveals that it is quite untenable. As explained in the introduction, the view has prevailed because of scholarly apathy and assumption. Indeed only one "fact"—a letter of Richard II to anti–grand master Richard Caracciolo—has been offered as support for the thesis that the English Knights adhered to the Roman faction of the order. Prior to the publication of this bit of evidence, supporters of the thesis relied wholly upon tradition and a firm belief in the strength of fourteenth-century nationalism.

The evidence presented in this study drives one inescapably to the conclusion that the exact opposite of the generally entertained opinion is

141. Rymer, *op. cit.*, IV, i, 130, and *CPR*, 1405–8, p. 430.

true. That is to say, the English Hospitallers did not dissociate themselves from their Clementine grand masters or the convent but remained loyal to both throughout the Schism. It has been shown, for example, that two English priors, John Radyington and Walter Grendon, owed their positions to appointments by "schismatics" and that both made repeated trips to Rhodes for military service and administrative purposes. During the time they held office there is massive evidence showing appointments of English brethren to preceptories by both Fernández de Heredia and Nailhac; the bulls of the former coming, in most cases, from the court of the Avignon pope. Under Radyington, Grendon, and their predecessor, Robert Hales, the *responsions*, mortuaries, *tailles*, and other dues were paid without question, sometimes to a collector from Avignon, sometimes by direct transportation to Rhodes.

In contrast to their friendly relations with Avignon, the English priors ignored the Roman faction of the order. Caracciolo and the later lieutenants not only had no power over the English but almost no contact with officers of the English *langue*. Even the Roman pontiff was unsuccessful in his efforts to secure control of the priory. When the pope summoned the English brethren to Rome, they did not appear; when he made appointments or sent bulls that touched their order, they appealed to the king and the pope was rebuffed.

From such behavior another conclusion follows: the English Hospitallers were not nationalistic. The emotionalism found in the early years of the Schism did not affect them, nor did they feel obliged to obey Urban VI simply because he was regarded as "our pope" by Englishmen. The appeal of Radyington in the parliament of 1384 is dramatic evidence that the order considered the maintenance of the "holy war" against the foes of Christendom more important than national considerations. Poverty in England and a divided church notwithstanding, the prior saw his first duty as the defense of Rhodes, the frontier of the faith. If the Schism is seen—as some have seen it—as a result of the clash of a growing nationalism with the older spirit of internationalism,[142] it is clear that the English Knights stood in the ancient ways. Their principle was ever unity, never nationality.

If the Hospitallers were not nationalistic, how were they regarded by their fellow Englishmen who supposedly were? On the basis of our evidence it appears that no one cared whether the Hospitallers obeyed a

142. There is a good discussion of this point in the first chapter of W. Ullmann, *The Origins of the Great Schism* (London, 1951).

Clementine or an Urbanite grand master, or whether they traveled to Rhodes or to Rome. Thus the strength of nationalism and the hatred of schismatics seems to have been considerably less than we have been led to believe.

It cannot be argued that Englishmen were ignorant of the Knights' activities. The petition of the commons in 1384 reveals that it was common knowledge that the *responsions* were being paid to Rhodes. Although it would also have been known that the convent was loyal to Fernández de Heredia, no great cry was raised on the issue of "schismatics." The commons were basically motivated by the desire to find some portion of society that could help them bear the cost of government; their favorite candidate was always some part of the church. When the king dashed their hopes of seizing the Hospital's revenues, however, nothing more was heard of the project.

The English church hierarchy knew what the Hospitallers were doing. Hales and Radyington, and to a lesser extent, Grendon, were important figures in political life, as were most of the bishops, and it is unthinkable that their movements could have escaped attention.[143] Despite the fact that the priors frequently went to Rhodes, accepted offices and orders from schismatics, and carried money from the realm, no English churchman attempted to carry out Urban VI's order to excommunicate everyone loyal to Fernández de Heredia. Nor is there any indication that an effort was made to enforce the pope's command that all contacts cease between England and the convent.

More important and more interesting than the attitude of parliament or the clergy is that of England's kings. Both Richard II and Henry IV were well aware of the "unnationalistic" conduct of the Knights. Still they preferred this conduct to control of the priory by Rome, as their intervention on several occasions testifies. But why should this be so if English policy during the Schism was firmly based upon support of the Roman papacy? The answer, of course, is that England's monarchs did not envision their support of Rome against Avignon in international politics as entailing the submission of the English church to the Roman pontiff. The Knights of St. John had always been fiercely independent, and, since the beginning of the century, had become even more independent as a

143. The Archbishop of Canterbury certainly knew that officers of the *langue* were in contact with Rhodes, and there is a letter that was written by Peter Holt, Turcopolier of Rhodes, to the archbishop c. 1401. The letter was carried to England by Walter Grendon, who was returning from the convent. (*Anglo-Norman Letters and Petitions*, ed. D. Legge [Oxford, 1941], p. 380.)

result of their sovereignty over Rhodes. To have allowed a pope to compromise that independence would have meant a diminution of the "liberties" of the English church, and this the island's crowned heads were understandably reluctant to do. It was consistent with royal interests and past policy to block papal maneuvers designed to bring the Hospital under Roman control, and the fact that there were two popes did not in the least alter the determination of England's rulers. The easiest way to thwart the pope was by allowing the Hospitallers to continue their obedience to the grand master and the convent.

Although all of these conclusions are "revisionist," the findings as a whole are not inconsistent with recent research upon the Schism. There has been a general scholarly awareness that nineteenth- and early twentieth-century historians have greatly overemphasized nationalism as a factor in the division of the church and of particular orders.[144] The explanation of virtually everything that happened during this era as the result of strong national sentiment—though still found in some textbooks—is gradually being recognized as a distorted interpretation.

144. H. M. Colvin's recent study of the Premonstratensian order places the blame for division within their ranks on "ecclesiastical profiteers" rather than on nationalism (*The White Canons in England* [Oxford, 1951], pp. 219–20).

BENZO D'ALESSANDRIA AND THE CITIES OF NORTHERN ITALY

Joseph R. Berrigan

University of Georgia

BENZO D'ALESSANDRIA AND THE CITIES OF NORTHERN ITALY*

By the beginning of the fourteenth century, northern Italy had several circles of lawyer-humanists, but the most promising circle was Padua, with such members as Lovato Lovati and Albertino Mussato.[1] Mussato, particularly, was a person of outstanding abilities, and was mentioned by Caluccio Salutati in his discussion of the origins of humanism.[2] The classics did more than charm Mussato, they challenged him to emulation; his work in history, poetry, and drama is of first-rate quality.[3]

Verona did not equal Padua in men of Mussato's stature; it was represented by such men as Guglielmo da Pastrengo and Giovanni Mansionario, and by Benzo d'Alessandria, who came to Verona from Milan.[4] All of the Veronese scholars flourished on the city's capitular library; indeed, Roberto Weiss believes that the "antiquarian" nature of early Veronese humanism is explained by the library and its "collection of classical texts unrivalled in Italy."[5] West of Verona was Lombardy, whose pre-humanist circle centered on Milan and Como. Lombardy was the weakest of the three circles, for—aside from Benzo—only Giovanni da Cermenate merits mention. Lombardy's interest was primarily historical, as the *Chronicon* of Benzo and the *Historia* of Da Cermenate testify.

The products of these circles vary—chiefly literary in Padua, antiquarian in Verona, and historical in Milan—but all represented different aspects of pre-humanism. Elements that were common to all three circles are legal training, appreciation of classical texts, a critical spirit, creative impulse, and many medieval forms and styles. Characteristic of pre-humanism is a lack of precision—a state between two relatively clear and

* The author expresses his thanks to Professor Charles Till Davis for his inspiration and constant encouragement, and to Professor Hans Baron for his close examination and determined betterment of the manuscript.

1. For an evaluation of one aspect of their work, see Guido Billanovich, "'Veterum vestigia vatum' nei carmi dei preumanisti padovani," *Italia Medioevale e Umanistica*, I (1958), 155–243.

2. See E. Garin, *L'Umanesimo Italiano* (Bari, 1952), pp. 27–28.

3. See G. Saitta, *L'Umanesimo* (Florence, 1961), p. 6.

4. For a general view of the Verona circle, see C. Cipolla, "Attorno a Giovanni Mansionario e a Guglielmo da Pastrengo," *Miscellanea Ceriani* (Milan, 1910).

5. R. Weiss, *The Dawn of Humanism in Italy* (London, 1947), p. 12.

distinct cultures. Pre-humanism shares in both what had been and what was yet to be.

The fusion of distinct qualities is profoundly characteristic of the work of Benzo d'Alessandria. Nothing—for example—could be more medieval than a bulky compilation of universal history. The *Chronicon*[6] begins with the creation, its manner of presentation is basically medieval, and evidence is admitted from authors whom tradition had established as authorities. The whole *Chronicon* proclaims a continuity with the past and the persistence of decisive elements that must be considered medieval, but all this is coupled with elements that herald the coming age.

Benzo, not satisfied with the conventional lore, sought new sources for his work; intending to write a book of permanent value, he made every effort to enrich it with the choicest quotations. Although the discovery of new texts often leads to an unquestioning acquiescence in the testimony they embody, this fault is not found in Benzo, who joined astute critical faculties to his other qualities. No name put him in awe; no text was exempt from his critical sense; he was awake to the possibility of textual corruption and to the inevitability of human error. No two authors are interchangeable—there is a hierarchy, with such historians as Livy ranked at the very top; discernment is one of Benzo's finest qualities.

A counterpart of his critical acumen is the clear-sightedness with which he viewed contemporary Italy. He could see the structure of society cracking apart. The evidence could be found in almost every city with which he dealt. The keen intelligence Benzo exerted when dealing with authors and texts did not desert him as he looked out on Italy. An age of violent transition found in Benzo a man who could understand its turbulence, at least partially because he was himself a transitional figure.

Benzo drew together two of the traditions of pre-humanism, those of Lombardy and Verona. Although he conceived the scheme of his greatest work in Lombardy, and carried it through to completion there, Verona provided him with indispensable material; and the best of these two circles is found in this notary-encyclopedist. Unfortunately, however, only a third of all his work is extant.

The *Chronicon* is a leatherbound volume of 285 parchment leaves in folio. The writing is in a fully developed fourteenth-century Gothic hand,

6. MS B 24 inf. of the Ambrosian Library, hereafter referred to as Benzo. The manuscript has been studied by such scholars as L. A. Ferrai and R. Sabbadini. Sabbadini quoted extensively from it in his *Le scoperte dei codici latini e greci ne'secoli xiv e xv* (Florence, 1914), and Ferrai published a transcription of the chapter on Milan in *Bullettino dell' Istituto Storico Italiano,* IX (1890), 15–36.

with colored capitals and chapter headings. On several pages the ink has faded badly, and on some of these pages there has been an attempt to trace over the letters—with consequent distortions. These poor pages are particularly frequent in Book XIV, the most popular of the entire work, but, although they are difficult to read, they are rarely illegible. There are many marginal notations in fourteenth- and seventeenth-century hands, particularly in Book XIV. It is clear from a passage in the chapter on Padua that Benzo did not write the body of the text himself, and a comparison of the extant samples of his handwriting shows that he did not write the notes.[7]

The twenty-four books of the *Chronicon* fall into four general sections. The first ten books are concerned with sacred history, from the Creation to the destruction of Jerusalem, and the last chapter of Book X is an encomium on Josephus—a well-deserved one, for the entire first section of the *Chronicon* is essentially based on Josephus's works (the *Antiquitates Judaicae* and the *De Bello Judaico*). Books XI to XIV are geographical and deal with bodies of water, nations and provinces, mountains, and the cities of the world (we shall say more of Book XIV shortly). The next five books are devoted to Macedonia, Alexander, and Alexander's successors. The final five books relate the early history of Greece, and the last book is a mythological as well as a historical treatise on the heroes of Greece.

Benzo did not compose a distinct work on the cities of northern Italy, which are treated within the framework of the book on the cities of the world (Book XIV) and which is part of the larger geographical section. There is material on all of the cities of the then known world, and many biblical and Greek cities are discussed. There are also some chapters on cities of western Europe, but the core of the book is the section on the cities of northern Italy. Benzo allots more space to these cities—and demonstrates a better knowledge of their history and a keener interest in their affairs—than to the cities of southern Italy and those that lay outside the peninsula.

7. Benzo, fol. 149*v*. We have autograph samples of his hand in two documents: Vatican Archives, AA Arm., C 539, and Milan State Archives, Fondo di Religione, in Raccolta delle pergamene, cart. 392 (Decumani del Duomo di Milano, perg. nr. 26). The Vatican document was first discussed by A. Ratti in "Intorno all'anno della scomunica di Matteo Visconti," *Rendiconti, Reale Istituto Lombardo di Scienze e Lettere*, ser. 2, Vol. XXVI (1903). The Milan document was analyzed by G. Biscaro in "Benzo da Alessandria e i giudizi contro i ribelli dell'impero a Milano nel 1311," *Archivio Storico Lombardo*, XXXXIV (1907). (Biscaro's designation of the document is wrong; Professor Giuseppe Billanovich graciously provided me with the correct one, which I supply above.)

It was perhaps Benzo's work as a notary that developed his interest in city seals and led him to refer frequently to them.[8] His everyday work brought him into contact with them on the documents that were his livelihood. The beauty of his hand, which one can appreciate if he compares it with those of contemporary notaries, testifies to the satisfaction that Benzo found in his vocation. Benzo's very apparent familiarity with these seals did not in any way lessen his interest in them as tokens of the seething political life of Italy.

There are twelve occasions upon which Benzo cited these seals. On three occasions he gave both the figure and the inscription: for Florence, for Genoa, and for Acqui; and all three of these seals reflect the violence of the age. Florence presents Hercules, armed with his club, and the warning: "*Herculea clava domat Florentia parva.*"[9] Genoa's seal is perhaps even more savage; a fierce griffin is shown crushing small birds: "*Griffus ut has angit, sic hostes Ianua frangit.*"[10] Acqui's has an eagle snatching up a hare and bears the words: "*Lector, Aquis dignum communis respice signum.*"[11]

The mottos of the seals of the other nine cities are less violent, and five have a religious cast. Brescia calls upon the Deity: "*Brixia sum mitis, Deus constans est michi basis.*"[12] Siena and Parma invoke the protection of the Virgin: "*Salve, Virgo, Senam veterem quam cernis amenam*";[13] and "*Hostis turbetur quia Parmam Virgo tuetur.*"[14] Bologna contents itself with St. Peter: "*Petrus ubique pater, legum Bononia mater.*"[15] Asti relies upon its patron, St. Secundus: "*Aste viret mundo sancto custode Secundo.*"[16] The city of Alessandria manages to straddle the gulf between these two types of seals: "*Deprimit elatos, levat Alexandria stratos*";[17] violence is suggested but it is cloaked in biblical phrases. The other three city seals hardly escape mediocrity: Pistoia, "*Que volo tantillo Pistoia celo sigillo*";[18] Ravenna, "*Urbis antique sigillum summe Ravenne*";[19] and Tortona, "*Pro tribus donis similis Terdona leonis.*"[20]

There are places in the *Chronicon*'s recital of authorities, facts, and dates at which Benzo could not suppress a groan as he recorded the sorry story of many cities. All were torn by the fierce, relentless savagery of civil war, and dissension, bloodshed, and the disruption of communal life is the thread that binds the disparate stories of many cities into a whole. On at least one occasion Benzo's grief offers us a symbol for this state of violence

8. Sabbadini (in *Le scoperte,* pp. 131–33) used these seals as evidence of Benzo's travels.

9. Benzo, fol. 139*v*. 10. *Ibid.*, fol. 150*v*. 11. *Ibid.*, fol. 151*r*.

12. *Ibid.*, fol. 149*r*. 13. *Ibid.*, fol. 139*r*. 14. *Ibid.*, fol. 149*v*.

15. *Ibid.* 16. *Ibid.*, fol. 151*r*. 17. *Ibid.*

18. *Ibid.*, fol. 139*v*. 19. *Ibid.*, fol. 140*r*. 20. *Ibid.*, fol. 150*r*.

and discontent that would do honor to Dante. While discussing the fate of Acqui, Benzo recalled that an old man had once told him Acqui was a golden shell filled with scorpions ("*aurea concha scorpionibus plena*").[21] The bright exterior of many prosperous cities only masked the political passion, vengeance, and violence within. Dante, Dino Compagni, and Giovanni Villani made the struggles of Florence the most famous example of this ambivalence, but Benzo does not even hint at the dreadful tensions that lay beneath the placid exterior of this city on the Arno. Most of the "scorpions" that Benzo pointed out were native to his northern Italy. This again confirms the great emphasis in the *Chronicon* upon that region.

Benzo referred to the blight of civil dissension on twelve occasions, and only one of the cities—Lucca—is not in northern Italy;[22] the center of the malady was north of the Apennines. In the chapter on Milan, Benzo mentioned an omen of the wrangling that was to mar the history of Lombardy. Noting that two of his sources said the Celtic migration into Italy was caused by "internal discord and constant domestic strife," Benzo said he would have given no thought to this "except that perhaps these [dissensions] were an unhappy omen of our internal discord and domestic strife."[23] Toward the end of the chapter on Milan, Benzo recalled the conflicts between its people and the aristocracy that had been resolved by Lanzo.[24]

Not every city was as fortunate as Milan in finding a solution to its internal difficulties, even if they had been of long duration; they seemed to suffer with no hope of solution. The citizens of Pavia were so engrossed in the shifting of political power that they could not be grieved over the loss of their cherished civic glory, *Rez Solium*,[25] but its loss was minor compared with that suffered by many of the other cities recorded in Benzo's pages—such as Tortona, Acqui, and Alessandria.[26] Vercelli had degenerated so far that it no longer deserved the designation of city.[27] Genoa's plight was even more wretched; its very existence was at stake. Benzo wondered whether the old superstition might not come to pass—that one day passersby would say "*Hec fuit Janua*."[28] Benzo's most telling description of the agonies of civil degeneration and dissension is sketched in the chapter on Bergamo.[29]

Benzo may well have welcomed the advent of Henry VII and did enrol in the emperor's service. Like Dante and many other Italians of his

21. *Ibid.*, fol. 151*r*.
22. *Ibid.*, fol. 139*r*.
23. *Ibid.*, fol. 144*v*.
24. *Ibid.*, fol. 147*r*.
25. *Ibid.*, fols. 147*v*–148*r*.
26. *Ibid.*, fols. 150*r*, 151*r*.
27. *Ibid.*, fol. 151*r*.
28. *Ibid.*, fol. 150*v*.
29. *Ibid.*, fol. 148.

day, Benzo had to choose between the agony, confusion, and utter anarchy of the Italian communes and the prospect of order and tranquility that would follow in the train of the idealistic emperor who crossed the Alps with the claim of bringing peace to the garden of the Empire.

Many of Benzo's sources are used both for northern Italy and for the rest of the peninsula, and, for the entire section, the two indispensable authors are Solinus and Isidore of Seville. Solinus, a fourth-century Latin historian who had written into his *Collectanea Rerum Memorabilium*[30] a jumble of history, myth, and sundry information, was much admired during the middle ages—as the great number of his manuscripts testifies. He provided the varied diet that suited the taste of the medieval man. The same was true of Isidore, his successor, whose *Etymologiae* was one of the standard texts of the age. The popularity of this work is attested by the many manuscripts that Lindsay lists in his edition.[31] Eusebius was another authority, as translated by Jerome and expanded by Miletus and Riccobaldus of Ferrara.[32] (Benzo employed several different methods to cite the latter work, which provided the chronological skeleton for his own narration.)

Rivalling all the preceding authorities in importance is the eleventh-century grammarian Papias, whose major work is a sort of dictionary-encyclopedia that held its own long into the fifteenth century.[33] Like Isidore, upon whom he relied for much of his information, Papias had assembled a potpourri of itemized knowledge, in alphabetical order. The handiness of this method appealed to Benzo, and page after page contains references to Papias.

These principal sources usually are accompanied by passages from many other authors, notably Justinus, the abridger of Trogus Pompeius,[34] who was particularly valuable to Benzo for his lists of the cities founded by the Gauls in northern Italy.[35] Justinus, however, was a supplementary

30. Ed. T. Mommsen (Berlin, 1895).

31. *Etymologiarum sive Originum Libri XX*, ed. W. Lindsay (2 vols.; Oxford, 1911), I, vii–xi.

32. Jerome, *Die Chronik des Hieronymus*, ed. R. Helm (Berlin, 1956). There is no modern edition of Riccobaldus's several works, the *Compendium* and two versions of the *Historie*, and I am indebted to Professor T. Hankey of London for my references to Riccobaldus's manuscripts.

33. Papias, *Vocabularium* (Milan, 1476).

34. Justinus, *Epitoma Historiarum Philippicarum Pompei Trogi.*

35. Benzo, fol. 144*v*.

engine, wheeled in and out of action as Benzo required his assistance; a much greater authority was Livy.[36] The most important instances of Livy's assistance are in Benzo's digressions upon the founding of Milan and Genoa; in both cases confronted with the legend of Noe-Janus, Benzo used Livy to demolish the myth. His esteem for Livy is further revealed in the praise he bestowed upon the ancient historian: "*maximus ystoriografus*"[37] and "*in cuius narracione tacet omnis oblocutor et gaudet elocutor.*"[38]

A late-Latin author who enjoyed great popularity in the middle ages and who was consulted several times by Benzo is Eutropius.[39] Paul the Lombard,[40] another favorite, was especially helpful for northern Italy, and his tales of the Lombards are repeated in the chapters on Pavia, Como, and Verona.[41] A more tranquil tone than that of the blood-curdling book of Paul was set by Cassiodorus, who is represented primarily by his correspondence.[42] Bearing all the traits of set-pieces, his letters are rhetorically embellished descriptions of cities and landscapes, which had a great appeal for Benzo. Benzo also quoted from Cassiodorus's *Historia Ecclesiastica Tripartita*[43] in referring to a synod held in Milan.[44]

Two twelfth-century ecclesiastics who wrote extensive chronicles appear now and then, Godfrey of Viterbo and Sicard of Cremona;[45] they supplied Benzo with useful scraps of information—although Sicard may say that Verona was named for a noble Trojan matron[46] or that Vercelli was founded by companions of Aeneas and Antenor.[47] Godfrey also is cited for Verona.[48] Two other ecclesiastical writers, of an earlier age—and of greater ability and influence—also are employed, Augustine

36. Livy, *Ab urbe condita*, ed. W. Weissenborn and H. J. Muller (10 vols.; Berlin, 1880–1924).

37. Benzo, fol. 149*v*.

38. *Ibid.*, fol. 144*v*.

39. Eutropius was the author of *Breviarium ab urbe condita*, ed. H. Droysen, *MGH*, *AA*, II (Berlin, 1879).

40. Paul the Lombard, *Historia Langobardorum*, ed. L. Bethmann and G. Waitz, *MGH*, *SRLI*, I (Hanover, 1878), 12–487.

41. Benzo, fols. 147*v*, 148*r*, and 149*r*.

42. Cassiodorus, *Variae*, ed. T. Mommsen, *MGH*, *AA*, XII (Berlin, 1894).

43. Cassiodorus, *Historia Ecclesiastica Tripartita*, ed. W. Jacob (Vienna, 1952).

44. Benzo, fol. 145*r*.

45. Although there are modern editions of portions of the works of Godfrey and Sicard, they do not contain the parts from which Benzo worked, and for those parts I have used microfilm that was generously provided by the Bavarian State Library (for Godfrey, the *Liber Pantheon*, Cod. Clm 43; for Sicard, the *Chronicon*, Cod. Clm 314).

46. Benzo, fol. 149*r*.

47. *Ibid.*, fol. 151*r*.

48. *Ibid.*, fol. 149*r*.

and Orosius;[49] both writers are cited for chronological information. Seneca's *Dialogues* are quoted for the foundation of Padua by Antenor,[50] and the *Historia Augusta* is used for the births of Valerian and Galienus.[51]

Much more significant for Lombardy, and particularly for Milan, are several medieval works and chronicles that Benzo cited frequently; they are the products of local pride and early instances of the historiography that was to find a great representative in Benzo. The *De Situ Urbis Mediolani*[52] provides information on the climate, geography, wines, and waters of the region, as well as on the physical characteristics and emotional makeup of its inhabitants,[53] and may also have supplied Benzo with information on the earliest phase of Christianity in Milan, as Ferrai supposes.[54] Three medieval chronicles—those of Landulph, Landulph of St. Paul, and Arnulph—were used, although Benzo quoted from the first under the name of Dacius, who provided facts on the walls and buildings of Milan and on its history after the death of Ambrose.[55] Landulph of St. Paul was quoted on the crown of iron in the church of St. Michael in Monza,[56] and Arnulph was used in describing the basilica of St. Laurence and the privileges of the archbishop of Milan.[57] For St. Ambrose's deeds, Benzo followed the biography by Paulinus of Nola.[58] Two other medieval works, although particularly relevant to Benzo's massive chapter on Rome, are cited occasionally in the section on northern Italy, especially in connection with the legend of Janus: the *Chronicon* of Martinus Polonus[59] and the *Graphia Urbis Auree*. The Janus legend is particularly significant for the early history of Genoa, and Iacopo da Varagine is Benzo's principal source—or rather whipping-boy.[60]

49. Augustine, *De civitate dei*, and Orosius, *Historiae adversus paganos*.

50. Benzo, fol. 149*v*. 51. *Ibid.*, fol. 147*r*.

52. "De situ civitatis Mediolani," in *RIS*, I–II (Milan, 1725), 203–27.

53. Benzo, fols. 145*rv*.

54. L. A. Ferrai, "Benzo d'Alessandria e i cronisti Milanesi del secolo xiv," *Bulletino dell'Instituto Storico Italiano*, VII (1889), 129.

55. Benzo, fols. 145*v*, 147*r*, and Landulph, *Historia Mediolanensis*, ed. L. Bethmann and W. Wattenbach, *MGH, SS*, VIII (Hanover, 1848), 32–100.

56. Benzo, fol. 146*r*, and Landulph of St. Paul, *Historia Mediolanensis*, ed. L. Bethmann and P. Jaffe, *MGH, SS*, XX (Hanover, 1868), 17–49.

57. Benzo, fols. 146*rv*, and Arnulph, *Gesta Archiepiscoporum Mediolanensium*, ed. L. Bethmann and W. Wattenbach, *MGH, SS*, VIII (Hanover, 1848), 1–31.

58. Benzo, fol. 146*r*, and Paulinus, *Vita S. Ambrosii*, *Patrologia Latina*, XIV (Paris, 1845), 27–46.

59. Martinus Polonus, *Chronicon*, ed. L. Weiland, *MGH, SS*, XXII (Hanover, 1872), 377–482.

60. Iacopo da Varagine, *Cronaca*, ed. G. Monleone (Rome, 1941).

The profusion of prose sources is in striking contrast with the paucity of quotations from poets. Several verses are quoted from city seals and a verse or two in the chapter on Milan. Benzo's favorite poet, however, was Ausonius, the author of a poem on the cities of the Roman empire in the fifth century[61] (Sabbadini forcefully contends that Benzo took the copy of this poem, which had been preserved in the capitular library of Verona[62]). A few lines on Mantua are quoted from Virgil;[63] a single line of Lucan is used; and a line from Ovid is cited without acknowledgment of its origin.[64]

Benzo also used his own observations. He wrote of an equestrian statue he had Seen in Pavia, of a garrulous old man from Acqui, and his description of Pisa seems something more than his usual adoption of a source.[65]

Benzo is usually exact in quoting his sources, although he occasionally paraphrased an author to make his meaning clearer to his readers. This process is usually reserved for the poets, but on one occasion Benzo paraphrased Livy.[66] Whoever the author or source, Benzo exercised his gift of critical acumen, for his training and experience had taught him the value of a critical spirit in the face of conflicting testimony and in the authentication of documents. His restraint and acumen are manifested throughout the *Chronicon*.

Benzo's demand for *autentici* allowed him to be convinced, but only on the evidence of a writer with sufficient credentials; moreover, Benzo sometimes went beyond the simple demand for authority and at times approached the level of textual criticism—if only in a tentative and rudimentary manner. He realized, of course, that even the texts of reliable authorities are subject to corruption. In discussing a passage from the *Tripartite History* and its reference to a city called Alba, which some authors had identified with Milan, Benzo suggested an error in the text.[67] When confronted with a difficulty on a text of Eutropius on Pavia, he noted that the source might be corrupt.[68] He gave the correct form of Genoa, *Genua* (instead of *Janua*) on the bases of the text of Livy and the "most ancient codices of the history of the Lombards."[69]

There were many medieval legends about the origins of Genoa,

61. Ausonius, "Ondo Urbium Nobilium," *Carmina*, ed. C. Schenkl, *MGH, AA*, V–II (Berlin, 1883), 98–103.

62. Sabbadini, "Bencius Alexandrinus und der Codex Veronensis des Ausonius," *Rheinische Museum für Philologie*, LXIII (1908), 234.

63. Benzo, fol. 149*r*. 64. *Ibid.*, fol. 147*v*. 65. *Ibid.*, fol. 139*r*.

66. *Ibid.*, fol. 144*v*. 67. *Ibid.*, fol. 145*r*. 68. *Ibid.*, fol. 147*r*.

69. *Ibid.*, fol. 150*v*.

legends that were amplified to embrace the beginnings of such other cities as Rome, Ravenna, and Milan. There had been no limit to the inventiveness of the creators of these fables, all based on the assertion that Noe and his son, Janus, had come to Italy and had founded the city of Janus or Janiculum.[70] The author who gave fullest expression to this collection of fancies was Iacopo da Varagine; not satisfied with one Janus, he designated three men with the same name, all of whom (he said) helped develop the city.[71] This enabled Iacopo to locate Janus in three different periods of history and thus attribute all the major advances made in the early history of Genoa to Janus.

Benzo, in his chapter on Genoa, indulged in a controversy with Iacopo when he proved that Janus could not have been a contemporary of Moses and Abraham, as Iacopo had proposed.[72] Iacopo's contention of a Trojan Janus, who either built or increased the size of Genoa, is countered with Benzo's declaration: "I have not found this in any reliable authors."[73]

Milan had not escaped this biblical founder-hunting and had been awarded a man named Subres as its mythical progenitor.[74] Benzo's response was effective and characteristic; he listed all authors who should have mentioned such an important occurrence and concluded that none of them had said anything on this matter. Of Subres he wrote: "*Deus novit, ego ignoro.*"[75]

It is interesting to compare Benzo's work and spirit with those of his contemporaries in northern Italy, but, unfortunately, there were only a few, and the foremost was an acknowledged borrower from Benzo—a Dominican named Galvaneo Fiamma. There is no parallel to Benzo's section on the cities of northern Italy in the works of Fiamma, but we can form a rather accurate idea of his abilities and methods in relation to those of Benzo by examining his information on Milan. Also, there are several brief references to other cities of Lombardy in the pages of Fiamma that we can contrast with Benzo's handling of the same subject. Fiamma's distinguishing characteristic is prolixity, which sets him apart from Benzo; the latter's chapter on Milan is minute compared with the number of pages written by Fiamma in his several resumptions of the Milanese theme. Fiamma's relationship to Benzo is that of dependence, but, when it came to writing a critical study that was based on the manipulation of

70. *Ibid.*, fol. 137*r*. 71. *Ibid.*, fol. 150*r*. 72. *Ibid.*, fols. 150*rv*.
73. *Ibid.*, fol. 150*v*. 74. *Ibid.*, fol. 144*r*. 75. *Ibid.*, fol. 144*v*.

many sources that had to be assigned varying weights, Fiamma turned away from Benzo's excellent precedent and indulged in uncritical fantasies.

A typical example of Fiamma's mind and work—which reveals the nature of the author all too well—is his employment of his fellow Dominican, Iacopo da Varagine. For Fiamma, the fact that Iacopo was a doctor of divinity guaranteed his reliability as a witness. Also, the bond of membership in the Dominican order may have been stronger than Fiamma's critical ability, but that he paid no attention to Benzo's strictures on the Genoese bishop is surprising.

Fiamma, who also employed other authors for his history of Milan, began his concoction with the Noe-Janus legend and many mythical kings and wars and invasions, outdoing even Iacopo.[76] Although Benzo mentioned the legend of Subres, son of Tubal, but rejected it,[77] Fiamma used the legend as the beginning of his treatment of Milanese history. Nor does the rest of Fiamma's history of early Milan find a counterpart in the sober pages of Benzo; the numerous kings, with their magnificent names, are either Fiamma's inventions or inventions of his sources. It is therefore quite incorrect to say—as Ferrai contended—that Benzo was the principal source of these wild stories of Fiamma.[78]

Fiamma treated later Milanese history as fully as the earlier, legendary period, and there is more solidity here, but it is not the sort of material Benzo recorded. There is much more of the chronicler in Fiamma than in Benzo. Benzo cut through webs of dispute with his trained mind, but Fiamma did not do this; there is no discrimination in the latter's work, only inclusiveness, which accounts for his great quantity of material.

Fiamma was just as prone to accept mythology and legend for the other cities of Lombardy. Manto, daughter of Tyresias, was the foundress of Mantua;[79] Piacenza was founded by Pucentius, and later was called Augusta;[80] Chrysopolus founded Parma, which for a while was called Julia;[81] Lodi was founded by a man called Laudus.[82] Fiamma also said that Lodi was a city at the time that Pompey settled the pirates there, and that Pavia was founded by emigrants who left Milan because of overpopulation and who named their new settlement Ticinum.[83]

76. Other works by Fiamma have been published, but the Politia Novella is available only in manuscript form; e.g., in Cod. A 275 inf. of the Ambrosian Library. Folios 1–30 of this manuscript contain the mythical portion of Fiamma's work.

77. Benzo, fol. 144*r*. 78. Ferrai, *op. cit.*, p. 102, n. 1.

79. Fiamma, "Manipulus Florum," in *RIS*, XI (Milan, 1729), 549.

80. *Ibid.*, cols. 548–49. 81. *Ibid.*, col. 549. 82. *Ibid.* 83. *Ibid.*, col. 548.

Another contemporary of Benzo, and one who almost certainly knew Benzo at Como, was Giovanni da Cermenate. A document for the creation of a special procurator—dated May 22, 1316, and now in the state archives of Milan—was notarized by Da Cermenate, "*notarius Cumanus et scriba domini episcopi*,"[84] for Lord-Bishop Leo dei Lambertenghi. This definitely places Da Cermenate in Como at the same time as Benzo and in the service of the same man. Also, Da Cermenate possessed a copy of Livy, which may be the manuscript Benzo employed in compiling his *Chronicon*.[85]

Da Cermenate's *Historia* deals principally with the events in Milan that were connected with the advent of Henry VII. Although Benzo never expressed his devotion to the imperial cause, his actions as a member of the imperial bureaucracy reveal where he stood; Da Cermenate, on the other hand, was explicit in his championship of the emperor.[86] Da Cermenate may well have been writing at the same time as Benzo if Ferrai's assumption is correct—that he had completed the first part of his work at least by 1317.

Although the subject matter of the *Historia* precludes comparison with the *Chronicon*, Da Cermenate related some of the legends that Benzo subjected to a critical examination; for example, that Tubal founded Ravenna, that Subres founded Milan, and that Janus built a town in the vicinity of Rome. Not all of Da Cermenate's introductory material is of such legendary character, however; he quoted the same passage as Benzo (from the fifth book of Livy) for the foundation of Milan by the Gauls.[87]

Another writer who must have known Benzo was Guglielmo da Pastrengo, whose *De Originibus Rerum*[88] contains a section on the cities of the world. Da Pastrengo, interested only in determining the founders of the cities with which he dealt, listed the names of the cities and the names of the founders,[89] so that this treatment is much shorter than Benzo's. The cities of the world are listed alphabetically, but many of the cities mentioned in the *Chronicon* are missing in the *De Originibus Rerum*—such as Capua, Florence, and Padua. For cities that appear in both works, Benzo's elaborate framework of quotations is lacking in Da Pastrengo,

84. State Archives of Milan, Fondo di Religione, cart. 112, nr. 2.
85. See Giovanni da Cermenate's *Historia*, ed. L. A. Ferrai (Rome, 1889), p. 7.
86. *Ibid.*, p. 17. 87. *Ibid.*, pp. 5–8.
88. Guglielmo de Pastrengo, *De originibus rerum* (Venice, 1547).
89. *Ibid.*, fol. 89*v*.

who simply gave the opinion of one or two authors on the foundation of each city.

It is significant that we often seem to hear echoes of Benzo's conclusions in Da Pastrengo, but this may be partially due to the latter's use of such authors as Solinus and Isidore, whom Benzo also cited and whose opinions he often followed (particularly when they were corroborated by such authors as Livy, Eutropius, or Eusebius). There are enough instances of similarity between the two works, however, that we suspect dependence: Da Pastrengo's acceptance of the testimony of Livy and Justinus for Milan,[90] and Lodi's creation by Pompey for the pirates—as well as the story of Manto.[91] The most striking similarities are found in the sections on Ferrara.[92]

Benzo's treatment of the cities of northern Italy is more inclusive than his contemporaries' (if we except the expatiations of Fiamma on Milan), and, despite similarities, his scope is wider than the others' and his grasp is firmer. Benzo, who had done extensive reading in ancient and medieval literature, ordered his work with admirable skill and harnessed his authorities to the task for which he was so well suited by temperament and training. This important work on the origins of the cities of northern Italy is notable for its freshness of viewpoint, its breadth of learning, its high level of competence, and its command of new material.

Note Prefatory to the Text

The main purpose of this edition is to present as accurately as possible the text of the *Chronicon* as it is found in Ambrosian MS B 24 inf., which is the only nonderivative source for Benzo that we possess. Two other manuscripts (Ambrosian O 83 sup. and Brera AD 14, 55) are apographs of B 24 inf., as has long been acknowledged and is clear from a comparative study. They contain only the chapter on Milan and their readings are questionable.

Because it is difficult to decide whether differences between the two apographs of Ambrosian B 24 inf. represent readings that are no longer legible in the original or misreadings or conjectures of the copyists—and because use of the apographs did not prevent Ferrai from producing a seriously deficient text—I have preferred to rely exclusively upon an intensive study of Ambrosian MS B 24 inf. Although I worked principally

90. *Ibid.*, fol. 98*v*. 91. *Ibid.*, fols. 97*v*, 98*r*. 92. *Ibid.*, fol. 95*v*.

from microfilm and photostats, I also consulted the manuscript, particularly in every place where the reading is difficult.

I have not changed the spelling or removed grammatical inconsistencies. Only occasionally have I ventured an emendation, when the text seemed to cry out for it, and these instances are recorded in the notes. Whenever possible, the sources of Benzo's information have been noted and standard editions have been used. Some of Benzo's authorities, however, have not been published, and for them I have employed manuscripts.

The Milan chapter constituted a special problem. Ferrai's edition (in *Bullettino dell' Istituto Storico Italiano*, IX [1890], 15–36), far from rendering the present effort needless, required correction, for it is marred by many errors, omissions, and insertions. Therefore every substantial discrepancy between Ferrai and the present text has been noted. (Although Ferrai followed the standard procedure of his day in turning medieval into classical Latin, I have not noted every discrepancy between the manuscript and Ferrai's classicized version.)

Liber XIV

CAPITULUM .CXXXVI.[1] DE MEDIOLANO FLORENTISSIMA CIVITATE [fol. 144*r*]

Mediolanum in Ytalia[2] olim Ligurum nunc Langobardorum florentissima et opulentissima civitas condita fuit a Gallis Senonibus, regnante Tarquinio Prisco quinto Romanorum rege, ut dicit Titus[3] Livius,[4] post scilicet .xxv.[5] annum regni eiusdem, anno nativitatis Abraam .miiii^{c}xxii.,[6] post excidium Troie .v^{c}xc., a mundi exordio circiter .v^{m}viiii^{c}lx.,[7] a diluvio circitir .mclxv., a divisione linguarum circiter .m.v^{c}xx.,[8] ab imperio Nini regis Assiriorum[9] circiter .m.iiii^{c}lx.,[10] ab urbe Roma condita circiter .clx.,[11] ante Christi ortum .vxc^{c}ii.[12] aut circiter.

Et hee[13] computaciones intelligantur factas esse iuxta quod supra computati sunt anni condite urbis Rome, et secundum eosdem auctores, additis singulis temporibus annis .clx., qui fluxerant ab ipsa urbe Roma condita usque ad .xxv. annum regni eiu'sdem Prisci Tarquinii; post quos .clx. annos Galli[14] Senones, ut infra docebitur, Ytaliam intraverunt. Fuerunt autem Galli Senones, ut scribit Papias et Ysidorus,[15] qui antiquitus Zenones dicebantur, eo quod Liberum, idest Bachum,[16] hospicio recepissent, postea z in s littera commutata est.[17] Hii[18] autem, ut refert Titus[19] Livius libro .v., cum sub duce Brenone illorum regulo Romam tunc primitus captam incendissent, preter arcem et Capitolium, restitit eis Manlius voce anseris excitatus; tandem, accepto auro ne Capitolium obsiderent, discesserunt. Quos insecutus Camillus, ita cecidit eos ut[20] et aurum et omnia que ceperant signa militaria revocaret.[21]

Cum autem de tempore fundacionis et de fundatoribus huius urbis Mediolani nonnulli moderni scribant et referant quedam que[22] meo iudicio, si quicquam[23] pensi est, immo patenter discrepant et valde

1. *L. A. Ferrai* ("*Bentii Alexandrini de Mediolano civitate opusculum ex chronico eiusdem excerptum,*" Bullettino dell'Istituto Storico Italiano, *IX* [*1890*], *15–36*) *omitted this chapter number. Ferrai's readings, where they differ from those in Ambrosian MS B 24 inf., are preceded by the letter* F.

2. F, Italia. 3. F, T. 4. *Livy,* V, 34, 9. 5. F, vigesimum quintum.
6. F, .MCCCCXXII. 7. F, .M^{v}VIIII^{c}LX. 8. F, .MDXX.
9. F, Assiriorum regis. 10. F, .MCDLX. 11. F, .MDLX.
12. F, .DXLII. 13. F, haec. 14. F, Galli . . . intraverunt *omitted.*
15. F, Isidorus. 16. F, Bacchum.

17. *Papias,* Vocabularium (*Milan, 1476*), *s.v. Senones; Isidore,* Etymologiarum sive Originum Libri, *XX* (*Oxford, 1911*), *IX, 11, 106.*

18. F, hi. 19. F, T. 20. F, eos (ita) ut. 21. *Livy, V, 33, 5.*
22. F, quaedamque. 23. F, quoque.

dissona sunt relatis scriptisque auctorum antiquissimorum[24] et[25] pariter autenticorum,[26] ut infra patebit, nitentes ad urbis huius laudem eius inaniter antiquitatem extendere, ego vero mallens in commendacione ipsius veridica relacione fulciri, quam[27] ex nimia vel inani prorsus laude et adversa veritati scripcione[28] antiquitatis eius pennis peregrinis, ne dicam adulterinis, tempora palliare, Titi Livii maximi et autentici[29] scriptoris, necnon Trogi Pompei sive Iustini eius abreviatoris, ac Orosii, Eutropii, Eusebii sive[30] Ieronimi et magistri in historiis, necnon Dacii et Ausonii ac Papie dicta sequar, et in medium proferam elucidancia plenissime huius urbis condite verissima tempora et acta magnifica.

Prius tamen inseram breviter eorum dicta sive scripta, qui nituntur, ostendendo probare Mediolanum vetustate precellere urbem Romam, non ut derogem antiquitati urbis huius sed ut tenebris erroris lucem erogem veritatis. Dicunt enim quod Noe, conscensa rate, une cum filio suo Iano biffronte et alio Iano bicorporeo, filio Iaphet, et maxima populorum multitudine in Ytaliam[31] veniens, venit ad Camesem[32] filium Nembroth gigantis pronepotis Noe, qui paterno mandato iam transfretaverat et ubi nunc est Roma elegerat sibi sedem.[33] Audiverat enim[34] Nembroth a Iuvan filio Iafeth[35] cunctas mundi monarchias sub italico imperio annullari et construendam[36] fore civitatem in Italia[37] orbi dominaturam. Noe igitur[38] cum venisset ibi iuxta locum in quo[39] nunc est Roma civitatem construxit et eam ex suo nomine appellavit, in qua et laboris et vite terminum dedit, cum regnasset in Italia annos .clii. Hoc autem testari dicunt Escodium[40] et in Graphia auree urbis contineri. Martinus Polonus.[41] Interea cum Noe per ora maris Romanorum ingrederetur Ytaliam,[42] ex parte altera per ora maris Adriatici sive Veneciarum Tubal filius Iafeth[43] in Italiam similiter[44] venit, et in ripa maris civitatem construxit, quam a ratibus et navibus et vento appellavit Ravennam.[45]

24. MS, *marginal notation, but not noted as such in F.*
25. F, et *omitted.* 26. F, authenticorum. 27. F, quod.
28. F, veritate scriptor. 29. F, authentici. 30. F, Eusebii et sancti.
31. F. Italiam. 32. F, Camensem. 33. F, sibi sedem *omitted.*
34. F, enim *as emendation for* an ejus *in the text.*
35. F, Nembroth Iano filio Iaphet.
36. F, constituendam. 37. F. Italiam. 38. F, igitur *omitted.*
39. F, ubi. 40. F, Excodius.
41. *Martinus,* Chronicon, *ed. L. Weiland,* MGH, SS *(Hannover, 1872), XXII, 399–400.*
42. MS, Ytaliam *is a marginal interpolation and was not noted by Ferrai.*
43. F, Iaphet.
44. MS, similiter *is a marginal notation and was not noted by Ferrai.*
45. *Iacopo da Varagine,* Cronaca, *ed. G. Monleone (Rome, 1941), p. 15.*

Filius vero Tubal nomine Subres planum Lombardie ingressus, civitatem construxit et ex suo nomine Subriam denominavit, a qua et cetera regio circumposita dicta est Subria.[46] Hec autem ex cronicis Sicardi Cremonensis episcopi haberi dicunt,[47] (et) quod[48] eciam ex Eutropio et Papia evidenter colligi.

Subiungunt eciam quod hec civitas Subria per Bellovesum Gallorum ducem postmodum reedificata dicta est Mediolanum, et hoc libro[49] .v. Titi Livi contineri, sicque probari manifeste astruunt[50] Mediolanum fuisse conditum antequam Roma conderetur per annos .viiii^c^xxxii. seu fere mille, Subriam pro Mediolano ponentes. Si autem in hac prioritate temporum condicionis urbis Mediolani sit huiusmodi /[fol. 144*v*] assercioni(s) adhibenda fides, re vera mirandum michi videtur qualiter a ceteris scriptoribus talia sint obmissa, vel quod ignoraverint, vel quod neglexerint, vel quod non meminerint, ut minimam[51] mencionem non fecerint, qui fuerunt in tantis et tam variis solliciti et eciam[52] curiosi, utpote Iosephus, Egesippus, Iustinus ex Trogo, Augustinus libro[53] De civitate dei, Orosius, Ysidorus,[54] Eutropius, Solinus, Papias et in cronicis[55] suis Miletus, Eusebius,[56] Ieronimus, Beda, Richardus[57] Cluniacensis,[58] Hugo Floriacensis, Methodius martyr, Cassiodorus in Tripartita vel in epistulis,[59] Ruffinus Aquilegensis,[60] et ut ad novissimos veniam, Vincencius, qui ex tam diversis auctoribus suum tanta sollicitudine[61] et curiositate opus conscripsit historiale libris .xxxii., Dacius quoque,[62] qui de gestis Mediolanensium scripsit, et non pretereundus, nullique suorum temporum secundus Paulus Langobardorum fidelis conscriptor historie,[63] quorum omnium auctorum libros seu cronicas[64] vel scripsi vel partim seriose, partim perfunctorie[65] legi. Quodque eciam validius est in toto veteri et novo testamento aut in historiis que scolastice dicuntur, aut in aliquibus eccleise doctorum glosis vel postillis[66] non legitur quod Noe eciam

46. *See F. Savio, "La Cronaca di Filippo da Castel Seprio,"* Atti della reale accademia della scienze di Torino, *XLI (1906), p. 10.*

47. *Sicard, fol. 12v*: Tubal, ex quo Iberes, scilicet . . . Itali.

48. F, quae.

49. F, libro *omitted.*

50. F, asserunt.

51. F, ignoraverint, vel quod minimam.

52. F, immo.

53. F, in libro.

54. F, Isidorus.

55. F, chronicis.

56. F, Eusebius *omitted.*

57. F, Ricardus.

58. MS, Clivacensis.

59. *See Ferrai, "Benzo d'Alessandria," p. 121. Misreading the text, Ferrai said the letters are by Rufinus rather than by Cassiodorus.*

60. F, epistulis Ruffini Aquilegensis.

61. F, sollecitudine.

62. F, quoque *omitted.*

63. *See Ferrai, "Benzo d'Alessandria," pp. 112–35, for a treatment of these medieval authorities.*

64. F, chronicas.

65. F, persunctorie.

66. F, aut postilis.

transiverit in Ytaliam[67] aut quod filium habuerit nomine Ianum, vel quod civitatem maxime sibi equivocam[68] alicubi edificaverit et quod Iafet[69] habuerit filliuḿ nomine Subrem. Unde igitur hoc habuerit Sicardus sive Escodius, scriptores novissimi, vel illius Graphie auree compilator Deus novit, ego ignoro. Orosius preterea scribit quod omnes ystorie[70] antique a Nino incipiunt,[71] qui fuit ante ortum Abre annis .xlii.,[72] secundum Augustinum a diluvio[73] .clxiiii.,[74] secundum Eusebium qui fuit Noe vite[75] .vii.lxv.,[76] ante vero eius mortem .clxxxv. secundum Iosephum,[77] et tamen nichil de hoc refert.[78]

Que autem novi a prefatis auctoribus, maxime a Tito Livio, omnium scriptorum et historiographorum[79] maximo, in cuius narracione omnis tacet oblocutor et gaudet elocutor,[80] de transitu Gallorum in Ytaliam[81] et eiusdem huius urbis[82] Mediolani fundatoribus et fundacionis tempore hec ipsius sunt verba, mutato non sentencia sed latino in aliquibus.[83] Prisco Tarquinio Rome regnante Celtarum gencium que pars Gallie tercia est penes Bituriges summa[84] imperii fuit; hii[85] enim regem Celticis[86] dabant. Eo tempore Ambigatus rex eorum fuit, virtute et fortuna tum sua tum publica prepollens,[87] eo quod in imperio eius Gallia adeo frugum et hominum fertilis fuit, ut habundans[88] multitudo vix regi posse videretur. Hic ipse iam magno natu a pregravante turba exhonerare regnum cupiens, Bellovesum ac Sigovesum,[89] sororis filios, impigros iuvenes, missurum[90] se esse dixit in quas sedes dii dedissent auguriis, et quantum ipsi vellent numerum hominum evocarent, ne[91] qua gens arcere illos advenientes posset. Tunc Segoveso sortibus dati sunt Hercinei[92]

67. F, Italiam.

68. F, maxime . . . , *with* sibi equivocam *in a footnote as the reading of the Ambrosian MS O 83 inf.*

69. F, Iaphet. 70. F, historiae.

71. *Orosius,* Historiae adversum paganos, *ed. C. Zangemeister (Leipzig, 1889), I, 1.*

72. *Jerome,* Die Chronik, *ed. R. Helm (Berlin, 1956), p. 20*a.

73. MS, ante diluvium.

74. *Augustine,* De civitate Dei, *ed. E. Hoffmann (2 vols., Vienna, 1889), XVIII, 22.*

75. F, vite *omitted.*

76. *Jerome,* Die Chronik, *p. 20*a; F, .DCCLXV.

77. *Josephus,* Antiquitates Judaicae, *I, vi, 5.*

78. F, nihil refert de hoc.

79. F, historiograforum. 80. F, et gaudet elocutor *omitted.*

81. F, Italiam. 82. MS, eisdem huius rebus.

83. *Livy here received the treatment Benzo usually accorded such authors as Claudian and Statius.*

84. F, ac summa. 85. F, ii. 86. F, Celticis regem. 87. F, pollens.

88. F, abundans. 89. F. Segovesum. 90. F, missurus.

91. F, hominum, ne. 92. F, Hercynei.

saltus; Belloveso autem non paulo latiorem in Italiam dii viam dabant. Qui Bellovesus id auod ex populis eius habundabat,[93] scilicet Bituriges, Arvennos,[94] Senones, Eduos, Ambaures, Carmites,[95] et Aulercos evocavit. Profectus igitur ingentibus[96] peditum et equitum copiis in Triscapinos[97] venit. Alpes inde opposite erant, quas inexsuperabiles ab eo[98] visas fuisse non equidem miror, dum nulla via quod quidem continens memoria sit, nisi de Hercule, si fabulis credere libet, constet[99] superatas fuisse. Ibi autem cum velut septos Gallos teneret moncium altitudo et circumspectarent quanam parte periuncta celo iuga in alium orbem terrarum transirent, religio illos eciam[100] tenuit, quia allatum est alios advenas querentes agros ab Salivium[101] gente oppugnari. Massilienses ibi tunc[102] erant in navibus a Phoca profecti. Id Galli fortune sue omen rati esse ibi eciam adiverunt[103] ut[104] quem primum in terram egressi occupaverant locum patentibus silvis communirent. Per Taurinos igitur montes saltusque Iulie Alpis[105] transcenderunt, fusisque acie Tuscis non procul a Ticino flumine, cum agrum in quo consederunt[106] Insubrium[107] appellari audissent cognomine Insubribus pago Eduorum,[108] ibi omen sequentes loci condiderunt urbem et Mediolanum appellarunt.[109] Alia subinde manus Germanorum Titonio duce vestigia priorum[110] secuta, eodem saltu, favente Belloveso, cum transcendisset Alpes, ubi nunc Brixia urbes sunt,[111] locos tenuerunt, ibique Libili considunt,[112] post hos Saluivi[113] qui prope antiquam gentem, scilicet Levos Ligures incolentes circa Ticinum amnem, montes Apenninos, deinde Boios[114] Liguresque transgressi, cum iam inter Padum atque[115] Alpes omnia tenerent,[116] Pado[117] ratibus traiecto, non Etruscos tantum sed eciam Umbros agro[118] pellunt; intra Apenninum tamen[119] sese tenuerunt; tunc Senones Galli recentissimi advenarum ab Utente flumine usque ad Arthesim[120] fines habuerunt.[121] Actor.[122] Hec ex Tito Livio, per que[123] patet primo Mediolanum a Gallis,

93. F, abundabat. 94. F, Arvernos.
95. F, Ambares, Carnutes. 96. F, cum ingentibus.
97. F, Tricastinos, *with note that the manuscripts read* Hernici.
98. F, ab eo *omitted.* 99. F, constat. 100. F, (etiam) illos.
101. F, ab Saluvium. 102. F, enim. 103. F, adiverant. 104. F, et.
105. F, Alpis *omitted.* 106. F, conscenderunt. 107. F, Insubriam.
108. F, Haeduorum. 109. F, appellaverunt. 110. F, prorsus.
111. F, sunt urbes. 112. F, consident. 113. F, Saluvii. 114. F, Boii.
115. F, et. 116. F, tenerent[ur]. 117. F, Padoque.
118. F, Umbros immo Perusinos et Spoletanos agro. *The manuscript has a marginal note (in a late hand) that explains Umbros:* Umbri fuerunt Perusini et Spoletani.
119. F, tamen *omitted.* 120. F, Athesim. 121. *Livy, V, 34–35.*
122. F, Actor *omitted.* 123. F, quem.

regnante Rome Tarquinio Prisco, conditam urbem Mediolanum et non reedificatam in agro Subrio, sive Insubribus[124] pago Eduorum, et non in civitate Subria, vel aliter dicta secuti quod destinaverant, primum[125] scilicet locum quem patentibus silvis occupassent, communire. Certum est eciam, testante Ysidoro,[126] et Papia, agrum non esse urbem vel civitatem.[127] Pagi autem sunt loca apta edificiis inter agros habitantibus, ut dicit Ysidorus,[128] vel potuit forte in loco illo esse villa, cum dicat Titus pago Eduorum. Pagi enim eciam[129] ville sunt dicte a fontibus, circa[130] quos ville consueverant condi; unde pagani dicti sunt, quasi une fonte potantes; pe(r)ge enim grece fons,[131] ut dicit Papias.

Sunt preterea et alii autentici testes manifeste scribentes Mediolanum a Gallis non reedificando sed edificando constructum vel conditum. Inquiunt enim Trogus Pompeius sive Iustinus eius abreviator, et Ysidorus[132] et Papias quod Galli, cum in Ytaliam[133] venissent, sedibus Tuscos expulerunt, et Mediolanum, Comum, Brixiam, Veronam, Pergamum, Tridentum, Vincenciam condiderunt.[134] Quibus eciam concordat Miletus sive Eusebius[135] vel Ieronimus. Quam vero magna esset eorum multitudo et quam effera gens insinuat eciam idem Iustinus dicens: Galli habundanti[136] multitudine cum eos non caperent terre que genuerant, trecenta milia hominum ad sedes novas querendas miserunt; et porcio in Ytalia[137] consedit, que urbem Romam captam incendit; porcio Illiricos sinus, idest[138] Adriaticum mare, in quo et Venecie, et in Panonia[139] consedit,[140] unde et Iustinus Tito concordat dicenti habundantem[141] Gallorum multitudinem vix regi posse.

Causam tamen transitus eciam aliam ponunt Iustinus et Ysidorus[142] et Papias, quam que[143] supra dicta est a Tito. Dicunt enim Gallis in Ytaliam[144] veniendi et sedes novas querendi causa[145] intestina discordia et assidue domi dissenciones fuere, quarum tedio cum venissent in Ytaliam prenominatas condiderunt urbes.[146]

124. F, Insulibus. 125. F, aliter dicta primum. 126. F, Isidoro.
127. *Isidore, XV, 13, 1; Papias,* s.v. *ager.* 128. *Isidore, XV, 2, 14;* F, Isodorus.
129. F, eciam *omitted.* 130. F, contra.
131. *Papias, s.v. paganus;* F, fons dicitur.
132. F, Isidorus. 133. F, Italiam.
134. *Justinus,* Epitoma Historiarum Phillipicarum Pompei Troji, *ed. O. Seal (Leipzig, 1935), XX, 5, 9.*
135. F, Euxebius. 136. F, abundanti. 137. F, Italia.
138. F, immo in. 139. F, Pannonia. 140. *Justinus, XXIV, 4, 1–3.*
141. F, abundantem. 142. F, Isidorus. 143. F, quamquam.
144. F, Italiam. 145. Causa *must be added for the sense of the passage;* F, causae.
146. F, *Justinus, XX, 5, 8.*

Sed quantum ad tempus edificacionis[147] seu ad ipsam urbis Mediolani condicionem adventus causa nil[148] discrepat. Neque ad hoc attendendum, nisi quod fortasse ipsi fuerunt nobis discordiarum intestinarum et dissensionum domesticarum infelix augurium. Ipse eciam quoque Titus aliam[149] adventus causam tradit, non tamen assertive, sic dicendo: Eam autem Gallorum gentem traditur ex fama dulcedine frugum et maxime vini nova tunc voluptate captam Alpes transisse[150] et agros ab Etruscis[151] ante cultos possedisse, et invexisse[152] in Galliam vinum, illiciende gentis causa.[153] Licet autem moderni non sint ex Gallorum progenie, Langobar- /[fol. 145*r*] di enim sunt, a Gallis tamen vino illectis[154] aliqui eciam[155] non degenerant.

Tempus vero ex quo Mediolanum conditum fuerit, idem Titus patenter insinuat. Ubi agit de oppugnacione Clusii et irruptione in urbem Romam facta per Gallos, duce tunc Brenone illorum, inquit ab[156] ducentis quippe annis antequam Clusium oppugnarent urbemque Romam caperent, in Italiam Galli transcenderunt;[157] et paulo post sequitur quod tempore illius irrupcionis transierant ab urbe Roma condita[158] anni .ccc.lx., quibus, ut idem scribit, omnibus bellis victrix fuerat ipsa Roma.[159] Si igitur recte calculando demantur ex annis .iii^c^lx. anni .cc., restabunt sine dubio .clx. anni, qui iam transierant ab urbe condita, regnante scilicet tunc Tarquinio[160] Prisco, anno scilicet regni eius .xxv. et in regum numero quinto. Iam enim per illos .clx. annos, demptis .xxv. qui fuerunt in regno Tarquinii Prisci, regnaverant Romulus, Numma[161] Pompilius, Tullus Hostilius, et Ancus Marcus, si recta calculacio fiat, quo annorum .clx. numero expleto ab urbe condita precedebant adhuc[162] Salvatoris nostri ortum anni .vi^c^xcii.[163] Secundum vero Eusebium[164] illa irrupcio sive invasio Gallorum Senonum fuit anno urbis Rome[165] .ccclxxi., hoc est .xvii. Artaxerxis cognomine Memnon Persarum regis, qui regnare cepit anno urbis .iii^c^iv.,[166] secundum eundem Eusebium.[167]

Utrum autem statim, ipso scilicet anno adventus eorum, condiderint Mediolanum nec (ne) expresse (non) invenio. Sed Titus per verba eius superius posita videtur innuere quod in ipso suo adventu electa sede

147. MS, edificacionem. 148. F, nihil. 149. F, aliam quoque.
150. F, transcendisse. 151. F, Hetruscis. 152. F, innexisse.
153. *Livy, V, 33, 2,* 154. F, illecti. 155. F, et.
156. F, enim. 157. *Livy, V, 33, 5,*
158. F, irruptionis iam transierant ab ipsa urbe condita Roma.
159. *Livy, V, 40, 1.* 160. F, regnante tum Tarquinio. 161. F, Numa.
162. F, ad hunc. 163. F, ortum .DC.XCII. 164. F, Euxebium.
165. F, urbis conditae. 166. F, .CCCLXV. 167. *Jerome, pp. 116, 118.*

condidisse urbem ipsam, et certe credendum est quod urbi condende non fuerunt diutius[168] immorari et per iniratas[169] vagasse sedes. Posito preterea quod in loco quo Galli Mediolanum condiderunt fuisse[170] ante Subria, vel alia civitas stans vel eversa, non propterea sequeretur quod Mediolanum antiquius esset Roma, cum eadem racione antiquitatis Subrie[171] satis contemporanea et Ianiculum civitas quam condidisse ferunt in eo loco ubi nunc est Roma Ianum, qui Noe filius esse dicitur, et si not satis contemporanea, non tamen esset[172] prioritas illa quam astruunt,[173] scilicet[174] mille ferme annorum, cum non nisi transisse dicant .clii. annos ex quo Ianus, defuncto Noe, regnum accepit et Ianiculum condidit. Sed si credatur assertis eciam[175] contemporanea[176] fuit ipsi Subrie alia civitas, quam, ut refert Martinus Polonus in cronicis,[177] traducere se dicens eciam ab Escodio,[178] condidit Noe in loco in quo nunc est Roma et a suo nomine denominavit.[179] Quod autem Mediolanum fuerit in Subria[180] regione non quod Subrium[181] fuerit civitas multi produnt auctores, maxime prenominati, Titus, Orosius, et eciam Eutropius, nam ex verbis precedentibus Titi demonstratum iam et alibi eciam fuerat.[182] Orosius vero cum de Marchi[183] Claudii Marcelli Romani[184] consulis victoria loquitur contra Gallos, quando scilicet .xxx. milia ex eis destruit,[185] subiungit dicens: Inter multa Insubrum que ad dedicionem coegerat[186] opida,[187] Mediolanum quoque urbem florentissimam cepit et hoc fuisse dicit anno[188] ab urbe Roma condita .dxx., qui fuit ante Christi adventum .cc.xxx(x)ii., addiditque[189] ex urbe ipsa Mediolani predam maximam reportavit;[190] et tunc, ut scribit Sicardus, archum illum triumphalem extra portam Romanam erexit in quo iussit inscribi, Qui vult modico tempore vivere, Mediolanum inhabitet, ubi vires[191] habentur pro legibus et iura describuntur in ossibus mortuorum.[192]

168. F, credendum non fuerit diutius. 169. F, incertas.

170. F, fuisset. 171. F, Subria.

172. F, antiquitatis Subria satis contemporanea; non tamen esset.

173. F, asserunt. 174. F, sed. 175. F, et. 176. F, temporanea.

177. F, chronicis. 178. F, dicens ab Excodio. 179. *Martinus, pp. 399–400.*

180. MS, Subrio. 181. F, Subria.

182. F, demonstratum est. Iam et alibi dictum est. *This part of the paragraph—to the section ending with* opida sive civitates*—has been spoiled by a later hand, which perhaps traced over the words in an effort to bring clarity to the text; it has achieved only confusion. I have attempted to make as much sense as I can out of the text.*

183. F, Marci. 184. F, Rom. 185. F, dederunt. 186. F, coegerant.

187. F, oppida. 188. F, cepit anno. 189. F, addidit et iam quod.

190. *Orosius, IV, 13, 15.* 191. F, mores.

192. F, [mortuorum]. *Sicard (fol. 29*r*) did not mention this arch and inscription.*

De arcu cum isto versu nichil[193] refert Orosius.[194] Hec eciam[195] Eutropius qui eciam expugnationem eandem recitat. Ipsi quoque ambo scriptores referunt alia vice Romanos[196] pugnasse[197] cum Insubribus et .xxiii. milia ex eis interemisse, quinque vero milia captivasse.[198] Patet igitur quod multa erant Insubrium opida[199] sive civitates, inter quas eminebat Mediolanum. Et forte adhuc pars[200] comitatus Mediolani Seprium dictum nomen inde sumpsit vel nomen retinuit, mutata litera u in e.

Erant eciam (eciam)[201] Insubribus populi confines, scilicet Boi et Cenomanni;[202] Boi autem,[203] ut dicit Eutropius, condiderunt Ticinum urbem que dicitur Papia.[204] Cenomannis[205] vero caput erat Brixia, ut dicit Titus.[206] Ipsi eciam Boi et Cenomanni,[207] ut dicit idem Orosius, contractis in unum viribus, Amilchare[208] Peno[209] duce, qui in Ytalia[210] remanserat, Cremonam et Placenciam vastantes dificil[l]imo bello victi sunt a Romanis.[211]

Nec est quorundam assercionibus,[212] immo confabulacionibus inherendum,[213] qui vel scribunt vel autumant Brenonem Gallorum regulum[214] Mediolanum edificasse. Nam, ut predictum est, .cc.[215] anni precesserant[216] iam ab adventu Gallorum qui Mediolanum edificaverant[217] Bellovisso[218] duce, quando Breno[219] ipse regulus erat Gallorum et Roman invasit; potuit tamen esse quod reparavit, prout vult Gotifridus[220] Viterbiensis.[221] Alibi[222] non legi. Aliqui eciam referunt hanc civitatem fuisse binominam;[223] quod [224] videlicet idem Breno[225] nomen Mediolanum mutaverit et vocaverit eam Albam a candore populi. Sed hoc eciam autenticum[226] non inveni. In legenda tamen de adventu apostoli Barnabe in civitatum Mediolani, que intitulatur secundum aliquos Paulino

193. MS, nichi. 194. *Ferrai omitted this sentence.* 195. F, eciam *omitted.*
196. F, Romanos alia vice. 197. F, (ex)pugnasse.
198. F, .XXIII. milia captivasse; *Orosius, IV, 13, 10; Eutropius* (*Paul*), Breviarium ab urbe condita, *ed. H. Droysen*, MGH, AA, *II* (*Berlin, 1879*), *III, 2, 2.*
199. F, oppida. 200. F, praesens.
201. F, etiam et. 202. F, Cenomani. 203. F, antea.
204. *Eutropius, IV, 2, 3.* 205. F, Cenomannis. 206. *Livy, XXXII, 30.*
207. F, Cenomani. 208. F, Amilcare. 209. F, Phoeno.
210. F, Italia. 211. *Orosius, IV, 20, 4.*
212. F, Nec est credendum quorundam assertionibus.
213. F, inherendum *omitted.* 214. F, ducem sive regulum. 215. F, ducenti.
216. F, processerant. 217. F, Mediolanum condiderunt.
218. F, Belloveso. 219. F, quum Brenus. 220. F, Gotefridus.
221. *Godfrey* of *Viterbo*, Liber Pantheon (*Bavarian State Library, Munich* (*Cod. Clm 43*) *fol. 49*v).
222. F, Sed alibi. 223. *De Situ Civitatis*, RIS, *I–II* (*Milan, 1725*), *col. 205*a.
224. F, quia. 225. F, Brenus. 226. F, authenticum.

Nolano episcopo, habetur quod Mediolanum a veteribus Albe primum nomen sortita est, usitato autem vocabulo Mediolanum dicta.[227] Ad huius eciam binominitatis assercionem adducitur quod scribit Cassiodorus Tripartite libro quinto[228] dicens, quod apud Mediolanum celebrata est synodus[229] in qua orientales convenientes ante omnia contra Athanasium decretum fieri commune poscebant. Quod dum sensisset Paulinus Gallicane Treverensis et Dyonisius[230] Albe metropolis Ytalorum[231] et Eusebius Vercellensis episcopus etc.[232] Sed cum reffellatur[233] primum quod scilicet[234] a veteribus sit Alba prius dicta, nam constant ut[235] premonstratum est a Tito fuisse primum eius nomen Mediolanum, nec aliqui ex ceteris prefatis auctoribus eam binominam fuisse insinuent, seu Albam dictam, potest a simili et secundum quod in legenda dicitur eciam[236] repugnari, cum non ibi insinuetur expresse, quod illa Alba in qua Dyonisius[237] episcopus fuerit Mediolanum et si Alba illa[238] fuisset Mediolanum qua racione predixisset[239] idem auctor sinodum illam fuisse apud Mediolanum, nisi addidisset quod et[240] Alba dictum est? Non legi eciam alicubi quod aliqua civitas fuerit metropolis Italorum Alba nomine; fortassis fuit error in scriptore, quia[241] alius textus habebat loco Albe alterius.

Cur vero hec urbs Mediolanum hoc nomen sit sortita, quod Titus non meminit, varia referuntur.[242] Alii enim ideo Mediolanum fuisse dictam astruunt[243] eo quod inter duo flumina, Ticinum videlicet et Adduam,[244] velut in medietate sitam[245] equa ab utroque lance[246] distare videatur.[247] Alii affirmant monstrum ibidem inventum, hoc est sus ex media parte corporis laneo tectus[248] vellere, nomen urbi indidit Mediolanum. Ad cuius rei indicium[249] mos inolevit ut quociens ab ipsa velut[250] ex principali urbium metropoli Romani consules ad bella prodibant, vexilla eos suillanea[251] preirent.[252]

Hee[253] autem due opiniones eciam scribuntur[254] dicto opusculo

227. De Situ Civitatis, *col. 205*a. 228. F, .V. 229. F, sinodus.
230. F, Dionisus. 231. F, Italorum.
232. *Cassiodorus,* Historia Tripartita, *V, 15.* 233. F, refellatur.
234. F, scilicet *omitted.* 235. F, et. 236. F, eciam *omitted.*
237. F, Dionisius. 238. F, illa Alba. 239. F, prodixisset.
240. F, ex. 241. F, quod.
242. F, Titus quamvis non referat, ab aliis tamen quamplurimis referuntur.
243. F, affirmant. 244. F, Abduam. 245. F, sita. 246. F, amne.
247. De Situ Civitatis, *col. 205*a. 248. F, tutus. 249. F, iudicium.
250. MS, urbe, *but* velut *is traced in.* 251. MS, sunillanea.
252. De Situ Civitates, *col. 205*a. 253. F, haec.
254. F, opiniones inscribuntur.

legende apostoli Barnabe,[255] cui ultime, scilicet de sue, concordat Isidorus et Papias, dicentes vocatum Mediolanum ab eo quod ibi sus media lanea perhibetur inventa.[256] Unde et quidam metrice[257] dixit:

> Sus fuit inventus ubi fixit castra iuventus
> In medio (tergo) lanam tulit [tergo]. Accidit ergo
> Nomen ut aptaret, Mediolanumque vocaret.

De situ quoque et qualitate loci urbis huius et bonorum copia tamen et multa[258] preclara et magnifica possent scribi; ego tamen paucula ex multis succincte inseram gracia brevitatis. Situs[259] namque huius civitatis uberrimus est fecunde matris Italie sinus,[260] in/[fol. 145*v*] ea dumtaxat provincie ipsius plaga que Ligurie nomen a veteribus sortita est, a legendis, idest[261] colligendis, leguminibus, quorum satis est fertilis, per quam a septentrionali ad orientalem[262] versus partem Addua et Ticinum ingencia flumina Padani gurgitis medium influunt gremium.

Loci qualitas circa fruges et fructus.[263] Qualitas vero loci urbis huius omittenda non est, que ita moderate[264] temperancie[265] per divinam providenciam in sese naturam possidet ut nisi delicta cohabitancium[266] impediant, necessarios usus congruis subministrare[267] temporibus et sue affluencia(m)[268] dignitatis patriotas iocundare[269] non desinat. In nonnullis namque regionibus aut solis fervor immensus iugi estu[270] virencia terre perurit, aut glacialis hiems sub nivea[271] crusta rigescens prohibet solum humano usui producere fetus, fitque ut quibus fruges suppetunt, dulcia vina negentur, item[272] quos vini potat dulcedo,[273] frugum inopia necet. At iste de quo loquor locus summa satis opulencia largus diversorum profert semina fructuum, et nunc has, nunc illas novellas[274] subinde fessus agricola colligit fruges. Sic quoque qui toto anni spacio non indulserat ocio, gaudebit passim[275] telluris ubere profluo.[276]

Vinum.[277] Quid eciam[278] de vini referam ubertate precipua qua[279]

255. F, apostoli beati Barnabae.
256. F, iuventa; *Isidore, XV, 1, 57; Papias, s.v. Mediolanum.*
257. F, Unde quidam sic metrice.
258. F, copia multa. 259. F, sinus. 260. F, prius.
261. F, immo. 262. F, orientem.
263. *Ferrai omitted this title.* 264. F, moderate *omitted.*
265. MS, temperanciam. 266. F, inhabitantium. 267. F, ministrare.
268. F, affluentia. 269. F, iucundare. 270. F, iugi estu *omitted.*
271. F, nimia. 272. F, itemque. 273. F, dulcedo potat.
274. F, et nunc has novellas, nunc illas. 275. F, passum.
276. F, profluo *omitted.* 277. F, Vinum *omitted.* 278. F, eciam *omitted.*
279. F, ubertate et copia praecipua quam.

per supernam largitatem usque adeo plurimas Romani nominis provincias exsuperat, ut multo amplius huic nonnumquam meraca[280] pocius quam sincera, quibus suis vel eciam aque salubris videatur inesse.

Plenitudo[281] Aque. Nam[282] et de aquis loci eiusdem quid primum mirer, que quam[283] sint ad potandum habiles,[284] atque omnium usu laudabiles, non tantum virorum peritorum, sed eciam pistorum et fullonum optime novit industria. Raro autem eidem urbi marine copie, raro diversorum stagnorum dapes affluentissime deesse potuerunt pro temporis accessu.

Civium Forma.[285] Et quod valde mirandum eius loci genium sive[286] natura concinens[287] ibidem satis ipsa equiparant forma corporea[288] eatenus ut longe dispariliter a ceterarum urbium distare videantur indigenis.[289] Inest nempe illis stature proceritas decens, que eminenciam secuture dignitatis prefiguret[290] in membris, nec[291] tamen modum excedat ornate prolixitatis; quin[292] eciam nativa sollercia[293] ex genitalis quadam sapiencie prosapia decurrens frons hilaris et ore roseo benignissima, eciam[294] si animus in mestitudine torpeat.[295]

Urbis menia et edificia. De meniis preterea et mirificis[296] edificiis urbis[297] huius in verissimis annalibus Dacius se reperisse testatur, qui fuit illius urbis episcopus, quod videlicet augustales, imperatores, consules, et patricii eius urbis acole, dum orbis uno regeretur imperio, olim[298] magisterio regali ipsam ornarunt,[299] locantes in ea, more patrio, eximium Augustorum dignitati regale palatium,[300] unde et illa ecclesia denominatur que dicitur[301] Sancti Georgii in Palacio, quod Traianus dicitur construxisse. Erat eciam in ea urbe theatrum, idest semicirculare[302] decentissimum edificium ad spectacula fabricatum, quod constructum erat in loco ubi nunc est monasterium. Aumacium quoque in ea urbe erat, idest secretus locus publicus sicut theatrum.[303]

Ypodromum.[304] Ubi vero dicitur Sancta[305] Maria ad Circulum erat ypodromum[306] circi, idest ubi equi currebant. Ypos[307] enim equus grece,

280. F, mera. 281. F, Inesse plenitudo. 282. F, Aque *omitted.*
283. F, quamquam. 284. F, habiles ad potandum.
285. F, Civium Forma *omitted.* 286. F, sive *omitted.* 287. MS, concines.
288. F, corporea forma. 289. F, indigenes. 290. F, praedgeret.
291. F, ne. 292. F, quam. 293. F, naturalis sive natura solertia.
294. F, etsi. 295. De Situ Civitatis, *col. 204.*
296. F, mirificis *omitted.* 297. F, urbis *omitted.* 298. F, imperatores olim.
299. F, ornari. 300. *Landulph,* Historia Mediolanensis, *II, 2.* 301. F, de.
302. F, semicirculare *omitted.* 303. *Landulph,* Historia Mediolanensis, *II, 2.*
304. F, Ypodromum *omitted.* 305. F, dicitur modo Sancta.
306. F, ipodromum. 307. F, ipos.

dromos strata, ibi enim equestres milites sua hastiludia[308] peragebant Romanorum more, et inde usque ad teatrum erat subterranea strata.[309] In ipso circo eciam levatus fuit rex Langobardorum Adoloaldus.[310]

Therme, idest[311] stuve. Erant et therme, idest[312] balnea calida, ubi regine, imperatorum coniuges urbem pro tempore incolencium, semotim a masculis nitide mundabantur, et universe civitatis multitudo, cum tempus et utilitas exigebat, ad lavandum, viris a mulieribus sequestratis, sedule concurrebant.[313]

Viridarium, idest Verzarium.[314] Deinde viridarium quasi[315] paradisus diversis insitum arboribus amenum erat iuxta menia civitatis, ubi senatores et consules[316] sua corpora recreabant, in quo fructuum et florum immensa diversitas aviumque inclusarum ingenio clarissima[317] melodia. In medio erat ydolum Februe dii Martis genitricis sedens in aureo throno, quod[318] super apparatu bellorum responsa dabat; hic locus hodie vulgo Verzarium dicitur.[319]

Arena que et Arengum. Erat insuper arena in urbe ipsa lapidibus et magisteriis diversis ornata, albo scilicet et nigro marmore distincta, tota rotunda, in cuius circuitu tot erant camere quot in anno sunt dies per occultos meatus incluse. Hec autem arena[320] tante erat capacitatis ut in ea tocius Ytalie[321] milites consedere et ab uno oratore audire et competenter intelligere possent et invicem se videre et iste locus hodie denominatur Arengum.[322]

Brolietum.[323] Non longe ab eo erat locus, qui hodie dicitur vetus Brolietum,[324] in quo habebatur capitolium, ubi senatores et consules morabantur iudicantes de causis et urbem gubernantes.[325]

Turres et porte.[326] Quin[327] eciam ipsam amplificantes civitatem ultra quam Senones Galli edificaverant .ccclxv. turres densissimas opere grandi edificarunt et compleverunt.[328] Preterea super sex civitatis portas domicilia

308. F, astiludia. 309. F, strata subterrenea.

310. F, Adaloaldus; *Paul the Lombard,* Historia Longobardorum, *ed. L. Bethmann and G. Waitz,* MGH, SRLI (*Hannover, 1878*), *IV, 30.*

311. F, et. 312. F, Erant etiam thermae et.

313. F, sedula concurrebat; *Landulph,* Historia Mediolanensis, *II, 2.*

314. *Ferrai omitted this title.* 315. F, viridarium seu verzarium quasi.

316. F, consules et senatores. 317. F, inclusarum . . . clarissima.

318. F, quae. 319. *Landulph,* Historia Mediolanensis, *II, 2.*

320. F, arena *omitted.* 321. F, Italiae.

322. F, Arenghum; *Landulph,* Historia Mediolanensis, *II, 2.*

323. F, Brolietum *omitted.* 324. F, Brolietum vetus.

325. *Fiamma,* Manipulus Florum, RIS, *XI* (*Milan, 1727*), *col. 555.*

326. MS, portas. 327. F, Qui. 328. F, complerunt.

altissima ac rotunda, ac anteportale altissimum et triangulare opere decentissimo edificantes, que hostibus barbaricis quasi natura munita introitum contenderent, agere satagerunt, ob quas causas sepissime ab eisdem postmodum Augustis hec urbs frequentari et incoli ac[329] honorari cepit, maxime quia[330] esset inibi[331] saluberrimi aeris aptissima temperies locusque ad usus domesticos irrefragabiliter paratissimus,[332] sicut legimus de Galieno, Maximiano, Valente, Valentiniano, Theodosio, et multis aliis. Fertur eciam quod ad leonis formam et sub ascendente astro Leonis murum civitatis fundaverunt, latitudinis .xxiiii. pedum, altitudinis .lxxiiii., et quod in singulis portis erant singula ydola, scilicet in porta que nunc Romana dicitur idolum Apolinis, idolum Veneris in porta Vercellina, idolum Iunonis[333] in porta Ticinensi, idolum Iovis in porta que vulgo dicitur Zobia,[334] cuius et nomen hodie retinet in latino, idola[335] preterea Saturni et Martis[336] et aliorum fuerunt in reliquis, sed in quibus certa non invenitur[337] scriptura.[338]

Ex hiis[339] et aliis innumeris eminenciis, hanc urbem secundam denominantes Romam, portis inscribi iusserunt:

Dic homo qui transis, qui porte limina tangis:
Roma secunda, vale, regni decus imperiale.
Urbs veneranda nimis, plenissima rebus opimis,
Te metuunt gentes, tibi flectunt colla potentes,
In bello Thebas, in sensu vincis Athenas.[340]

Unde eciam Decius Magnus Ausonius[341] vir illustris in cathalago[342] urbium nobilium post Romam, Constantinopolim, et[343] Carthaginem, Antiochiam, Alexandriam atque Treverim, loquens de urbe Mediolani ic ait:

Et Mediolani mira omnia copia rerum,
Innumere[344] culteque domus, facunda virorum

329. F, et. 330. F, cum. 331. F, ibi.
332. *Landulph,* Historia Mediolanensis, *II, 2.*
333. F, scilicet in porta Vercellina ydolum Iunonis.
334. F, in porta Ticinensi ydolum Iovis, et in porta quae hodie dicitur Zobia.
335. F, ydola. 336. F, et Martis *omitted.* 337. F, non invenitur certa.
338. *Fiamma,* Manipulus Florum, *col. 554.*
339. F, his.
340. *See V. Forcella,* Iscrizioni delle chiese e degli altri edifici di Milano dal secolo VIII ai giorni nostri, *X* (*Milan, 1892*), *pp. 33–34.*
341. F, Unde Decius Ausonius Magnus. 342. F. cathalogo.
343. F, et *omitted.* 344. MS, innumero.

Ingenia et mores leti,[345] cum[346] duplice muro
Amplificata loci species, populique voluptas
Circus, et inclusi moles cuneata teatri;[347]
Templa palatineque arces, opulensque moneta
Et regio Herculei celebri[348] sub honore lavacri,
Cunctaque marmoreis ornata peristula[349] signis,
Meniaque in valli formam circumdata limbo:[350]
Omnia que magnis operum velut emula formis
Excellunt nec iuncta premit vicinia Rome.[351]

Notandum est quod iste Ausonius[352] fuit contemporaneus Theodosio iuniori,[353] qui cepit imperare anno Domini /[fol. 146*r*] .iiii^c^xxv.[354] Hunc eciam cathologum[355] Ausonii repperi in archivo[356] ecclesie Veronensis, in quo erant libri innumeri et vetustissimi.[357] Quod autem dicit Ausonius duplici muro, intelligas quum ipsa civitas ampliata fuit, quia tunc secundus fuit murus erectus. Quod vero dicit regio Herculei, intelligas contratatam vel provinciam seu provincie partem vel hic[358] fuisse hanc urbem Herculei, idest Maximiani imperatoris, qui dicebatur Herculeius[359] Maximianus, nam in ea coronatus, fanum[360] Herculis mirificum, de quo infra dicetur, fabricavit. Et dum ibi venisset et Christianos persequeretur et[361] huiusmodi emisit edictum: Imperator Cesar[362] Herculeius Maximianus semper augustus invictus triumphator maximus advenit. Ecce, concurrite, cives, deos reportate patrios; concurrite, cives, et veneramini nos.[363] Vos[364] vero[365] ab urbe prophani, vobis[366] dicitur, recedite, Christiani. Ordinavit eciam ut[367] ibi corona imperii ferrea remaneret.[368]

De templis autem sive ecclesiis et monasteriis, ex multis que scribi possent hec pauca inseram; sed prius de primordio metropolico et matricis ecclesie exordio succincte exordiar, secundum quod in eodem opusculo de adventu Barnabe et in aliis libris et cronicis eiusdem urbis habetur. Cum Sancto dispensante Spiritu, ut apostolorum sacra narrat

345. MS, et mores leti *omitted.* 346. F, tum. 347. F, theatri.
348. F, celebris. 349. F, peristyla. 350. F, Labro.
351. *Ausonius,* Ordo Urbium Nobilium, *Carmina, ed. C. Schenkel,* MGH, AA, *V–II (Berlin, 1883), VII (on Milan).*
352. F, et notandum quod Ausonius. 353. F, minori.
354. F, .CCCCXXV. 355. F, cathalogum. 356. F, archivio.
357. *Here Benzo testifies to his use of the Capitular Library in Verona.*
358. F, vel hic *omitted.* 359. F, Herculeus. 360. F, phanum.
361. F, et *omitted.* 362. F, Imp. Caes. 363. MS, vos. 364. MS, nos.
365. F, et veneramini. vos vero. 366. F, nobis. 367. F, et quod.
368. *See Fiamma,* Manipulus Florum, *col. 563.*

historia, Paulum et Barnabam in opus verbi quo eos assumpserat, anno .vii.[369] post Domini passionem fundata in[370] Iacobo fratre Domini primitiva Hierosolimorum ecclesia, per manuum imposicionem apostoli[371] ad apostolatus fastigium extulerunt, editum divinitus oraculum segregari iussisset, horum alter, scilicet[372] Barnabas, Ciprius[373] genere, Cyprum[374] insulam suam repetiit[375] patriam, iniunctum[376] sibi predicacionis evangelice opus non desinens exercere. Non multo post navem ascendens Romam adiit, velut ad tocius dominam orbis, cum esset annus a constitucione eiusdem urbis Rome .vii.^{c}xcv.,[377] qui fuit Claudii imperatoris primus, post Domini ascensionem octavus. Stansque in loco urbis Rome celeberrimo, ubi populus Romanus concurrerat, cepit primus ex apostolis inopinatum filii Dei adventum libere protestari. Tunc nonnulli derisui eius verba habere ceperunt, nonnulli eciam amplexati illa fuerunt, inter quos Clemens qui postea beato Petro in apostolica sede Rome successit. Cumque idem apostolus Barnabas Roma egressus ceteras provincias lustraretur,[378] audiens quod Mediolanensis[379] secunda post Roman augustales occidentis imperii infulas retinebat, ad eandem[380] assumpto secum Anathelone[381] quodam genere Greco morumque probitate et fidei vigore precipuo cursus sui tramitem destinavit. Qui dum ibidem predicacioni verbi Dei operam daret, Anathelonem[382] sui itineris comitem Brixiam misit, que est una ex Veneciarum urbibus non ignobilis. Cognito tandem apostolus Barnabas quod ibi Anathelon[383] proficeret, imponens illi manum, episcopalem curam Mediolanensium ac[384] Brixiensium communiter delegavit. Unde factum est, ut quoad viveret[385] utriusque ecclesie plebibus pari tenore pastoralem impenderet curam; preterea quidem sanxit ut Mediolanensis ecclesia, quam ipse fundaverat, aliarum[386] in ea provincia ecclesiarum metropolis haberetur, verbisque solatus[387] apostolicis virum Dei Anathelonem,[388] ad Palestine gremium repedavit. Anathelo[389] vero in pastorali cura utrarumque sedium .xiii. annis fuit, ab anno scilicet .vii. Claudii usque ad .viii.[390] Neronis; in quo tempore sibi successores duos ordinavit, alterum Mediolanensis, alterum Brixiensis civitatis episcopum, nichilque[391] a suo institutore discrepans metropolit-

369. MS, dum .vii.; F, anno quartodecimo.
370. F, a. 371. F, a(p)postoli. 372. F, s. 373. F, Cyprius.
374. F, Cyprium. 375. F, repetit. 376. F, invictum.
377. F, .DCCXCV. 378. F, lustraret. 379. F, Mediolanensis civitas.
380. MS, eande. 381. F, Anathalone. 382. F, Anathalonem.
383. F, Anathalon. 384. F, et. 385. F, ut quod adiuveret.
386. F, quum ipse aliarum. 387. F, consolatus. 388. F, Anathalonem.
389. F, Anathalon. 390. F, octavum. 391. F, nihilque.

anam in urbe Mediolani[392] cathedram[393] pro futuris temporibus Christi statuit esse fidelibus, quatenus affinium populorum antistites, hoc est Venecie, Ligurie, Emilie, Recie, Alpis Cocie, post Romanum pontificem habere debeant Mediolanensis sedis presulem caput quondam[394] et decus insigne.[395]

Quod autem[396] apostolus Barnabas fuerit Mediolani[397] episcopus testatur eciam Ieronimus[398] in epistola ad Cromatium et Theodorum; item Silvester papa, necnon et beatus Dorotheus.[399]

Ferunt eciam[400] nonnulli hac consideracione apostolum instituisse urbem Mediolani metropolim, quia[401] secundum Romanorum ritum eciam archiflamines Mediolani tempore gentilitatis preerant aliis flaminibus Italie. Dicebantur enim tunc archiflamines et flamines apud gentiles qui nunc archiepiscopi et episcopi a Christianis dicuntur.[402] In hoc eciam credendum est ideo Brixiensem episcopum ad dexteram[403] archiepiscopi Mediolanensis sedis obtinere locum, ut primitiva ipsarum sedium unio denotetur.[404] Licet autem ipse archiepiscopus tantis refulserit insignibus dignitatum, ut difficile foret retexere, tamen hiis[405] paucis eius potest adverti sublime fastigium.[406] Nam, sicut predictum est, tam diffusam metropolim habuit, licet sit hodie defalcata,[407] ut non nisi .xiiii. presit presulibus. Ad ipsum quoque, ut testatus est Conradus imperator huius nominis secundus, prout scribit Arnulphus in cronicis suis, regalis eleccio et consecracio spectat, et demum representacio ad imperialis culminis infulas.[408] Nam, sicut in quibusdam scribitur cronicis,[409] fertur quod Maximianus imperator cum eius predecessores ac ipse ferrea corona[410] consuevissent coronari, et eius tempore aureo dyademate[411] coronari cepissent, instituit ut ferree corone[412] Mediolani coronacio fieret, Roma vero aurei dyadematis[413] coronacionem possideret, ut scribit Sicardus.[414] Fertur eciam quod beatus Gregorius privilegio concessit archiepiscopo Mediolanensi quod semper vacante imperio de consensu

392. F, Mediolanense. 393. F, catedram.
394. F, quoddam. 395. De Situ Civitatis, *cols. 205*a–*207*e.
396. F, antea. 397. F, Mediolanensis. 398. F, Hieronimus.
399. *Nothing in these men's extant writings supports the Barnabas legend.*
400. F, Dorotheus ferunt et. 401. F, quae.
402. *See Fiamma,* Manipulus Florum, *col. 552.* 403. F, dextram.
404. F, sedium . . . denotetur. 405. F, his. 406. F, fastigium sublime.
407. F, diffalcata.
408. *Arnulph,* Gesta Archiepiscoporum Mediolanensium, *II, ii.*
409. F, chronicis. 410. F, corona ferrea. 411. F, diademate.
412. F, corone *omitted.* 413. F, diadematis.
414. F, Sycardus. (*There is nothing in Sicard on this.*)

suorum suffraganeorum, posset eligere Italie comitem, qui vice regis Longobardis preesset, et in ecclesia sancti Ambrosii corona insigniretur triticea per eundem archiepiscopum vel eius vasallum,[415] eique comiti prelati Lombardi tenerentur .iii.c. marcis[416] auri purissimi. Ipse vero comes continuatis dietis, non contrahendo moram in aliqua urbe ultra tres dies, festinando Romam deberet per papam vel cardinales coronari argentea corona,[417] et tunc dici debeat[418] non comes sed rex. Iterum[419] Modoeciam veniens, debebat ferrea insigniri corona,[420] demum Romam reversus aureo diademate coronari, dicique non rex sed imperator. Quo privilegio feruntur usi fuisse nonnulli archiepiscopi, scilicet Valpertus, Heribertus, et alii plures. Hec habentur[421] ex cronicis[422] Philippi comitis Castri Seprii; sed in cronicis Martini Poloni habetur quod Conradum tercium benedixit, unxit, et coronavit in regem Italie Anselmus archiepiscopus Mediolani origine Mediolanensis de[423] progenie Pusterlengorum, in ecclesia sancti Michaelis de Modoecia,[424] in qua est primus locus corone Italice, et postea in ecclesia sancti Ambrosii Mediolani, ut legitur in quodam libro qui dicitur Copia[425] Landulfi de Sancto Paulo, qui Mediolani habetur.[426] Sic tamen servatum non fuit in coronacione de regno Italico Henrici VII, quia solum in ecclesia sancti Ambrosii coronam ferream accepit, quamquam multum fuerit disceptatum an Modoecie fieri deberet, et ob id locum illum postmodum sollempniter[427] visitavit.

Nec ad minorem, immo verius ad maiorem huius ecclesie metropolitane spectat excellenciam quod eius presules ipsam metropolitanam ecclesiam circa[428] divinum officium et ipsius ministros mirifice et laudabiliter ordinarunt. Inter quos maxime beatus Ambrosius preminuisse dignoscitur. Ad instar enim[429] .lxxii. discipulorum Christi .lxxii. instituit sacerdotes, qui episcopi dicebantur, ferula et anulo insigniti,[430] ex quibus unum primicerium, idest co(r)episcopum nuncupavit, qui de virtutibus ceteros instituebat[431] sacerdotes.[432] Iuxta[433] eciam .xxiiii. seniorum et .xxiiii. horarum naturalium ordinem,[434] .xxiiii. cardines[435] /[fol. 146*v*] qui hodie

415. F, vassallum. 416. F, Longobardi tenerentur marchis.
417. F, corona argentea. 418. F, debebat. 419. F, item.
420. F, corona insigniri. 421. F, trahuntur. 422. F, chronicis.
423. F, origine Mediolanensis, et de origine Mediolani et de.
424. *Martinus'* Chronicon *does not contain this information.*
425. F, Copia *omitted.*
426. *Landulph of St. Paul,* Historia Mediolanensis, *p. 44.*
427. F, solemniter. 428. F, archa. 429. F, eius.
430. *Landulph,* Historia Mediolanensis, *I, 2.*
431. F, instruebat. 432. *Landulph,* Historia Mediolanensis, *I, 3.*
433. F, instituit. 434. F, instituit *added.* 435. F, cardinales.

ordines[436] nuncupantur,[437] archipresbyterum[438] quoque cum .vii. dyaconibus,[439] item subdyacones[440] .xxiiii.[441] et acholitos,[442] idest[443] notarios sui palacii, multos instituit, similiter et lectores,[444] similiter et primicerium puerorum, qui cum ferula corio[445] ornata in ecclesia hyemali[446] filios marchionum et comitum vel eciam capitaneorum[447] iniciales litteras edocebat. In scola[448] beati Ambrosii erant .x. viri clerici[449] cum quibus mulieres vetule vinum et hostias ministrabant. In latere aquilonari ecclesie hyemalis[450] erant philosophorum scole, que longa archiepiscoporum consuetudine ipsorum sustentabantur stipendiis.[451]

De philosophis autem qui Mediolani studuerunt, habentur eximii[452] Virgilius Mantuanus, qui ibi togam suscepit,[453] et magnus Augustinus, qui ibi rethoricam docuit et veram didicit philosophiam. Sicque[454] Mediolanensi urbe velut unum templum facta, proverbium inolevit quod Mediolanum in clericis, Papia in deliciis, Ravenna in ecclesiis, Roma in edificiis anteiret.

Adhuc accedit ad decus insigne metropolitane urbis huius quod tam antique tamque nobilis ecclesie Ravenatis[455] metropolitanum precedit, ut patet ex decreto ubi agitur quod archiepiscopus Mediolanensis in synodo[456] pape Symachi[457] primo se subscripsit, postea pater[458] Ravenas archiepiscopus,[459] quod ecclesie Cumane primum[460] dedit episcopum beatus Ambrosius nomine Felicem, quod beatus Simplicianus sanctum Gaudencium primum Novarium[461] consecravit episcopum. Nonnulli quoque qui cardinalatus apicem adepti fuerant,[462] facti fuerunt huius urbis archiepiscopi, sicut de beato Galdino legitur.

Sequitur de certis[463] edificiis et locis insignibus urbis et dyocesis[464] et

436. F, ordinarii. 437. *Landulph,* Historia Mediolanensis, *I, 4.*
438. F, archipresbiterum.
439. F, diaconibus; *Landulph,* Historia Mediolanensis, *I, 5.*
440. MS, subdiaconi; F, subdiacones.
441. *Landulph,* Historia Mediolanensis, *I, 5.*
442. F, acolitos. 443. F, scilicet.
444. *Landulph,* Historia Mediolanensis, *I, 7.* 445. F, corio ferula.
446. F, hiemali. 447. F, praedictus primicerius *added.* 448. F, schola.
449. F, erant et viri electi. 450. F, hiemales.
451. *Paulinus,* Vita S. Ambrosii, *PL, XIV, 27.*
452. F, eximius. 453. *Jerome, p. 155.* 454. F, sic.
455. F, Ravennatis. 456. F, sinodo. 457. F, Simachi.
458. F, pater *omitted.*
459. *See P. F. Kehr,* Italia Pontificia *(Berlin, 1911), V, 53, n. 170.*
460. F, ecclesiae omnis primus. 461. F, Novariae. 462. F, fuerunt.
463. F, caeteris. 464. F, et dyocesis *omitted.*

fundatoribus ac[465] fundacionis temporibus eorundem.[466] Iuxta fontem qui est apud Sanctum Eustorgium,[467] sanctus Anathalon, beati Barnabe successor, divina officia sub divo, non in templo celebravit.[468] Unde et creditur primum ibi qua[469] in Liguria et eciam in Ytalia[470] hostia Deo Patri fuisse oblata;[471] hunc eciam fontem sanctus successor eius Gaius benedixit et in eo Christi fideles instituit baptizari.[472] Inter quos fuerunt Vitalis cum Valeria coniuge et Gervasio et Protasio filiis. Item Philippus cum Fausto et Porcio filiis.[473] Castricianus quoque de Oldanis ex domo Philippi[474] extra civitatem[475] sita templum construxit Deo dicatum et intitulatum postmodum sanctis Nabori et Felici martiribus, hodie vero glorioso confessori Francisco; cuius templi tanta extitit virtus ut non solum gentiles sed et fideles tam ex urbe quam ex suburbanis, vel eciam ex Subriensibus viculis concurrentes, omnium languorum medelam[476] reciperent.[477] Nec misterio carere videtur quod sicut locus primus oracionis et missarum conventui predicatorum cessit, sic locus prime constructe ecclesie minorum fratrum conventui adveniret; et uterque locus egris medelam[478] corporibus daret,[479] significans ibidem animarum veros medicos futuris temporibus habitare.

Ecclesiam sancti Vitalis, olim dictam Faustam, et ecclesiam sancti Victoris ad Corpus, que Porciana dicebatur, Faustus et Porcius Philippi[480] iam dicti filii construxerunt, in quibus Castricianus archiepiscopus clericorum choros Daviticos ymnos[481] personantes instituit. In hac eciam Porciana ecclesia beatus Ambrosius ab Arrianis[482] obsessus divinum composuit officium, primoque fuit in toto occidente cantatum.[483] Ecclesia sancti Laurentii fuit fanum[484] Herculis, quod Maximianus imperator construxit. Ibi enim erat Herculis simulachrum in throno eburneo[485] sedens, dabatque responsa. Ante fanum .xvi. marmoreas columpnas[486] erexit, quas laminis ereis deauratis vestivit, in quibus erant sculpture avium, piscium et diversorum monstrorum. Contigit autem postmodum ut cum ipsum fanum[487] in honorem beati Laurentii dedicatum fuisset a Christi fidelibus, uno et horrendo concremaretur incendio

465. F, et. 466. F, eorumdem. 467. F, Euxtorgium.
468. De Situ Civitatis, *col. 207*d. 469. F, qua *omitted.* 470. F, Italia.
471. F, oblatum. 472. De Situ Civitatis, *col. 208*c.
473. *Ferrai omitted this sentence.* 474. MS, Plilippi. 475. F, tunc *added.*
476. F, medel(l)am. 477. De Situ Civitatis, *col. 212*e.
478. F, medel(l)am. 479. F, daret *omitted.*
480. F, Portius et . . . Faustus Filippi. 481. F, hymnos. 482. F, Arianis.
483. *Paulinus,* Vita S. Ambrosii, *col. 31.* 484. F, phanum.
485. F, trono heburneo. 486. F, colupnas. 487. F, phanum.

cum pluribus aliis basilicis, imperante Henrico .iiii.,[488] ut scribitur in libro Arnulfi,[489] qui cepit imperare anno Christi .mlvii.,[490] et sic omne illius operis decus consumptum est.[491] Refert enim idem Arnulfus[492] quod adeo omnium speciosissima fuit sancti Laurencii ecclesia, ut relatu difficile videatur[493] que fuerint lignorum lapidumque sculpture[494] et eorum altrinsecus compaginate iuncture que (suis)[495] columpne[496] cum[497] basibus, tribunalia quoque per girum ac desuper tegens universa musium,[498] idest opus depictum.[499]

Ecclesiam sancti Nazarii fundavit beatus Ambrosius in honorem .xii. apostolorum; ecclesiam quoque que nunc suo dedicata est nomini, idem[500] fundavit Ambrosius in honorem sanctorum Gervasii et Protasii et omnium martyrum.[501] Monasterium vero quod dicitur sancti Ambrosii fundavit Petrus archiepiscopus Mediolani anno Christi .viii^{c},[502] in quo et serpens eneus Moysi, de quo in ipsa Moysi historia dictum. Ibi eciam Herculis marmorea statua venuste formata.[503] Est enim Hercules amictus leonina pelle[504] in una[505] clavam tenens per aliam et[506] cauda leonem. Hec eciam statua cum esset iacens post cancellos[507] inclusa fuit muro iuxta[508] maius altare, tempore quo Heinricus[509] .vii. coronatus fuit Mediolani, ita ut supina iaceret, et supra eam imperatoris et regine consortis eius ymagines,[510] quod ideo factum vulgo ferebatur, quia dum vultu in terra demisso[511] iaceret, non posset Ytalie[512] imperium sublimari; quod fabulosum credatur.

Ecclesiam que modo dicitur sancti Dyonisii[513] fundavit[514] idem in honorem omnium confessorum; monasterium vero quod dicitur sancti Dyonisii[515] fundavit Heribertus de Interamne Mediolani episcopus anno Domini .mxxiii.;[516] ecclesia que nunc dicitur sancti Simpliciani fundata fuit ab ipso eciam beato Ambrosio in honorem beate Marie et omnium virginum. In ecclesia sancti Michaelis prope Sanctum Ambrosium coronabantur reges Langobardorum, iuxta privilegium Theodorici, a

488. F, IV. 489. F, Arnulphi. 490. F, .MCVIII.
491. *Arnulph,* Gesta Archiepiscoporum Mediolanensium, *III, 24.*
492. F, Arnulphus. 493. F, explicare *added.* 494. F, sculpture.
495. F, *. 496. F, columnae. 497. F, vel. 498. F, universa * *.
499. *Arnulph,* Gesta Archiepiscoporum Mediolanensium, *III, 24.*
500. MS, nomine, idem; F, nomine, item. 501. F, martirum. 502 F, .DCCI.
503. MS, firmata. 504. F, pelle amictus. 505. F, manu *added.*
506. F, ex. 507. F, canzellos. 508. F, post. 509. F, Henricus.
510. F, imagines. 511. F, dimisso. 512. F, Italiae.
513. F, Dionisii. 514. F, fundavit *omitted.* 515. F, Dionisii.
516. *Arnulph,* Gesta Archiepiscoporum Mediolanensium, *II, 20.*

nobilibus Mediolani, sicut de Perideo dicitur Mediolanensi[517] duce. Sed Paulus Langobardus nichil[518] de hoc meminit. Ecclesiam sancti Georgii in Palacio fundavit Anathaleon.[519] Alii dicunt quod fuit beatus Vitalis archiepiscopus Mediolani anno Domini. vii^c^l.[520] Monasterium sancti Vincencii fundavit Desiderius Langobardorum rex;[521] similiter et monasterium sancti Petri de Clavate dyocesis[522] Mediolani anno Domini .vii^c^lxxx.iii. Ecclesia sancte Marie Pedonis fundata fuit anno Domini .viii.xxxvi.[523] Ecclesia sancti Satyri[524] fundata fuit ab Ansperto de Confaloneriis[525] archiepiscopo Mediolani anno Domini. viii^c^lxxxvii.[526] Monasterium de Arona fundavit Amizo comes urbis stacione[527] anno Domini .viii^c^lxiii.[528] Ecclesia[529] sancti Sepulcri fuit fundata a Benedicto de Rozo de Cortexella sive de Canzelariis anno Domini .mxxxvi., .xvi. Iulii. Monasterium sancti Celsi fundatum fuit a Landulpho de Carcano[530] anno Domini .viiii.xcii.[531] Ecclesia sancti Mathei ad Banchetam[532] fundata fuit ab Anchifredo de Fagnano[533] anno Domini .ml. Ecclesiam sancti Hilarii[534] fundavit Anselmus de Badagio archiepiscopus Mediolanensis, qui fuit papa Romanus, anno Domini .mlvi.[535] Monasterium Claravallis[536] fuit fundatum anno Domini .mcxxxv. Hospitale de Brolio[537] fundatum fuit a Guifredo de Buxero[538] anno Domini .mcxlv., qui et hospitale sancti[539] Barnabe similiter fundavit. Ecclesia beati Petri de Vicoboldono fuit fundata anno Domini .mclxxvi.

De Sanctis Corporibus.[540] Hec et alia multa sunt in hac urbe insignia loca, quibus et ipsa urbs egregia redditur, sed non minus gloriosa redditur ex sanctorum corporibus ibi quiescentibus, quibus noscitur predotata, de quibus alique[541] corpora nominabo[542] et loca in quibus quiescunt. Corpora sanctorum Gervasii et Protasii et sororis beati Ambrosii nomine Marcelline quiescunt in ecclesia beati Ambrosii. Corpus vero beati Satiri[543] fratris eiusdem Ambrosii quiescit in ecclesia que decitur sancti Satiri,[544] contigua ecclesie beati Ambrosii. Corpora sanctorum Naboris et

517. F, Mediolanense. 518. F, nihil. 519. F, Anathalon.
520. F, .DCCL. 521. *Landulph*, Historia Mediolanensis, *II, 2.*
522. F, diocesis. 523. F, Mediolani anno Domini .DCCCXXXVI.
524. F, Satiri. 525. F, Confalonieriis. 526. F, .DCCCLXXXVII.
527. F, stacione *omitted.* 528. F, .DCCCLXIII.
529. *Ferrai reversed the positions of this and the following sentence.* 530. F, Carchano.
531. F, .DCCCXCII.; *Arnulph*, Gesta Archiepiscoporum Mediolanensium, *I, 10.*
532. F, Matthei ad Banchettam. 533. F, Fugnano. 534. F, Ilarii.
535. F, .MLVIII. 536. MS, Carevellis. 537. F, Brolii.
538. F, Guffredo de Bussero. 539. F, beati. 540. *Ferrai omitted this title.*
541. F, aliqua. 542. F, nominabo corpora. 543. F, Satyri.
544. F, Satyri.

Felicis quiescunt in ecclesia eorundem.[545] Corpus sancti Victoris quiescit in ecclesia eiusdem, que dicitur sancti Victoris ad Corpus. Corpus sancti Eustorgii quiescit /[fol. 147*r*] in eiusdem ecclesia. Ibi eciam visitur[546] archa grandis marmorea, in qua iacuerunt magorum trium[547] corpora gloriosa. Corpus quoque beati Petri martiris in eadem ecclesia honorabiliter[548] quiescit. Corpus sancti[549] Celsi in eiusdem monasterio iacet. Corpus sancti Nazarii in ipsius habetur ecclesia. Corpus sancti Dyonisii in monasterio eiusdem humatum est.[550] Corpus sancti[551] Simpliciani in eiusdem veneratur ecclesia. De reliquis taceo; ista enim famosiora habentur.

De prelatis, principibus, ducibus, capitaneis, et valvasoribus huius civitatis.[552] Sed nec pretereundum est quod in hac urbe multi cives nec[553] infimis dignitatum titulis claruerunt. Et ut de ceteris taceam, tres ex eis usque ad apostolatus cathedram prodierunt; multi cardinalatus apicem adepti sunt; duo dicuntur[554] Romanum nactos imperium et unus regnum ytalicum.[555] Sed hoc autenticum non inveni expresse. De imperatoribus enim,[556] scilicet Valeriano et Galieno[557] eius filio, quos asserunt fuisse origine Mediolanenses et de progenie Soresinorum,[558] hoc tantum invenio ex historiis Iulii Capitolini, quod Valerianus duos habuit filios ex diversis uxoribus, scilicet Valerianum et Galienum,[559] et cum ipse Valerianum captus fuisset a Sapore rege Persarum, qui et in captivitate consenuit, alter Valerianus circa Mediolanum occisus et sepultus est, adito[560] titulo iussu Claudii, Valerianus imperator;[561] Galienus quoque circa Mediolanum dicitur esse percussus.[562] Eutropius vero dicit expresse quod Galienus[563] cum fratre Valeriano occisus est Mediolani.[564] Ex hiis[565] quod placet elicito.[566]

Duces preterea multi in ea fuerunt; capitaneos et valvasores[567] et[568] habuisse eam urbem constat antiquitus et in ea hodie esse. De ducum autem officio, et capitaneorum ac valvasorum[569] exordio hec pauca

545. F, eorumdem. 546. F, videtur. 547. F, tria.
548. F, honorabiliter ecclesia. 549. F, s.
550. *Ferrai omitted the preceding two sentences.* 551. F, s.
552. *Ferrai omitted this title.* 553. F, non. 554. F, dicunt.
555. F, Italicum. 556. F, vero. 557. F, Gallieno.
558. F, Sorexinorum. 559. F, Gallienum. 560. F, addito.
561. F, Valerianus imperator *omitted.*
562. *See* Scriptores Historiae Augustae, *ed. H. Peter* (*2 vols.; Leipzig, 1884*), *II, 77, 92–93.*
563. F, Gallienus. 564. *Eutropius, IX, ii.* 565. F, his.
566. F, eligite.
567. F, valvassores. 568. F, nam. 569. F, et valvassorum.

subiungam, ad modernorum notitiam, que in Dacio legi et in aliis cronicis.[570] Duces post mortem beati Ambrosii Mediolanum regebant, qui per eleccionem, sicut Veneciis fit, assumebantur ad vitam; quibus eciam conferebantur ducatus Burgarie, comitatus Seprii et marchionatus Martexame.[571] Sui eciam iuris erat communitatis statera, hereditas quoque sine liberis decedencium et alia multa; prout autem eorum dignitas exigebat, per tempora quedam anni in palaciis iuxta sancti Prothasii[572] ecclesiam habitantes, ubi et hodie dicitur Curia Ducis. Quod honestum erat civitati curiose procurabant, et quod incaute fractum[573] studiose ac sapienter consolidabant, et quod iniuste actum in aliquo fuerat continuo per aliquam causam emendare et satisfacere iniuriantem procurabant. Presidium erant orphanis, adiutorium tribulatis, viduis subsidium, parvulis munimentum. Lex erant iniustis, iusticia perfiddis,[574] timorque latronibus; ecclesiarum ac clericorum honoribus erant quippe solliciti, sicque, prosperantibus omnibus, in pace universi vivebant; contigit ut quibusdam increbescentibus malis, honorificenciam atque suarum[575] dignitatum magnificenciam duces ipsi noviciis capitaneis dantes, paulatim se nudarunt, et ad postremum eorum reverencia viluit apud omnes, et quos ipsi sublimaverant capitaneos, cepit populus revereri. Maiora[576] tamen ducibus manu et consiliis adhuc regentibus, capitanei[577] subelegerunt valvasores, ut sibi nova[578] dona tenerent. Interea populus Mediolani advertens ex novis dominis nova sibi mala exorta[579] fuisse, et gravius ferens dominium concivium suorum quam ducum, adversus capitaneos et valvasores[580] ut liberi fierent bella gravissima concitarunt, ita ut multe cedes hinc inde[581] fierent. Tandem, ductore et protectore populi quodam Lanzo nomine, de capitaneorum[582] stirpe, cum prevaleret populus, capitanei et valvasores[583] urbe[584] cesserunt; castraque metati sunt ab urbe per miliare,[585] quam non ut cives, sed velut hostes assidue impugnabant. Demum Lanzo populi ductor compassus patrie[586] affliccionibus, cum tractassent[587] apud imperatorem Henricum de habendo subsidio, et adverteret requisiciones[588] imperatoris posse perniciosas sibi et suis esse, facta cum capitaneis et valvasoribus[589]

570. F, chronicis. 571. F, Marthexanae. 572. F, Protaxii.
573. F, factum. 574. F, perfidis. 575. MS, suorum.
576. F, civitatis *added, although it was canceled in the manuscript.*
577. F, capitaneis. 578. F, valvassores sibi, ut nova. 579. F, exhorta.
580. F, valvassores. 581. F, hinc inde multae caedes. 582. F, Curte.
583. F, valvassores. 584. F, urbem. 585. F, mi[l]liare.
586. F, patriam. 587. F, tractasset. 588. F, acquisitiones.
589. F, valvassoribus.

ad ultimum pace, illos recepit in patriam.[590] Hec acta sunt, scilicet[591] de discordia et reconciliacione populi et nobilium, imperante Henrico huius nominis . . . , qui cepit imperare anno Domini . . . ,[592] et sedente[593] in archiepiscopatu Heriberto[594] de Interampno[595] ex capitaneis de Arziaco[596] de ultra Adduam.[597]

Quanta vero hec et alia, et quam gravissima forensia et civilia bella sit[598] perpessa, et quociens senserit ferrum et ignem, non est presentis materie hiis[599] locis inserere. Nam scire cupiens legat ipsius civitatis annalia. Referunt enim aliqui quod ultra vicesies[600] sit excisa sive expugnata, scilicet a Tuscis, Gallis, Hunis,[601] Romanis, Vuandalis, Ruthenis, Gothis, Francis, Langobardis,[602] ultimo autem a Cremonensibus, Papiensibus, Navariensibus,[603] Laudensibus, Cumensibus, Sepriensibus, et Marcesanis,[604] iubente imperatore Federico cognomine Barbaruffa,[605] qui eam urbem quadripartivit in burgos anno Christi .mclxii. Fuit quoque post hoc reedificatum anno .v.[606] ab eversione, assistentibus Pergamensibus, Cremonensibus,[607] Brixiensibus, Mantuanis, et Ferrariensibus.

Capitulum .cxxxvii. De Papia Urbe

Papia, civitatum Italie deliciosa proceris, decora turribus, Ticinum a Ticino flumine antiquitus denominata perhibetur, supra quod noscitur situata. De tempore autem quo fundata fuerit hec civitas nil autenticum sive certum inveni. De fundatoribus vero diversimode legi. Nonnulli enim scribunt quod anno decimo ab urbe Mediolani condita habitantes in ripa Ticini ipsam edifficaverunt civitatum Ticinensem. Alii scribunt quod Boii et Cenomanni opidum edificaverunt non multum longe a fluvio Ticini, multas sustinentes infestaciones atque molestias a quibusdam montes ultra Eridanum, qui et Padus dicitur, inhabitantibus, et quod dum illud opidum edificarent et quicquid per diem construerent nocte sequenti destrueretur, apparuit uni ex eis, viro magis prudenti, nomine Ticinensis, scedula tria .n. continens, quam[608] ille ita interpretatus est:

590. F, patria. 591. F, scilicet *omitted.*
592. *These dates are not given in the manuscript.* 593. F, Henrico et sedente.
594. F, Henrico. 595. F, Antimiano. 596. F, Arciago.
597. F, Abduam; *Landulph,* Historia Mediolanensis, *II, 26.*
598. F, sic. 599. F, his. 600. F, viceties. 601. F, Hunnis.
602. F, Franchis, Longobardis. 603. F, Novariensibus, Papiensibus.
604. F, Martexanis. 605. F, Barbarubea. 606. F, quinto.
607. F, Cremonensibus, Pergamensibus. 608. MS, quod.

per primum enim dixit nidus significari, per secundum nidorum, per tercium non, hoc est dicere nidus nidorum non edificabitur ibi. Et cum vellet urbis situm alio transferre relatum est interpreti quod secus erant apices exponendi, scilicet pro primo .n. Nineve civitas magna, pro secundo[609] nidus, pro tercio nidorum ne debellantibus ipsam. Hec inveni in antiquis scripturis apud ipsam urbem, quibus quante fuerit[610] fidei ignoro. Si autem sic se habuit veritas, credo illud fuisse grandis et potentis civitatis future presagium, quia sicut in antiquorum reperitur annalibus, urbs fuit quondam potentissima et debellantibus eam varias intulit strages.

Eutropius vero ystoriographus scribit quod Insubres Boii Ticinum civitatem condiderunt,[611] et hoc intelligo vel quod Insubres et Boii fuerunt unus populus vel quod in solo quod erat in Subrio civitatem hanc edificaverunt vel forte corruptus est textus exemplaris. Alibi enim invenio quod Ticinum in Ytalia a Gallis Bois conditur, ut habetur in cronicis Mileti sive Eusebii. Cenomannorum autem populorum caput erat Brixia.[612]

Alii referunt quod, sicut dictum est, anno .x. post Mediolanum conditum Boii et Cenomanni gentes ferocissime de urbe Mediolani egressi pre multitudine inhabitancium, construxerunt civitatem quam a vicinitate fluminis (eam) Ticinum denominantes.

Ticinus autem fluvius dictus est quasi Taginus, ut quidam notant, a Tago fluvio aurifluo, cuius et hic naturam imitatur, sabulum ha- /[fol. 147*v*] bens in quo plus ceteris Ytalie aurum colligitur, cuius fons oritur in monte ubi dicitur loco magnus iuxta Curvaliam.[613] Idem eciam dicitur Athax ab acta, quod est litus, quia grandia habet littora et diffusa,[614] de quo Lucanus in .i., Mitis Athax Lacias gaudet non ferre carinas.[615] Nonnulli dicunt Athax esse Verone flumen, sed errant, quia secundum quod dicit Papias, flumen illud Verone non Athax sed Arthesis appellatur.[616] Utrum autem Atthax sit Ticinus pro constanti non habeo, quia Papias dicit quod Athax fluvius est inter Laudanum et Remos iuxta Roceium.[617] Horum autem relaciones de tempore huius urbis autenticas non inveni. Sed quod autenticum videri debet refert Paulus dyaconus, qui Langobardorum gesta conscripsit, quod Galli dum Ytaliam invasissent, Ticinum et Mediolanum, Pergamumque Brixiam quoque

609. MS, secunda. 610. MS, fuit.
611. *Eutropius, IV, 2, 3.* 612. *Livy, XXXII, 30, 6.*
613. *The text apparently is corrupt here.* 614. *Papias, s.v.* Athax.
615. *Lucan,* Belli Civilis Libri Decem, *ed. C. Hosius (Leipzig, 1913), I, 403.*
616. *Papias, s.v.* Arthesis. 617. *Papias, s.v.* Athax.

construentes et Salpinam Galliam regioni nomen dederunt.[618] Alibi dicit eciam quod secunda Ytalie provincia Liguria dicitur in quo Mediolanum et Papia.[619] Per quod eciam innuitur quod, licet primitus sit dicta Ticinum, et ab antiquo tamen et antiquitus eciam Papie nomen sortita est.

Cuius denominacionis sive nominis mutati causam et ethimologiam varii varie ponunt. Alii enim circa ethimologyam vel derivacionem dicunt quod dicta sit a pape, quod est admirabilis. Alii quod Papia, quasi pauperibus pia. Alii quasi parum pia. Alii quasi patri pia, et hanc ultimam ethimologiam fertur dixisse beatus Petrus martir.[620] Papias vero dicit quod Papia dicta est a pape, eo quod habundet in multis quasi mirabilis et addit quod civitas est iuxta Ticinum fluvium a Gallis edita.[621] Alii ferunt quod sit dicta a Papirio quodam, Karoli Magni nepote, qui post annos .vi^{c}iiii. a Christi nativitate in Ytaliam venit et in ea civitates optinuit preter Mediolanum, Veronam et Placenciam, et cum in Ticino resideret et eius optineret dominium, Ticinenses urbem suam ab ipso Papirio Papiam denominarunt. Hoc eciam autenticum non inveni, quia eciam qui hoc scripsit multa inseruit non vera que obmisi.

Ex verbis Eutropii, Pauli, et Papie constat satis fuisse hanc urbem Mediolano contemporaneam. Potest eciam et hoc per Ysidori verba firmari, qui dicit, Gallos Mediolanum atque alias urbes condidisse,[622] licet alias non nominet quam Mediolanum. Trogus vero sive Iustinus nominat alias, scilicet Comum, Pergamum, Brixiam, Veronam, Vincenciam, et Tridentum.[623] Que igitur de tempore fundacionis et fundatoribus huius civitatis inveni, fideliter conscripsi, nullas obmittens opiniones ut quisque quid maluerit eligat.

Huius civitatis episcopus suffraganeus fuisse asseritur archiepiscopi Mediolani, quod patet ex eo quia beatus Protasius archiepiscopus Mediolani consecravit beatum Epifanium episcopum Papiensem, Sancti Crispini successorem, anno .cclxix. Sed quia tempore Longobardorum qui erant infideles, timore eorum, archiepiscopi Mediolani apud Ianuam residebant, sicut de Honorato legitur,[624] episcopi Papienses consecrari ceperunt a Papa, unde cum Benedictus archiepiscopus Mediolani anno Domini .vi^{c}lxxxviii. in curia Romana cantet episcopum Papiensem suum ab antiquo suffraganeum, succubuit.[625] Unde et hodie Papiensis, Placenciensis, et Ferrariensis episcopi subsunt immediate dominio Pape. Patet

618. *Paul the Lombard, II, 23.* 619. Ibid., *II, 15.*

620. *For another treatment of the etymology of Pavia,* see De Laudibus Papiae, RIS, *XI (Milan, 1727),* 44.

621. *Papias, s.v.* Papia. 622. *Isidore, XV, i, 57.* 623. *Justinus, XX, 5, 9.*

624. *Kehr, VI–I, 32, n. 23.* 625. *Landulph,* Historia Mediolanensis, *II, 15.*

eciam quod episcopus iste Papiensis uti cruce et pallio consuevit unde in cronicis Martini habetur quod Alexander III episcopum Papiensem eo quod imperatori Frederico primo adheserat crucis et pallei dignitate privavit circa annos Domini .mclx.[626]

Quante autem hec civitas potencie et quanta sit perpessa scire cupidus legat antiquitatum ystorias. Hoc unum non omitto, quod dum Albuinus, Langobardorum rex primus, intrasset Ytaliam, civitas hec eius obsidionem per triennium est perpessa, ut dicit Paulus Longobardus,[627] ex cuius et aliorum scriptis constat in ea urbe Longobardorum reges sedes regias habuisse et tam ipsi quam alii principes templa, palacia, turres, et alia edificia edifficasse, ubertate et salubri aere et amenitate regionis urbis illius plurimum delectatos.

Nam condiderunt eciam ibi plures regias sepulturas et, ut dicit idem Paulus, palacium ibi regale construxit Theodoricus rex in quo eciam sedem habuit Alboinus.[628] Monasterium quod novum dicitur construxit Bertarit Longobardorum rex. Ecclesiam Sancte Marie ad Porticas extra muros fundavit Rodelinda regina, eiusdem regis consors.[629]

In hac preterea urbe gloriosa pignora requiescunt. Inter que doctor maximus Augustinus et Syrus primus eiusdem civitatis episcopus et vir illustris Severinus Boecius ibidem relegatus, quorum corpora preciosa in venerabili basilica que dicitur Sancti Petri in Celo Aureo honorabiliter sunt humata, similiter et corpus regis incliti Liuthprandi.

Eminuit eciam longis in urbe illa temporibus ereus ille equs fusilis et deauratus[630] cum insidente ereo equite, qui vulgo Rez Solium dicebatur. Erat enim loco patenti et eminenti ante matricem ecclesiam supra latericiam columpnam. Eques autem una manu freno regebat equum, alteram tenebat extensam. Equi pes unus a catulo ereo tenebatur erectus. Et quod mirifice commendebat artificem, tanta quippe militari doctrina et tam docta tamque venusta industria videbatur eques equo insidere ut non solum eius decora insessio sed et regulata scapediacio contemplantes ad equitandum instrueret verum eciam provocaret, unde et nobiles pariter et ignobiles cives et hospites adveneque tanta eum aviditate contuebantur ut eciam longa mora contuentibus fastidium non pararet. Incole vero urbis eum habebant decus eximium civitatis. Hec que loquor oculis meis vidi et novi. Legi eciam in cronicis ecclesie Ravennatis quod

626. *Kehr, VI–I, 182, n.* 40.
627. *Paul the Lombard, II, 27.*
628. Ibid. 629. Ibid., *V, 34.*
630. MS, fusilis et deauratus *added in the margin.*

hoc simulachrum fabricari fecit rex Italie Theodericus apud Ravennam et in ponte Austri Ravenne locari et sicut in Pontificali libro eiusdem ecclesie legitur Karolus Rex Francorum et Romanorum Augustus inde eum sustulit ut transferret in Franciam.[631]

Qualiter vero Papie delatum fuerit diverse narratur. Vulgo fertur quod Papienses Ravennam hostiliter invadentes illud inde sustulerunt unde processu temporis Ravennates hostiliter aggressi Papiensem urbem, portas contectas laminis ereis et deauratis aput basilicam beati Petri in Celo Aureo in reconpensam sive talionem prefati simulacri Ravennam exportarunt et ibi hodie haberi dicuntur.

In aliquibus cronicis legi quod cum Theodericus prefatus rex una cum Mediolanensibus Odovacrum Ytalie regem apud Ravennam oppressisset, Mediolanenses statuam hanc contra Padi fluenta usque Papiam perduxerunt, quam Papienses occulte subtractam occupaverunt. Sed vulgacior est fama opinionis prioris.

Mansit autem statua hec equestris tam Ravenne quam Papie per annos circiter .viii^{c}., computando annos a tempore regni Theodorici, qui regnabat circa annum Domini .v^{c}., usque ad annum nativitatis Christi .mcccxv. Tunc enim Papia a Mediolanensibus furto optenta, statua ipsa equestris per equestres, videlicet mercenarios Mediolanenses, adhibitis equis funem trahentibus, fuit solo prostrata et postea in fragmenta conversa Mediolanumque delata.

Licet autem, ut dixi, Papienses hoc civitatis sue decus prestantissimum reputarent et propterea de illius turbanda ruina. . . .[632] tanta tamen fuit oborta stupefaccio ex urbe furata tamque merens et tristis pars civium que urbem amiserat, tam vero gaudens pars que exulaverat ex patria acquisita, ut ruine statue preponderaverit meror et gaudium conceptum ex urbis /[fol. 148*r*] (urbis) subita et incredibili novitate.

Non miretur autem quis si prolixiori sermone immoratus sum de hac narrando statua. Ad hoc enim et vetustas eius et vulgata celebrisque fama me induxit.

Capitulum .cxxxviii. De Como civitate

Comum Langobardie civitas, que olim in Liguria est dicta, supra Lacum Larium sita est. Lacum autem ideo Larium puto dictum quod lauris habundet. Hec a Gallis Senonibus condita fuit et urbi Mediolanensi

631. *Riccobaldus,* Compendium, *Vatican Library, Cod. Ottob. Lat. 2073, fol. 108*v.
632. *A word seems to be missing here.*

contemporanea, ut scribit Trogus Pompeius sive Iustinus eius abreviator dicens quod Galli, Tuscis sedibus suis pulsis, Mediolanum, Comum, Pergamum, Brixiam, etc. condiderunt.[633]

In huius autem civitatis commendacionem maxime quoad situm multa scribit Cassiodorus in epistula ad Gaudiosum Cancellarium, inter que refert civitatem ipsam preter moncium devia et laci purissimi vastitatem quasi murus esse plane Ligurie, que licet munimen claustrale probetur esse provincie, in tantam pulchritudinem perducitur ut ad solas delicias instituta esse videatur. Hec post tergum campestria culta transmittit amenis vectacionibus apta et victualibus copiis indulgenter accomoda, a fronte .lx. milibus dulcissimi equoris, idest laci amenitate, perfruitur, ut et aliis recreabili delectacione sacietur et piscium copia nullis tempestatibus subducatur. Merito ergo Como nomen accepit, que tantis letatur compta muneribus.[634] De ipso vero lacu ex eadem epistula dictum est supra ubi de lacubus agitur.[635]

Huius eciam civitatis primus episcopus extitit Felix nomine circa annos Domini .iiii^{c}xlviii., dum Ambrosius Mediolanensem ecclesiam regeret. Post vero annos .xxii. prefuit Habundius in episcopatu eiusdem civitatis, qui multos in fide convertit errantes.[636] Multi preterea imperatores ac reges maximis privilegiis Cumanam dotarunt ecclesiam et pariter civitatem et ipsius antistitem principem et comitem ordinarunt et contulerunt eciam temporalis gladii potestatem sicut in archivis eiusdem urbis et ecclesie fidem faciunt publica documenta.[637]

Imperante autem Lothario anno scilicet Domini .mcxxvii. Mediolanenses, suffragantibus sibi Cremonensibus, Papiensibus, Brixiensibus, Pergamensibus, Vercellensibus, Astensibus, Novariensibus, Veronensibus, Ferrariensibus, Mantuanis, Parmensibus, et nonnullis aliis, castra metati[638] sunt circa civitatem hanc, exercitu trifariam diviso, scilicet in Alebio, Zergo, et Classio, de mandato archiepiscopi Mediolanensis nomine Iordanus prosapie capitaneorum de Clivio, et cum guerra hinc inde diu perdurasset acerrima, non sine altriutrius strage maxima, tandem prevalentibus Mediolanensibus, civitatem ipsam everterunt .v. Kal. Aug.

Causa autem guerre huius fuit propter eleccionem quandam de Cumano episcopo in discordia celebratam. Nam imperator Heinricus .iiii. investiverat Landulfum de Cartano de ipso episcopatu Comano. Canonici autem elegerant Guidonem de Grimoldis de Cavaliasca magis

633. *Justinus, XX, 5, 9.* 634. *Cassiodorus,* Variae, *XI, 14.* 635. *Benzo, fol. 94*r.

636. Errantes *is a marginal insertion with manuscript.*

637. *See* Privilegia Cumane Ecclesie, *Cod. G 164 of the Ambrosian Library.*

638. MS, merati.

Cumanis acceptum. Unde Cumani, armata manu, expugnato castro Sancti Georgii Pleberatus Agnii Cumane dyocesis, in quo dictus Landulfus habitabat, ipsum Landulfum et nepotes interemerunt et Guido episcopatum optinuit. Propter quod commotus archiepiscopus dictum exercitum adunari et civitatem hanc everti mandavit. Non multo post[639] reedificata fuit ita ut hodie opulenta et ditissima civitas habeatur.[640]

Munitissima quoque duplici muro fossa lata distanti et lapidibus quadris compacto cincta turribusque decenter erectis. Ex cuius fundacionis figura nonnulli forme cancrine volentes alludere, dicunt semicivitatis corpus ipsum cancri esse, suburbium vero porte turris caudam, alia vero duo suburbia, Vici scilicet et Curignolio, ipsa duo cancri brachia presentare.

Insula Comacina. Non longe ab hac civitate fuit opidum famosum quippe et natura munitissimum quod dicebatur insula Comacina. Erat enim in colle saxeo firmissimoque qui lacu Lario sive Cumacino ambiebatur. Et quia sic erat naturaliter munitum opidum, multi ad hanc insulam confugiebant tanquam ad asylum, sicut legitur in historia Longobardorum, maxime de Cuniperto Langobardorum rege et de Ansprando. Nam de Cuniperto scribit ibi Paulus quod in insulam que intra lacum Larium, que non longe a Como est, confugit ibique se fortiter communivit.[641] De Ansprando vero scribit quod in tutorem regis parvuli datus ab Ariperto filio Raginperti Taurinensium ducis, regni invasore, fugere coactus est in hanc insulam Comacinam, ubi dum se fortiter communisset, tandem Raginpercius exercitus insulam invadens eius opidum diruit sed Ansprandus per Curiam Rethorum, idest civitatem Curiensem, fuge beneficio in Baioarium evasit.[642] Acta sunt hec temporibus Iustiniani imperatoris huius nominis secundi, qui cepit imperare circa annos Domini .vii^{c}. Demum cum reedificatum esset opidum, tandem anno .mclix. eversum est iterum a Cumanis, decreto adhibito ne unquam reedificaretur quod usque in presentem eius testantur ruine.

Hec que de Como civitate ex cronicis et epistulis Cassiodori repperi; plura tamen alia in laudem civitatis huius possent scripture mandari, si temporum antiquitate et malicia hominum deleta non essent illius urbis annalia.

Et vero libenter urbis illius insisterem laudibus, cum in ea gratum et quietum sim domicilium nactus ad compilandum presens opus et maiora alia, exacto iam fere septennio.

639. MS, post *inserted in a smaller hand.* 640. *Landulph of St. Paul, p. 41.*
641. *Paul the Lombard, V, 38.* 642. Ibid., *VI, 21.*

Sed quod non occultandum est subiungo quia inibi multa gloriosa corpora requiescunt et sollempni habentur reverencia, scilicet corpus gloriosi confessoris Abundii, eiusdem civitatis antistitis, quod in sollempni monasterio eius dicato nomini requiescit et in omni secunda feria a cuncto populo devote visitatur ibidem. Ibi similiter corpus beati Adalberti quiescit, quod annua eciam reverencia frequentatur: corpora preterea gloriosorum martyrum Prothi et Iacinctii et sanctarum virginum Faustine et Liberate in matrici ecclesia condignis sepulchris recondita devotissime visitantur. Corpus eciam beati Felicis primi episcopi eiusdem urbis in monasterio sancti Carpofori, beati Fidelis martyris et beati Probini in ecclesiis suis dicatis[643] nominibus requiescunt. Corpus quoque Christi militis gloriosi Carpofori in monasterio eiusdem servatur humatum et alia plura transeo causa brevitatis.

Habet eciam et civitas ista singulare quoddam[644] valde usibus humanis accomodum, lapides videlicet singulares quibus fabricantur vasa precipua ad cibaria decoquenda, quorum toti provincie fere copie habunde ministrat. Gignit preterea lacus inter pisces alios optimas torrenticias. Sciendum preterea est quod alia est eciam civitas non longe a Neapolis Cume dicta, de qua supra dictum est.[645]

CAPITULUM .CXXXIX. DE PERGAMO CIVITATE

Pergamum Ytalie civitas olim in Venecia provincia sive Gallia Cisalpina[646] nunc in Longobardia provincia sita est. De tempore autem fundacionis ipsius et fundatoribus satis constat per dicta Trogi sive Iustini, dicens, Gallos, expulsis Tuscis eorum sedibus, Mediolanum, Comum, Pergamum, etc. condiderunt.[647] Idem testatur /[fol. 148*v*] Paulus in Longobardorum hystoria, qui eciam ibidem asserit in annalibus libris Pergamum esse Veneciarum civitatem,[648] Venecie autem tunc erat nomen provincie antequam civitas eiusdem nominis fundaretur. Unde per hoc convicitur fuisse civitatem hanc Mediolano contemporaneam, de quo supra dictum est fuisse conditum anno urbis condite .clx., qui fuit ante Christi nativitatem anno .v^{c}xcii.

Quare autem hec civitas huiusmodi sit sortita vocabulum non legi; racione(m) tamen loci et situs et edificiorum sic eam autumo denominatam; Pergama enim grece dicuntur alta ediffìcia. Hec autem civitas et

643. MS, dicate. 644. MS, quodam.
645. *See* capitulum .cix., *fol. 138*v. 646. MS, Galliam Cisalpiam.
647. *Justinus, XX, 5, 9.* 648. *Paul the Lombard, II, 14.*

in alto sita est, colle videlicet eminenti, et alta habuit in edifficiis et turribus menia, vel forte a principe aliquo ex Gallis sic denominata fuit.

Est eciam alia civitas dicta Pergamum cui predicavit sanctus Iohannes et a Pergamo opido dictum est carte genus pergamenum, quod prius Pergameni reges excogitaverunt, ex membris pecudum detrahentes.[649]

Pergamum civitas ubi olim Venecie provincia dicebatur, nunc Longobardie dicitur situm habere; hec, ut scribit Paulus in Longobardorum historia, in Venecia, que fuit antiquitus provincia prima Ytalie, condita fuit, ut predictum est, (civitas hec) et finis erat illius provincie,[650] et sicut recitat Iustinus ex Trogo ibi a Gallis Senonibus constructa fuit quando ipsi Galli Mediolanum et urbes reliquas condiderunt.[651] Ex quo patet Mediolano sit in fundacione contemporanea.

Quare autem dicta sit Pergamum non legi expresse sed racio adduci potest quam de hoc nomine ponit Ysidorus dicens Pergama esse alta menia unde et Troiana illa edificia propter altitudinem dicta sunt Pergama,[652] et sic a simili de hac civitate dici potest, quod propter meniorum altitudinem, seu ex situ, sewex parietibus dicta sit Pergamum. Fuit enim olim prealtis edificiis mirabiliter decorata, que collis ex tuberacione venustatem suam eciam procul intuentibus demonstrabant.

Hec in clivo, limpidine foncium et consitu virgultorum ameno quasi in throno sedens, planiciem provincie velut ab arce prospectat et aeris salubritate, agrorum fecunditate, virentis collis pinguedine, metallorum minera, gregibus, armentis, volucribus ac ingeniorum prestancia, vulgari assercione reputatur insignis.

Hec abolim innate ubertatis dyadema gestans, post relique provincie convulsionem, diu in pacis pulchritudine ac rerum omnium ubertate quievit. Populi frequenciam augebat advenarum cetus, qui facciosa vi propriis pulsis Laribus ad eam tanquam ad portum publicum et tutum refugium confluebant. Securos prebebat sompnos, ius affluens supra omnem iniuriam positum. Ignorabatur predo; consodalem aut cohabitatorem vix ibi homicida inveniebat. Clipeorum retinacula pre vetustate soluta erant et loricis superfusa rubigo. Tympano et tybia strepebat[653] theatrum. In cythara et psalterio atrium exultabat. Qualiter autem tantorum beneficiorum congeriem a Deo largitore cognoverit civitas, ut commessaciones, ebrietates, ceterumque preterea luxum, ipsa municipalis testatur edicio, que fenus patrocinia munit sacerdociumque proscribit. Proinde nimirum eterni iudicis inconcussa iusticia, civium ingratitudinem

649. *Papias, s.v.* Pergamum. 650. *Paul the Lombard, II, 14.*
651. *Justinus, XX, 5, 9.* 652. *This is not in Isidore.* 653. MS, strepabat.

animadversione digna percuciens, civitatem ipsam fato permisit. Tantarum itaque diviciarum lascivia civium enervante virtutem, susurrium, livor, cupiditas, ambicio, libido, aliaque vicia succreverunt. Sicque depravatis moribus et subinde civium interrupta concordia, indulgencius fota nobilitas in facciones scissa conspicitur, ad quarum zelum velut ad cotem plebe sua in diversum acuente studia, cura communis utilitatis negligitur et res publica vallo roboris exarmatur. De substancia plebis quasi preda in medio iacente certatur. Civile bellum omnia miscet, gladiorum furit[654] impunitas; planicies, colles, et valles civium madent cruore. Luctu, pavore, et tremore inibi universa complentur. Presens status est[655] huius civitatis, quando videlicet actor presentis compilacionis de hac et ceteris urbibus scripsit. Est alia civitas huius nominis in Asya ad quam predicavit evangelista Iohannes.[656]

CAPITULUM .CXL. DE CIVITATE LAUDE

Laude civitas olim in agro Insubribus sive Ligurum, nunc Longobardorum provincia dicta sita fuit hac de causa, que in Romanorum sic habetur hystoriis. Dum enim pyrate Cilices maxima classe mare totum vexarent, non solum commeatus navium, idest alimenta que navibus vehebantur, intercipiendo sed insulas eciam diripiendo et cottidie scelerata manus eorum augeretur, missus ad eos Gneius Pompeius cum classe, qui bimestri tempore eos in fedus recepit, quibus secundum fedus Pompei datus est ager ad coloniam deducendam. Est autem colonia locus culture deditus, coloni vero cultores advene.[657] Cum autem agitaretur in Senatu quis ager eis assignaretur ad coloniam ponendam decreto senatus actum est ut Insubribus ager daretur, ea scilicet causa ut ibi feroces cum Insubribus ferocibus colliderentur et provisum est ut coloniam ponerent, idest sedes statuerent, in loco qui pari intercapedine abstat a tribus opidis, scilicet Mediolano, Ticino, idest Papia, atque Cremona; ea vero colonia nominata est Laude Pompei.[658] Alii addunt duo opida, scilicet Augustam, que hodie Placencia, et Brimoniam, cuius hodie vocabulum ignoro, credo quod sit Cremona.

Quod autem utrique, scilicet pirate et Insubres sive Ligures, feroces

654. MS, fuerit. 655. MS, est *added in the margin.*
656. *This sentence is a marginal notation in the manuscript.*
657. *Isidore, XV, ii, 9.*
658. *Riccobaldus,* Historie, *Vatican Library, Cod. Vat. Lat. 1961, fol. 180*v.

essent patet et ex effectu piratarum et Ligurum moribus seu natura. Sunt enim bella piratica sparsa latronum manus per maria non solum navium commeatus sive merces sed eciam insulas provinciasque vastantes. Ligures autem erant rebelles, bellicosi, feroces animo, gens indomita et Romano semper imperio resistentes. Locati preterea fuerunt iuxta fluvium, qui Silicon dicebatur, propter sicalis habundanciam, sed ab ipsis sceleratis piratis dictus est Scelera. Non solum autem ea consideracione ut suppeditarentur a Liguribus sed ut Ligures Romanis exosi per eos detrimenta et incommoda paterentur. Non autem consonare Romanorum videtur hystoriis quod aliqui scribunt dicentes, Laude a quodam viro sedicioso urbi Mediolani exule fuisse conditum et ab eius nomine sit denominatum post .lxxvi. annos conditi Mediolani et postmodum in ea civitate per Pompeium piratas fuisse locatos, qui in ipsis hystoriis dicitur quod ipsis piratis datus est ager Insubribus. Si igitur ager, ergo non civitas. In hoc tamen quisque sentiat prout placet.

Mansit autem hec civitas in primo situ annis circiter .m.ccxxx. Nam constat per Romanorum annalia fuisse edificatam post annos ab urbe condita .vi^{c}lxxix.; post annos vero nativitatis Christi .mclviii. a Mediolanensibus eversam, cuius usque in presentem apparent ruine; nam eodem anno a Frederico imperatore huius nominis primo reedificata sive de novo constructa fuit in odium Mediolani loco qui mons Ghizonis dicebatur iuxta Addue flumen, in quo et hodie perseverat, multipliciter vexata tamen[659] sedicionibus intestinis, non procul ab antiquo situ. Unde quidam, Laudensem turrem statuit Fridericus in urbem. Quam quidem civitatem Heinricus huius nominis[660] septimus imperator /[fol. 149*r*] donavit Henrico Flandrensi, titulo comitatus.

Capitulum .cxli. De civitate Cremona

Cremona Ytalie quondam potentissima et famosissima civitas. Nunc vero talis nescio qualis. Fertur tamen quod ibi sint formose domine et mulieres.

Capitulum .cxlii. De Brixia civitate nobili

Brixia Ytalie nobilis civitas in provincia Longobardie sita est, quam Galli Senones condiderunt, unde provinciam ipsam Cisalpinam Galliam nominarunt, similiter et Mediolanum, sicut testantur Iustinus et Paulus

659. *This section has been traced over; I have tried to reconstruct the preceding three words.*
660. MS, nominis *was added in the margin.*

Langobardus, ut in multis superius dictum est, unde apparet Mediolano, Como, et Pergamo aliisque ibi nominatis contemporaneam fuisse.[661] Hoc idem testatur Miletus sive Eusebius. Hec autem civitas, ut scribit idem Paulus magnam semper nobilium Langobardorum multitudinem habuit.[662] Hanc eciam foncium ubertas speciosam et famosam reddidit. In cuius sigillo talis est versus, Brixia sum mitis, Deus constans est michi basis.[663]

CAPITULUM .CXLIII. DE CIVITATE MANTUA

Mantua vetustissima Ytalie civitas in provincia que quondam Venecia, que et Gallia Cisalpina vel Pannonia secundum alios dicebatur, sita fuit, secundum quod refert Ysidorus et Paulus Langobardus.[664]

Hanc autem civitatem Manto, Tyresie filia, post interitum Thebanorum, in Italiam delata condidisse dicitur et dicta Mantua, quod manes tueatur, ut scribit Ysidorus.[665] Ab ipsa eciam Mantho dicta est Mantua civitas.

Virgilius vero, qui ex hac urbe traxit originem, non minimum civitati decus, dicit quod filius eiusdem Manthois Ognus nomine eandem civitatem a matris nomine Mantuam appellavit.[666] Ipsa autem dicta est Mantho vel Manthos quasi divinatrix a manes et tueor, quia manes, idest mortuorum deos, tueretur. Hec, ut alii dicunt, de quodam viro nomine Tiber filium habuit, qui dictus est Obnus et idem dictus est Bianor, idest bis fortis, scilicet animo et corpore,[667] unde Virgilius, Sepulchrum incipit apparere Biaononis.[668] Hic, ut quidam volunt, condidit Mantuam, quam ex Manthois matris nomine Mantuam nominavit.

Fuit autem Tyresias huius Manthois genitor magnus Thebanorum vates, de quo neminit Statius in Thebanorum hystoria.[669] Hec de exordio urbis huius inveni ex auctoribus memoratis.

Tempus autem fundacionis eius expressum in tantum habetur. Antiquissimam enim opinari potest, ex quo a Manto, Tyresie vatis filia, vel a

661. *Justinus, XX, 5, 9; Paul the Lombard, II, 14.*
662. *Paul the Lombard, V, 36.*
663. *This sentence is a marginal insertion in the manuscript.*
664. *Isidore, XV, i, 57; Paul the Lombard, II, 14.*
665. *Isidore, XV, i, 59.*
666. *Virgil,* Aeneid, *X, 198–200.*
667. *Papias, s.v.* Bianor.
668. *Virgil,* Eclogues, *IX, 59–60.*
669. *Statius,* Thebaid, *ed. H. W. Garrod (Oxford, 1906), VII, 416.*

filio ipsius Manthois constat conditam; nam interitus Thebanorum sive Thebarum expugnacio facta per Grecos post diutinam obsidionem pro concertamine regni inter Ethioclem et Polinicem, Edippi Thebanorum regis filios, Troianum precessit excidium per annos circiter .lx. hoc modo. Edippus enim tempore Abimelech iudicis Israel erat. Troia vero excisa fuit anno tercio Abdon, iudicis Israhel; ab ultimo vero anno Abymelech usque ad tercium Abdon fuerunt anni .lx. Troie vero excidium precessit condicionem urbis Rome per annos .iiii.xxxi. secundum Ieronimum.[670] Condita autem fuit Roma ante Christi adventum per annos .dcclii. secundum Orosium.[671] Et sic eciam non computatis annis qui precesserunt ab interitu Thebanorum, post quem, ut dictum est, fuit Mantua edificata, usque ad excidium Troianum, si recte calculabitur, invenientur .mclxxxiii. anni preteriti a Mantua condita usque ad Salvatoris adventum.

In cronicis autem Mileti sive Eusebii habetur quod condita fuit Mantua anno nativitatis Abraam .v^{c}xxx., qui annus ante urbem conditam .vi^{c}lxx. Nam Abram nativitas precessit urbem conditam secundum Augustinum circiter .mcc. annos, quod testatur libro .xviii. De civitate Dei.[672] De quibus si detrahantur anni .v^{c}xxx., qui fuerunt a nativitate Abraam usque ad edificacionem Mantue, ut dictum est, restat fuisse ab edificacione Mantue[673] usque ad condicionem Rome .vi^{c}lxx. Quibus si addantur anni .vii^{c}lii., qui fuerunt ab urbe condita usque ad Christi adventum secundum Orosium,[674] erunt ab edificacione Mantue usque ad ipsum Christi adventum, recte calculando, anni .miiii^{c}xxii.

Hanc civitatem preterfluit amnis Mincius Padum influens, quam eciam munitissimam et inexpugnabilem reddit lacus eam ambiens. In suburbano quoque pago supra ripam ipsius lacus sito, qui Polectolis dicitur, natus fertur fuisse Virgilius, urbis Mantuane decus eximium, sicut et Verone Catullus, unde illud monosticon, Mantua Virgilio gaudet, Verona Catullo.[675] De hac eciam urbe habetur hoc elogium: Manthois Tyresie Thebarum filia Lagi alibi regis vel vatis condidit ista suis bene menia pertha futuris.[676]

Capitulum .cxliiii. De civitate Verona

Verona in Ytalia feracissima civitas a Gallis condita est, qui et Mediolanum et alias urbes condiderunt, ut testatur Iustinus et Miletus sive

670. *Jerome, p. 88*a. 671. *Orosius, V, 19, 1.*
672. *Augustine, XVI, 1, 7.*
673. MS, ut dictum est, . . . Mantue *is repeated in the text.* 674. *Orosius, V, 19, 1.*
675. *Ovid,* Amores, *III, xv, 7.* 676. *This passage seems to be corrupt.*

Ieronimus sicut supra demonstratum est de urbe Mediolani, anno post urbem Romam conditam .clx., qui fuit ante Christi ortum.v $.^{c}$xcii., fuitque ipsi Mediolano, Pergamo, et Brixie[677] contemporanea, sicut scribit idem dicens quod Galli, expulsis sedibus suis Tuscis, Mediolanum, Comum, Pergamum, Brixiam, Veronam, Tridentum et Vincenciam condiderunt[678] et per hoc non videtur verum quod[679] in modernis cronicis scribitur, maxime a Sicardo episcopo Cremonensi, dicens quod a quadam nobili Troiana nomine Verona constructa et denominata fuit;[680] quod si ita fuit, ergo Galli eam non condiderunt sed reedifficaverunt.

Gotifridus Viterbiensis in cronicis suis dicit quod Brennus dux Gallorum victus a Romanis, duce Camillo, contra urbem Romam Veronam[681] condidit dictam quasi Ve Roma. Insuper Brixiam, Ticinum, et Mediolanum et Senogalliam urbem maris Illirici et quod has urbes Suevi tenuerunt primi, sub quibus Allobrogi, idest Burgundiones, et Senones habitatores fuerunt illorum.[682]

Quod autem dictum est, Brennum Veronam et alias urbes condidisse, credo intelligendum de reparacione, non de fundacione illarum, cum constet secundum Titum Mediolanum longe ante Breni adventum fuisse a Gallis, tum duce Belloveso, fundatum[683] et secundum Trogum sive Iustinum constat Veronam et alias predictas urbes Mediolano contemporaneas esse.[684]

De urbis autem huius nomine feruntur illi duo versiculi, ethimologiam et antiquitatem insinuantes eiusdem: Ve/vere surgens, Ro/rotas per circuitum, Na/nam antiqua urbs est vocata Verona. Hanc preterea urbem preterfluit fluvius Artesie[685] nomine, secundum quod dicit Papias,[686] licet aliqui eum Athacem vocant, dicentes illum esse de quo meminit Lucanus;[687] alii dicunt Athacem esse Ticinum. Sed Papias dicit quod Athax est fluvius inter Laudunum et Remos iuxta Roceium, Arthesius vero Vero Verone fluvius.[688]

In hac urbe /[fol. 149*v*] sepultus fuit Alboinus, qui primus ex Langobardorum regibus Ytaliam intravit,[689] a quibus et Liguria provincia dicta est Longobardia.

Laberinthum eciam quod nunc harena dicitur ibi habetur, quod

677. MS, Brixia. 678. *Justinus, XX, 5, 8.* 679. MS, quia.
680. *Sicard, fol. 18*v.
681. Veronam *is added in the margin of the manuscript.* 682. *Godfrey, fol. 49*v.
683. *Livy, V, 34, 9.* 684. *Justinus, XX, 5, 8.*
685. Artesie *is a marginal insertion in the manuscript.* 686. *Papias, s.v.* Arthesia.
687. *Lucan, I, 403.* 688. *Papias, s.v.* Athax.
689. *Paul the Lombard, II, 28.*

constructum fuit anno Octaviani Augusti .xxxix., ante Christi ortum tercio, cuius pars exterior terre motibus corruit. De ipsis autem ruinis, scilicet lapidibus quadris, constructa fuit pars muri urbis que est inter portam qua itur Mantuam ad monasterium Sancti Zenonis,[690] qui fuit ipsius civitatis octavus episcopus circa annum Domini .iii^c^xxii.

Capitulum .cxlv. De urbe Vincencia

Vincencia civitas non procul a Verona ab eisdem Gallis condita est, ipsi eciam urbi Verone contemporanea sicut per eundem Iustinum et Miletum constat. Causam quare sic denominata fuerit non inveni.

.cxlvi. Padua

Facit querere retro in decimo folio; quesivi et non inveni.[691]

Padua in Ytalia condita fuit ab Anthenore Troyano, prius dicta Patavium, anno nativitatis Abraam .viii^c^xxvii. secundum Miletum sive Ieronimum qui fuit annus ante Christi ortum circiter .mc.lx. Quod autem ab Anthenore fuerit condita testatur Titus Livius, maximus ystoriografus et huius oriundus urbis, necnon Solinus et Seneca. Inquit enim Titus, Casibus variis, Anthenor cum multitudine Enetum, qui seditione ex Pafflagonia pulsi, et sedes et ducem, rege eorum Philemene a Troyam amisso, querebant, in intimum maris Adriatici sinum venit et Euganeis qui inter mare et Alpes incolebant pulsis Eneti et Troyani eas tenuerunt terras. Locus vero in quem primo egressi sunt Troya vocatur et inde pago Troyano nomen est. Gens universa Veneti sunt appellati.[692] Ergo Anthenor in Venetia urbem condidit quam Patavium appellavit, nunc Padua.

Seneca autem sic refert, Quid interest enumerare Anthenorem Patavii conditorem et Evandrum in ripa Tiberis regna Archadis collocantem?[693]

Solinus vero capitulo de Ytalia, ubi loquitur de conditoribus urbium dicit similiter Patavium ab Anthenore constitutum.[694] Sepulchrum[695]

690. *Riccobaldus, Historie (Florence), fol. 45*r.

691. *This notation is the only material on Padua in the body of the text; the chapter on Padua was written by another hand at the foot of the page.*

692. *Livy, I, 1, 2–3.*

693. *Seneca,* Dialogues, *ed. F. Haase (Leipzig, 1881), XII, 7, 6.*

694. *Solinus, 2, 10.* 695. MS, sed pulchrum.

quoque eiusdem in ea urbe etiam usque in presens ostenditur, et quod eius conditur fuerit illud dysticon continens sermone pene vulgi titulum, quod est, Hic iacet Anthenor, conditor urbis, etc. Actor.

Hanc urbem, fortissimis in ea repugnantibus militibus cum Langobardis diutissime revelasset, usque videlicet ad tempora Agilulfi eorum regis circa annum Domini .vi^{c}., flame vorantes uno totam incendio consumpserunt et usque ad solum eversa fuit, iussu regis eiusdem, ut scribitur in ystoria Langobardorum.[696]

Hodie autem civitas ista licet olim potentissima et famosissima tum opibus et divitiis ac liberalium artium studiis quam innumeris populis fuerit inter urbes Ytalie, tandem peste seditionis strageque illata a Cane Grande Verone et Vincentie dominatore subsequentibus, pristinam gemit felicitatem consideratione presentium.

CAPITULUM .CXLVII. DE URBE FERRARIA

Ferraria Ytalie civitas est, quo autem tempore, a quibus condita fuerit non legi nisi quod ordinata fuit civitas, dato ipsi urbi primo episcopo a Vitaliano papa, tempore Constantini imperatoris huius nominis tercii, qui imperabat anno Christi .vi^{c}.lxx. ante et post.[697]

CAPITULUM .CXLVIII. DE URBE BONONIA

Bononia pinguis est Italie civitas quam et soli fertilitas fecundam reddidit et studii cultura famosam effecit. Hanc, ut scribit Miletus vel Ieronimus, Romani condiderunt. Dicit enim Bonania colonia a Romanis in Gallia conditur anno ab urbe condita .v^{c}.li., qui fuit annus circiter .cc.

Huius matricis ecclesie titulus beato Petro apostolo inscriptus est, unde in sigillo communitatis inscriptus est eciam talis versus, Petrus ubique pater, legum Bononia mater.

Alia de huius urbis antiquitate non inveni. De laudibus preterea ipsius notare michi videtur superfluum cum fere cuncti maxime litterati studentes quantis bonis affluat sint experti. Est eciam et alia civitas Bononia in maris littore situata sed aliud de illa non repperi.

696. *Paul the Lombard, IV, 23.*
697. *Riccobaldus,* Compendium, *Vat. Lib., Cod. Ottob. Lat. 2073, fol. 113*r.

De urbe Mutina Capitulum .cxlix.

Mutina civitas Ytalie inter Bononiam et Mantuam sita et a Gallis condita fertur. De qua dictum est mutineque labores. Quod autem a Gallis condita fuerit certum quid sive autenticum non inveni. Miletus autem, cuius adherendum est testimonio, scribit Mutinam coloniam fuisse conditam a Romanis in Gallia Togata, anno urbis condite .v.^{c}lxvii., qui fuit ante Christi adventum .clxxxv.[698] Fertur autem dictam fuisse Mutinam a moneo quodque olim grande fuerit passa diluvium, unde quidam, Mutina submersa fuit olim gurgitis unda.

Capitulum .cl. De urbe Regio

Regium[699] Ytalie civitas inter Mutinam et Parmam habetur, que secundum Paulum Langobardum sita est in provincia que Emilia dicebatur, a Liguria incipiens, que modo Langobardia dicitur, inter Appenninas, Alpes, et Padi fluenta versus Ravennam pergit, in qua Emilia eciam Placencia, Parma, Mutina, Bolonia, et Ymola habebantur, ut dicit idem.[700] Tempus vero quo hec civitas Regium et a quibus condita sit non legi. Est eciam alia huius nominis civitas in Calabria sita, de qua dictum est supra.

Capitulum .cli. De civitate Parma

Parma civitas in Emilia, que nunc in Longobardia dicitur, sita, Mutine contemporanea fuit. Nam scribit Miletus sive Ieronimus vel Eusebius quod Parma et Mutina colonie a Romanis condite[701] sunt in Gallia Togata, anno urbis condite .v.^{c}lxvii., qui fuit ante Christi ortum .clxxxv.

In quibusdam quoque scribitur cronicis quod de civitate Placentia civis egressus Grisopolis nomine, Bellovesi ducis Gallorum commilito, civitatem Parmam construxit eamque suo nomine Grisopolim dixit, que eciam et Iulia postmodum fuisse dicitur nominata a Iulio Cesare, unde et in lapide grandi ante basilicam beati Domini in burgo eiusdem sunt antique littere, scilicet Iulia civitas Grisopoli; distat a corpore beati Donini per .xv. miliaria.

698. Ibid., *fol. 59*v. 699. MS, Regnum.
700. *Paul the Lombard, II, 18.* 701. MS, condita.

Nunc Parma a flumine, quod[702] eam preterfluit dicitur. Unde quidam, dicitur a Parma labenti flumine Parma. Super[703] quo flumine lapideus pons testudineatus habetur, opere insignis, et sic videtur quod fuerit satis Mediolano contemporanea. Certum tamen sive autenticum auctorem ex hoc non inveni. Fama tamen tenet vulgaris quod fuerit dicta Grisopolis, idest civitas aurea, crisis enim grece aurum, polis civitas.

Hanc civitatem Parmensem Fredericus imperator huius nominis secundus obsedit, anno Christi .mccxlviii. et in eius suburbiis civitatem condidit quam Victoriam appellavit. Victoribus tandem Parmensibus, fortuna illis arridente, civitas ipsa Victoria victa et deleta nominis amisit effectum. Inter spolia vero coronam habuerunt imperatoris Frederici, que Henrico imperatori huius nominis .vii. fuit postmodum restituta in castris ante Brixiam, anno Christi .mccc.xi.

Cathedralis huius ecclesia decoro opere fabricata nomini Virginis dicata est, unde et in sigillo ipsius civitatis versus habetur qui talis est, Hostis turbetur, quia Parmam Virgo tuetur.

CAPITULUM .CLII. DE CIVITATE PLACENCIA

Placencia placida urbs (et) Ytalie in Emilia sita, ut scribit Paulus, que nunc Longobardia dicitur,[704] iuxta est Padi fluenta. Hanc, ut in aliquibus cronicis habetur, conmilito quidam Bellovesi Gallorum ducis, Peucencius nomine, construxit et a suo nomine Peucenciam appellavit. A quodam fonte Augusta nomine inter ipsam civitatem et Padum plurimum inundante, Augusta est nuncupata. Fons vero Augusta dictus est ab Augusto Cesare, qui eundem fontem suo supposuit interdicto. Sua denique amenitate et pulchritudine tam ex situ quam ex incolis eiusdem urbis fuit Placencia dicta.

Alii ponunt quod primo fuit appellata Augusta, postea Peucencia, demum Placencia. Unde quidam, a verbo placeo sumpsit Placencia nomen. Sed si verum fuit quod a conmilitone aliquo Bellovesi fundata fuerit, non potuit esse quod causa predicta fuerit nuncupata Augusta, quia (quia) nondum Augustas aliquis Cesar erat, cum a Belloveso usque ad Augustum Octavianum fuerint anni ferme .vi^{c} et ideo videtur quod a fundatore Peucencio fuerit prius Peucencia dicta. Titus Livius ubi de Hannibalis transitu in Alpibus loquitur, nominat eam Placenciam, quod fuit circa annum urbis Rome .v.xxiii.[705]

702. MS, qui. 703. Super *was added in the margin of the manuscript.*
704. Dicitur *was added in the margin.* 705. *Livy, XXI, 56.*

Utrum autem Ysidorus de hac Peucencia intelligat, in dubio sum. /[fol. 150*r*] Inmediate enim postquam de condicione Mediolani locutus est, subiungit sic. Historiis placet a Messapo Greco Messapie datam originem, versa postmodum in nomen Calabrie, quam in exordio Enotrii frater Peucentius Peucentiam nominaverat.[706] Forte intellexit de civitate illa de qua dicit Papias, Peucen est civitas iuxta mare ubi currit Danubius in mare.[707] Est eciam et alia civitas dicta Placencia sub metropoli archiepiscopi Emeritensis in Hispania, ut habetur in Pontificali Romane ecclesie.

Capitulum .cliii. De Bobio civitate (ma)

Bobium civitas Ytalie est, que secundum Paulum Longobardum habetur in quinta Ytalie provincia, que Alpescocie dicitur, a Liguria usque ad mare extensa, nominatque hanc civitatem monasterium Bobii.[708] Causam autem nominis et fundacionis tempus et quis fundaverit expresse non inveni. Sed ex[709] exempli posicione quam Paulus facit, innuitur fore satis antiqua et eciam multum famosa, licet hodie sit incolis plurimum vacuata. Est eciam inter montes sic situata ut a montibus cernatur obsessa et forte tunc edificata fuit quando ipsum monasterium fuit constructum.

De monasterii enim fundacione constat per eundem Paulum, qui refert quod Sanctus Columbanus genere Gothicus in Ytaliam veniens et a Longobardorum rege Agilulfo, qui et Ago, gratanter exceptus, cenobium quod Bobium appellatur in Alpibus Cociis edificavit, quod .xl. milibus ab urbe dividitur Ticinense, circiter annum Domini .vic.[710]

Capitulum .cliiii. De Terdona civitate

Terdona Ytalie civitas in provincia eiusdem que Alpes Cocie dicebatur. Secundum quod scribit Paulus Langobardus sita est colle ameno. De huius civitatis fundacione et fundatoribus qui et quo tempore fuerint[711] autentice non legi. In quibusdam tamen cronicis, si fides dari possit assertis, inveni quod Galli hanc civitatem eciam edifficarant, eam Altiliam nuncupantes. Hoc eciam, de nomine videlicet, vulgata tenet antiquitas.

706. *Isidore, XV, i, 58.* 707. *Papias, s.v.* Peucen.
708. *Paul the Lombard, II, 16.* 709. MS, ex *added in the margin.*
710. *Paul the Lombard, IV, 41,* 711. MS, fuerit.

Fuit autem destructa et eversa per Fredericum imperatorem cognomine Barbaruffam, cum ipsi Terdonenses, Papiensibus exosi eo quod Mediolanenses favebant, Papiensibus procurantibus, banno fuissent imperiali suppositi anno Christi .mcliiii., sed eodem anno per Mediolanenses reedificata fuit. Hodie intestinis facientibus sedicionibus fere desolatus est locus habitacionibus antiquis et burgus in radice collis inhabitatur.

Fertur quoque quod hec civitas ab antiquo tribus singularibus donis eminuit, quibus dici poterat leoni conformis; propterea, mutato priori nomine,[712] dicta est Terdona. Dona autem fuisse dicuntur quod loco qui Paerna dicitur petra oleum desudabat; apud Garbagnum fons erumpebat in die Iohannis; apud petram Brixariam quorundam nobilium agnacio tale consuevit instantis mortis habere presagium, nam ex inciso pane sanguis emanabat et tunc paulo post unus ex illa prosapia moriebatur. Unde et hodie in sigillo communitatis insculptus est huiusmodi versus, Pro tribus donis similis Terdona leonis. Alii volunt eam dictam esse Tergonam, quia in tergo collis sita.

De priori autem nomine, scilicet Altilia, asseruit michi quidam iam etate grandevus, fere scilicet septuagenarius, quod ita a primordio fuerit Altilia dicta. Si vero causam narraverit non recolo. Hoc unum tamen michi cordi est quod veluti mirabile quoddam[713] non silebo. Deus scit quod non mentior. Nam licet illitteratus esset et homo rusticus utpote oriundus de Aquensi episcopatu, qui conterminis est episcopatui Alexandrino, ipse tante erat memorie ut nomina omnium civitatum Ytalie et tempora fundacionum et qui fundatores fuerant cursim recitaret ac si perfecte litteratus cronicas haberet et legeret coram se positas, et ni fallor eciam hoc idem recitabat de provinciis reliquis orbis sed in hoc certus non sum.

CAPITULUM .CLV. DE IANUA CIVITATE

Ianua Ytalie civitas secundum Plinium libro de naturali ystoria,[714] in provincia est Ligurie, que nunc Longobardia dicitur; scribit enim Plinius, ut testatur Iacobus de Voragine, quod provincia Ligurie ex parte ore maritime protendebatur a Vintimilio et flumine Merula usque ad Sigestrum et flumen Magre, in qua provincia est Ianua et flumen Pulcifere.[715]

712. MS, nomine *added in the margin.*

713. MS, quodam.

714. MS, ystoria *added in the margin.*

715. *Iacopo, pp. 223–24.*

Paulus vero Langobardorum scriptor historie scribit quod est in quinta Ytalie provincia, que Alpes Cocie dicitur, et quod ipsa provincia a Liguria usque ad mare extensa, ab occiduo Gallorum finibus copulatur, in qua Terdona, monasterium Bobii, Ianua, et Saona civitates habentur.[716] Hos autem ideo adduxi testes eo quod ipse Ianuenses in nulla esse harum se dicunt, verum pocius Marchiam se appellant.

De tempore autem quo fundata fuit et quo auctore varia senciuntur. Scribit enim Iacobus de Voragine in cronicis suis, quas de urbe ipsa compilavit, quod Ianus quidam princeps Moysi contemporaneus de orientis partibus in Ytaliam veniens, ibi primus omnium regnavit, quamvis ut idem dicit alie ystorie videantur asserere quod Abrae tempore regnaverit. Hic Ianuam civitatem construxit, et de suo nomine Ianiculam appellavit,[717] et ad hoc probandum adducit Solini verba dicentis, Quis ignorat vel dictam vel conditam vel a Iano Ianiculam, a Saturno Saturniam?[718]

Alius Ianus Troianus origine post Troie excidium in Ytaliam venit, et dicit eciam quod cum idem Ianus dum navigaret et ventum prosperum haberet loci qui Albarium dicitur, obscuritas grandis in aere apparuit, que vulgo albasia dicitur, apud alios cigaria, que et loco nomen Albarium dedit. Procedens vero loco qui Calignaum dicitur cum terre situs illi placuisset, vela calavit. Unde et locus sic dictus est. Locus vero qui Sarzanum dicitur saltatus in terram descendit et ex illo saltu Sarzanum vulgo quasi saltus Iani locus ille nomen accepit.[719] Veniens autem ad civitatem ipsam Ianiculam castrum ibi edifficavit loco qui nunc castellum vocatur.[720] Fecit quoque turres et fortilicias ubi nunc est archiepiscopale palacium et muris fortissimis communivit et sic eam ampliavit Ianus secundus; convenientibus eciam ibidem diversis habitatoribus civitas magnificari cepit. Quod autem de Iano cive Troie refert dicit se tantum per famam publicam et antiquam novisse.

Subiungit quoque quod Ianua fuit edifficata per annos .vii^{c}vii. ante urbis Rome condicionem et ante adventum Christi per annos .mv^{c}xlvi. et in tercia mundi estate.[721] Hec autem constare dicit et per supradicta verba Solini, scilicet quod Ianus Ianiculam, que modo Ianua dicitur, edificavit et per cronicas autenticas, sed auctorem sive scriptorem non nominat, quod Ianus Moysi regnabat temporibus, quando populi in deserto tenebat ducatum et quod Roma condita fuit tempore Achaz iudicis Israel, unde si a tempore Moysi usque ad Achaz tempora quibus

716. *Paul the Lombard, II, 16.* 717. *Iacopo, p. 16.* 718. *Solinus, 2, 5.*
719. *Iacopo, p. 26.* 720. Ibid., *p. 27.* 721. Ibid., *p. 32, n.* s.

Roma fuit condita computabuntur, invenientur anni fluxisse .vii^{c}vii., quibus Ianue edificacio precessit Rome condicionem. Si autem a Moyse usque ad Christum tempora computabuntur, invenientur, ut dictum est, anni qui fluxerunt .mv^{c}xlvi. Istam autem computacionem annorum dicit se fecisse secundum assignacionem Ieronimi, qui minorem numerum ponit; Beda enim et Me- /[fol. 150*v*] thodius maiorem numerum ponunt.[722]

Hec sunt que scribit de origine Ianue idem Iacobus, concludere volens Ianuam primo conditam a quodam Iano de partibus orientis et Ianiculam dictam teste Solino, sed hoc non videtur verum quia non dixit Solinus Ianiculam sed Ianiculum.[723] Preterea in cronicis Escodii, ut scribit Martinus Polonus, habetur quod Ianus ubi nunc est Roma civitatem construxit nomine Ianiculum.[724] Hoc idem et in Graphia urbis auree continetur.[725] Ieronimus quoque sive Miletus in cronicis scribit quod Ianiculum a Iano in Ytalia conditum est.

Quod eciam concludere nititur, Ianum contemporaneum Moysi et primum in Ytaliam regnantem ediffícasse Ianuam, hoc eciam esse non potest. Nam scribit Eusebius in cronicis et Magister in historiis quod Eneas regnavit in Ytalia anno tercio vel quinto, ut quidam volunt, post excidium Troie, in qua Italia prius regnaverunt Ianus, Saturnus, Picus, Faunus, Latinus, annis circiter .cl.[726] Cum ergo .cl., ut dictum est, anni fuerint a Iano ipso usque ad annum tercium excidii Troie, ut probatur per Eusebium et Magistrum, nequaquam Moysi temporibus esse potuit Ianus quia secundum Eutropium sive Paulum eius abreviatorem a Moysi nativitate usque ad Troie excidium fluxerunt anni .iiii^{c}x.,[727] vel secundum Eusebium fluxerant ab egressu Moysi de Egipto usque ad tempus Labdon iudicis Israel, cuius principatus, anno tercio excisa est Troia, anni .iii^{c}xxviii.,[728] nisi forte Moyses tot annis vixisset, qui non nisi .cxx. fuit annorum, vel ille Ianus quando cepit regnare fuisset annorum .cclx. vel clxxviii. vel fuerit alius Ianus qui ante Ianum de quo locuntur Eusebius et Eutropius regnaverat, de quo latini tamen scriptores nec de illius successione autentici apud nos non habentur.

Quia igitur per hos testes refellitur quod Ianus non fuerit Moysi contemporaneus, multo magis refelli potest quod non fuit temporibus Abrae, qui precessit ortum Moysi, secundum Eusebium, per annos .iiii^{c}xxv.,[729] excidium vero Troie precessit, secundum Ieronimum, .viii.xxx.[730] Constat eciam per Eusebium sive Ieronimum quod Ianiculum

722. Ibid., *pp. 33–34.* 723. *Solinus, 2, 5.* 724. *Martinus, pp. 399–400.*
725. Graphia, Urbis Auree, *ed. R. Valentino and G. Zucchetti (Rome, 1946), p. 78.*
726. *Jerome, p. 62*b. 727. *Eutropius, p. 6.* 728. *Jerome, p. 60*a.
729. Ibid., *p. 43*a. 730. Ibid., *p. 60*a.

a Iano in Ytalia fuit conditum anno nativitatis Abraam .vi^{c}x.[731] et sic si Ianus Ianiculi conditor fuisset Moysi contemporaneus, iam videretur Moysen vixisse annis .ccxv., qui non vixit nisi tantum .cxx. Utrum autem a Iano Troiano vel edificata vel ampliata fuerit in aliquibus scriptis autenticis non inveni.

Sunt eciam qui dicunt fuisse Ianuam dictam vel quod ianua, idest porta, quod quasi sit Lombardie introitus,[732] vel a Iano,[733] qui ibi colebatur, cuius hodie in ecclesia Sancti Mathei statua in loco eminenti manet, et cum statua illa fuerit bifrons, Ianuenses, Romanorum morem secuti, quociens aliquod opus iniciare volebant, fronti anteriori ex animalibus vel avibus sacrificia offerebant, sortito autem operis alicuius effectu, fronti posteriori prebebant libamina. Viri preterea anteriorem, femine posteriorem faciem adorabant.[734]

Tempus quoque fundacionis et quis eam fundaverit in certo auctore non legi. In quadam tamen cronica inveni quod Galli quorum dux fuit Bellovesus eam edificarunt.

Titus Livius preterea non nominat eam Ianuam sed Genuam dicitque ipsam civitatem anno ab urbe condita .dxxxiiii. a Magone Penorum, idest Affricanorum, duce cum .xxx. navibus rostratis et multis honerariis in quibus erant .xii. milia peditum et ferme duo milia equitum, multis munitam presidiis cepit et pene destruxit, circa que tempora Mediolanum fuit expugnatum eciam a Marcello;[735] per quod patet quod saltem per annos .ccxxx. fuit Ianua ante Christi adventum. Alibi dicit quod Scipio frater Publii Cornelii Scipionis navibus Genuam venit in occursum Hannibalis Alpes transgressuri.[736] Refert eciam Titus idem quod Lucrecio prorogatum est imperium a Romanis ut Genuam opidum a Magone pene disruptum reedificaret anno ab urbe Roma condita .v^{c}xlv.[737] Et sic videtur annis .xi. dirupta permansisse.

Scribit eciam idem Titus quod Quintus Minucius consul Romanus in leva Ytalie ad inferum mare flexit iter et contra[738] Genuam exercitu educto orsus est bellum.[739] Vetustissimi preterea codices hystorie Longobardorum habent ubi agitur de Ytalie provinciis Genuam.[740] Per hec igitur patet hanc urbem non Ianuam sed Genuam antiquitus nuncupatam et sic non a Iano dictam vel conditam, quamquam et hodie Ianua appelletur.

731. *This is not found in Jerome.*
732. *Iacopo, p. 53.* 733. Ibid., *p. 52.* 734. Ibid.
735. *Livy, XXVIII, 46, 7.* 736. Ibid., *XXI, 32, 5.* 737. Ibid., *XXX, 1, 10.*
738. *I have supplied this word for the sense of the passage.*
739. *Livy, XXXII, 29, 5.* 740. *Paul the Lombard, II, 16.*

Quando autem fuerit ad Christi fidem conversa expresse non patet; videtur quod tempore Neronis, quia in legenda Nazarii habetur quod anno a passione Christi .xxxv., a nativitate .lxviii., iubente Nerone idem, martyres in mari submersos ab angelo exceptos; naute certe facti, Ianuam perduxerunt.[741]

Quando vero primum habuit episcopum, hoc se non invenisse dicit idem Iacobus.[742] Sed de primo archiepiscopo patet quia cum subesset archiepiscopo Mediolani, Innocencius Papa II Syrum primum ei ordinavit archiepiscopum anno Domini .mcxxxii., cum solum antea episcopos habuisset, deditque ei suffraganeos episcopos Maranensem, Robiensem, et Actiensem, qui fuerant Pisane metropolis, item Bobiensem et Brumacensem.[743] Postea Alexander tercius, Albigano dato episcopo, eum illi submisit.[744] Innocencius IIII Naulo episcopum constituit et ipsi archiepiscopo assignavit et ex tunc vocata est provincia Ianuensis.[745]

Eius in mari maxime gesta magnifica modernis ferme temporibus patenter insinuant quam claris claruerit viris et quam ditissima, opulentissima, ac potentissima fuerit. Que quidem transeo cum non sit presentis materie. Hoc tamen breviter referri potest, quod ex ea urbe duo prodierunt qui summi apostolatus adepti sunt cathedram.[746] Alii qui prelaturas et principatus et principum affinitates optinuerunt, non pauci fuerunt.

Unde ad insinuandam eius potenciam, habent in sculpturis sigilli communitatis ymaginem griffi aves pedibus conculcantis sive unguibus constringentis et versum talem, Griffus ut has angit, sic hostes Ianua frangit. Sed factum est dolorosis et dolosis civium sedicionibus ut urbs ipsa ferrum in se convertens et sibi ipsi hostis effecta a civili angatur hoste pariter et forensi, secundo iam labente anno ex quo obsessa miserabiliter labitur, se ipsam ruinis deformans et rapinis evacuans, cedibus consumens. Quam sint igitur inscrutabilia et terribilia Dei iudicia, quis hec videns non videt? Forte instat quod in vulgi ore solet versari, velut quodam fatali augurio. Predictum enim, inquiunt, futurum esse ut dicatur a transeuntibus, Hec fuit Ianua.

CAPITULUM .CLVI. DE CIVITATE SAONA

Saona Ytalie civitas iuxta mare in provincia que Alpes Cocie dicitur sita est, ut scribitur a Paulo in ystoria Longobardorum.[747] Quo autem tem-

741. *Iacopo, pp. 68–69.*
742. Ibid., *p. 215.*
743. *Kehr, VI–II, 266, n. 5.*
744. Ibid., *p. 262.*
745. Ibid.
746. *Innocent IV and Adrian V.*
747. *Paul the Lombard, II, 16.*

pore fuerit fundata et a quibus autentice scriptum non inveni. Legi tamen in quibusdam cronicis quod Galli qui fuerunt dicti Senones eam edifficaverunt sicut et de aliis dictum est.

Capitulum .clvii. De civitate Aquis Lombardie

Aquis civitas est Ytalie de qua scribit Papias quod sita est in Alpibus Cocie, ubi sunt aque calide, unde aliqui autumant sive volunt eam dictam Aquis ab aquarum copia.[748] Nam iuxta eam labitur flumen; ibi sunt fontes calidi, ex quo optima balnea /[fol. 151*r*] habentur in civitate ipsa, tabulis lapideis decenter constructa et per gradus disposita ut prout balneantes delectat possit se aquis immergere. Et mirum est de natura horum foncium. Vidi enim fontes ibi calentes et in margine eorum immo in eorum aquis calidis herbas virentes. Tante autem sunt caliditatis ut ad usum eorum pistores, tonsores, et macelarii operentur; medicinales eciam sunt cum quosdam morbos repellant.

Huius civitatis menia antiquissimam eam esse demonstrant et ut eorum testantur cronice fuit egregia civitas referta deliciis semperque presulibus decorata. Delicias autem hodie nullas ibi esse cognosco nisi ex balneis, ex quibus fortassis deliciis enervati et effeminati habitatores et ad sediciones concitati ipsam urbem ad statum hodie miserabilem redigerunt. Paucissimos enim incolas habet et pauperes, civili faciente discordia, et que dominari consuevit, nunc istis nunc illis nunc istis subicitur dominis, utpote Alexandrinis et Montiferrati marchionibus, unde verificari videtur quod narrabat michi antiquus ille admirabilis in memoria sicut dictum est in capitulo de Terdona civitate, quod Aquis civitas erat aurea concha scorpionibus plena.

Episcopatum tamen nobilem habet, qui olim per summum pontificem fuit unitus episcopatui Alexandrino ita quod episcopus unus preesse debebat ambobus episcopatibus et sedere Alexandrie mensibus .viii. anni, reliquis .iiii. Aquis, ut testantur publica documenta in archivis ecclesie Alexandrinorum recondita sed non servata.[749]

Civitatis huius sigillum habet aquile figuram leporem unguibus sustinentem et versum talem, Lector, Aquis dignum communis respice signum. Quid autem significet talis sculptura ego non novi. Sunt preterea et alie due civitates huic equivoce, una in Provincia non longe a Massilia et ab Avinione, alia in Alamannia, ubi regum coronacio celebratur, que dicitur Aquis Grani.

748. *Papias, s.v.* Aquis. 749. *Kehr, VI–II, 203, n. 4.*

CAPITULUM .CLVIII. DE ALEXANDRIA CIVITATE LOMBARDA

Alexandria colonia in Liguria, que nunc Longobardia dicitur, condita est temporibus Friderici imperatoris dicti Barbaruffa et Alexandri pape huius nominis tercii, anno Christi .mclxviii., mense Madii, qui fuit annus dicti imperatoris .xv., Alexandri vero .viiii., ultimi autem excidii Mediolani .vi., reedificacionis vero primus. Hanc autem Mediolanenses, Cremonenses, et Placencienses in Papiensium odium condiderunt, conductis ibi colonis ex oppidis Gamondio, Marenco, Roboreto, et Bergolio, et ut famosior fieret, ab Alexandro papa, qui tunc, ut dictum est, presidebat et qui populis favebat in imperatoris odium, Alexandriam nominarunt. Cui eciam civitati ipse Alexander ad Lombardorum ipsorum instanciam episcopum illi instituit nomine Ardoinum, dyaconem suum, multisque civitatem ipsam graciosis dotavit privilegiis. Ardoino autem primo episcopo successit Benedictus, quo defuncto, vacavit sedes usque in presentem diem.[750]

Hanc civitatem idem imperator anno .vi. edificacionis eius obsedit, eductis ibi magnis copiis ex Teutonicis, Papiensibus et Montisferrati marchionatu sed nichil proficiens .vi. obsidionis mense discessit.

Situs autem et soli ubertas civitatem hanc rediderunt uberem pariter et amenam. Est enim inter duos amnes Durmidam et Tanarum qui iuxta eam, immo per eam labitur. Solum vero sive tellus feracissimum est frumenti et vini, leguminum atque lini, planicie amena fecundum. Quam vero populosa et quod maximum sui districtus terminos ampliavit, opida munitissima possidens. Unde et in sigillo civitatis talis consueverat esse versus, Deprimit elatos, levat Alexandria stratos. Sed hodie intestina sedicio civitatem exinanivit incolis, iurisdiccionis vero terminos angustavit. Unde sacius est de preterita eius felicitate silere quam loqui.

CAPITULUM .CLIX. DE CIVITATE NOVARIA

Novaria civitas Ytalie in Liguria, que hodie est provincia Lombardie, cuius fundacionis tempus et fundatores non legi. Quod autem antiqua fuerit constat inter alia quia beatus Ambrosius archiepiscopus Mediolani beatum Gaudencium eidem civitati consecravit episcopum circa Domini. . . .[751]

750. Ibid., *p. 202, n. 1, and p. 203, n. 4.*

751. *This date is not supplied.*

CAPITULUM .CLX. DE CIVITATE VERCELLENSI

Vercelle Ytalie civitas in Liguria, que nunc Longobardia dicitur, sita est. Que, ut in gestis beati Eusebii legitur Liguriarum primatum urbium retinebat, quem postea primatum Mediolanum optinuit. Erat autem, ut in eisdem gestis habetur, Vercellis nobilissima civitas opibus fecunda, arboribus et vineis nemorosa, pascuis ubertina, aquis salutaribus irrigua sed Arriana peste fedata.[752] Fluit iuxta eam amnis qui Sarus dicitur. Quando autem fuerit constructa et a quo vel a quibus non inveni, sed antiquitus constat esse fundatam.

Sicardus tamen Cremonensis episcopus in cronicis suis dicit quod socii Anthenoris et Enee fundaverunt eam,[753] sed unde hoc habeat ibi non legi. In descripcione quoque orbis tempore nativitatis Christi facta, ipsius civitatis nomen eciam continetur.[754]

Per hoc autem quod in gestis beati Eusebii legitur, Vercellis Ligurie civitatum optinuisse primatum,[755] asseritur a quibusdam quod fuit metropolis sedemque archiepiscopalem optinuit. Alii dicunt quod hoc non fuit ab antiquo neque de iure primitivo sed casu urgente pocius et ad tempus. Nam cum Arriana invalesceret pestis et quidam archiepiscopus tunc Mediolani Auxanus nomine esset perfidissimus Arrianus, Silvester papa, Constantino contemporaneus, episcopum Vercellensem Eusebium, confortata ecclesia Romana propter eiusdem imperatoris Constantini favorem, quasi fidei Catholice columpnam super totam Italiam ordinavit qui eciam beato Dyonisio archiepiscopo Mediolani dixit, Te precedo tempore et auctoritate, quod verum fuisse dicunt quantum ex etate quia senior et officio quia a papa specialiter fuerit ceteris antelatus. Huius ego ambiciosam et inutilem questionem diffinire neque scio neque curo, cum magis deflendus sit miserabilis hodie status tam nobilis civitatis predicte. Nam civilis in ea civitate discordia, rerum prodiga hominumque perdicio in tantum inter partem et partem prevaluit ut unam civitatem sediciosi cives in duo castra redigerint, igne et ferro cuncta vastantes et sic unitate profugata civitatis decorum et gloriosum pariter nomen amisit. Est enim civitas secundum Ysidorum hominum multitudo societatis vinculo adunata.[756]

752. "*Passio S. Eusebii, episcopi Vercellensis*," *in F. Ughelli*, Italia Sacra (*10 vols.; Venice, 1717–22*), *IV, 751.*

753. *Sicard, fol. 18*v. 754. MS, concurrit (continetur *is a correction in the margin*).

755. "*Passio S. Eusebii*," *p. 751.*

756. *Isidore, XV, ii, 1.*

CAPITULUM .CLXI. DE CIVITATE AST

Ast Ytalie civitas est et in Liguria, que et Longobardia est; eam constat esse constructam sed a quo vel quando non legi. De ea tamen meminit Paulus Langobardus dicens, quod Gremoald germanus Theolinde regine dux erat in civitate Astensi.[757] Alibi dicit quod Franci cum Longobardis confligentes superati sunt tantaque ibi cedes Francorum fuit ut rivus qui non longe distat ab Astensis civitatis liminibus ab eis cognominetur usque hodie rivus Francorum, vulgo autem Rifrancor.[758]

Hec autem civitas edificiis speciosa, deliciis et diviciis affluere consuevit, unde et in sigillo eiusdem habetur hic versus: Aste viret mundo, sancto custode Secundo. Sanctus enim[759] Secundus vocabulum illius matricis ecclesie.

Hodie autem ci- /[fol. 151*v*] vilia discidia et civitatem deformarunt et civium delicias et divicias tenuarunt.

CAPITULUM .CLXII. ALBA ITALIE CIVITAS

CAPITULUM .CLXIII.

Yporegia Ytalie civitas in Liguria, que nunc Longobardia, constructa extitit.

CAPITULUM .CLXIIII. TAURINUM

CAPITULUM .CLXV. SECLUSIA

CAPITULUM .CLXVII.

Augusta civitas est non longe ab Yporegia, que in Pontificali Romane ecclesie ponitur sub archiepiscopo Tarantasie in Burgundia. Fuit autem edificata ab Augusto in Italia secundum quod scribit Ieronimus sive Miletus et cognominatur Augusta Pretoria. Condita vero anno urbis .vii^{c}xxiiii., qui fuit ante adventum Christi .xxviii.

757. *Paul the Lombard, IV, 40.*

758. Ibid., *V, 5.*

759. MS, enim *was added in the margin.*

MEDIEVAL CITIZENSHIP: THE INDIVIDUAL AND THE STATE IN THE COMMUNE OF SIENA, 1287–1355

William M. Bowsky

University of California, Davis

MEDIEVAL CITIZENSHIP: THE INDIVIDUAL AND THE STATE IN THE COMMUNE OF SIENA, 1287–1355*

A problem fraught with far-reaching implications confronted the Tuscan commune of Siena in 1324. The magistracy of the Nine Governors and Defenders of the Commune and People of Siena (the commune's ruling oligarchy from 1287 to 1355) received a petition from the leading members of a powerful noble family, the Abati del Malia, the de facto rulers of Grosseto. Although recognizing that they were subject to Sienese taxation for real property they possessed within the Sienese state, the Abati del Malia denied that this made them liable to taxation upon their movables.

Rather than decide this delicate matter themselves, the Nine ordered that the petition be analyzed by a legal expert. The jurist selected was the famed Cino of Pistoia, then teaching at the Sienese university. The "General Council" (City Council, or "Council of the Bell") then decided the case on the basis of Cino's *consilium*.[1]

As the jurist ruled in favor of the petitioners, it is of interest to note the principal argument upon which their case depended

> It is said on behalf of the said Malia that he is not held to pay because he is not a citizen, nor one of the contado,[2] nor a person subject to the

* This study is based in part upon a paper that was read at the annual meeting of the Midwest Medieval History Conference in Chicago on October 23, 1965. A Guggenheim Fellowship, a fellowship from the Social Science Research Council, and a leave of absence from the University of Nebraska made the necessary research possible.

Unless otherwise indicated the unpublished documents cited below are found in the Archivio di Stato of Siena.

1. For the background of this case and for the relationships between Cino of Pistoia and the government of the Nine, and the text of the *consilium*, see W. Bowsky, "A new *Consilium* of Cino da Pistoia (1324): Citizenship, Residence and Taxation," *Speculum*, *XLII* (1967); see also pp. 233–34 (below).

2. The contado was the portion of the state outside the city and its boroughs that was most fully subject to the jurisdiction of the commune; and whose inhabitants,*co mitatini* or *comitatinenses* (herein called "contadini," in contrast to modern Italian usage), and territories ordinarily were bound to the dominating city in the relationship of *comitatinantia* or *comitatinanza* (see G. de Vergottini, "Origini e sviluppo storico della comitatinanza," *Studi Senesi*, XLIII [1929], 347–481). De Vergottini also demonstrated that by the early thirteenth century the inhabitant of a borough (by that time usually included within the

> commune of Siena. . . . It seems to me, Cino of Pistoia, now teaching at the Sienese university, and I so counsel, that the aforesaid Malia cannot be forced to pay . . . by the aforesaid reason of the movables, because he is neither a citizen nor an inhabitant of Siena, but is a citizen and resident in his city of Grosseto, where he has his person, family and movables . . . . Nor is it an obstacle that the city of Grosseto has some pacts with that city [Siena], because it is not perpetually subjected to the jurisdiction of Siena and its territory, as is not the land of Montepulciano and other similar lands.

In essence, the outcome rested upon the plaintiff's plea that he was not a citizen, an inhabitant, or a legal resident of the Sienese state. What, then, was the status of a member of a late-medieval or early-renaissance Italian city-state? What groups legally comprised the membership of this body politic? What were the prerequisites for and the privileges and obligations of membership in each group? How and why did these change? And what were the relationships of the individual members of each group toward the state?

Citizens, of course, were the privileged members of an Italian city-state and formed the heart and core of the communes. Surprisingly, however, little scholarship has focused upon the nature of such citizenship, and most particularly, not citizenship in abstract theoretical or juristic terms, but citizenship as understood and treated in a specific city-state. This paper is a pilot study that arose in connection with a general examination of Sienese government and society during the regime of the Nine.[3]

Even during the early decades of the rule of the Nine, the Sienese par excellence was the citizen, especially the urban citizen who regularly

---

city walls and defenses) was a "burgensis" in only a topical sense, while in law he could be a "civis optimo iure."

3. The only major scholarly study that treats medieval Sienese citizenship to any great extent is D. Bizzarri, "Ricerche sul diritto di cittadinanza nella costituzione comunale," *Studi Senesi*, XXXII (1916), 19–136, which was reprinted in her *Studi di storia del diritto italiano* (Turin, 1937), pp. 61–158. (My references are to the reprint, which is cited "Cittadinanza.") For Siena, see "Cittadinanza," especially pp. 109–34.

The sources for most of Bizzarri's assertions concerning Siena are to be found, however, in L. Zdekauer (ed.), *Il constituto del comune di Siena dell'anno 1262* (Milan, 1897 [cited as Zdekauer]), and A. Lisini (ed.), *Il costituto del commune di Siena volgarizzato nel MCCCIX–MCCCX* (2 vols.; Siena, 1903 [cited as Lisini]). Overreliance upon these two compilations is a serious shortcoming in the work of Bizzarri and her predecessors, who were almost exclusively legal historians.

resided within the city or one of its boroughs. He either was a citizen by birth (if his father was a citizen at the time of his birth), or he acquired citizenship if his petition was approved by a two-thirds vote of the City Council,[4] after which he knelt before a communal magistrate—ordinarily the podestà—who granted him citizenship in the name of the commune.[5]

These urban citizens enjoyed the fullest measure of privilege and protection that the commune could offer. They alone could participate fully in the functions of government and in the creation of public policy, and could hold influential and potentially lucrative offices.[6] Carefully shielded by the commune's courts (which specially assisted them against their debtors), they received the state's full support against all external temporal jurisdictions.[7]

Although, like non-citizens, they served Siena in time of war, citizens alone were guaranteed free medical treatment of war wounds and illnesses, payment of ransom by the commune if their resources were insufficient, and even maintenance for life at public expense (by the Hospital of Santa

4. Lisini, Dist. I, r. clxxxvi. The Constitution of 1262 did not call for this Council approval; see Zdekauer, Dist. IV, r. xxxxvii.

5. An extant record of the ceremony of initiation into Sienese citizenship during the regime of the Nine is Diplomatico Riformagioni [DR], No. 1574, Sept. 19, 1329, which states that ser Credo di Berto of Tatti had fulfilled the legal requirements for attaining citizenship, summarizes the requirements, and adds that, at a General Council session: "dominus potestas et dominus capitaneus [populi] ipsum ser Credum flexis genibus coram eis astantem et volentem et devote petentem se admicti et recipi in verum et legiptimum civem civitatis senensis in presentia voluntate et assensu consilii memorati auctoritate etiam eorum et cuiusque eorum offic[iorum] potestarie et capitaneatus admiserunt et receperunt ipsumque ser Credum per se et filiis suis recipientem de omnibus et singulis privilegiis gratiis beneficiis auxiliis honoribus et factionibus quibus alii veri cives de civitate comuniter participant fruuntur et gaudent per virgas quas manu gestabant solempniter investiverunt." Such a dual grant by the podestà and the captain of the people was rare; the podestà ordinarily performed this act alone (see below, pp. 207, 214).

On some occasions, one or more of the Nine performed the ceremony, acting upon authorization by the City Council (see e.g., G. de Vergottini, "Origini e sviluppo," 348). DR, No. 1704, Apr. 21, 1353, records that on Apr. 22, 1353, seven of the Nine granted Sienese citizenship to Lamberto di Tino of Montepulciano: "se presentem et se de dicta civilitate investarii [sic] petentem humiliter et devote coram eis existentem capite discoperto cum bacchetta quam habebant in manu tangentes singuli eorum capud eiusdem de ipsa civilitate investiverunt omni jure et modo quibus melius potuerunt, dicentes exto civis verus et legiptimus Civitatis Senarum." See also below, p. 220.

6. See W. Bowsky, "The *Buon Governo* of Siena (1287–1355): A Mediaeval Italian Oligarchy," *Speculum*, XXXVII (1962), 368–81 *passim* (cited below as "*Buon Governo*").

7. See, for example, Lisini, Dist. II, r., xix, lxxiii, lxxx, lxxxi, lxxxvi.

Maria della Scala) if they were so disabled by war injuries that they became incapable of earning a living and had no private means of support.[8] Within the state, they had special immunity and protection from harassment by local lords and communities—for themselves, their properties, laborers, sharecroppers, and renters[9]—and even were exempted from the cruel injunction that persons mutilated as part of the sentence of conviction for specified crimes had to leave the city within three days after this mutilation.[10]

Compared with his advantages the citizen's few liabilities were minor; for example, he might be compelled to serve in some of the less lucrative public offices and had to pay double the fine exacted of non-citizens for the commission of various major crimes, such as perjury in criminal cases[11] or harboring a condemned homicide.[12]

Before the accession of the Nine, urban Sienese citizens—like those of many other communes—were divided into various classifications: "ancient, true and natural citizens" (*cives antiqui veri et naturales*) or "ancient, true and original citizens," who were citizens by birth and whose forebears had been citizens for a long (but legally undefined) period, and "continual citizens" (*cives assidui*), who themselves had long been citizens and who lived in the city all year—or dwelt outside the city only during the harvest season.[13]

8. See Lisini, Dist. I, r. lxxv, cdlxx, and Dist. I, r. 342 (fol. 76*r*), of Statuti, Siena, No. 26 (the latter is a major constitutional redaction of Sienese statutes, for whose dating see the Appendix [below]).

9. See, for example, Lisini, Dist. I, r. cdxcvi, Dist. IV, r. xxxix, xlv, Dist. V, r. lxx, cclxix, Dist. VI, r. lxxiii.

10. Lisini, Dist V, r. ccviii. Cf. Dist. V, r. ccxli, of the Constitution of 1262, ed. L. Zdekauer, *Bullettino Senese di Storia Patria* [*BSSP*], III (1896), 90. Zdekauer, who edited final fragments of the 1262 Constitution (see *BSSP*, I [1894], 131–54, 271–84; II [1895], 137–44, 315–22; III [1896], 79–92), believed they were probably compiled between 1262 and 1270 (*BSSP*, I, 131–35). U. G. Mondolfo has shown, however, that the fragments were redacted in September, 1262 ("La legislazione statutaria senese dal 1262 al 1310," *Studi Senesi*, XXI (1904), 230–56, p. 236, and "L'ultima parte del constituto senese del 1262, ricostruita dalla riforma successiva," *BSSP*, V (1898), 124–228).

11. See, for example, "Consiglio Generale, Deliberazioni [CG], No. 53, fol. 122*r–v* (June 11, 1298).

12. Lisini, Dist. V, r. cclii; cf. Dist. V, r. clxxxviiii, of the 1262 Constitution (in *BSSP*, III [1896], 80). The reward for the capture of a citizen who had committed homicide was twice that offered for the capture of a non-citizen (Lisini, Dist. V, r. ccxlviii).

13. For a discussion of these categories in Siena and elsewhere, see Bizzarri, "Cittadinanza," pp. 82–84.

These special classes of citizens had long enjoyed a particularly privileged status, as many rubrics of the Constitution of 1262 clearly indicated. They received greater legal protection than other citizens and had such valuable prerogatives as the right to serve in leading governmental positions: as councillors of the City Council, as contado rectors, as the chiefs and supervisors (*Provveditori* or *Provisores*) of the *Biccherna* (the highest financial magistracy), and on the signory itself—for example, as members of the Twenty-four Priors of the Sienese People and Commune or the Thirty-six Governors of the City and Commune of Siena (predecessors of the Nine).

Although it has been assumed that these basic separations and distinctions within the membership of the urban citizen body continued to be very important throughout the late thirteenth and the first half of the fourteenth century, this assumption is unwarranted for Siena. Even an examination confined largely to the communal Constitution of 1309–10 indicates that these distinctions had become blurred and were diminishing in significance early in the regime of the Nine. Rubrics that seem to have granted such citizens advantages in eligibility for office are confused and ambiguous, and, on occasion, were vitiated by major exceptions. Membership on the City Council, for example, was limited to "men, good Catholics, and of good reputation," each of whom was at least twenty-five years of age and had resided "in the city of Siena as a continual citizen for ten years"; however, judges from the city or the contado as well as contadini who had become citizens, also could be appointed councillors.[14]

Rubrics for the special protection of the rights of continual citizens over their serfs are a holdover (in far less elaborate form) of legislation of an earlier epoch—as early as the twelfth century. Even the important rubric that villeins of continual citizens could become citizens but could have no farm or holding other than one to which they furnished proof of allodial rights was not an innovation but a carryover from the Constitution of 1262.[15] So, too, was the podestà's promise not to honor the sale of a lord's properties by his villein if the lord was a continual citizen.[16] A rubric for the treatment of villeins of "*assiduali cittadini*" who had warred against their lords was a composite of several rubrics of the 1262 Constitution

14. Lisini, Dist. I, r. ccxliii; cf. Dist. I, r. xlviii, cccxxxix.

15. Lisini, Dist. IV, r. xlix; Zdekauer, Dist. IV, r. lviii.

16. Lisini, Dist, IV, r. lxvi; 1262 Constitution, Dist. IV, r. lxxviii (in *BSSP*, I [1894], 137).

—at least one of which goes back to 1222.[17] Indeed, on December 18, 1286, when the City Council for the last time considered by statutory precept the question of how the taxable worth of the villeins of continual citizens was to be evaluated, it tabled the matter indefinitely—as the recording notary wrote, "because the said statute is ancient."[18] The 1309–10 Constitution also distinguished between urban-continual and other citizens on the penalties for some of the lesser crimes of physical violence. (Although the distinction was clearly stated in the 1262 Constitution, the wording of the 1309–10 Constitution obscures the difference.[19])

The very definition of *civis assiduus* is elusive. The term was not defined in the Constitution of 1262, but it appears to refer to citizens who had lived in the city continuously for at least three years and were in good standing; that is, were listed in the occasionally prepared tax registers and performed the expected services for the commune.[20] Similarly, the 1309–10 Constitution did not clearly define *civis assiduus*, but in the rare references that possibly link this form of citizenship to a specific time span, five years is the shortest period mentioned.[21]

The "ancient," "true and original" or "natural" citizens were recognized by the Constitution of 1309–10 as a special category—as descendants of forebears who were distinguished by "long and continual and great residence" in the city.[22] The only privilege left them, however—

17. Lisini, Dist. IV, r. lxvii; cf. 1262 Constitution, Dist. IV, r. lxxx, lxxxi (*BSSP*, I [1894], 137–38).

18. CG, No. 33, fols. 8*r*–9*v*. On this issue of "allibramento villanorum civium senarum adsidualium," the Council accepted the advice of the notary ser Jacobus Sardus (Jacomo Sardo): "quod cum dictum statutum sit antiquum quod super hiis debeat supersedere."

19. See, for example, Lisini, Dist. V, r. ccxxxv–ccxxxviii, cclxxvii, cclxxviii; the 1262 Constitution, Dist. V, r. ccxiiii, ccxv (*BSSP*, III [1896], 84–85). Statuti, Siena, No. 26, Dist. III, r. 265 (fol. 169*r*), removed an obscurity from the 1309–10 text.

20. Zdekauer, Dist. I, r. cclxx, cclxxxviii.

21. See especially Lisini, Dist. VI, r. xxix: ". . . che ciascuna d'esse comunanze elega tre notari de la città di Siena li quali sieno essuti cittadini et abiano fatte tutte le fazioni, secondo che cittadini, continuamente per V. anni ne la città di Siena . . . ." Cf. Lisini, Dist. I, r. ccxxxiii. Statuti, Siena, No. 26, Dist. IV, r. 19, fols. 201*r*, 201*v*, 202*r*, notes that several offices are reserved for those who have resided in the city for ten years "pro cive assidue per decem annos . . . ." This does not however define the length of time required for qualification as a *civis assiduus*, particularly as some of these same restrictions applied in the 1309–10 Constitution (cf. above, n. 14).

22. Lisini, Dist. IV, r. lix: ". . . quelli huomini et persone è quali avuti sono per antichi cittadini per longa et continua et grande abitazione, la quale fecero essi et li loro antecessori ne la città di Siena et li quali sono avuti ne la città di Siena per cittadini antichi et veri . . . ."

although even this is uncertain—was exemption from the periodic investigations that were made of naturalized citizens.

Any advantage possessed by the formerly privileged "ancient," "natural," "true," and "original" citizens lost its importance through still another phenomenon. By the period of the Nine—or certainly a few years after 1287—it became customary for persons seeking citizenship to include within their petitions the request that they and their heirs enjoy all of the rights of true, ancient, and original citizens.

Legislation of the 1320s shows how the various shades of urban citizenship were being fused into a single form of citizenship. According to a measure of November 10, 1328, after various types of persons fulfilled specified conditions, they were to be

> received as citizens and invested with the benefit of citizenship by the lord podestà of Siena, and so be publicly received and admitted in the General Council of the said commune, [and] a public instrument should appear concerning this reception, lest such persons pass by unnoticed; and thus received *ipso facto* they are, and are to be understood to be, true Sienese citizens (*veri cives senenses*), and are to be treated as true citizens . . . .[23]

An act of the following November, which stemmed directly from the measure of 1328, reveals the meaning of "true Sienese citizens." Anyone who complied with the requirements therein set forth was to be granted citizenship and henceforth "held to be a true and legitimate citizen of the city of Siena and [considered] as if he were of Sienese origin." Such persons, it continued, are to be held to be "legitimate" citizens, exactly as if they were "natural" citizens of the city.[24]

A grant of citizenship to a person of special importance often contained a clause that equated him with "natural" citizens. Several such acts were passed in favor of members of the famous Franzesi family of the Florentine contado—the family of "Biche" and "Mouche," sometime personal bankers to King Philip the Fair of France.

23. Statuti, Siena, No. 23, fols. 194*r*–96*v* (quotation on fols. 194*v*–95*r*). This measure was designed particularly for persons of from moderate to great wealth from the Masse and the contado who had not yet acquired Sienese citizenship after prolonged residence in Siena. (For the Masse [various communities immediately adjacent to the city], see W. Bowsky, "*Buon Governo,*" 375 n. 32, and "The Impact of the Black Death upon Sienese Government and Society" ["Black Death"], *Speculum,* XXXIX [1964], 5–10, 21 n. 116, 22 n. 123, and below [pp. 227–30].)

24. See CG, No. 108, fols. 75*r*–79*v* (Nov. 27, 1329). ". . . et habeatur verus et legiptimus civis civitatis sen. ac si esset oriundus de dicta civitate Sen." (fol. 78*r*).

As early as 1295 the Sienese City Council accepted a petition

> on behalf of the noble men, Albizzo, called Biche, and Ciampolo, called Musciatto [Mouche], and Niccoluccio, brothers, sons of the late lord Guido Franzesi of Pian di Valdarno in the Florentine contado [in which it is stated] that these men intend and wish to be and become Sienese citizens and to purchase possessions in the Sienese city and contado, to the honor and good state of the Commune and People of Siena.[25]

On June 27, 1301, the Council formally approved the application for eligibility for citizenship presented on behalf of lord Musciatto del fu Guido dei Franzesi[26]—an unusual procedure, perhaps adopted because of the Franzesi's importance and their close relationship with the Florentine state. Mouche's citizenship petition was approved by the City Council the following month, and it included the statement that "he can have and receive and exercise [public] offices and honors in the city of Siena like other natural Sienese citizens . . . ."[27] Eight days later his brother, Biche, received a grant of citizenship in exactly the same form.[28]

25. CG, No. 47, fols. 96*v*–98*v* (Apr. 12, 1295) (quotation on fol. 96*v*); summarized in R. Davidsohn, *Forschungen zur Geschichte von Florenz*, III (Berlin, 1901), 53, No. 227. The Franzesi also requested exemption from all dazi (certain direct taxes that were based upon official evaluations of one's properties), from prestanze or preste (forced loans), and from other real and personal obligations, and they asked that they be bound to pay only the gabelles (various forms of excise and customs duties and miscellaneous other taxes) paid by Sienese citizens. Although three of the councillors who participated in the ensuing discussion were Noveschi (members of the oligarchy of the Nine), their opinions differed. Pane Squarcialupi advised that the matter be delegated to the Nine and the other "Orders." [The Orders consisted of the Nine, the "Four *Provveditori*" of the Biccherna, the Consuls of the Knights (occasionally called "Captains of the Party," meaning the Guelf Party), and the Consuls of the *Mercanzia* or Merchant Guild. (See, e.g., Lisini, Dist. I, r. cccxl.)] Judge Meo di Tigo di Leo (or Tigolei) counseled that the Franzesi receive immunity from dazi and prestanze for five years. Memmo di Viviano Vignari suggested that they be given citizenship and a ten-year immunity (presumably in the form they had requested). The Council, however, agreed with Bartolomeo Manetti (not one of the Noveschi), who counseled that the Franzesi receive citizenship and only five years' immunity from dazi and prestanze. For the Franzesi and their Sienese and Florentine citizenships, see also R. Davidsohn, *Geschichte von Florenz*, II, Part II (Berlin, 1908), 382–90.

26. CG, No. 59, fol. 108*r*.

27. CG, No. 60, fols. 34*r*–35*v* (July 14, 1301) (quotation on fol. 34*r*); summarized in Davidsohn, *Forschungen*, III, 78, No. 372. Mouche also received immunity from dazi and prestanze, and from service in the army and on cavalry expeditions for a period to be set by the Nine.

28. CG, No. 60, fol. 40*r*–*v* (July 22, 1301); cf. Davidsohn, *Forschungen*, III, 78, No. 372.

If these grants of Sienese citizenship to Florentine citizens cause surprise, let us recall that, although not common, dual citizenship was not unknown in late-medieval Italy.[29]

Even the few newly acquired communities whose members received Sienese citizenship as a part of the community's pacts of submission or of incorporation into the contado might find that their members were designated "true and natural" and "legitimate" citizens, even though they did not become urban citizens who were required to live in Siena. Although we cannot be certain, it is likely that the members of those few communities of the Masse that received full urban citizenship also received this designation.[30]

An instance that seems to contradict the development of a single urban citizenship is that of the new or naturalized citizen. This exception is only apparent. Although the commune placed restrictions upon new citizens their citizenship did not differ in kind from that of older citizens—whether by birth or by naturalization. A new citizen was subjected to a specific probationary period during which the government attempted to ascertain that he was fulfilling the obligations and the promises he had undertaken when he had applied for citizenship.

Well might the commune have cause for concern. In 1296, for example, the City Council treated the problem of the

> many men from outside the contado and jurisdiction of the commune of Siena [who] continually become citizens of Siena for the twenty *soldi* that one who wishes to become a Sienese citizen pays to the commune. And by reason of having this citizenship, when it is advantageous, such citizens export their merchandise, and cause it to be exported, through the territory of Siena without paying any export duty to the said commune of Siena. And thus . . . the commune is deceived and defrauded.[31]

This problem, of course, was not confined to Siena. To cite only a random example, in 1316 the government of Florence dealt with a complaint tendered by "many citizens"

> That foreign-born persons, under false colors and not with true causes alleged, are found to have been made citizens of Florence . . . , especially so that as citizens they may pay less taxes at the gates of the

29. See, for example, Bizzarri, "Cittadinanza," pp. 96–97; F. A. Freiherr von der Heydte, *Die Geburtstunde des souveränen Staates* (Regensburg, 1952), pp. 387–88.

30. See below, pp. 220–23, 228.

31. CG, No. 49, fols. 49*v*–50*r* (Feb. 15, 1296), fol. 49*v*.

city; which taxes paid by those foreign-born should often be greater, because higher taxes are paid by Florentines in their cities.[32]

Sienese legislation of March 10, 1324, reveals another of the many forms of deception that were often practised by new citizens: evasion of their obligation to build a new house in the city.

> Since it is publicly manifest both to Sienese citizens and contadini that many frauds are continuously committed, deceiving the commune of Siena, by some men who become citizens of the city of Siena, from the fact that houses are constructed in their name, when in truth they belong to and are the property of another person, and this is a grave harm to the commune of Siena . . ., [it is] provided and ordered that all and each who become . . . citizens of the aforesaid city are held to and must build a house, or cause a house to be built, in accordance with the form of the statutes and ordinances of the commune of Siena, in the city of Siena or its boroughs, in that part and place of the city or boroughs in which it will be ordered them by the Nine or other Orders of the city who will then be in office, which order must be made before the said person [*sic*] is received as a citizen.[33]

A Sienese law that was passed April 9, 1333, and that was incorporated a few years later into a major constitutional redaction, is especially interesting.[34] The enactment provided that the captain of the people, a high communal magistrate, would investigate every new citizen once each year for the first six years after the acquisition of citizenship; then, if all went well, the investigation would cease and the new citizens henceforth were to be regarded as "natural and ancient citizens." (Again the term "ancient citizen"!)

Even this six-year period was a lightening of the burden on new citizens. As recently as 1330 they had been subjected to ten years of

32. Archivio di Stato di Firenze, Provvisioni, No. 15, fols. 28*v*, 30*r*, 30*v* (quotation on fol. 28*v*). Florence, on this occasion, provided that citizenship privileges conceded to foreigners were to be canceled if within the next six months they did not prove they had lived in Florence continuously from their reception of citizenship to the present, that their properties were listed in the Florentine tax registers, and that they were performing all of their obligations to the commune.

33. Statuti, Siena, No. 23, fols. 71*r*–75*r* (quotation on fol. 72*r*). There is another copy of this measure in Capitano del Popolo, No. 1, fols. 142*r*–46*r*. Folios 91*r*–94*r* of CG, No. 99 (Mar. 10, 1324), do not include the contents of these provisions, which were advised by Judge Meo di Tigo di Leo and approved 185–50.

34. See W. Bowsky, "*Cives Silvestres*: Sylvan Citizenship and the Sienese Commune (1287–1355)," *BSSP*, LXXII (1965).

annual investigation, and only at the end of this probationary period were those found to have fulfilled their obligations "treated in all things as natural and ancient Sienese citizens."[35] Among the most important obligations of new citizens were those of entering their names and properties on the tax registers, of building a house in the city or one of its boroughs, and of residing there with their families and performing the services required by the commune.

This decrease in the probationary period for naturalized citizens and their equation with "ancient citizens" is of a piece with the other developments we have examined. By the end of the fourth decade of the fourteenth century, then, the distinctions that had earlier been made among urban citizens had become blurred, ill defined, and of little significance. Within the space of about a half-century the Sienese government had altered the nature of urban citizenship and had completed the fundamental steps for amalgamating the gradations of urban citizenship for those citizens who dwelt within the city and its boroughs.

The urban citizens were men who possessed a specified minimum wealth, resided within the city, demonstrated willingness and ability to pay taxes, and who performed the other real and personal services that the commune demanded of its citizenry. But when we ask what sort of men were attracted by the lure of citizenship and were capable of meeting its requirements, or in what ways the commune facilitated or hindered the entrance of new members into its inner core, we enter upon two areas of policy and legislation that—in the Siena of the Nine—were inextricably interwoven and treated as one: immigration and naturalization.

The commune was in fact concerned with the volume and the nature of immigration into the city and state, and with the types of persons it most favored as additions to the citizen body; and it treated all this as a single problem. The first five decades of the regime of the Nine—at least until the late 1330s—saw a great influx of population into the city, from the

35. Statuti, Siena, No. 23, fols. 281*r*–83*v* (Dec. 28, 1330), especially 281*r*–*v*. This systematization of the investigation process was achieved, in part, because of complaints made to the government by new citizens irritated at the capricious nature of repeated and unwarranted investigations to which they claimed to have been subjected. On February 9, 1328, for example, the City Council received a petition on behalf of naturalized citizens who complained that they had been subjected to repeated investigations by successive captains of the people. To end this inconvenience, the Council decided that the name and surname of each new citizen should be listed in two identical books, one to be kept in the Biccherna and the other by the captain of the people (CG, No. 105, fols. 29*v*–36*r*, esp. 29*v*–31*v*).

contado and from neighboring states.[36] During this period the government elaborated a complex body of naturalization legislation in order to attract new citizens and to make certain that it obtained the greatest benefit from them. If we touch upon only a few of the major steps in this process the general development nonetheless becomes clear.

In 1281, citizenship could be acquired through the payment of a 20-*soldi* fee—and, of course, the enrollment of one's properties on the tax registers, as was required even of non-citizens who resided within the state. But the fee was increased fivefold, to 100 *soldi* (£5) in 1295; still not a forbidding sum. By 1306 a new citizen faced the added and considerable burden of building a new house evaluated at a minimum of £100 in the city or its boroughs no later than one year after receiving citizenship. This house, furthermore, was obligated to the commune for ten years to ensure that the new citizen performed the services that all citizens owed the commune. Failure to meet these commitments entailed payment of double the value of the house, which became the property of the commune. A new citizen's promises also had to be guaranteed by two men who pledged themselves as sureties. Dina Bizzarri correctly assumed that these obligations, particularly the construction of a new house, were also imposed to improve the city's appearance, and to enrich it with new construction, as well as to prevent new citizens from defrauding the government by entering into fictitious purchase agreements.[37]

Two folios of a Biccherna register contain a unique account, hitherto unnoticed, that recorded the process undertaken by an individual in acquiring citizenship while the legislation of 1306 was in force.[38]

1. On October 26, 1311, the Nine approved the petition for citizenship submitted by Gerino di ser Tano of Casole. The notary of the Nine recorded this decision on an instrument that was given to Gerino.
2. Gerino appeared before the leading Biccherna officials the same day: the *Camerarius* (treasurer) and the Four *Provveditori*. He paid them 100 *soldi* and promised to build a new house that would be worth £100 or more, or to have one built, within one year; Ser Nello di Giovanni, a notary, and Cino di messer Tinaccio, probably a notary, appeared as his guarantors. A notary of the

36. W. Bowsky, "Black Death," [cited above, n. 23], 5–9.

37. Bizzarri, "Cittadinanza," pp. 128–29. See Lisini, Dist. I, r. clxxxvi, cccxlvii, and Dist. IV, r. xxxviii.

38. Biccherna, No. 1058, fols. 17*r*–18*r*.

Biccherna gave Gerino an instrument that recorded these actions.

3. On October 28, 1311, the City Council voted that Gerino be made a citizen, a notary extracted a copy of this decision for Gerino's use from the records of ser Fone del fu Ranaldo of San Gimignano, the "Notary of the Riformagioni"—or notary in charge of the redaction of the acts of the principal Sienese councils.
4. Later the same day, the podestà of Siena, Ranieri di Sasso Gabrielli of Gubbio, granted Gerino citizenship and gave him a notarized instrument of citizenship.
5. Gerino immediately returned to the *Camerarius* and the Four *Provveditori* and declared that he wished to be "*allibratus*"—to have his properties entered on the tax-assessment registers—as a Sienese citizen. He was enrolled as "*Gerinus ser Tani de Casulis civis senensis de populo Sancti Petri Castri Veteris ---- XXV lb. denariorum senensium allibratus.*"
6. On October 21, 1312, almost one year later, Gerino appeared at the Biccherna before the *Camerarius* and the Four *Provveditori*, with his two guarantors. He deposed that, as part of his citizenship requirement, he had caused a house to be built in the city of Siena in the "*popolo*" (district or ward) of S. Pietro in Castelvecchio, and he described its exact location by reference to the adjacent properties.
7. On October 26, 1312, Gerino returned to the Biccherna officials and gave them a notarized instrument in which he declared that he had been received as a citizen in the "Council of the Bell," had paid the 100-*soldi* fee to the Biccherna, and within a year of receiving citizenship had caused a house to be built in S. Pietro in Castelvecchio that he now offered as security to the commune against debts that he might incur to it. He requested that the house be received by the Biccherna officials.
8. The next day, October 27, Gerino's proctor, Cino di Tinaccio, appeared before the Biccherna officials and displayed a receipt from the seller indicating that on September 28, 1312, Gerino had purchased from Pietro di Ugolino Giliotti "de Boscolis" the square in the *popolo* of S. Pietro in Castelvecchio upon which the aforesaid house had been built. He showed a second instrument, of October 21, 1312, that appointed him, Cino, as Gerino's proctor. He then requested that the Biccherna send a master *operarius* (supervisor) to appraise the new house.
9. Two Biccherna officials appeared before the *Camerarius* and the Four *Provveditori* that same day, and, in the presence of Master Andrea del fu Ventura, a master *operarius* of the Opera of the

Hospital of Santa Maria della Scala, reported that he had seen the house that had been built for Gerino and had evaluated it at £100 "and more."

10. At the petition of Gerino's proctor, Cino, the *Camerarius* and two of the Four *Provveditori*—also on October 27—stated that they accepted and approved the report on the house, which had been presented by the aforesaid two Biccherna officials.

In this way did Gerino fulfill the formal obligations he had assumed in order to obtain citizenship.

The system under which Gerino became a citizen, which was embodied in the legislation of 1306, underwent a major modification in 1324—the last major revision of Sienese naturalization policies during the regime of the Nine. In the legislation of March 10, 1324, the 100-*soldi* fee was eliminated and a new system was created.

> [It is provided that] no one from the Sienese contado can be received or admitted as a citizen of the aforesaid city [Siena] unless he first pays the Biccherna of the said commune 6 *denari* in counted coin for each *lira* of the evaluation made of his real property in the table [of possessions], and also the taxation made of his movable property in the said table or by occasion of the said table. However, [it is provided] that no one can pay less than £25, even though his evaluation and taxation do not ascend to the sum of £25 at the said rate. And if anyone from outside the Sienese contado and jurisdiction wishes to become a Sienese citizen, [it is ordered] that he cannot be received or admitted unless he first pays to the Biccherna £10 of Sienese *denari* in counted coin. And nonetheless, both the contadino and the person from outside the Sienese contado and jurisdiction who wishes to become a citizen is held to build a house, or to have a house built, and to pay the dazi, impositions, and collections and other single obligations, both real and personal, according to the form of the statutes and ordinances of the commune of Siena.[39]

For those who came from within the Sienese state, this new legislation based the citizenship fee on a proportion of an applicant's taxable wealth—2.5 per cent to be exact—and particularly sought to attract persons of considerable means, of £1,000 or more, though recognizing that many seeking and deserving citizenship would not be so well off. Foreigners were to pay a flat rate, and need have wealth only to the extent of £400,

39. Manuscripts cited above, n. 33 (quotation on fol. 74*r*).

if the same tax ratio was assumed. The government recognized that it was more difficult to attract foreigners into the state and into accepting citizenship, but that their acquisition would strengthen the state. The system created in 1324 was included in the major redaction of communal statutes of the late 1330s,[40] and, as far as can be ascertained, it remained in force throughout the remainder of the regime of the Nine.

The expanding body of naturalization requirements during the late thirteenth and early fourteenth centuries did not stem the tide of men who sought citizenship, nor was this the intent. On the contrary, there are many indications—some overtly expressed by the Sienese lawmakers—that the government wished to attract more immigrants and more new citizens during this period.[41]

It has long been known that special efforts were made to attract persons from rival communities—to induce them to immigrate to Siena and to acquire Sienese citizenship. But it has been overlooked that while measures such as that of 1292, exempting from reprisal legislation persons from the Maremma and the Bishopric of Volterra who wished to become Sienese citizens, named specific communities, those same provisions included phrases that extended their application to those coming "from other places."[42] Similarly, a temporary enactment of 1328 granted special treatment to men from Chiusi and Grosseto, but it also applied to men from other dioceses.[43]

40. Statuti, Siena, No. 26, Dist. I, r. 239, fol. 60*r*; cf. Bizzarri, "Cittadinanza," p. 129. On November 10, 1328 (Statuti, Siena, No. 23, fols. 194*r*–96*v*), the City Council modified the system of 1324 in order to make citizenship possible for persons from the Masse and the contado who already were resident in Siena and who possessed less than £1,000 in property but more than £100. Such persons were exempted from the obligation of building a house and from the £25 fee, and were ordered to pay a flat 6 per cent of the valuation of their property. A measure of November 27, 1329 (CG, No. 108, fols. 75*r*–79*v*), indicated that this system was difficult to execute and noted that errors of less than 20 per cent in valuations were too trifling to be corrected. The variant of 1328 must have been abandoned soon after mid-1331, and was not included in Statuti, Siena, No. 26; cf. below, pp. 215–16.

41. Lisini, Dist. IV, r. lxiv. This, an undated rubric, ordered the podestà to receive and defend as a citizen anyone from outside the state who might wish to come to Siena, become a citizen, and reside there as a citizen.

42. Lisini, Dist. IV, r. lxv; see also Bizzarri, "Cittadinanza," p. 128. For reprisals, see below (n. 106).

43. CG, No. 105, fols. 77*r*–81*v* (Mar. 28, 1328). In discussing this measure in "Black Death," 7–8, I did not mention that persons who benefited from this provision had to pay a £25 citizenship fee.

An act of December 28, 1330, that was intended in part to further the policy of immigration, noted that

> the commune of Siena has in the past been seen to induce with all its ability its contadini, and foreigners as well, to return to and come to the city of Siena, and has offered them various graces and privileges so that they might become citizens of the said city, from which new citizens the common weal of the city (*res publica civitatis*) is increased in manifold ways.[44]

Although there is an apparent paradox between statements that the commune wanted new citizens and the heavier financial burdens it placed upon these citizens, we must recall that the commune wanted only those who would fulfill their obligations as citizens—not the tax-evaders against whom the City Council inveighed in 1296 or of whom the Florentines complained in 1316.

This becomes even clearer if we turn our attention to the body of legislation directed toward a unique type of citizen who posed a special problem for Siena (as for her sister communes), *cives silvestres* or *cittadini selvatici*—the "sylvan citizens."[45]

In Siena, as in many other cities, "sylvan citizens" were men from the contado who acquired urban citizenship and obligated themselves to live in the city, with their families, for a fixed portion of the year. Unlike some communes, however, this period was the same in Siena as that required of other citizens—the entire year, with the exception of harvest times—and this is in keeping with the Sienese attempt to create a single urban citizenship.

Although this often sizable group of citizens formed one of the strongest personal bonds that linked the major commune with the component parts of the state, the sylvan citizens created serious problems because, in actual fact, they frequently remained in the contado, but claimed the privileges of urban citizenship and immunity from local jurisdiction, or, when they moved to the city, they failed to enter themselves and their properties on the tax registers and perform the obligations incumbent upon all citizens. From its inception until its collapse, in 1355, the government of the Nine was concerned with this problem and rapidly developed a consistent policy, which it refined particularly in the 1320s

44. Statuti, Siena, No. 23, fols. 281*r*–83*v* (quotation on fol. 281*r*).

45. For more about sylvan citizenship, see W. Bowsky, "*Cives Silvestres*" [cited above, n. 34]; see also below, n. 101.

and 1330s, but which it applied—with varying degrees of rigor—throughout the entire period.

Although the Pisan commune's principal concern and sole interest in its sylvan citizens was essentially fiscal, that was not the case in Siena; the Sienese interest was broader and more constant. Siena wanted taxes from its sylvan citizens but it also wanted their personal services. Its interest also extended to the protection of contado communities from the abuses and deception practised by their erstwhile citizens. Protection was sorely needed, for the sylvan citizens frequently were the richest and most powerful members of their local communities—men whom those small towns could not easily control or deal with.

The Sienese government ordered that sylvan citizens who did not reside in Siena with their families for the greater part of each year must perform all personal and real obligations in and with the contado communities where they possessed their properties or had their hearths. It created practical methods for implementing this policy and established procedures by which a contado community could petition Siena for redress of evasions or defiance and obtain it.

The Sienese government also initiated a systematic investigation of sylvan citizens to discover whether they were conducting themselves properly and to punish those who, for one reason or another, were not prosecuted by their native communities and those who avoided being listed on the special tax registers that often were created for sylvan citizens. Those who received a clean "bill of health" after a specified probationary period were no longer investigated.

The commune did more than attempt to link immigration to naturalization and to enlarge the ranks of the citizen body with true and effective members: policies of the 1320s, in particular, attempted to regulate the pattern of the city's growth. Legislation was enacted that offered new citizens special inducements to settle in Borgo Santa Maria, a new development in the southeastern tip of the *Terzo* of San Martino, the southeastern third of the city. The commune purchased land in Borgo Santa Maria (in 1324) so that those citizens might build their homes there.[46] This was certainly intended to simplify the surveillance of new citizens, but the lawmakers must also have been aware of the

46. See W. Bowsky, "Black Death," 7–8. Biccherna records of 1327 seem to indicate that lots in this district may have been transferred by the commune to new citizens without charge, particularly to those of contado origin (Biccherna, No. 154, fols. 31*r*, 33*r*, 39*r*), but by 1332—at the latest—the lots were sold at prices set by the Biccherna: CG, No. 111, fols. 40*r*–45*v* (Feb. 21, 1332).

topographical implications of this policy—in a city that had very elaborate legislation for urban development.[47]

A further question to be posed is whether or not the Sienese government demonstrated a preference not only for certain areas for settlement by new citizens, but for gaining certain types of persons as citizens—other than wishing to attract foreigners, and, generally, persons with means sufficient to contribute to the functioning of the state.

Provisions written by a legislative commission appointed by the Nine to "provide in what way and how those persons from outside the contado and the jurisdiction of Siena who wish in the future to become citizens of the aforesaid city are to be treated," received overwhelming approval in the City Council on June 17, 1324.[48] They began with the statement that

> it is hoped and held for certain that . . . many men and persons of various and diverse occupations (*ministeriis*), conditions, and capabilities (*facultatibus*) from outside the contado and jurisdiction of Siena will in the future become citizens of the city of Siena. At present, a certain form, mode, or arrangement cannot be given or made for or against them, especially as their occupations, conditions, and capabilities are unknown.

The Nine and other Orders of the city therefore were instructed to undertake investigations "of the condition, state, occupations, and capabilities of such persons" and make specific recommendations that would include whatever each such foreign candidate for citizenship should be ordered to do for the commune beyond those things required by statute. The City Council would then act upon these recommendations in its consideration of citizenship petitions.

This apparent concern over the occupations of prospective citizens is not further elucidated in the act of June 17, 1324, however—or in other extant measures. If the government had specific predilections for or against specific trades or occupations—other than those favored by most communes—this is not indicated in Sienese legislation. Nor did Siena offer special favors to guilds or guildsmen. There is no Sienese parallel to a Luccan statute of 1311 that offered citizenship to guild masters, but

47. Most of Distinction III of the Constitution of 1309–10 is devoted to these matters; see also W. Braunfels, *Mittelalterliche Stadtbaukunst in der Toskana* (2d ed.; Berlin, 1959), and R. Rocchigiani, "Urbanistica ed igiene negli statuti senesi del XIII e XIV secolo," *Studi Senesi*, LXX (1958), 369–419.

48. Statuti, Siena, No. 23, fol. 97*r*–*v* (quotation on fol. 97*r*); CG, No. 100, fols. 12*v*–14*r*.

denied it to their apprentices and workers.[49] This is consistent with what we know of the role of the guilds in Sienese government and society.

The instances in which Sienese citizenship and immigration policies indicate a clear preference for certain types of persons are peculiar neither to Siena nor to the regime of the Nine. In Siena, as elsewhere, teachers at all levels, important judges and notaries, jurisconsults, and well-known physicians frequently received special privileges and immunities as part of their grants of citizenship. Most common was exemption for five or ten years from various taxes and, occasionally, from personal services, and from the obligation to build a new house.[50] The extent of the privileges varied, according to the reputation of the petitioner and the commune's estimate of its need for men of his profession.

Illustrative of both of these considerations is the exceptionally well-documented case of the physician, Master Onesto, son of the late Master Bartolomeo of Montepulciano. On October 6, 1315, the Sienese City Council received a petition that—together with a physician from Pistoia and a surgeon from Poggibonsi—Master Onesto receive immunity from all real and personal obligations to the city and commune in order that he might take up residence in Siena, as he desired, for this would redound "to the honor of the commune of Siena [and] to the convenience and utility of the men and persons of the said city and of all men dwelling in it." Upon the recommendation of the Nine and the other Orders, the Council granted the physicians immunities for five years.[51]

Only fifteen months later the Council heard Dr. Onesto's petition for citizenship, and the brevity of his residence in the city is an indication of the commune's special interest. A Biccherna receipt dated December 4, 1316, noting that on that day Onesto had paid his 100-*soldi* fee and provided surety that he would build a house worth £100 in the city or one of its boroughs, or have one built, was read to the councillors. They

49. G. Luzzatto, "L'inurbamento delle populazioni rurali in Italia nei secoli XII e XIII," *Studi di storia e diritto in onore di Enrico Besta,* II (Milan, 1939), 202.

50. See, for example, CG, No. 33, fols. 63*r*, 64*r*–65*r* (May 21, 1287): a ten-year immunity from dazi and other exactions was granted with his citizenship to a judge from Massa Marittima; CG, No. 43, fols. 77*v*–78*r* (June 21, 1292): a similar ten-year immunity from all "honeribus" was granted to judge Corrado da Stradella; CG, No. 44, fols. 48*r*–49*v* (Oct. 14, 1292): a similar ten-year immunity and a ten-year exemption from army service was granted "judge Porrina"; CG, No. 66, fols. 95*r*–99*r* (March 10, 1305): a five-year immunity from all real and personal obligations—including the privilege of keeping his properties off the tax rolls—was granted a physician from Massa Marittima. Cf. Bizzarri, "Cittadinanza," pp. 132–34.

51. CG, No. 86, fols. 98*v*–102*r*; published, in part, in G. Cecchini and G. Prunai (eds.), *Chartularium Studii Senensis,* I: (*1240–1357*) (Siena, 1942), 117–19, No. 136.

then voted (240–2) that he be granted citizenship. At another Council session, a week later, the podestà invested Onesto with citizenship, preserving intact however his immunities and privileges.[52] In 1317, Onesto built a house in the city, in the district of San Pietro di Ovile di Sopra, in the Terzo of Camollia; and in 1330 still another, valued at £125, "*in borgo novo Sancte Marie*"—the district particularly intended for new and recent citizens.[53]

An instructive sequel to the story of Dr. Onesto occurred on October 15, 1326, when the City Council heard his petition that he be freed from all real and personal obligations and given a domicile worth £30 a year at the commune's expense. The Council accepted the recommendation of the Nine and the other Orders that Onesto receive a ten-year immunity from all but communal gabelles; for, as the doctor had noted in his petition, Siena now had an abundance of men of letters, of experts in civil and canon law, and of practitioners of other professions and occupations, but it lacked men of experience and knowledge in medicine. Physicians, moreover, were "more necessary in every city than are other lettered men and the practitioners of other occupations."[54]

Because no major constitutional revision was undertaken after that of the late 1330s, and because we lack large collections of provisions and ordinances for the last twenty-seven years of the regime of the Nine, we cannot trace the elaboration of citizenship, naturalization, and immigration policies in detail. The small amount of indirect evidence that is available for the years 1340 to 1348 (until the onslaught of the Black Death), however, shows no basic change of direction. And what we know of the last years of the Nine, from the onset of the Black Death until 1355, indicates that the statutes of the 1330s remained in force and that the commune still wished to attract new citizens, especially from foreign lands. The government continued to develop policies for its contadini that would permit it to replenish the urban citizen body with wealthy contadini and that would prevent the destruction of the rural communities as a result of the movement of their wealthiest members to the city—a very difficult task.[55]

However informative even so brief an analysis may be in its own right

52. CG, No. 88, fols. 40*r*–42*v* (Jan. 13, 1317), and fol. 228*r*–*v* (Jan. 21, 1317).

53. Biccherna, No. 1058, fol. 31*r*.

54. CG, No. 103, fols. 74*r*–81*r* (published in Cecchini and Prunai, *Chartularium*, I, 353–58, No. 277) (quotation on p. 354).

55. See especially W. Bowsky, "Black Death," 31.

we should now attempt to test theory against reality despite the paucity of documentation. What were the actual effects of policy?

Although in Siena as elsewhere, citizens—whether native-born or naturalized—were a minority in the total population, the lack of adequate population and citizenship data makes it idle to speculate on the proportion of citizens to non-citizens, or even the number of citizens at a particular time. Fragmentary records, such as a woefully incomplete list with the names of 130 men who pledged to build new houses for the period 1307–1338, or the names of eighty new citizens who were received by the City Council between 1340 and 1348, or of another ninety-eight citizens who were received between 1348 and 1355—included in demonstrably incomplete registers, can do little more than pique the historian's curiosity and arouse irritation at torch-brandishing revolutionaries, foreign occupations, and a foolish eighteenth-century archivist.[56] Some useful observations can be made, however, of some of the men who sought and obtained citizenship.

A Biccherna entry of December 31, 1329, lists the payment of £2,321 to the commune by 123 new citizens who had paid at a rate of 6 per cent of the assessed valuation of their wealth and who were not obliged to build a new house in the city, as each man possessed more than £100 but less than £1,000 in taxable property.[57] More than half of these men had less than £300 and only twenty-six men paid on assessed valuations of £400 or more. They came from all parts of the Sienese state and from satellite and allied communities from the Maremma to the Valdichiana. They had not settled in any one area, but in no less than twenty-eight boroughs or districts of the city. Eighteen men—the largest group—had established residence in the district of San Marco, near the city gates at the southernmost tip of the Terzo of Città, the southwestern third of the city. The occupations of only thirty-one of the 123 men are indicated even indirectly. No less than ten are designated "*sere*," and therefore may have been notaries. Nine are called "*magister*" (Master), and may have been physicians, jurists, or teachers—but could equally well have been stonemasons or master carpenters. Among the remainder four were shoemakers; two were bakers; and there was a wool manufacturer, an innkeeper, and an animal dealer and butcher.

56. *Ibid.*, 7, 31; see also G. Cecchini, "La legislazione archivistica del Comune di Siena," *Archivio Storico Italiano*, CXIV (1956), 224–57, for a brief history of the Sienese archives.

57. Biccherna, No. 162, fols. 82*r*–87*v*. For the 6 per cent requirement, which was established November 10, 1328, see n. 40 (above).

A Biccherna entry of June 30, 1331, records payments from another 184 naturalized citizens whose places of origin were similar to those of the preceding group and who also were scattered throughout the city and its boroughs.[58] For only thirty of the 160 men who paid a total of £2,084/16/– (at the 6 per cent rate, without the obligation to build a house) do we have indications of their occupations. Thirteen are called "*sere*" (one of whom is specifically designated as a notary), and their assessments ranged from £100 to £800—£800 being the highest valuation for any of the 160 men. There were four *pizzicaioli*, merchants who dealt in bulk in a variety of items and who were members of the powerful *Mercanzia* or Merchant Guild. (Three of the four, including two brothers, came from lands that were under the temporal jurisdiction of the Bishop of Siena.) Two men, each assessed £300, were wool manufacturers; another, who was assessed £100, was a *rigattiere*, a retailer (somewhat similar to the keeper of a general store). A physician was assessed £500 and a *speziale*, or dealer in dyes, drugs, and other pharmaceuticals, was assessed £350. The remainder of the 160 men included artisans and guildsmen: two smiths, assessed £600 and £400; two shoemakers, £100 each; two vintners, £200 and £50; three bakers, £400, £100, and £50; a butcher and animal dealer, £200; and a horseshoer, £100.

The vintner and the baker who were assessed only £50 illustrate an important point: twelve of the 160 naturalized citizens owned properties that were valued at less than £100, ten properties were valued at £50, and a tanner's property was valued at only £30. Thus, although communal-citizenship legislation aimed at acquiring men who were at least moderately wealthy, wealth was not the only criterion: men of very modest means could sometimes obtain citizenship—perhaps because their particular skills were in short supply.

The remaining twenty-four men (in addition to the 160) whose payments were recorded in the entry of June 30, 1331, paid a total of £2,290 at the rate of 2.5 per cent of their assessed worth and each had the obligation of building a new house with a minimum value of £100 in the city or one of its boroughs. These, as we have seen, were the more well-to-do of the recent citizens—those who were assessed on no less than £1,000. They, too, had settled throughout the city, but none resided in Borgo Santa Maria; however, the size of our sample precludes attaching great significance to this fact. All but one of the twenty-four originally came from towns in the Sienese Masse or contado. The single exception

58. Biccherna, No. 168, fols. 117*r*–18*r* and 118*v*–26*r*; see also W. Bowsky, "Black Death," 7 n. 38.

had come originally from Chiusdino, a town that was subject to Siena in the diocese of Volterra, compelled to select its podestà from the Sienese citizenry with the sanction of the Sienese City Council. But even he had been a resident of Sovicille, in the Sienese contado, at the time of his application for citizenship. Of the six men whose occupations are indicated, three are called "*sere.*" Ser Ligo di ser Mori, from Montichiello, was assessed £18,000—the highest assessment in the entire group. The other three men were Master Neri di Francesco, from Asciano, assessed £10,500; a smith from Rosia, assessed £1,100; and, curiously, Nuccio di Lorenzo, "*marinario,*" from S. Mamilliano in the Masse of Siena. The seaman seems to have fared extremely well, as he had taxable assets of £3,000.

The information available for others who sought and attained citizenship during the remainder of the regime of the Nine shows little variation from the pattern we have outlined—except that more of the applicants may have come from outside the state, particularly from the neighboring state of Florence.

The data that can be gleaned from all sources, including City Council deliberations—although skimpy—show that men of the law—jurists, judges, and notaries—and men in the high-ranking strata of commerce, banking, and manufacturing (to which many of the Noveschi belonged) are much in evidence, but new citizens also included teachers, physicians, and practitioners of many trades. As is to be expected, the new citizens do not seem to include apprentices, shop boys, day laborers, and transients—in other words, the bulk of the urban populace.

The great majority of men—within and outside the city—did not belong to the most highly privileged group, the urban citizenry, but they cannot be thought of as a single entity. They comprised various groups and had different degrees and types of rights and duties, and different qualities of membership in and relationship to the Sienese state. Even a cursory examination of the most important of these groups will by contrast and nuance bring the special condition of the urban citizen into sharper focus.

Citizenship sometimes was granted to persons without the obligation that they become urban citizens; they could remain in their regular places of residence, and were not compelled to build a house in Siena. Often they could keep their properties off the Sienese urban tax registers—or could enter them for a fixed sum that could not be increased. The concession of such grants during the period of the Nine was an intensified continuation of earlier communal policy.

Some of these recipients of citizenship were contado nobles and some were nobles who had entered into special pacts of submission to Siena, even though their lands did not become a part of the contado.[59] In this situation the commune conferred benefits of citizenship upon powerful persons whose support it desired or whom it wished to bind to it with the closest bonds. Although such men did not hold office in the Sienese commune or serve as councillors, they found the other perquisites of citizenship—especially the right to be treated as citizens in communal courts—worth obtaining.

Some of the most powerful of the noble lords of the Maremma lands (along the Tyrrhenian coast, southwest of Siena) were the Pannocchieschi counts, and among these were the Counts of Ilci. Their ten major properties that Siena held to be within her contado were evaluated at more than £140,000 about 1318.[60] On June 30, 1322, the Sienese City Council considered a preliminary agreement that the Nine had negotiated with five of the leading Pannocchieschi lords.[61] The nobles would restore to Siena the castle, land, and *curia* of Travale[62] (in the important mining district of Montieri, near the Cecina River)—as well as full jurisdiction (*merum et mixtum imperium et jurisdictionem*) and their rights over all of the inhabitants of Travale. In return, Siena would defend the Pannocchieschi properties in that district, would cancel sentences that had been passed against the five lords and their followers, and would receive these Pannocchieschi and their descendants "as and for citizens of the city of Siena" (*in cives et pro civibus civitatis Senarum*). Perhaps because the terms were believed to be too generous, or for reasons of diplomacy, the Council —by a vote of 113–96—refused to ratify the negotiations.

The atmosphere was different, however, when—seven years later—twenty-seven Pannocchieschi petitioned the City Council that they, their castles, and lands be restored to the "benevolence" of Siena, that all

59. For the legal process of the assumption of lands into the contado, see G. de Vergottini, "I presuppositi storici del rapporto di comitatinanza e la diplomatica comunale con particolare riguardo al territorio senese," *BSSP*, LX (1953), 1–34. For contado nobles, see below, pp. 231–32.

60. MS C. 46 pp. 361–71; this is almost certainly the text summarized by A. Lisini in *Miscellanea Storica Senese*, I (1898), 198–203.

61. CG, No. 96, fols. 159*r*–163*r*.

62. For Travale, see e.g., E. Repetti, *Dizionario geografico, fisico, storico della Toscana* (6 vols.; Florence, 1833–45), V, 582–83. The Pannocchieschi had retaken Travale from Siena in 1320: see CG, No. 94, fols. 77*r*–78*v* (Aug. 4, 1320), and the chronicle of Agnolo di Tura del Grasso, in *Cronache senesi*, A. Lisini and F. Iacometti (eds.), *Rerum Italicarum Scriptores*, n.s., XV, Part VI (Bologna, 1931–37), 379.

sentences against them and their followers be canceled, and that they receive citizenship for themselves and their descendants. The City Council was receptive to this proposal, probably because of worsening conditions in the Maremma, which soon would lead to a war with the greatest independent nobles with whom Siena had contended, the Aldobrandeschi counts.

Acting upon the recommendations of the *Camerarius* of the Biccherna, Don Ranieri, monk of the Cistercian abbey of San Galgano, the Council agreed—by an overwhelming majority—to the cancelation of sentences without charge. It also authorized the Nine to receive those Pannocchieschi and their descendants as citizens of the city of Siena, with all of the privileges and immunities of citizenship and with exemption from the requirement of building houses in Siena. All of their properties at Travale and its court, and all of their possessions outside the Sienese state were assessed £3,000—a sum that could never be increased and that was substituted for all contributions and services to which citizenship might otherwise obligate them. Other properties, however, if held in the city or state, were to be evaluated separately and bear whatever burdens would be incumbent upon any citizen.[63]

Siena accorded similar treatment to another group of Maremma lords, the nobles of Sticciano (in the valley of the Ombrone River and the diocese of Grosseto), when their rich lands—evaluated at £33,333/6/8—were made part of the Sienese cantado.[64] On October 8, 1324, the City Council authorized the Nine to conclude formal arrangements for the subjection of Sticciano and its district, which "for a long time and in a certain way" had been subject to Siena, and to make them an integral part of the contado and their inhabitants "true contadini." On October 31 the seven lords of Sticciano and their heirs were made "true and legitimate citizens" of Siena, and were granted concessions similar to those the Pannocchieschi would receive in 1329.[65]

On February 1, 1332, in recompense for the submission of their Maremma castle of Colonna and in return for promised annual payments (*censi*) of £500, the nobles of the family of the Lombardi of Buriano

63. CG, No. 107, fols. 110*v*–16*r* (June 30, 1329); see also Capitoli, No. 1 (Caleffo Vecchio), fols. 857*r*–64*r*.

64. For Sticciano, see Repetti, *Dizionario,* V, 473–75; for the evaluation, see MS C. 46, p. 371, and *Miscellanea Storica Senese,* I (1898), 203.

65. CG, No. 101, fols. 110*r*–14*r* (Oct. 8, 1324), and 132*v*–34*r* (Oct. 31). Cf. Capitoli, No. 2 (Caleffo Bianco or Caleffo dell'Assunta), fols. 723*v*–26*r*, for the pacts of 1314 between Siena and the lords of Sticciano.

received Sienese citizenship at the hands of the prior or chairman of the Nine. He also exempted them perpetually from the obligation of building a house in Siena and from all other burdens that might be imposed upon their patrimonial holdings. Properties they had acquired or would acquire within the state, however, were subject to the impositions that were applied to citizens in general.[66]

Even the major capitulation to Siena in 1345 by the once-mighty Aldobrandeschi Counts of Santa Fiora, for centuries enemies of the commune, included the grant of citizenship to the five participating brothers. Acting upon the authorization of the City Council, the prior of the Nine, Campana di Jacomo, invested the counts with citizenship through their proctor, Conte di messer Manno Squarcialupi (a Noveschi noble), exempted them from the obligation of building a house in Siena and enrolled all of their patrimonial holdings in the Sienese tax registers for a total evaluation of £10,000—a sum that could not be increased.[67]

Siena also conceded citizenship to members of several communities at the time of their submission to the commune through special pacts, or with their incorporation into the contado, as an inducement to accept such new status.

66. See DR, No. 1589, Jan. 12, 1331 (Sienese style), for the submission of Colonna, and DR, No. 1593, Feb. 1, 1331 (Sienese style), for the citizenship granted the Lombardi of Buriano. G. de Vergottini, in "Origini e sviluppo," [cited above, n. 2], 348 [= 347 n. 2], published a portion of this citizenship formula, taken from a copy in Capitoli, No. 1, but he incorrectly dated it March 1. For copies of the documents for the submission of Colonna and the Lombardi citizenship, see Capitoli, No. 1, fols. 909*r*–21*r*, and No. 2, fols. 569*v*–71*r*. (Siena followed the Florentine style of dating, that of the Annunciation, beginning the year on March 25—almost three months after the style that we presently use. For Colonna, see, e.g., Repetti, *Dizionario*, I, 783–86.)

67. See DR, No. 1689, June 22, 1345; No. 1690, Aug. 15, 1345; and No. 1691, Aug. 15, 1345, for grants of proctorship to Conte di messer Manno Squarcialupi. (For his position on the Nine, see W. Bowsky, "*Buon Governo*," 375 n. 30.) For the entire submission, see Capitoli, No. 3 (Caleffo Nero), fols. 203*r*–12*v*, and No. 61 (June 22–Aug. 18, 1345 [unpaginated]). CG, No. 137, fols. 11*v*–12*r* (Aug. 12, 1345), records the appointment of Campana di Jacomo as the Sienese proctor for receiving their submission and for granting citizenship to Andrea, Giovanni, Piero, Binduccio, and Enrico, sons of the late Count Enrico of Santa Fiora. The submission included half of the land and castle of Santa Fiora, two-thirds of the castle of Samprugnano, one-third of Scansano, three-eighths of Magliano and half of the Wood of San Donato and of Tombolo, one-fourth the castle and Isola del Giglio, one-fourth of the castle and land of Capalbio, and half the castle and land of Petreto. There are short summaries of these concessions in O. Malavolti, *Dell'Historia di Siena* (2 vols.; Venice, 1599), II, 106, and in G. Tommasi, *Dell'Historie di Siena* (2 vols.; Venice, 1625–26), II, 301–2. The best single work on the Aldobrandeschi remains G. Ciacci, *Gli Aldobrandeschi nella storia e nella "Divina Commedia"* (2 vols.; Rome, 1935).

The policy of the Nine in these affairs marked an extension and intensification of more limited earlier practice. In 1227, for example, Siena had granted citizenship to the men of the commune and castle of Mensano (Menzano) di Casole in exchange for their submission.[68] When, in 1314, Casole capitulated to Siena, the "Guelf men of Casole" received Sienese citizenship in terms that exempted them from the obligations of paying the 100-*soldi* citizenship fee and building residences in the city or its boroughs.[69]

Three years later, in November, 1317, the proctor of the men and commune of the Maremma castle of Travale "submitted, subjected, placed beneath, and subjugated" the castle, its district, persons, and properties to Siena in a series of pacts. The first article of these conditions stated that "the Sienese commune receives the said commune and men of Travale as citizens and for citizens of the city of Siena with all the immunities and privileges that other Sienese citizens use and enjoy." It seems clear that the Travalesi were exempted from the obligation to build houses, pay the citizenship fee, and enroll their properties on the tax rolls—all this despite the fact that Travale was not technically incorporated into the contado at that time. Siena further promised not to exact taxation or impositions other than those specifically stated in these pacts, which were limited to carefully defined terms of military service, an annual payment of £100 (*censo*), and a ceremonial recognition of the relationship of subjection at the annual Sienese festivities in honor of the Assumption of the Virgin Mary.[70]

In October, 1318, the nearby castle and commune of Gerfalco submitted to Siena on similar terms and its men also obtained Sienese citizenship, with the right to "enjoy all and each of the privileges and

68. See G. Cecchini (ed.), *Il Caleffo Vecchio del Comune di Siena* (3 vols.; Florence, 1932–34, and Siena, 1942), I, 356–60, Nos. 251–53; see also Bizzarri, "Cittadinanza," p. 130. Although the men of Mensano promised "solvemus datium seu libram de nostris allibramentis eo tempore quando datium colligetur per civitatem et solvent alii cives Senenses," they retained "iurisdictionem dicti castri tam in mittendis signoriis quam in faciendis constitutis et in maleficiis puniendis et maliis queremoniis congnoscendis et finiendis et recipiendis et aliis negotiis explicandis, que pertinent ad consuetudinem et iurisdictionem dicti castri de Menzano et curtis eius." (G. Cecchini, *Caleffo*, I, 357–58.) For Mensano see also Repetti, *Dizionario*, III, 191–92.

69. Bizzarri, "Cittadinanza," p. 129 n. 1; Capitoli, No. 39.

70. For the pacts of Nov. 27, 1317, between Siena and Travale, see Capitoli, No. 1, fols. 849*r*–52*v*; and for Travale's appointment of a proctor, see fols. 853*r*–54*v*, and DR, No. 1467, Nov. 22, 1317.

immunities that true citizens of the city of Siena (*veri cives civitatis Senarum*) enjoy and can enjoy."[71]

In 1326, when Siena acquired the mining community of Montieri in the diocese of Volterra and incorporated it into the Sienese contado, the formal pacts stated that

> The Montieresi, or men of the commune of Montieri, will be received solemnly by the commune of Siena, and according to the form of the statutes and ordinances of the city of Siena, as citizens and for citizens of the city of Siena. And they will be treated and held as true and natural citizens of the said city . . . and enjoy all and each of the privileges, immunities, and graces, benefits, and honors in the Sienese city and contado that true and legitimate citizens of the city of Siena enjoy and should enjoy.

Siena further guaranteed the Montieresi that their total taxation would always be only the nominal sum of £40 a year. Nor were they held to pay extra citizenship fees or build houses in Siena.[72]

71. See especially CG, No. 91, fols. 118*r*–23*v* (Oct. 11, 1318), and DR, No. 1475, Oct. 11, 1318. Gerfalco was to pay Siena £200 a year. For later submissions by Gerfalco to Siena, in 1319 and 1331, see Capitoli, No. 2, fols. 504*v*–5*r*, 513*v*–16*v*. For Gerfalco see also Repetti, *Dizionario*, II, 430–31.

72. See CG, No. 103, fols. 108*r*–13*r* (Nov. 11, 1306), for the ratification of the pacts between Siena and Montieri (quotation on fol. 104*v*). The document of submission, DR, No. 1538, Oct. 18, 1326, notes that representatives of Montieri will bring candles to the annual festival of the Assumption of the Virgin Mary in Siena "ut moris est et erit et faciunt et facient alie comunitates comitatus Sen.," and it describes the £40 payment due each January 1 as "pro taxatione et datii nomine et libre dicti comunis et hominum de Monterio et ultra dicto nomine gravari non possit nec dicta quantitas de cetero pro predictis possit augeri." Montieri also promised to make war and peace at Siena's bidding, and not to offer refuge to men sentenced by Siena. The vicissitudes of warfare and diplomacy made it necessary for Siena to reassume Montieri into the contado in 1341, for which see G. de Vergottini, "I presupposıti storici," [cited above, n. 59], 13–14, Capitoli, No. 3, fols. 155*r*–60*v*, CG, No. 128, fols. 75*r*–80*r* (June 15, 1341).

For Montieri as an object of the conflicting interests of Siena, Massa Marittima, the bishop of Volterra, and the Tolomei nobles of Siena, see, e.g., G. Volpe, "Montieri: costituzione politica, struttura sociale e attività economica d'une terra mineraria toscana nel secolo XIII," which has been reprinted in his *Medio Evo Italiano* (2d ed.; Florence, 1961), pp. 319–423, *idem*, "Per la storia delle giurisdizioni vescovili e dei rapporti fra Stato e Chiesa nelle città italiane dei secoli XII e XIII. Vescovi e Comune di Massa Marittima (Documenti)," in Vol. XIX of *Studi Storici*, ed. A. Crivellucci (1910), 261–327. See also M. Cavallini, "Il vescovo Rainuccio Allegretti (1320–1348)," *Rassegna Volterrana*, XX (1952), 39–72; N. Rodolico and A. Panella (eds.), *Ordinamenta super arte fossarum ramerie et argenterie Civitatis Masse*, R. Deputazione di Storia Patria per la Toscana (Florence, 1938); and S. Cocconi, "L'espansione della Republica di Siena nella Maremma

The Sienese government took a slightly different tack in arranging the definitive submission of Massa Marittima. It ordered that the Massetani be treated as Sienese citizens in the Sienese courts, and granted all Massetani who so wished the right to become Sienese citizens without the obligation of building a house in Siena or fulfilling the other statutory requirements.[73]

The privileges accorded the Massetani in the Sienese courts suggests another of the many possible relationships that could exist between special categories of persons and the Sienese state. The government conceded some rights of citizenship to various groups because of their value or special, though temporary, role. Protection against molestation or physical violence was the most common concession. Privileges of 1287, for example, granted teachers and scholars who came to Siena protection for their persons and properties that was equal to the protection enjoyed by continual citizens. And this privilege remained enshrined in the major constitutional redaction of the late 1330s.[74] The principal foreign magi-

---

e la sottomissione di Massa Marittima," Università degli Studi, Firenze (Facoltà di Magistero, Anno Accademico 1947–48) (MS F. 7, Archivio di Stato di Siena). D. Marrara, in *Storia istituzionale della Maremma Senese* (Siena, 1961), treats the period from the eighth to the nineteenth centuries; L. Petrocchi's *Massa Marittima. Arte e Storia* (Florence, 1900), must be used with caution.

Valuable documentation is contained in G. Cecchini, *Caleffo*, [cited above, n. 68], I, 219–24 (No. 159), 224–26 (No. 160), and II, 766–68 (No. 560), 768–70 (No. 561). See also Capitoli, No. 2, fols. 12*r*–23*r*; CG, No. 44, fols. 75*r*–76*r* (Dec. 30, 1292); Concistoro, No. 1, fols. 26*r*, 38*v*–39*r* (Jan.–Feb., 1339); DR, No. 1130—Dec. 31, 1292, No. 1319—Jan. 30, 1303, No. 1320—Feb. 1, 1303, No. 1547—Mar. 31, 1327, No. 1572—June 19, 1329; and Archivio Vescovile di Volterra, Diplomatico, Apr. 2, 1327, July 28, 1329, Sept. 29, 1329, Nov. 19, 1352, and Mar. 28, 1355.

73. DR, No. 1663, Oct. 5, 1335, DR Massa, Oct. 5, 1335; Capitoli, No. 2, fols. 582*v*–87*v*. For Siena and Massa Marittima, see the bibliography cited above, n. 72; E. Cristiani, "Il trattato del 27 febbraio 1314 tra Roberto d'Angiò, Pisa e la lega Guelfa toscana alla luce di nuovi documenti," *Bullettino dell'Istituto Storico Italiano per il Medio Evo e Archivio Muratoriano*, No. 68 (1956), 259–80; G. Cecchini, *Caleffo*, I, 1064–101 (Nos. 879–94); Capitoli, No. 1, fols. 933*r*–34*r*, No. 2, fols. 563*r*–66*r*, No. 3, fols. 67*r*–94*r*, 140*r*–44*r*, and 255*r*–56*r*, and Capitoli, Nos. 10, 36, 45, and 57–58; DR, June 13, 1319, June 27, 1319, Oct. 13, 1326, Oct. 18, 1326, July 13, 1333, July 16, 1333, Sept. 18, 1333, Sept. 25, 1333; CG, No. 114, fols. 5*r*–12*v* (July 7, 1333.) See also Archivio di Stato di Pisa, Comune A, No. 29, fols. 24*r*–36*r* (Aug. 12, 1329), 56*r*–58*r* (June 3, 1331), 61*r*–67*r* (June 12–Sept. 4, 1333), and Comune A, No. 204, fols. 36*r*–*v*, 39*v*, 40*r*–*v*, and 41*v*–42*r* (Jan., 1333); and Atti Pubblici (Sept. 4, 1333).

74. See G. Cecchini and G. Prunai, *Chartularium*, [cited above, n. 51], I, 47–48 (No. 64); Statuti, Siena, No. 26, Dist. III, r. 197, fols. 158*v*–59*r*. Statutes also exempted teachers from military service and from guard duty. See, e.g., Lisini, Dist. IV, r. xviii:

strates and officials concerned with the execution of criminal sentences—the podestà, captain of the people, and the war captain—were protected by extremely severe measures against those who physically harmed them; and in judging crimes committed against them they were held to be "true and legitimate citizens and continual inhabitants of the city of Siena" through their terms of office and the succeeding three years.[75]

Within the city of Siena, as in some other communes, the condition of still another group—although only vaguely or imprecisely defined by the late thirteenth century—lay somewhere between that of urban citizenship and non-citizenship. These were the *habitatores* or *habitatores assidui*—permanent residents who enjoyed some of the privileges of citizenship and who were distinguished from the *habitantes* or ordinary inhabitants. Although the minimum period of residence necessary for qualification as *habitator assiduus* cannot be determined with certitude for the years that preceded the accession of the Nine, a definition of five years appears in the records of an important City Council session of January 9, 1314.[76]

A sensitive and crucial issue was under consideration and both the councillors' suggestions and the Council's formal statements and action must be taken seriously and should not be treated as casual or unreflected judgments and opinions. At stake was the treatment to be accorded persons who were accused of having acted treasonously against Siena by aiding its enemy, Emperor Henry VII, who had died less than five months earlier near the Sienese contado town of Buonconvento.[77]

The prior of the Nine, Vanni di Bartolomeo, informed the Council that on December 15, 1313, the podestà had completed an investigation of these persons, especially the knights of the city and contado who had served in the late emperor's army (*steterunt in exercitu domini Henrici olim imperatoris Romanorum*).[78] He declared that the Nine and the other Orders urged the speedy dismissal of all false accusations.

"Che chi insigne li fanciulli a legere non vada in oste o cavalcata"; and Dist. I, r. xcv: "Che li maestri de la grammatica non facciano la guardia di notte." Anyone who offended or harmed foreign professors of civil or canon law or of medicine teaching at the Sienese university was subject to double the penalty that would have been exacted "si aliquem civem senensem et dicte civitatis habitatorem offendisset." Statuti, Siena, No. 26, Dist. II, r. 362, fol. 78*v*: "De pena offendentium doctores et scolares."

75. Statuti, Siena, No. 26, Dist. III, r. 167–72, fols. 152*v*–53*v*, and see especially r. 172, fol. 153*v*: "Quod potestas et capitaneus guerre et populi habeantur pro civibus."

76. CG, No. 83, fols. 35*r*–37*v*; the definition is on fol. 36*r*.

77. For the Italian expedition of Emperor Henry VII and his relations with Siena, see W. Bowsky, *Henry VII in Italy. The Conflict of Empire and City-State, 1310–1313* (Lincoln, Nebr., 1960).

78. CG, No. 83, fol. 35*r*.

Well might the Guelf government have wished to end this entire episode as quickly and quietly as possible in a city that had a long tradition of steadfast Ghibellinism, from the days of Frederick Barbarossa in the twelfth century to the death of the ill-fated Conradin of Hohenstaufen after the battle of Tagliacozzo in 1268. In the early fourteenth century many Sienese still looked back with fierce pride to the battle of Montaperti, in 1260, when Ghibelline Siena had crushed the Guelf hosts of Florence on the day that the Arbia River flowed red with blood.[79] The very roots of the regime of the Nine lay not in glory, but in that last, disastrous defeat inflicted by Florence upon Ghibelline Siena at the battle of Colle di Valdelsa in 1269.

It is not surprising, then, that the Italian expedition of Dante's "*alto Arrigo*" provoked enormous unrest in Siena, and that scions of old Ghibelline families in the city and contado nobles answered the imperial call. One of Henry VII's important Italian administrators was the Sienese noble, Niccolo di Bonifazio dei Bonsignori, a leading member of the family that controlled the "Great Table"—one of Europe's greatest banking houses until the closing years of the thirteenth century. During Henry's stay in Tuscany, the city of Siena itself had been in danger of betrayal to the emperor.

It was against this historical background that Vanni di Bartolomeo reported that at a meeting of the "secret council" of the Nine, attended by approximately 130 of the best and wisest men of the city (*de melioribus et sapientibus*),[80] the Nine and the other Orders had recommended that during the present month the podestà, his court, and all other Sienese officials proceed no further in any action or investigation against those suspected of aiding the late emperor until the Orders had examined each case and decided whether each accusation was good, legal, and true. In addition, all future and similar accusations against "citizens, contadini, or continual inhabitants of the city of Siena" (*assiduos habitatores civitatis Senarum*)[81] were to be judged and decided by the Nine and the other Orders rather than by the regular communal courts. The City Council

79. Dante, *La Divina Commedia*, *Inferno*, X, 85–86: "Lo strazio e 'l grande scempio / che fece l'Arbia colorata in rosso."

80. The "secret councils" of the Nine were "secret" in that the participants were bound not to reveal their discussions or decisions to outsiders, not because the councillors' names were held secret. These councils were ad hoc groups, of greatly varying size, that were selected and called upon by the Nine for consultation and advice whenever the Nine deemed such assistance would be useful.

81. CG, No. 83, fol. 36*r*.

ratified these proposals 212–37, and adopted the special committee's declaration that "by continual inhabitants of the city (*assidui habitatores Civitatis*) are to be understood those who have lived continuously in the city of Siena for the past five years." Nor do we find any other time period designated throughout the remainder of the regime of the Nine.

The equivalence of this length of time with that apparently prescribed for qualification as a "continual citizen"[82] supports Dina Bizzarri's suggestion that the *assidui habitatores* were gradually being transformed into "continual citizens" of the city.[83] It is further supported by the scant reference to *habitatores* and lack of documentation concerning them.

Particularly illuminating is a rubric of December, 1281, still retained in the Constitution of 1309–10, which enjoins that "Anyone who is not *allibrato* [does not have his possessions entered in the occasional tax registers] as a citizen, or as an *abitatore*, or as a contadino is not to be defended nor can he be served by any privilege of citizenship or of residence, nor laws [*ragioni*] or statutes of the commune of Siena, except in [cases involving] crimes."[84] With this single exception, such persons could claim only the rights of "common law" (*le ragioni comuni*) in civil and criminal cases.[85] And in Siena as elsewhere in Tuscany "common law" meant specifically Roman or imperial law.[86]

It should not be assumed, however, that the protection of Sienese statute law was denied to the great mass of inhabitants (*habitantes*) of the city who did not possess the financial or other qualifications for citizenship. For all residents were required to enroll their possessions (with the exception of some exempt household items) in the tax registers if they met minimal requirements—requirements decided upon anew for each general tax evaluation ordered. A measure approved by the Nine on July 7, 1324, for example, declared that no head of a family could be

82. See above, p. 200.

83. See Bizzarri, "Cittadinanza," pp. 86–90, "Gli '*habitatores*'," (especially pp. 89–90 for Siena).

84. Lisini, Dist. I, r. cccxlvii; see also Statuti, Siena, No. 26, Dist. I, r. 267, fol. 64v.

85. Lisini, Dist. II, r. cclviii.

86. For *ius comune* as Roman law, see, e.g., U. Gualazzini, *Considerazioni in tema di legislazione statutaria medievale* (2d ed.; Milan, 1958), pp. 9–49; F. Calasso, "Il problema storico del diritto comune," *Studi di storia e diritto in onore di Enrico Besta*, II (Milan, 1939), 459–513, and especially p. 498; "Il diritto imperiale è sempre *comune ius*: ma esso vige soltanto *ubi cessat statutum*." See also W. Brynteson, "Roman Law and Legislation in the Middle Ages," *Speculum*, XLI (1966), 420–37. For Siena, see Zdekauer, p. liv; cf. G. Prunai, "Notizie e documenti sulla servitù domestica nel territorio senese (secoli VII–XVI)," *BSSP*, XLIII (1936), 133–82, 245–98, 398–438, and especially p. 141.

assessed at less than £60 for his movables unless he attested to and furnished proof of poverty and of living on alms.[87]

Far from being deprived of their legal rights, those who were too poor to be included on the tax rolls were represented during the regime of the Nine by the so-called "Advocates of the Poor." These were three judges who were appointed by the commune (one for each Terzo or third of the city) whom the law bound to serve as lawyers for the poor in civil and criminal cases. They exacted no fees from their clients but received a salary that was established by the chief Biccherna officials. If an Advocate failed to accept a client he was subject to a fine of ten *lire*.[88] In May, 1324, the Nine themselves were charged with the regular appointment of these judges.[89] Although we may wonder how effective three judges might have been—and although we have no records of their activities—it is nonetheless intriguing that medieval Siena adopted so "modern" a device as the "Public Defender," and assigned the task to judges rather than to simple advocates.

Distinct and differentiated relationships to the state also marked the vast population that dwelt outside of the city and its boroughs. The so-called

87. Statuti, Siena, No. 23, fol. 29*r*. For an *allibramento*, or general tax evaluation, of 1289, "poor persons" were defined as those "allirati" for forty *soldi* or less (CG, No. 37, fol. 61*r* [Mar. 17, 1289]). See also fol. 56*v* [Mar. 10, 1289]: "Item cum hoc anno eodem modo fuit reformatum quod nullus posset esse allibrator [a tax assessor] presentis libre nisi esset allibratus XXV lb. vel ab inde supra, et in libra [tax district] de Malborghecto non possit reperi aliquis allibrator qui sit allibratus in XXV lb. vel ab inde supra. . . ." [The Council decided at the suggestion of the Noveschi noble, Memmo di Viviano di Guglielmo Vignari, which was seconded by messer Scozia di messer Renaldo Tolomei, that the Nine could select a man from another district, who was *allibratus* at £25 or more, to serve as an assessor for Malborghetto.] See also above, pp. 207, 216.

The erroneous assertion by Bizzarri ("Cittadinanza," p. 124) and by C. Falletti-Fossati (*Costumi senesi nella seconda metà del secolo XIV* [Siena, 1881], pp. 25–26) that the poor were automatically entered on the tax rolls with an evaluation of £50 each is derived from a misreading of L. Banchi, "Gli ordinamenti economici dei comuni toscani nel medioevo e segnatamente del Comune di Siena: Parte Prima. La Lira o l'Estimo," *Atti della Regia Accademia dei Fisiocritici di Siena* Ser. III, Vol. II (Siena, 1879), 1–80, pp. 55–56: "E circa alle persone miserabili, la legge pose un limite all'arbitrio degli Allibratori, ordinando che non dovessero iscriversi nell'Estimo per somma superiore alle cinquanta lira." (For this assertion Banchi cited a document of February 8, 1369.) Unfortunately the extant "Tables of Possessions" for the city and the contado include only persons who possessed real property and therefore exclude much of the population, especially the poor. See also W. Bowsky, "*Buon Governo*," 375–78, and "Black Death," 6–7.

88. Lisini, Dist. I, r. ccxxxviii; Biccherna, No. 1, fols. 50*v*–51*r*.

89. Biccherna, No. 1, fol. 50*v*. See also Statuti, Siena, No. 26, Dist. I, r. 139, fol. 41*r*, "De electione advocatorum pauperum."

"Masse," "Massa," or "Masse and Cortine" constituted a separate and peculiar entity since earliest recorded communal history.[90] During the regime of the Nine these consisted of from forty-one to fifty-one towns immediately adjacent to the city, separated into three administrative groupings, each assigned to one of the Terzi.[91] Although legislation of 1324 indicates that a distinction was still occasionally made between the towns of the Masse and those of the Cortine, we do not know the basis for this distinction—or even the names of the communities that belonged to the Cortine. Ordinarily, the term Masse or Massa alone was used, and it applied to both.[92]

Although very few communities of the Masse obtained full Sienese citizenship, as did Montecchio in 1292 and Monistero S. Eugenio at an undetermined earlier date,[93] the principal advantage enjoyed by the

90. See, e.g., L. Zdekauer, "La vita pubblica dei Senesi nel dugento," *Commissione Senese di Storia Patria nella R. Accademia dei Rozzi. Conferenze*, III (1897), 75–191, especially p. 103.

91. A Biccherna entry of Jan.–June, 1292, recording the collection of a presta or forced loan of 2 *soldi* per *lira* of each taxpayer's assessed property valuation includes a total of forty-one Masse communities, of which seven were in the Massa of Città, eighteen in the Massa of San Martino, and sixteen in the Massa of Camollia (Biccherna, No. 107, fols. 125*r*–36*r*). Possibly other communities were not listed because the presta was not collected in them. By the late 1330s at least four communities had been added to the Masse and Cortine (Statuti, Siena, No. 26, Dist. I, r. 266, fol. 64*r*). The Masse contained at least fifty-one communities by the time of the compilation of a list of persons owing Siena forced loans from 1348 to September 1, 1364: fifteen communities in Città, sixteen in San Martino, and twenty in Camollia (Lira, No. 423, fols. III*v*–IV*r*).

92. Statuti, Siena, No. 23, fols. 100*r*–6*v* (June 29, 1324). Folio 103*r* contains a provision that, every June and December, "quando eliguntur sindici infra Massam et Cortinas Civitatis Senarum," the *Camerarius* and Four *Provveditori* of the Biccherna were "eligere seu eligi facere sex bonos et legales homines de vignariis et pensionariis habitantibus infra Massam et Cortinas Civitatis Senarum, videlicet duos in quolibet terzerio, silicet unum de Massa et alium de Cortinis," and to confer with the "notarius camparie," his armed men and messengers, entrusted with the protection of property in the Masse and Cortine; and to present the Biccherna with a secret book containing any complaints against these custodians. This clear statement that there were "Cortine" and a "Massa" assigned to each Terzo casts doubt upon the interesting speculation offered me by the late Giovanni Cecchini that the Cortine might refer to lands in the Valdarbia, particularly those between Asciano and Castelnovo Berardenga—most especially near Taverna d'Arbia. There was, in fact, a small commune called Cortina approximately equidistant between Siena and Asciano. See MS D. 82, p. 86: "Visita fatta nell'Anno 1676 alle città, terre, castella, comuni e comunelli dello stato della città di Siena dall Ill.mo Sig.re Bartolomeo Gherardini auditore generale in Siena per l'A. S. di Cosimo III de Medici Gran Duca VI. di Toscana . . . ," vol. I, copied in 1723.

93. See Lisini, Dist. IV, r. xlvi–xlvii; Statuti, Siena, No. 26, Dist. I, r. 267, fol. 64*r*. For Montecchio, see Repetti, *Dizionario* [cited above, n. 62], III, 367; for Monistero

inhabitants of the Masse was that they were subject directly to the jurisdiction of Siena and could have no lords or rectors. The Constitution of 1262 assured them this privilege,[94] which they retained during the regime of the Nine.[95] It should also be noted that the Masse were not included in the general taxation of the contado; rather they were taxed separately—usually at the same time as taxes were imposed in the city itself, although not necessarily at the same rates.[96]

A City Council deliberation of September 27, 1342, further clarifies some of the peculiar characteristics of the Masse.[97] On that day the Council considered a petition submitted by certain unnamed communities that had been transferred from the Masse and Cortine to the contado and desired to be restored to their former status. They argued that such a restoration would be advantageous to the city of Siena, in part, "because in the aforesaid Cortine and Massa jurisdiction pertains to the city alone and not to any lord." They further contended that the produce of the Masse and Cortine was only sent to the city for sale, and not marketed

---

S. Eugenio, see G. Prunai (ed.), *Statuti dei Comuni di Monastero S. Eugenio (1352), Monteriggioni (1380) e Sovicille (1383)*, Fonti sui comuni rurali toscani, I (Florence, 1961). Among the nineteen "Libre" [Lire] or administrative and tax districts in the Terzo of Città whose "sindici" received regular stipends from the Biccherna in the second semester of 1354 were "Monastero" and Montecchio (Biccherna, No. 231, fol. 208*v*). For the sindici see W. Bowsky, "The Medieval Commune and Internal Violence: Police Power and Public Safety in Siena, 1287–1355," *American Historical Review*, LXXII (1967).

94. Zdekauer, Dist. III, r. cccxxxxviiii, "De electione rectorum castrorum et villarum comitatus senarum." This rubric ordered that all castles, lands, and villages of the Sienese contado and jurisdiction select as their rectors "cives Senenses assiduos habitatores. . . . Salvo et intellecto quod castra, terre et ville, que sunt, quantum ad iurisdictionem, alicuius, predictos rectores eligere non teneantur, sed possint esse ipsi iidem, qui ius habent, rectores in dictis locis . . . et omnibus et singulis sit salvum ius eorum. Et exceptis villis et terris, que sunt de Massa Senensi, que non teneantur eligere vel habere rectores sibi, nec potestas eis dare, sed dicta loca de Massa habeant sindicos, qui debeant respondere comuni Senarum de hiis, que comune eis imposuerit."

95. Lisini, Dist. I, r. cccxxvi, ". . . a li uomini de la Massa di Siena, non si dia rettore, nè rettore avere possono."

96. See, for example, W. Bowsky, "*Buon Governo*," 375 n. 32. The only exception to this practice that I have found occurred after the onslaught of the Black Death. Rubric XV of a seventeen-rubric omnibus money bill, approved by a vote of 87–40 in the City Council on October 7, 1350, was entitled: "Quod Massa et Cortine taxentur ut comunitates comitatus." CG, No. 147, fols. 21*v*–23*r* (quotation on fol. 23*r*). Unfortunately, we know only the rubric titles and not their contents, and thus do not know the details of this measure and whether it was meant to effect a permanent or a temporary arrangement.

97. CG, No. 131, fols. 56*r*–58*r*.

elsewhere. They unfortunately did not state whether this was so because of a legal restriction, as seems improbable (and I have found no indication of such a law), or, as seems more likely, through a combination of custom, convenience and informal urban pressure. The petition further claimed that persons from the Masse and Cortine often were called upon to guard the city (*presepius vocantur ad custodiam civitatis*); adding that the city would suffer harm if those communities remained a part of the contado, for being so close to Siena they could not escape the burdens of direct taxes and gabelles.

The City Council was informed that the Nine, the other Orders, and the Executors of the *Gabella* (a financial magistracy second in importance only to the Biccherna) had examined the petition and sent it to the Council with a recommendation for approval subject to their addition: that if any person in the affected communities owned property located in a contado community he must confer in all obligations with that community—though only for that specific property. The passage of this measure by a vote of 180–62 tends to indicate the City Council's basic approval of and agreement with the argumentation presented in the petition.

A point well worth considering with regard to the status of these suburban communities is that, in fact, we find exceedingly little reference to them in the legislation of the period of the Nine. Enactments are not said to apply to "the city, Masse and Cortine, and contado and jurisdiction of Siena," but rather to "the city, contado and jurisdiction of Siena." The Masse and Cortine seem to have had little juridic or political significance by the late thirteenth century. They probably were ordinarily thought of as being an appendage of the city whose communities still retained some special characteristics, particularly with regard to taxation and the imposition of rectors; but whose inhabitants were commonly viewed as quasi-contadini.

As for those contadini themselves, the vast majority did not of course enjoy the special privileges of citizenship. But although juridically and politically inferior to Sienese citizens and denied much direct participation in the policy-making activities of the Sienese commune, the contadini received Sienese military, political and to some extent economic protection and had special advantages over persons from outside of the state and certain rights upon which they could rely.[98]

98. The Sienese contado, in all of its aspects, requires more study. R. Caggese's "La Repubblica di Siena e il suo contado" (*BSSP*, XIII [1906], 3–120), must be thoroughly revised, as must its English summary, which comprises the major portion of F. Schevill's *Siena* (London and New York, 1909, and New York, 1964), Chap. VIII,

Citizen and contadino paid the same tolls, customs duties and other gabelles in the state and at the city gates.[99] Contado communities possessed a separate corporate existence with strictly limited rights of self-government, recognized and guaranteed by the Sienese commune. Contadini had the right to make representations to the Sienese courts and magistracies, both as individuals and as the representatives of their communes. Sienese statute was designed to protect the contadini against violence and fraud. It is perhaps worth noting that in the Constitution of 1309–10 the penalty for slaying a contadino was the same as that for killing a citizen: death, or a fine of £3,000 if the homicide occurred during a fight or brawl—with the criminal condemned to remain chained in a communal prison until his fine was paid in full.[100] Over and above such rights possessed by all contadini, we have seen that some of them also enjoyed advantages of the Sienese citizenship granted to their local communes, and that the members of certain communities had the special privileges that had been guaranteed or conceded in the pacts incorporating them into the contado.

Before and during the regime of the Nine a special status also accrued to some so-called "contado nobles." But in essence this amounted to the fact that ordinarily they were assessed and taxed separately from the communities in which they had their principal residence or which at

---

"The Contado," pp. 229–49. See the review of Caggese in G. Volpe, *Medio Evo Italiano* (2d ed.; Florence, 1961), pp. 241–56. For the contado see G. de Vergottini, "Origini e sviluppo storico" [cited above, n. 2]; and "I presupposti storici" [cited above, n. 59]; W. Bowsky, "*Buon Governo*," and "Black Death," and E. Fiumi, "Sui rapporti economici tra città e contado nell'età comunale," *Archivio Storico Italiano*, CXIV (1956), 18–68.

99. Gabella, No. 1, r. 127 (fols. 62*v*–63*r*), notes that Siena had acceded to the request of the commune of Montepulciano, and "concederetur quod dicti comune et homines et persone de monte puliziano in civitate comitatu et iurisdictione senarum et eius districtu tractentur et habeantur in passagiis et kabellis tamquam cives et comitatini civitatis et comitatus senarum. Et ideo mandato dictorum dominorum Novem. Statutum et ordinatum est quod comune et homines et persone castri de monte puliziano et eius districtus tractentur et habeantur in civitate comitatu et iurisdictione senarum et districtu eius et sua fortia tamquam cives et comitatini eiusdem civitatis et districtus in passagiis et kabellis, et quod solvant homines et persone dicti castri de monte puliziano passagia et kabellas sicut solvunt et solvere debent cives et comitatini civitatis et comitatus senarum et non aliter." Rubric 127 is undated, but the two following rubrics are dated December, 1292. Gabella No. 1, which was developed from Gabella statutes of 1273, was written between November, 1297, and November, 1298. It contains many additions and corrections of Nov., 1297 (e.g., fols. 32*v*, 126*v*, and 132*r*). The earliest marginal additions were made in Nov., 1298 (e.g., fol. 54*r*).

100. Lisini, Dist. V, r. ccxlviii.

times they controlled or held as fiefs. Any other advantages they possessed derived basically from their de facto strength, either as individuals or as members of powerful landholding *consorterie* or family federations, with numerous vassals, armed retainers, renters, laborers, sharecroppers and servants—for such power commanded communal respect, or at least cautious treatment.[101]

101. For the contado nobles, see, e.g., Estimo, No. 93, a register (now mutilated) that was compiled in the second decade of the fourteenth century and that lists some of the immovables of contado nobles, and pages 346–57 of MS C. 46 ("Nobili del Contado"), a brief table of contents of Estimo No. 93.

For their special tax status, see Gabella, No. 1, r. 87, fol. 44*r–v* ("De solutione fienda a nobilibus comitatus"). See also Biccherna, No. 103 (July–December, 1290, fols. 40*r*–41*r*), which states that £632/13/4 was collected from twenty-eight contado nobles: "Infrascripta est intrata cabelle imposita nobilibus de comitatu de mense julii anno LXXXX pro kabella vini et bladi et farine." This is quite distinct from the entry (fols. 27*r*–39*r*) that £17,322/16/4 was collected from 256 contado communities: "Infrascripte sunt intrate XX[M] lib. imposit. comunitatibus comitatus Senarum de mense julii anno LXXXX pro eorum cabella bladi et vini recolletti et farine que comedunt tempore domini Iohannis de Camerino Sen. potestatis et inceperunt solvere de mense julii in ultimis VI mensibus sui regiminis" (fol. 27*r*).

The contado nobles retained this separate status after 1291 and the major change in the nature of contado taxation. See, for example Biccherna, No. 223 (Jan.–June, 1348, fol. 78*r* [June 18]) noting the collection of £5,838/19/4 "da Simone di ser Jacomo, banchiere, per mille cinque[C] due fiorini doro e mille cento sette lb. tredici s. quatro d. che ricolse de la presta del terzo di Citta con certi residui che si ricolsero in biccherna . . . ."; £5,592/16/3 "da Neruccio Tornanini e compagni" for 1,471 gold florins and £949/3/11 from the presta of the Terzo of San Martino "con certi residui"; £6,550/17/3 "da Neri Bruni e compagni" for 1,793 gold florins and £902/18/3, from the presta of the terzo of Camollia, etc. Folio 80*r* (June 30) records £24,737/18/– "da Petro di Tofano Buonamichi . . . ricolse de le cabelle e rendite a lui asegnate per pagha la presta imposta per li Nove de quali a certi stanziamenti, in sette miglia ottocento trentuno fiorini doro e settanta lb. cinque s. tre d. . . .". Folio 81*r* (June 30) records £1,980/6/6 "da Lonardo di Chola e compagni per cinquecento novantadue fiorini doro e cento settante quattro lb. e quatordici s. sei d. ricolsero de la presta del contado del mese di giugnio del terzo di Citta,"; £2,258/2/– "da Neri Bruni e compagni" for 740 gold florins and £1/2/–, "de la presta del contado del terzo di S. Martino . . . ."; £1,692/16/8 "da Ciecho Bartalomei e compagni" for 545 gold florins and 4*s*. 8*d*., "ricolsero de la presta del contado del terzo di Kamollia," and £137/5/– from the same "Cieccho e compagni" for 45 gold florins collected "de la presta de nobili del contado . . . ."

For the final years of the regime of the Nine, see, e.g., Biccherna, No. 228 (July–December, 1351, fol. 87*r* [Dec. 31]), which records the collection of £60,907/11/10 "a presta civium in dictis sex mensibus" (for 18,167 gold florins and £209/7/6), £10,364/10/– "a presta Masse et civium silvestrium" (for 3,105 gold florins and £14/10/–), £1,149/19/6 "de presta nobilium comitatus" (for 342 gold florins), and £2,706/13/4 "de presta clericorum" (for 812 gold florins). Cf. E. Fiumi, "Fioritura e decadenza dell'economia fiorentina" (Part III), *Archivio Storico Italiano*, CXVII (1959), 451. [N.B. Despite the

Still others in the contado had special privileges and some unique relationships to the state because of their own relationships to its most favored members, the citizens. Thus, for example, servants, armed retainers, and sharecroppers of citizens received Sienese protection against certain exactions demanded by the rural communes in whose territories they lived and worked. But this status can best be conceived of as another of the privileges of citizenship, rather than as a reward or favor granted to those contadini for their own sake.[102]

Apart from the contado, although frequently surrounded by it, were those towns and lordships that had submitted to Siena with special pacts and agreements but had not, or perhaps better, had not yet been formally incorporated into the contado. We have seen this in the case of Travale in 1317, and will recall that it was the condition ascribed to Montepulciano and Grosseto by Cino of Pistoia in 1324.

Although Cino may indeed have been correct in legal theory—and one could argue convincingly that by law such places were bound only to the contents of their pacts with Siena—Cino's contemporaries could not have been blind to practical realities. And, in actual fact, whatever their pacts and agreements, such places frequently were completely subject to Siena in all but name.

We need look no farther afield than to the very commune of Grosseto, just fourteen years before Cino's observations. In 1310 Grosseto rebelled against Sienese control, inspired by the approach of the forces of the Emperor Henry VII. But a brief show of Sienese military strength brought the rebels to heel, and on June 17, 1310, Grosseto appointed a proctor empowered to notify the Sienese government that the rebel commune would do whatever Siena wished.

The formal arrangements that Siena drew up unilaterally for the regulation of Grosseto were approved on June 22, 1310, by a vote of 374–40 in an extremely well attended session of the Sienese City Council. These provisions included the Grossetans "among the true subjects of the commune of Siena . . . ." It was as such that most Sienese probably regarded them. How well could any theoretical Grossetan independence accord with the provision in the same regulations "that the lords Nine Governors and Defenders of the Commune and People of the City of Siena are held

---

statement in some of these entries that they represented so many gold florins and so many *lire*, the Sienese *lira* of course was nonetheless a money of account and did not indicate a "*lira*" coin.]

102. See above, n. 9.

to and must in perpetuity select the podestà and foreign rector of the City and Commune of Grosseto," and establish his salary, following and term of office? And Siena not only ordered that one-fourth of Grosseto's walls be leveled before the Sienese troops left the occupied city—so that the Sienese might have free access to that portion of Grosseto lying towards their own city—but forbade Grosseto to rebuild or even repair the walls and other defenses unless they received explicit permission from the Nine of Siena and from three-fourths of the Sienese City Council at a session attended by no fewer than 400 councillors![103]

As in other city-states, so throughout the lands that Siena controlled—

103. For the City Council's approval of the provisions for Grosseto, see CG, No. 76, fols. 177*r*–78*r* (June 22, 1310); for the actual provisions, see Statuti, Siena, No. 15, fols. 431*r*–33*v* (June 22, 1310). A commission of twelve men (four from each Terzo), selected by the Nine wrote this measure "In primis pro honore civitatis Senensis . . . providerunt . . . quod domini novem gubernatores et defensores comunis et populi civitatis sen. teneantur et debeant in perpetuum eligere potestatem et rectorem forensem Civitatis et Comunis Grosseti . . . ." (fol. 431*r*). See especially fols. 432*v*–33*r*: "Item ut inter veros subditos comunis sen. pax et unitas observetur provisum et ordinatum est quod omnes homines de Montepescali [in the Sienese contado] qui nunc sunt in banno civitatis Grosseti in dicta civitate debeant rebanniri et earum condempnationes et banna de libris comunis Grosseti debeant cancellari et cassari sine aliqua solutione pecunie facienda / dicto comuni Grosseti." See also CG, No. 76 (fols. 152*r*–55*v* [June 5, 1310]), which records the session in which the Sienese City Council, having been notified of the Grossetan rebellion, ordered the Nine to take whatever measures were necessary to quell the uprising and to surround Grosseto with Sienese troops within three days, and (fols. 174*r*–76*v* [June 20, 1310]) which authorized the Nine to have the provisions for the regulation of Grosseto drawn up. See DR, June 17, 1310 for the appointment of a Grossetan proctor. For Montepescali as a part of the Sienese contado by May 26, 1310, see Capitano del Popolo, No. 1, fol. 26*v* and Statuti, Siena, No. 15, fol. 406*r*, cf. Statuti, Siena, No. 26, fol. 189*v*. For Montepescali, see also Repetti, *Dizionario*, III, 456–57.

Originally a fief of the Aldobrandeschi, Grosseto was already a commune (though not independent) by the thirteenth century, but made partial submission to Siena in 1224 as a result of Aldobrandeschi machinations. Conquered by Siena in that year, Grosseto rebelled in 1254, 1259, 1266, and 1310. After the collapse of the rebellion of 1310, Grosseto again rebelled against Siena—in 1312, under the leadership of Bino di Abate del Malia. After his death, in 1317, Grosseto became nominally an ally of Siena, while under the informal signory of Bino's sons, Vanni (Malia) and Abbatino, who, however, carefully followed Sienese directions, especially in foreign policy. Another brief rebellion against Siena was suppressed in January, 1334. Another of July, 1335, led by the Abati del Malia in alliance with Pisa, was crushed July, 1336. Thereafter, until the fall of the Nine, Grosseto remained subject to Siena. See G. Cecchini, *Caleffo*, I, 309–17 (Nos. 213–14), 317–18 (No. 216), II, 1107–13 (Nos. 899–900); Capitoli, No. 2, fols. 31*v*–45*r*; No. 3, fols. 62*r*–63*r*, 242*r*–*v*; CG, No. 115, fols. 18*r*–19*v* (Jan. 23, 1334), 39*r*–40*r* (Feb. 11, 1334), No. 117, fols. 10*r*–12*v* (July 31, 1335), No. 119, fols. 11*r*–17*r* (July 19, 1336), 33*r*–34*r* (Aug. 24, 1336), and Repetti, *Dizionario*, II, 525–55—to be used with caution, city, Masse, contado, and subject towns and lordships—three other groups had distinct and separate relationships to the state.

The first of these was the clergy, both regular and secular. While the commune attempted with varying success to hold clerics accountable in the taxation of their personal patrimonies, and on occasion claimed jurisdiction over them in criminal cases, on the whole it recognized their special status and their direct dependence upon the ecclesiastical hierarchy and jurisdiction—if not always with great enthusiasm. For other than their personal patrimonial possessions, Siena requested voluntary contributions and loans from the clergy and their institutions. Much of the government's concern was to make certain that it was not defrauded by persons who claimed the privilege of clergy in order to defraud the commune of taxes and services, while in reality they remained laymen. But on the other hand, the state clearly recognized its special obligations to the truly religious. Siena extended regular alms, occasional subventions and exemption from certain communal regulations to numerous religious orders and institutions and to individual hermits and holy persons of both sexes.[104]

---

as are: the chronicle of Agnolo di Tura del Grasso [cited above, n. 62], and the works of Malavolti and Tommasi [cited above, n. 67], *ad annum.*

104. See, e.g., L. Zdekauer, "Statuti criminali del fôro ecclesiastico di Siena (secoli XIII–XIV)," *BSSP*, VII (1900), 231–64; Lisini, Vol. II ("Indice," e.g., *s.v.*, "Cherici," "Chiese," "Duomo," "Elemosine," "Gaudenti," "Libertà ecclesiastica," "Monasteri," "Protezione di luoghi pii e religiosi"); Statuti, Siena, No. 26, Dist. I, r. 260, fol. 60*v*: "Quo modo solvant clerici et non subpositi de possessionibus et bonis eorum patrimonialibus." On January 14, 1345, the City Council voted 207–16 that in the interest of justice those clerics who had been "allibrati" for their patrimonial possessions, but whom communal officials had forced to pay the dazi and prestanze imposed upon those properties despite their personal clerical privileges, should no longer remain outside the protection of the Sienese commune—even if they had not paid willingly (CG, No. 136, fols. 5*r*–9*v*, especially fols. 6*r*–7*r*). The apostil to this item reads, "pro clericis qui sunt extra protectionem comunis." See also W. Bowsky, "The Medieval Commune and Internal Violence" [cited above, n. 93].

The relationships between Siena and its clergy and the Sienese church, which have not yet received the scholarly attention they merit, are considered in my forthcoming general study of Siena under the Nine. For the separate issue of the lands directly subject to the temporal jurisdiction of the Sienese bishop, see N. Mengozzi, *Il Feudo del Vescovado di Siena* (Siena, 1911), which was first published in *BSSP*, XVI–XVIII (1909–11); V. Lusini, "I confini storici del Vescovado di Siena," *BSSP*, V (1898), 333–57, VII (1900), 59–82, 418–67, and VIII (1901), 195–273; and G. A. Pecci, *Storia del vescovado della città di Siena* (Lucca, 1748). For comparison, see, e.g., M. Becker, "Church and State in Florence on the Eve of the Renaissance (1343–1382)," *Speculum*, XXXVII (1962), 509–27, and "Some Economic Implications of the Conflict between Church and State in *Trecento*

Foreigners too received separate treatment. With the exception of visiting dignitaries, ambassadors and other officials, and foreigners in Sienese service, the situation of the foreigner who did not own property that was registered in the Sienese commune, or have the required minimum length residence in the state, was unenviable. And in the clearest reference I have found, that residence was a lengthy ten years.[105]

The foreigner constantly risked becoming the object of a reprisal—of legally being seized or robbed by a Sienese who had been injured by someone from that foreigner's own land or commune.[106] His access to courts was limited, and even his life was protected by less severe penalties than those reserved for the slayer of a Sienese citizen or contadino. In both the Constitution of 1309–10 and in that redacted three decades later a £1,000 fine was exacted for the murder of a foreigner—except that it was less if that foreigner's state exacted a lesser penalty for the same crime. And that same limitation applied in the case of all blows and wounds inflicted upon a foreigner.[107]

Florence," *Mediaeval Studies*, XXI (1959), 1–16; G. Brucker, *Florentine Politics and Society, 1343–1378* (Princeton, 1962), pp. 131–40, 157–59, 302–5, 317–19; P. Partner, "Florence and the Papacy, 1300–1375," in J. R. Hale, J. R. L. Highfield, and B. Smalley (eds.), *Europe in the Late Middle Ages* (Evanston, Ill., 1965), pp. 76–121 (especially pp. 90, 102); and N. Rubenstein, "Marsilius of Padua and Italian Political Thought of His Time," in Hale, Highfield and Smalley, pp. 44–75 (especially pp. 47–48).

105. G. G. Cantucci, "'*Ordinamenta Scomputi*' in margine alla legislazione statutaria senese in materia penale," *Studi Senesi*, LXVIII–LXIX (1956–57), 492–516: "Et intelligatur forensis omnis persona que non sit civis senensis vel que sit de extra civitatem et comitatum Senarum, nisi habitavarit in civitate vel comitatu Senarum per tempus decem annorum, et singulas factiones ut cives civitatis vel comitatini senenses fecerint in eadem . . . ." (p. 505). Although this definition, which was set forth in general-amnesty and composition legislation of April 23, 1354, may have been valid only for that specific measure, it strengthens my disbelief in M. Kovalevsky's contention that, after the Black Death, Siena adopted a liberal citizenship policy similar to that of Venice (see W. Bowsky, "Black Death," 31). Note, too, that according to a measure adopted by the Nine on July 7, 1323, a foreign notary was not to be considered as foreign if he acquired Sienese citizenship and could prove this with an "instrumentum cittadinatus," or if he "in civitate senarum aut burgis habitaverit per decem annos vel ab inde supra . . . ." (Statuti, Siena, No. 23, fol. 30*r*.)

106. See D. Bizzarri, "Le rappresaglie negli statuti del comune di Siena," *BSSP*, XX (1913), 115–39, 217–45 (reprinted in her *Studi di storia del diritto italiano* [Turin, 1937]); Q. Senigaglia, *Lo statuto dell'Arte della Mercanzia Senese* (*1342–1343*) (Siena, 1911), pp. 27–28, 43–47 (originally published in *BSSP*, XIV [1907], 235–36, 251–55). The entire subject of reprisals, in law and in practise, has not yet been examined. The bibliography in A. Sapori, *Le Marchand Italian au Moyen Age* (Paris, 1952), pp. 97–98, still is useful.

107. Lisini, Dist. V, r. ccl; Statuti, Siena, No. 26, Dist. III, r. 265 (fol. 169*r–v*),

Foreigners who remained within the state for any length of time also found themselves the object of considerable Sienese pressure to contribute to the maintenance of the state in the same ways and to the same degree as its other inhabitants. One measure, for example, approved by the Nine July 7, 1323, stated that "since many foreigners have come with their families to dwell and stay in the Masse and Cortine of the city of Siena," but pay no taxes or other impositions; henceforth, regardless of their origins or status they were to pay the "gabelles on flour, grain, wine, and all other things and victuals for which all other persons of the said Masse and Cortine are held to and must pay."[108]

The third group that remains to be considered is one about which probably less is known than any of the others: the slaves.[109] Not only is there a paucity of clear references to slaves, but, as quickly becomes apparent to any investigator, difficulties are compounded because the word "*servus*" used in Sienese legislation to designate a slave is the same term that was applied to servants, and this although the two were recognized to be quite distinct.

We have no precise idea of the number of slaves in the Sienese state during the regime of the Nine, but it seems to have been small and most perhaps served as domestic servants. The few statutory dispositions concerning slaves that remained in the Constitution of 1309–10 were not novel, but carried over from much earlier statutes. The passage of a measure of October 16, 1355, which possibly refers to slaves may indicate that their number had increased; but I think it more likely that the law was intended to prevent servants, persons of base occupations and perhaps ex-slaves from attempting to infiltrate into governmental positions during the confusion and social upheaval that followed the Black Death of 1348 and the violent overthrow of the government of the Nine in March, 1355.

---

includes the statement: "Salvo quod si in terra de qua esset occisus esset minor pena statuta contra aliquem occidentem forensem illius terre tunc in illa minori pena occidens talis debeat contempnari, et item observetur de aliis percussionibus et vulneribus que inferuntur in forensem predictum." See also above, p. 231, and Statuti, Siena, No. 26, Dist. III, r. 238, fol. 163*r–v*, "Qualiter procedatur contra forensem vel vagabundum."

108. Statuti, Siena, No. 23, fols. 25*r*–34*v* (quotation on fol. 32*v*).

109. This summary is taken from G. Prunai, "Notizie e documenti sulla servitù domestica" [cited above, n. 86], who does not, however, express doubts concerning the legislation of October 16, 1355. See also I. Origo, "The Domestic Enemy: The Eastern Slaves in Tuscany in the Fourteenth and Fifteenth Centuries," *Speculum*, XXX (1955), 321–66 (which, for Siena, is based upon Prunai's "Notizie e documenti").

Sienese legislation concerning the status of slaves was a curious mixture of Roman, medieval imperial, Germanic, and indigenous statute law. Thus a Sienese judge had been bound to declare "And for those who are born of a slave father and a free belly I shall hold to the custom of the Empire (*morem imperii*)." Hence such offspring were accounted as free born. Contrary to Roman law, however, Sienese courts accepted testimony given by a slave without torture.

That the slave's lot was a sorry one need hardly be emphasized. Not only was he excluded from office and denied the right to enter into the numerous transactions open to free men—purchase, sale, contract, donation—but his master might whip him, and even have him incarcerated in the communal prisons for so long as he desired. In addition, of course, for all crimes punishable by communal law the Sienese courts claimed jurisdiction over the slave.

From the Valdichiana to the Maremma coasts and from the borders of Florence and Volterra to the boundaries of the Papal States, all, from slave to citizen, were subject to various degrees of Sienese control by 1355. After almost seven decades, the government of the Nine Governors and Defenders of the Commune and People of Siena had fused the various forms of urban citizenship into a single mold. Siena had elaborated consistent policies that linked immigration to naturalization—policies that encouraged continued recruitment into the citizen body, and that favored the elements of society that were most sought after by the ruling oligarchy. Although the problem of overseeing the new citizens had not been satisfactorily solved, it had been clearly recognized and defined, and legislation was being formulated that recognized the needs and rights of these new citizens as well as those of the state and its component parts.

Even so brief and introductory an examination as this reveals more perhaps than that sweeping generalizations of earlier scholarship concerning citizenship cannot be accepted at face value, but must be tested against specific historical situations. If we are to arrive at a more accurate and comprehensive knowledge of the phenomenon of citizenship in the late-medieval or early-renaissance Italian city-state, we must not view the matter solely from the vantage points of political theory and *Rechtsgeschichte*. Research must account for actual practice and must relate a study of citizenship to immigration and naturalization, socio-economic conditions, and the structure and aims of government.

APPENDIX

The Sienese Constitution of 1337–1339

The last of the three great Sienese constitutions, ranking in importance with that of 1262, edited by Lodovico Zdekauer[1] and with the vernacular redaction of 1309–10 edited by Alessandro Lisini,[2] is in Statuti, Siena, No. 26, in the Archivio di Stato of Siena. Described in a modern guide to the Sienese archives as "*Constitutum Comunis Senensis.* Compiled in 1337 by Niccola of Orvieto and by Michele of Prato,"[3] it remained the basic Sienese constitution until 1544[4]—only eleven years before the collapse of the independent republic of Siena.

Statuti, Siena, No. 26, contains four major "distinctions" or divisions—rather than the five distinctions of the Constitution of 1262 or the six distinctions of the Lisini Constitution (the sixth distinction contains the principal rubrics for the office of the Nine). A poem on folio 2*r* summarizes each of the four distinctions.

Ecce statutorum distinctum dogma novorum
  Quo Sena mando vetus, ut vivet quisque quietus.

Dico Dei iura, fiscalia publica cura *Cui datur et quales, sibi subsint officiales.*	} Dist. I
Ordine dispono, civilia iura pono *Litibus optatum reprimens dispendia fatum.*	} Dist. II
Ne quis ledatur proprio set iure fruatur *Iustitie frenis dignis premo crimina penis.*	} Dist. III
Pacis cultores roborans, expello furores *Corrigit et gesta male, syndicat hec mea sesta.*[5]	} Dist. IV

1. L. Zdekauer (ed.), *Il constituto del comune di Siena dell'anno 1262* (Milan, 1897), and the fragments published by Zdekauer and by U. G. Mondolfo, cited above, 198 n. 10.

2. A. Lisini (ed.), *Il costituto del comune di Siena volgarizzato nel MCCCIX–MCCCX* (2 vols.; Siena, 1903). Lisini's discussion of the Constitution of 1337–39 is in Vol. I, xvi–xvii.

3. *Ministero dell'Interno. Pubblicazioni degli Archivi di Stato,* V: *Archivio di Stato di Siena, Guida-Inventario,* I (Rome, 1951), 69.

4. Statuti, Siena, Nos. 48–64. See also *Guida-Inventario*, I, 73–75.

5. Printed in Lisini, I, xvi; which I have compared with Statuti, Siena, N. 26, fol. 2*r*, and found to be accurate.

The statutes are preceded by a separately paginated table of contents or *rubricario* (fols. I*r*–XIX*v*). The body of the text is on folios 1*r*–261*v*, with provisions of June, 1389, and an addition of May 21, 1395, on folios 263*r*–65*r*, corrections and changes of August, 1355, on folios 267*r*–88*r* and 291*r*–94*v*. Other, undated additions are on the last written folio, 295*r*.[6]

Written in a beautiful Gothic minuscule, this carefully executed compilation is not without error despite having been subjected to numerous readings and revisions.[7] Nor can we always rely upon the frequent marginal enumeration of the rubrics.[8]

The dating attributed to these statutes, however, needs revision. Both the "compiled in 1337" of the archival guide and Lisini's earlier assertion that "in August, 1337, the General Council [of Siena] ordered two jurisconsults, namely messer Niccola d'Angelo of Orvieto and messer Benamato di Michelle, citizen of Prato, to undertake a new compilation. . . ." are but a part of the truth.

A City Council deliberation of August 11, 1337, states that the compilation assigned to those jurists had been completed, but still needed to be examined and revised. The Council therefore ordered the Nine to make arrangements so that the men already selected to revise this constitution could reexamine and redact it together with messer Niccola d'Angelo of Orvieto. This accomplished, they were to present their completed work to the Council for its consideration and action.[9] On August 29 a provision prepared by this commission was read and approved in the Council, but—unfortunately—its contents are not included in the records of that deliberation.[10]

The task was not yet completed. Biccherna records of November and December, 1337, and February, 1338, show payments made to men who

6. The Prologue is on folios 1*r*–2*r*, Distinction I is on folios 3*r*–87*r*, Distinction II on folios 89*r*–126*r*, Distinction III on folios 127*r*–95*v*, and Distinction IV on folios 197*r*–261*v*; folios 2*v*, 87*v*–88*v*, 126*v*, 196*r*–*v*, 262*r*–*v*, 266*r*–*v*, 288*v*–90*v*, and 295*v*–96*v* are blank.

7. For example, Dist. IV, r. 317 contains the same rubric as r. 318 (fols. 245*v*–46*r*), and the rubricario reveals that no rubric was omitted there. The rubricario itself is imperfect; for example, on folio XIV*v* it omits the rubric that should be listed between rubrics 33 and 34 in Distinction IV: "De audientia tenenda per dominos novem qualibet die Jovis" (fol. 205*v*)—a shortened version of Lisini, Dist. VI, r. xxx.

8. The last rubric of Distinction IV (fol. 261*v*), for example, should be numbered No. 442 rather than No. 438.

9. CG, No. 121, fols. 14*r*–15*v*.

10. *Ibid.*, fols. 25*r*, 27*r*.

had been entrusted with "arranging" and "correcting" the communal statute.[11] On June 19, 1338, the City Council approved still another provision that had been drawn up by the men the Nine had chosen "*ad perficiendum opus compilationis nove facte per dominum Niccholam Angelis de Urbeveteri*,"—although, again, we have no record of the contents.[12]

That the statutes were not completed until—at the earliest—the late summer of 1338 is also suggested by the final group of provisions in the fourth distinction (rubrics 435–42, fols. 260*v*–261*v*), which deal principally with the regulation of prostitution in Siena. Rubric 435 restricted prostitutes and procurers to a particular area within the city, the *contrada* or district of S. Salvatore in Piano di Valdimontone in the Terzo of San Martino. This, clearly, was derived from a City Council decision of August 13, 1338, that restricted prostitutes to Valdimontone and prohibited them from living in the other two areas of the city in which they had formerly been permitted: the *contrada* of Valle Piatta in the Terzo of Città and the street near the Campansi Gate in the Terzo of Camollia.[13]

It might be supposed that as these are the final rubrics in the Constitution they also provide a terminal date. A passage in the chronicle of Agnolo di Tura del Grasso might also be construed to mean that a major redaction of Sienese statutes was compiled in 1338.[14]

11. According to Biccherna, No. 187 (fol. 124*v*, Nov. 27, 1337), £52 was paid to "domino Francisco Bonaventure et domino Francisco de Montalcino pro eorum salario XXVI dierum quibus steterunt ad ordinandum statutum Comunis Senarum ad rationem XX s. pro quolibet et qualibet die."; £13 was paid to "Andree domini Bindi et Fredi de Ponzis pro eorum salario XXVI diebus quibus steterunt ad ordinandum dictum statutum ad rationem V s. pro quolibet et qualibet die."; and £4 was paid to "Niccolao domini Stricche pro suo salario XVI dierum quibus stetit cum predictis ad ordinandum dictum statutum ad rationem V s. pro die." Folio 133*r* (Dec. 31, 1337) shows that £46 was paid to messer Francesco of Montalcino for 46 days of work, £43 to messer Francesco di Bonaventura for 43 days, £11/10/– to Andrea di messer Bindo for 43 days, £6/15/– to Fredo Ponzi for 27 days, and £6/15/– to Niccolo di messer Stricca for 27 days—all "ad corrigendum statutum comunis." Biccherna, No. 191 (fol. 96*r*, Feb. 28, 1338) records additional payments to these five men for several days' work in January and February "ad corrigendum statutum." Here Francesco di Bonaventura and Francesco di messer Guido (of Montalcino) are specifically called "judicibus." For these two judges—(and perhaps for the remaining three men, or for their homonyms), see G. Cecchini and G. Prunai (eds.), *Chartularium Studii Senensis*, I: *1240–1357* (Siena, 1942), *s.v.*

12. CG, No. 122, fol. 52*r*.

13. CG, No. 123, fols. 16*r*–*v*. This arrangement had been decided upon by communal officials in the autumn of 1336 (fol. 16*r*).

14. Chronicle of Agnolo di Tura del Grasso, in *Cronache senesi*, A. Lisini and F. Iacometti (eds.), *Rerum Italicarum Scriptores*, n.s., XV, Part VI (Bologna, 1931–37), 523:

Careful study of the entire compilation disproves this assumption. Rubric 71 (fol. 100*r*) of the second distinction reads *Quod debitores personaliter capi non possunt. Rubrica. Nulla persona occasione alicuius obligationis contrahende ab hodie in antea anno domini Millesimo trecentesimo trigesimo nono Indictione septima die vigesimatertia mensis aprelis possit personaliter capi, deteneri vel molestari*. . . . This rubric, clearly dated April 23, 1339, Indiction 7, written in the same hand as the other rubrics and an integral part of the statutes, provides a *terminus post quem* for the completion of the Constitution. One might surmise that this occurred by mid-1339. This dating is also suggested by payments that the Biccherna made for copies of vernacular translations of the communal statutes prepared for various officials.[15]

The so-called *volgarizzamento* of these statutes poses a mystery. As early as 1903 (and later), Lisini asserted that a complete copy of the vernacular translation of this Constitution was in the Vatican Library, a part of the Fondo Chigi. He reported that it had been taken from the Sienese archive by a Guglielmi, and later given by the Guglielmi to Pope Alexander VII (Fabio Chigi). Later, it was added to the Vatican Library, together with the Biblioteca Chigiana.[16]

One of the cards in the Vatican Library catalogue (which was prepared prior to the transfer of the Biblioteca Chigiana) describes Fondo Chigi, G. II. 54, as vernacular Sienese statutes—"*Statuta senensia in volgare*." But I have ascertained that this manuscript is a miscellaneous collection of *Gabella* regulations (c. 1290–1332). An examination of the other Chigiana documents that pertain to Siena proved only that they correspond to their descriptions on the catalogue cards.[17] Whatever the facts

"In Siena in detto anno [1338] fu ordinato e consoli e camerlenghi a molte arti, a féro statuti e legi per vivare con justitia."

15. See Lisini, I, xvi n. 1. Lisini, however, does not indicate that these payments were made during the first semester of 1340 and on December 20, 1341—when no fewer than four complete copies were paid for. (One copy was assigned to the Biccherna, one to the war captain, one to the captain of the people, and one to the maggior sindaco of the commune.)

16. Lisini, I, xvi n. 1; and Lisini's note 1 on p. 523 of the Chronicle of Agnolo di Tura del Grasso. Quinto Senigaglia also wrote that a copy of the vernacular constitution was in the Chigiana, but he may simply have been repeating Lisini (see *BSSP*, XIV [1907], 214).

17. The Chigiana documents from the period of the Nine are Vatican Library, Fondo Chigi, G. I. 7, "Scritture diverse . . . 1339–1554," (of which only folios 1*r*–9*v* are dated between 1339 and 1355, and record miscellaneous land transfers and receipts and the appointments of private proctors), and G. II. 58, "Rogiti di notai del 1346–1347,

at the time Lisini wrote, the vernacular version of the constitution seems to be missing or lost.[18]

1355, 1361, 1372," (fols. 1*r*–57*v* record miscellaneous notarial acts between Feb. 5, 1346, and May 10, 1347).

18. It is a pleasure to thank the Reverend Marie Hyacinte Laurent, O.P., for his generous assistance in my search for the missing statutes at the Vatican Library. Father Laurent, himself a scholar of Sienese history, brought to the task the experience of years of study at both the Sienese archives and the Vatican Library.